Dimensions
of the
Hospitality
Industry

Dimensions
of the
Hospitality
Industry

▶ **An Introduction**

SECOND EDITION

Paul R. Dittmer
New Hampshire College

Gerald G. Griffin
New York City Technical College
The City University of New York

VNR VAN NOSTRAND REINHOLD
I⟨T⟩P ® A Division of International Thomson Publishing, Inc.

New York • Albany • Bonn • Boston • Detroit • London • Madrid • Melbourne
Mexico City • Paris • San Francisco • Singapore • Tokyo • Toronto

I (T) P® A division of International Thomson Publishing Inc.
    The ITP logo is a registered trademark under license.

Printed in the United States of America

For more information, contact:

Van Nostrand Reinhold
115 Fifth Avenue
New York, NY 10003

Chapman & Hall GmbH
Pappelallee 3
69469 Weinheim
Germany

Chapman & Hall
2-6 Boundary Row
London
SE1 8HN
United Kingdom

International Thomson Publishing Asia
221 Henderson Road #05-10
Henderson Building
Singapore 0315

Thomas Nelson Australia
102 Dodds Street
South Melbourne, 3205
Victoria, Australia

International Thomson Publishing Japan
Hirakawacho Kyowa Building, 3F
2-2-1 Hirakawacho
Chiyoda-ku, 102 Tokyo
Japan

Nelson Canada
1120 Birchmount Road
Scarborough, Ontario
Canada M1K 5G4

International Thomson Editores
Seneca 53
Col. Polanco
11560 Mexico D.F. Mexico

1 2 3 4 5 6 7 8 9 10 QEB-FF 01 00 99 98 97 96

Library of Congress Cataloging-in-Publication data

Dittmer, Paul.
    Dimensions of the hospitality industry: an introduction / Paul R.
Dittmer, Gerald G. Griffin. — 2nd ed.
        p.   cm.
    Includes index.
    ISBN 0-442-02082-1
    1. Hospitality industry—Management.   I. Griffin, Gerald G.,
1936– .   II. Title.
TX911.3.M27D583   1996
647.94′068—dc20

96-14906
CIP

Contents

Preface

The second edition of this text is intended for courses that introduce students to the broad world of hospitality and tourism and to the curricula that will prepare them for managerial careers in these fields. This newly revised edition consists of fourteen chapters divided into seven parts. Each of the seven parts provides coverage of a primary area commonly treated in introductory courses, as indicated below.

Part	Area Covered	No. of Chapters
I	Introduction/overview	1
II	Historical foundations	2
III	Food and beverage	3
IV	Lodging	3
V	Hospitality management	1
VI	Travel and tourism	3
VII	Future perspectives	1

The number of chapters has been reduced to fourteen to facilitate the use of the complete work in a one-semester course. The strong positive features of the first edition have been retained and, in response to suggestions from users, several important features have been added throughout the book. These include excerpts from current periodicals designed to provide current industry-based illustrations and excerpts intended to show technological applications of significant points in the chapters. In addition, hospitality profiles, appearing only in the historical chapters, will provide students with interesting sketches of some of the giants who have made dramatic and lasting contributions to our field.

In addition to the new elements described above, this revised edition offers several case studies at the end of each chapter. These cases, identified as Moments of Truth, provide opportunities for students to engage in some chapter-related critical thinking under the guidance of their instructor and to discuss their varying views openly in the classroom setting. Finally, the statistical information from the first edition has been updated to provide students and their instructors with the very latest available data.

In developing and revising the text, we have attempted to make flexibility a key feature. For example, elimination of any one of the seven major parts will not make it difficult to use others. Thus, instructors in programs that do not include foodservice courses can choose to ignore "Part III: Food and Beverage Perspectives." In programs without lodging courses, instructors may prefer to skip "Part IV: Lodging Perspectives." And in programs without travel and tourism components, instructors can disregard "Part VI: Travel and Tourism Perspectives."

Although instructors in many programs will choose to include the parts of the text that introduce the principal areas covered in their curricula, some may prefer to take a contrary approach: to assign the parts that are not linked to the specifics of their programs. Instructors in programs that do not offer courses in food and beverage management, for example, may choose to assign the relevant chapters in this text to provide their students with some introduction to this important area.

In addition, because the number of end-of-chapter questions is more than most will be inclined to assign, instructors will be able to make selective use of these for written response or for in-class discussion. Answers for all end-of-chapter questions can be found in the *Instructor's Guide*, which also includes a number of other materials designed to assist those adopting the work. The *Instructor's Guide* is available on request from the publisher: Van Nostrand Reinhold, 115 Fifth Avenue, New York, NY 10003.

Overview

The following is an overview of the text.

Part I gives a profile of the hospitality industry and is intended to provide a sense of its scope. At the same time, it introduces the three principal areas addressed in college majors—foodservice, lodging, and travel and tourism—and two key concepts—*moments of truth* and *cycles of service*. Finally, it addresses some issues of particular concern to students: career opportunities, education, and the experience required to pursue those opportunities; and both the advantages and disadvantages of working in these fields.

Part II traces the history and development of travel and hospitality in the Western world. Chapter 2, the first of the two chapters in this part, sketches the growth of travel and hospitality from earliest times through the Greek and Roman empires, the Middle Ages, and the period up to the Industrial Revolution in England and in the United States from colonial times through the nineteenth century. Chapter 3 is concerned with twentieth-century developments in transportation and hospitality services principally in the United States.

Part III offers a broad introduction to food and beverage. Chapter 4, the first of three chapters, identifies the size and scope of the industry, describes many characteristic types of food and beverage operation, and explains a system for classifying establishments in the food-service industry. Chapter 5 deals with food and beverage facilities and defines the terms *product line* and *service product*. Chapter 6 describes food and beverage operations from purchasing through service.

Part IV provides a broad introduction to lodging. Chapter 7, the first of three chapters, identifies the size and scope of the industry, describes many characteristic types of lodging establishment operations, and discusses various ways of classifying and rating lodging establishments. Chapter 8 deals with lodging facilities and shows how the terms *product line* and *service product* relate to the lodging industry. Chapter 9 describes the basic operations that all lodging establishments require and identifies a number of services found in various lodging operations.

Part V provides an introduction to operations management in the hospitality industry. Using examples taken from the world of foodservice and lodging, the chapter introduces operations management in the following key areas: management, marketing, human resources, accounting, and computers.

Part VI introduces travel and tourism. Chapter 11 discusses various travel motivators, describes the role of governments in travel and tourism, and identifies the size and scope of the industry as well as its several components. Chapter 12 focuses on the people and businesses that sell travel, defines the term *package*, and describes various types of travel packages. Chapter 13 defines the terms *recreation* and *entertainment* and describes various recreation, entertainment, and other tourism attractions on which the travel industry depends.

Part VII consists of a single chapter devoted to a number of significant issues that are likely to be of increasing concern to managers in the hospitality and tourism industries in the years ahead.

Acknowledgments

In developing this text, we were fortunate to have the cooperation and assistance of the people whose names and affiliations are here recorded. Some of these individuals may feel their contributions were minor. We strongly disagree: even brief comments and the most casual of conversations can suggest ideas and change views, and thus have profound impact on a work in progress. With that in mind, we sincerely and publicly acknowledge and thank the following for their assistance: Patricia S. Bartholomew, Frank C. Constantino, Allen M. Freedman, Stephen K. Holzinger, Fedele J. Panzarino, and Carol Soloff of the Hospitality Management Department, New York City Technical College, The City University of New York; William Peterson and Fred Walter of the Division of Hospitality Management, and Julie Rain, Administrative Assistant in the division, as well as Richard Pantano, Library Director, and Edward Daniels, Research Librarian, all of New Hampshire College; Francis M. Domoy, Richard F. Marecki, Warren Sackler, and Carol B. Whitlock of the School of Food, Hotel, and Travel Management, Rochester Institute of Technology; Robert A. Heath and Edward F. McIntyre of the Birmingham (United Kingdom) College of Food, Tourism, and Creative Studies; Kevin Bedard, General Manager of Canopy's Training Restaurant, Rochester, New York, operated by the Educational Opportunity Center, State University of New York, Brockport; Andrew R. Schwarz of the Hospitality Division of Sullivan County Community College; David C. Dorf of Dave Dorf Associates; Marianne Gajewski and Lisa Gates of the Educational Foundation of the National Restaurant Association; Allan Sherwin of the Lundeberg Seamanship School; Kathryn K. Griffin of The Big Twinkie; James Bardi, Director, Hospitality Management Program, Pennsylvania State University, Berks Campus; Gus Katsigris, Director, Food and Hospitality Services Institute, El Centro College. We would also like to thank all the reviewers whose expert guidance helped shape this second edition: Frank J. Ambrozic, City College of San Francisco; Richard J. Doyon, Quincy College; Fred R. Hawk, Chaparral College; Richard M. Lagiewski, State University of New York, Plattsburgh; Fred Laughlin, Northwestern Michigan College; Christine D. Letchinger, Kendall College; Chris Mottern, College of Southern Idaho; Michael R. Pepper, Transylvania University; Mokie Steiskal, Columbus State Community College.

Through the many months required to produce this work, the extraordinary professional staff of Van Nostrand Reinhold has been most patient, helpful, and supportive. In particular, Mimi Melek, Melissa Rosati, Amy Beth Shipper, and Michelle Agosta all deserve a public salute for their special efforts on our behalf. So do Maxine Effenson Chuck, our developmental editor, and Elyse Rieder, who did an exceptional job of researching and collecting the photographs used in the book. Without their dedicated, professional help, this work would never have made it past the planning stage.

Finally, we gratefully salute our wives, Barbara and Charlene, who soldiered on in so many ways for so many months. Their understanding as the work progressed was a blessing. Without their cooperation and support, the manuscript could never have been completed.

If this text is successful—that is, if it is a useful addition to the growing number of professional texts available for students planning managerial careers in hospitality and tourism—much of the credit will be due to the people whose help we are delighted to have had this opportunity to acknowledge. If not, the responsibility is wholly that of the authors.

Paul R. Dittmer
Gerald G. Griffin
April, 1996

Dimensions
of the
Hospitality
Industry

Part One

Introduction

O n e

Dimensions of the Hospitality Industry

A Career Overview

After reading and studying this chapter, you should be able to:

1 Distinguish between the manufacturing and service sectors in an economy.

2 Define *hospitality* and describe the scope of the hospitality industry.

3 Identify the two principal segments of the hospitality industry and list the major types of businesses in each.

4 Describe the relationship between the hospitality and the travel and tourism industries.

5 Discuss the historic role of entertainment in the hospitality industry.

6 Distinguish between travel agents and tour operators.

7 List and explain the elements that make the hospitality industry unique.

8 Discuss the special characteristics that distinguish hospitality and other service businesses from those that manufacture products.

9 Define the terms *moment of truth, cycle of service,* and *employee empowerment* and then discuss the significance of each for the hospitality industry.

10 Identify the principal thrust of total quality management and its significance for hospitality management.

11 Discuss career opportunities in the hospitality industry and the qualifications commonly sought by hospitality employers.

12 Describe the advantages and disadvantages associated with careers in the hospitality industry.

▶ Introduction

Imagine yourself in an occupation that allows you to work in almost any part of the world, gives you the chance to meet famous people—movie stars, recording artists, political leaders, and others—offers an elegant work environment in luxurious surroundings, and lets you climb that well-known ladder of success, advancing in rank and position as fast as your abilities will allow. Don't think of it as only a dream; it's reality for many people just like you—people who decided on careers in hospitality, a worldwide industry that continues to grow faster than most people can imagine and that cries out for young men and women to help manage the hotels, restaurants, and related businesses springing up in every corner of the world. There are vast numbers of opportunities for anyone interested in people and willing to work hard. And it's one of the most interesting industries in the modern world economy.

Hospitality is just one part of a larger group of industries that make up the service sector of the economy. The economy can be divided into two sectors: the first includes companies that make real physical items that people can touch—these are known as products, and the sector that makes them is known as the manufacturing sector; the second—the service sector—is made up of individuals and organizations that perform services for people and businesses. The service sector includes a broad range of fields—law, interior decorating, dentistry, accounting, nursing, automobile repair, foodservice, haircutting; the list goes on and on, almost without end. Hospitality is a major part of the service sector.

In years past, the manufacturing sector was the major force in the economy, accounting for the largest part of the economic growth that so changed the United States in the nineteenth century and the first half of the twentieth century. However, in the years since 1950, the service sector of our economy has been growing much faster than the manufacturing sector, and the hospitality industry has been growing faster than most other service industries. All kinds of career opportunities are opening up every day in every part of the hospitality industry, and the number of jobs keeps growing.

Ever since the 1950s, hospitality has been a key industry in the economic life of many nations. It has become a world leader in providing jobs and new opportunities for people from every age group and from all ethnic, racial, and socioeconomic groups. Most economists predict that hospitality will continue to grow worldwide in the years ahead. That would mean ever greater numbers of career possibilities for the men and women who train to become hospitality professionals and prepare to seize these new opportunities.

As we begin our investigation into the hospitality industry, we will devote this first chapter to some basic elements: identifying the scope of the industry, contrasting it to other industries, and pointing out its distinctive characteristics. Finally, we will point out some of the opportunities the hospitality industry offers the men and women who prepare to take advantage of it.

▶ A Definition of Hospitality

The word **hospitality** has ancient roots, dating from the earliest days of Roman civilization. It is derived from the Latin word *hospitare,* meaning "to receive as a guest." Several related words come from the same Latin root, including *hospital, hospice,* and *hostel.* In each of these, the principal meaning focuses on a host who receives, welcomes, and caters to the needs of people who are temporarily away from their homes. *To receive as a guest* is a phrase that implies a host prepared to meet a guest's basic requirements while that guest is away from home. The requirements of a guest in these circumstances have traditionally been food, beverages, and lodging or shelter. Many would add to this some form of incidental entertainment, even though a number of hosts clearly have limited or ignored this as an element of hospitality.

▶ The Basics

The traditional view takes us to the heart of the hospitality industry. If the word *hospitality* refers to the act of providing food, beverages, or lodging to travelers, then the **hospitality industry** consists of businesses that do this. Some may offer entertainment, incidental or otherwise. But we choose to treat this as part of travel and tourism rather than food, beverage, and lodging—the basic elements of hospitality. The reason for that will become apparent later in this chapter. For this text, we will define the hospitality industry as businesses that provide food, beverages, or lodging to travelers.

This brings up two important distinctions between the hospitality industry and other service enterprises.

1.   The hospitality industry provides food, beverages, lodging, or some combination of the three that other businesses would provide only on the most incidental basis.

2.   The hospitality industry provides services primarily to travelers in a broad sense of the term. By contrast, other service businesses ordinarily deal with customers who are local residents rather than travelers.

Our definition also distinguishes the hospitality industry from businesses in the manufacturing sector of our economy. Manufacturers do not normally sell services. Instead, they make products that are sold to consumers through regional systems of local wholesalers and retailers, with some notable exceptions.

There are those who will be quick to point out a potential problem with our view of the industry. Clearly, sometimes a service provided for travelers is also provided to local residents. Restaurants and hotels that provide food, beverages, lodging, or some combination of these to residents of their local neighborhoods are excellent examples.

Those concerned with the question of the residential or nonresidential nature of customers in a hotel dining room will soon recognize the futility of attempting to make useful distinctions. Regardless of where the customers live, the staff must offer the same menus and provide the same level of service to all. Although the hospitality industry evolved as a means of providing food, shelter, and entertainment for travelers, these services appeal to local residents as well, and increasing numbers have come to take advantage of them over time. Today, some hospitality enterprises may service local residents only and never attend to the needs of any travelers. For practical and definitional purposes, then, those providing food, beverages, and shelter are considered part of the hospitality industry whether or not their customers are actually travelers.

▶ Scope of the Hospitality Industry

From the previous material, it quickly becomes apparent that there may be any number of businesses in the hospitality industry. The definition is really quite broad; therefore, at this point we will discuss some of the varied enterprises that make up each of the two principal segments of the industry—food and beverage on the one hand, and lodging on the other.

▶ Food and Beverage Segment

Everyone is aware of the seemingly limitless array of organizations that provide food and beverage service to the public. Today, these include every conceivable type of establishment between a brightly colored fast-food[1] restaurant and one offering elegant, ultraexpensive continental or French cuisine. No matter what type of food travelers and nontravelers alike desire, there must be foodservice available to them at the appropriate hour for breakfast, lunch, dinner, supper, snacks, and so on.

The public looks for foodservice everywhere: hotels, motels, factories, dormitories, highways, cruise ships, city streets, trains, offices, airlines, national parks, airports, bus terminals, shopping malls—any place outside the home where people can be found shopping, driving, working, or playing. There are commercial restaurants of every description around us every day: fast-service restaurants selling hamburgers, chicken, pizza, pasta, and hero sandwiches; ethnic restaurants selling Chinese, Mexican, Italian, Latin American, German, Indonesian, Indian, and dozens of other types of meals; specialty restaurants serving seafood, steaks, pasta, chicken, and vegetarian items; restaurants organized around particular themes, such as railroad cars, English pubs, railroad stations, medieval pageants, opera, and the circus; and a range of others—expensive, inexpensive, noisy, quiet, elegant, dingy, brightly lit, and dark; serving great food, decent food, terrible food, and every other kind you can imagine.

---

[1]Although the term *fast food* is very common, many believe *fast service* or *quick service* are more suitable terms. We will use all three interchangeably in this text; those learning about the hospitality industry should be familiar with all three.

No matter what type of food people desire—fast food, ethnic cuisine, or the finest in continental cuisine—the foodservice segment of the hospitality industry is there to provide it. Shown above are Chiam Chinese Cuisine, New York City; Le Regence Restaurant in the Plaza Athenee Hotel, New York City; and a Burger King restaurant. (Photos courtesy of Chiam Chinese Cuisine, New York City and Exclusive Hotels by Forte. The photograph of the Burger King® restaurant is reproduced with permission of Burger King Corporation, 1996, Miami, Florida.)

There are all sorts of foodservice establishments outside the usual restaurant settings. Examples are found in Disney World and other theme parks, in schools and colleges, in hospitals and homes for senior citizens, in prisons and halfway houses, and in shelters for the homeless. There are carts in the streets and vending machines everywhere; even supermarkets and other food stores are offering in-store foodservice.

Those familiar with the history of our industry will recognize that taverns traditionally have been establishments that sold both food and beverages and provide some form of entertainment, however limited. Some taverns even made overnight accommodations available for travelers. In fact, in the seventeenth century, laws were passed in New England requiring that each community provide a tavern for the "entertainment of travelers."

The tavern, pub, inn, ale house, or public house served as a social center—a place to which travelers and local residents could go to find "entertainment," and it served society in this manner throughout the eighteenth and nineteenth centuries, long before the invention of such pervasive modern devices as phonographs, movies, radios, televisions, videos, tape decks, and compact disc players. People gathered in the taverns, where local residents could mingle with travelers, to share news of wars, plagues, famines, or natural disasters and to discuss local politics or gossip about their neighbors. Sometimes it was only to find a quiet, warm place by the fire; normally it created an occasion for a mug of beer, a tankard of ale, or even a glass of wine.

During the twentieth century, the role of the establishments selling beer, ale, wine, and other beverages has changed to some extent. As we shall see, the role of taverns has expanded and evolved in the modern world. Their role as entertainment centers has diminished, but they are meeting new needs in society, needs that did not exist before the introduction of some of the modern world's technological innovations. Most are no longer called taverns; they are now known as bars, clubs, and cocktail lounges.

Hotels and restaurants have long been in the business of selling drinks—as accompaniments to food, or because their customers began to expect it, or because they discovered it was profitable. The terms *food* and *beverage* became ever more closely linked, and both hotels and restaurants began to use terminology that illustrated the linkage; "food and beverage manager" and "food and beverage department" became common and remain so. Because our industry treats food and beverages together as one segment of the industry, we will do the same in this text.

▶ The Lodging Segment

The lodging segment of the hospitality industry includes the more familiar kinds of establishments that have long offered shelter to travelers—-the hotels and motels that we see on city streets; along highways; near beaches; and close to airports, ski slopes, theme parks, lakes, and national parks. Those who are less familiar with the indus-

The lodging segment of the hospitality industry includes hotels, motels, inns, and other familiar kinds of establishments that have long offered shelter to travelers. Shown above are some of the best-known names in lodging—Red Roof, Hyatt, Embassy Suites, and Sheraton. (Photos courtesy of Red Roof Inns, Inc.; Hyatt Hotels and Resorts; Embassy Suites Hotel photo courtesy of Promus Hotel Corporation; and ITT Sheraton Corporation, Boston.)

try may not realize that some lodging facilities—called inns, motor hotels, lodges, or motor inns—are simply hotels or motels using different names. There are also lodging establishments using some very different terms and selling some very different lodging concepts from those of the traditional hotels and motels, such as the bed and breakfast, resort hotel, resort condominium, conference center, extended stay, time-sharing, and all-suite—all terms that must be addressed in a discussion of the lodging segment. Then there are lodging establishments that are known for the special facilities they offer: ski lodges in Colorado and casino hotels in Las Vegas and Atlantic City are good examples. Definitions and discussion of the various types of lodging establishments are found in chapter 7.

In many ways, campgrounds and transient trailer parks are lodging establishments and, in their own special ways, so are school and college dormitories, summer camps, and health spas. All attend to the lodging needs of those away from home.

In other parts of the world, the signs for lodging establishments may display some unfamiliar words. Some examples include parador—an old Spanish monastery or castle converted for use as a hotel; pension or pensione—a French or Italian home at which guests are provided with room and board; chateau—a French castle or elegant country home used as a hotel; ryokan—a Japanese inn at which traditional customs are observed; and hostel—a lodging facility at which inexpensive accommodations are provided for students and others, typically on a not-for-profit basis.

Lodging signs also bring us some of the world's best-known names in hospitality: Hilton, Sheraton, Holiday Inn, Marriott, Ramada, Days Inn, Quality Inn, and Hyatt, to name just a few. All these, and many others, help make up the dynamic and growing lodging segment of the industry.

▶ Travel and Tourism

Two key terms that arise in any discussion of the hospitality industry are **travel** and **tourism.** They are typically used together as an umbrella term to refer to those businesses providing primary services to travelers. These include the traditional hospitality businesses and a number of others closely linked to them. The term *travel and tourism* includes food and beverage operations, lodging operations, and related enterprises in the fields of entertainment, recreation, and transportation, as well as travel agencies and tour operators.

▶ Entertainment and Recreation

Entertainment has its roots in the traditional duty of a host to entertain his guests, whether neighborhood residents or travelers from afar. Hosts have always felt an obligation to minister to any of their guests' needs, not only for food and beverages and for lodging but also for entertainment.

Beginning centuries ago, innkeepers, tavern keepers, and their descendants have attended (in varying degrees) to guests' needs for entertainment. Some simply talked to their guests; others told stories (some truthful, others interesting or humorous lies); some provided games (e.g., darts, draughts, backgammon, or chess); and others hired jugglers and traveling minstrels.

Today, entertaining guests includes the modern equivalents of these ancient traditions, but it has not been limited to these. The concept of entertaining guests is far broader. Guests are being offered all manner of inducements in the form of entertainment and recreational activities to attract them to particular properties; golf, tennis, casino gambling, backpacking, concerts, swimming, boating, and handball are all examples of this.

In some cases, governments and businesses have worked together to turn communities into desirable destinations for travelers. For example, casino gambling and celebrity entertainment are two of the principal reasons that people go to Las Vegas, Nevada. The more tradi-

Sometimes government and business work together to turn communities into desirable destinations for travelers. Las Vegas, Nevada, famed for casino gambling and celebrity entertainment, is a prime example. (Photo courtesy of The Las Vegas News Bureau.)

tional elements of the hospitality business are almost incidental players there.

Disney World has taken a logical next step, developing a resort environment that includes a vast array of food and beverage, lodging, and entertainment facilities. The entertainment facilities include shows, rides, and exhibits so spectacular that guests have no interest in looking for any entertainment outside the Disney environment during their visit. This is one example of a complete recreational center that, in itself, has become a travel destination. To guests, the food, beverage, and lodging is relatively incidental; they travel to Disney World for the spectacle of it all.

▶ Transportation

All travelers require some means of getting from one place to another. That is a major purpose of the transportation business—making it possible for people to go from one place to another. There are many ways to do this, from the primitive and simple to the modern and complex. One can ride on the back of an animal or in a supersonic jet, or select from among any number of other possibilities. The more common possibilities are automobiles, recreational vehicles (RVs), buses, ships, trains, and airplanes.

Those preparing for professional careers in any part of the traditional hospitality industry should be aware of the long-standing importance of transportation to the survival of hotels, motels, restaurants, and closely related enterprises. Links between the transportation and hospitality businesses are as old as history, and developments in one have normally brought about changes in the other. Nations and states with the best transportation networks have usually developed the healthiest economic systems and the most advanced hospitality industries.

▶ Travel Agencies and Tour Operators

Travel agencies and tour operators are comparatively modern additions to the world of travel and tourism. Neither existed before the middle of the nineteenth century, but both have become central to the survival of many businesses in the hospitality industry.

A **travel agent** is one who sells travel services in a travel agency. Transportation and lodging are the most common services they sell, although meals are sometimes included in the price of lodging. Although a travel agent makes a large number of individual reservations for airline tickets and hotel rooms for some clients, much of the business volume in travel agencies normally consists of selling travel services assembled by others into *packages*. In the travel business, a **package** is a bundle of related travel services offered to a customer at a single price.

There are many types of packages available through travel agencies. Some include only a limited number of services—an airline ticket and a rental car, for example, or a hotel room and tickets for a ski lift. Other packages are more inclusive and may provide the buyer with a round-trip airline ticket, rental car, hotel room, all meals, access to such features as golf courses and tennis courts, and tickets to various events.

Most travel agencies selling packages do not put the packages together. This is done by **tour operators**—wholesalers who make the necessary contacts with hotels, airlines, and other providers of travel services. They devise packages that they believe will appeal to retail buyers. Like all wholesalers in all businesses, they are volume purchasers who are able to negotiate lower prices because of their high-volume purchases. They are typically able to offer any collection of travel services at a price lower than the individual consumer or his travel agent would be able to arrange.

Many resorts owe their survival to travel agents and tour operators. So too do other hospitality enterprises that depend on the sales volume provided by guests at these resorts. Resorts on some of the Caribbean islands, for example, find that up to 80 percent of their guests have been booked by travel agents. The vast majority of other international travel arrangements are made by travel agents.

▶ Special Characteristics of Hospitality Management

People who manufacture durable goods almost never meet the final purchasers of their products. Toy manufacturers do not see the children who use their toys and seldom know the real extent to which children are pleased or disappointed with their toys. Some customers may write the toy manufacturer to express pleasure or disappointment, and some may return toys to the manufacturer for repair or replacement, but that is usually the extent of their customer contact.

By contrast, people in the service industries typically deal directly with their customers, meeting them face-to-face on an ongoing basis. Hotel employees, for example, provide services directly to customers.

They are in daily contact with guests and often receive immediate feedback about the hotel's quality of service. Many customers express their feelings about the service by complimenting or complaining to the staff. For many customers, the level of service is defined by a specific event or by contact with a particular member of the staff. A clean room may lead a guest to believe that he is staying in a hotel that offers excellent service. Poor service in the dining room may lead another guest to think that all service in the hotel is poor. A friendly and helpful desk clerk or a housekeeper unwilling to provide extra towels may make a world of difference in the minds of guests distinguishing between excellent and poor service.

A customer has particular expectations about the level and quality of service to expect. If the service meets or exceeds those expectations, the customer is likely to be satisfied. If not, she is likely to be unhappy. In fact, an opportunity to transform a first-time customer into a loyal customer may be lost because of poor service. The quality of service is critical in the success and survival of a hospitality business.

Hospitality managers have traditionally tried to ensure the quality of service by providing training to staff. That training was aimed at uniformity. Most believed that by training each staff member to use certain specific service techniques and procedures, they were establishing standards for excellent service.

Some hospitality managers—the more enlightened ones—have come to realize that service need not necessarily be exactly the same for every customer. Service should be of high quality, of course, but some have found it advantageous to tailor service to the specific needs and perceptions of individual customers.

▶ Moments of Truth

Jan Carlzon, former president of Scandinavian Airlines, wrote a book published in 1987 in which he employs the term **moments of truth.** This term describes contacts between customers and businesses that give customers impressions of the businesses and from which customers make judgments about the businesses.[2]

A customer makes a judgment about a business each time he has contact with any element of that business. For example, in a hotel, a guest may first make contact with the hotel business when his taxicab

---

[2]Jan Carlzon, *Moments of Truth* (Cambridge, Mass.: Ballinger Publishing Co., 1987).

stops in front of the entrance. The initial impression made by the outward physical appearance of the building may be the first moment of truth. If the guest expects the taxi door to be opened by a doorkeeper, his presence or absence may be the next moment of truth. The next may be found in the doorkeeper's attitude or demeanor or the manner in which the job is performed. Other moments of truth come from guests' contacts with desk clerks and bellstaff, rides in the self-service elevator, and first reactions to their assigned rooms.

Many other moments of truth occur during the course of a guest's stay in a hotel. Finally, a guest's overall impression reflects every contact made during the period and includes a number of judgments about the business: how efficiently it is run, whether or not it is customer oriented, how competent the employees are, how well the establishment meets the needs of its customers, and the level of its service quality. In a fully occupied hotel of five hundred rooms, there are thousands of moments of truth occurring every day.

The sum total of the customers' moments of truth becomes the perception and impression of a hospitality business and its service quality. If the majority of customers judge the moments of truth to be positive, the business will have a positive reputation. If not, the business's reputation will be negative, and decreasing levels of sales will be likely.

▶ Cycles of Service

Karl Albrecht, in his 1988 book, *At America's Service,* carries this concept further. He states that a customer views an organization in terms of the chain of events from the beginning of his experience with an organization to the end of the experience. He refers to this chain of events as a **cycle of service.** Albrecht states that a cycle of service "is a natural, unconscious pattern that exists in the customer's mind, and it may have nothing in common with your 'technical' approach to setting up the business."[3]

Albrecht points out that service businesses are often set up and run in a fashion designed to achieve some specific goals established by owners or managers and that working to achieve these goals may impede one's ability to provide positive moments of truth and satisfy customers' needs. For example, a hotel may be run to achieve maxi-

---

[3]Karl Albrecht, *At America's Service* (Homewood, Ill.: Dow Jones-Irwin, 1988), p.33.

▶ The St. Regis Best on Pampering Guests ◀

The St. Regis Hotel in New York City pampers its guests like no other hotel in the city. It has a staff of forty-two *maître d'étages* (butlers) on call twenty-four hours a day to handle guests' requests. All *maître d'étages* must speak at least two languages. The 322-room hotel patterns its service after service-oriented hotels in Asia and caters to each of its guest's special needs.

Each *maître d'étages* is trained for two months by Ivor Spencer, who trains the staff at Buckingham Palace. They learn everything from how to serve proper English tea to how to inspect guest rooms. The checklist for each guest room has about three hundred details that must be inspected.

One couple checked into the St. Regis and wanted to watch a baseball game on cable. The St. Regis did not get that cable channel, but it worked out a one-time deal with a cable company to bring in the proper channel to meet the needs of this couple. Guests' preferences are recorded so that the next time they stay at the hotel, the staff will be able to anticipate their needs.

Adapted from an article in USA Today, *July 15, 1992.*

mum profit. In the eyes of management, this may mean that they should establish policies that minimize staff and maximize their efficiency. This may translate into instructions that the housekeeping staff should be intent on getting rooms ready for occupancy each day without regard for special requests of arriving guests. It may mean establishing policies in the kitchen and bar that do not allow servers to take orders for items other than those listed on the menu. Or it may lead to minimizing supervisory staff to a point where customer problems cannot be appropriately handled.

The guests, on the other hand, are not aware of these policies and are concerned with their own comfort and enjoyment of the hotel facility. They experience moments of truth from the beginning of their stay to their departure and, taken together, these represent a cycle of service that leaves an overall impression of satisfaction or dissatisfaction with the hotel.

It is important to note that the policies identified above may work very well in an enterprise producing durable goods. There, a good manager may be considered one who is best able to establish and carry out specific policies and routines that minimize costs and maximize output. In the production of durable goods, important goals include producing appropriate numbers of units at the minimal cost, each of which meets the quality standards established for the item. In that setting, disaffected workers and difficult working conditions may not be of real consequence as long as the products sold to customers meet the quality standards established by management and production volume can be maintained at suitable levels.

The results of such policies in a service enterprise, however, would necessarily be very different. In hospitality, where our products are service, policies must be customer oriented and service oriented. If both managers and staff members do their best to ensure positive moments of truth for customers, the resulting cycles of service are more likely to produce satisfaction. Policies and procedures must be sufficiently flexible so that staff members have the ability to provide individualized service for guests.

▶ Total Quality Management

In recent years, growing numbers of hospitality managers have begun to take the moments of truth concept very seriously and are now taking steps to ensure that more of the moments of truth in their establishments are positive. To accomplish this, many have changed the way they go about managing. A number of managers and organizations have adopted a management style that some refer to as **total quality management** (TQM). Some use the term **service quality management** (SQM) to refer to the same set of basic ideas. Regardless of the term one uses, the underlying principles are the same.

One of these principles is considered key: offering customized rather than standardized service; in other words, tailoring service to the needs of guests and customers. To accomplish this, management must delegate the authority to satisfy guests' needs to the employees who come into direct contact with guests: servers, housekeepers, desk attendants, etc. Managers give employees in these and similar job titles wide latitude to do what is necessary to meet guests' needs and solve their problems without obtaining specific permission from management. The term used to describe this is **employee empowerment.** Employees are said to be empowered when they have the power to make decisions about how best to meet the particular needs of a guest or customer in a particular instance. One effect of this is to provide employees with the ability to transform guests' moments of truth from negative to positive.

Empowerment does not mean that employees have unlimited power to make any changes they choose in any phase of operations. There are reasonable limits. Employees are commonly limited to making decisions about their own jobs. Additionally, there are some commonsense boundaries; housekeepers can satisfy the needs of guests who request extra towels, but they can not respond positively to a transient guest's request for the walls of his room be painted a different color.

While the details of TQM programs vary from one establishment to another, one example drawn from a luxury hotel in an eastern city will serve as a useful illustration. At this hotel, high standards of service are the norm. New employees are required to complete a weeklong training program during which they are instructed that all guests' needs always should be anticipated and satisfied. They also learn that any employee who receives a request or complaint from a guest "owns" that request or complaint; they are expected to fulfill that request or satisfy that complaint, even if they must interrupt other work to do so. If the request can only be met by an employee of another department and therefore must be turned over to another employee, the first employee is responsible for verifying that appropriate action has been taken.

Another feature of TQM programs is their approach to problem solving. Committees are formed to deal with the varied operational problems. In hotels, the members of these committees are drawn from several departments. The committees meet regularly to discuss changes in policies and procedures that might improve employees' abilities to serve the guests' needs. They have the authority to reach decisions and to implement new policies and procedures, as long as it can be demonstrated that guest service will improve.

It is very important to run hospitality operations in a manner that maintains service quality at suitable levels. This is one of the great challenges in hospitality management, a field that demands great dedication and a commitment to solving problems positively. For those prepared, the rewards can be great.

At this point, it will be useful to look at some of the many career opportunities available in the hospitality industry.

▶ Career Opportunities in the Hospitality Industry

Until the late 1950s, management personnel in the hospitality industry were not normally college educated. Those interested in hospitality management typically began their careers by taking lower-level jobs to learn the business and eventually worked their way up through the organization. This process often took many years. In hotels, men typically started as elevator operators, information clerks, or bellmen; by contrast, women began as reservations clerks or typists. Career development followed much the same approach in restaurants: people started as servers, order clerks, or bookkeepers and then progressed slowly to jobs with higher levels of responsibility and higher salaries.

▶ Educational Requirements

Although it is still possible to begin a career in hospitality without formal education in the industry, the opportunities for doing so are diminishing each year. Today, those starting careers in hospitality management are more and more likely to have some formal education obtained in one of the postsecondary programs developed over the last thirty years to prepare men and women for hospitality careers. Whether they have earned certificates, diplomas, or degrees at the associate, baccalaureate, or graduate level, growing numbers of hospitality managers and management trainees have studied formally to prepare for their chosen careers.

▶ Experience Requirements

It is important to note that starting positions are typically not filled solely on the basis of educational background. Experience in the field is still an important consideration to many employers, and a number of students have found that good work experience gained while attending classes has been instrumental in their finding good jobs after graduation. In many instances, those in the industry insist that graduates gain real work experience in conjunction with education, and most hospitality-management students today should seek part-time employment during the academic year or full-time employment in the summer. Potential employers are typically more inclined to offer good starting jobs to students with valid work experience behind them. For example, a student who has worked at the front desk of a local hotel while earning a degree is much more likely to obtain a favorable position in the front office of a hotel upon graduation than one who has not had prior front-office experience.

▶ Entry-Level Management Positions

The multifaceted nature of the hospitality industry suggests that the opportunities available are in a number of different areas. In hotels, individuals might be given such job titles as management trainee, assistant front-office manager, night auditor, banquet sales representative, assistant restaurant manager, assistant food and beverage controller, assistant housekeeper, and assistant steward. In some motels and smaller hotels, the available job titles could include assistant manager, banquet manager, and assistant food and beverage manager. In restaurants and similar foodservice operations, analogous positions might carry such titles as management trainee, assistant manager, dining room manager, unit manager, steward, bar manager, banquet manager, or food and beverage cost controller, depending on an individual's level of experience.

The size of an operation often determines the particular job title, and the authority and responsibility associated with a job title will vary greatly with the size of a property. For example, an assistant manager in a fifty-room motel might be the only person on duty in the front office, and therefore she would be responsible for taking reservations, operating the switchboard, checking guests in and out, and solving guests' problems. An assistant manager in a five-hundred-room hotel would have very different, higher-level responsibilities, such as supervising a sizable staff of specialists, each of whom is responsible for one of the many tasks required in lodging operations.

The specific job that a particular individual is offered may be heavily dependent on overall qualifications. After all, employers are likely to consider many aspects of an applicant, trying to match them to the requirements of a particular job. In order to do this successfully, they must attempt to assess all of an applicant's attributes, not simply her technical knowledge.

▶ Qualifications and Employer Assessment

Some of the factors commonly considered when assessing potential candidates include grades, outside interests, participation in organizations, past employment record, ability to communicate effectively, attitudes, and interpersonal skills. Each employer will weigh them differently—some will emphasize good grades, others will emphasize past employment record, and others will stress good communications skills.

▶ Lodging Jobs Will Increase at a Rapid Rate ◀

The number of jobs in the lodging industry will increase from 1.572 million to 2.209 million between 1992 and 2005, according to a study by the National Certification Commission of the U.S. Department of Labor. This is an increase of 40.5 percent over the ten-year period. The lodging industry ranks tenth among the forty major employment classifications.

Adapted from an article in Lodging Magazine, *June 1995, Page 20.*

Good grades demonstrate dedication to achievement and willingness to work hard as well as ability. A broad range of interests in sports, music, drama, and other areas normally indicates that the applicant is well rounded. Participation in organizations such as fraternities and sororities, student government, and professional groups gives the employer some idea of a person's social skills and leadership abilities. Past employment is examined to see if the applicant has a stable work record, which can be indicative of future reliability. Employers also assess the attitudes of applicants, looking for those who are willing to devote the necessary time and effort to a task, even if it means temporarily sacrificing other activities. They look for

▶ Managerial Careers Booming in Foodservice and

Of all the industries in the United States, the foodservice and lodging industries together employ the largest share of all types of managers. In 1990, there were nearly one million managers employed in the foodservice and lodging industries. This is the largest group of managers and accounts for 0.9 percent of all managerial professions as measured by the Bureau of Labor Statistics. In fact, the number of foodservice and lodging managers is greater than the number of financial managers or administrative managers. It is even greater than the number of marketing and advertising managers!

Adapted from an article in Restaurants USA, *March 1995, Page 44.*

applicants who are willing, cooperative workers, able to do the work required of them.

Finally, employers search for those with good interpersonal skills. During the course of a typical workday, hospitality employees are likely to come in contact with a diverse population. This includes guests from many regions of the country and from many parts of the world as well as coworkers whose native language is different from their own. Because hospitality is a service business that requires ongoing contact with a variety of people, it is critical that employees are able to communicate effectively with guests as well as with coworkers.

▶ Advantages and Disadvantages of Working in the Hospitality Industry

All jobs have positive and negative elements, and those in the hospitality industry are not exceptions. People view the characteristics of jobs quite differently. Although one aspect of a given job may be considered positive by one individual, another may view that same aspect in a negative light. For example, evening work suits some people well, but others dislike it intensely. Similarly, clerical work suits many, while others find it tedious. Rather than attempt judgments about what may be positive and negative, we will merely outline the conditions generally found in the industry.

▶ Wages and Salaries

Generally, wages and salaries are determined by such factors as the adequacy of the labor supply, the level of skills required for particular jobs, the extent to which unions influence wages, and various regional considerations. The hospitality industry is labor intensive, and many of the jobs require relatively low levels of skill and education. Generally, entry-level jobs requiring neither specific education nor previous experience tend to command the lowest wages. Jobs that do require specific training or previous experience, such as cook or night auditor, are paid somewhat higher wages. Starting salaries for recent college graduates with majors in hospitality management tend to be average when compared with similar jobs in other industries. Salaries for jobs in middle and upper management are often considered quite good, and many regard them as excellent. In general, larger organizations often pay more than smaller organizations for similar work and, within a given region, wages and salaries in affluent urban areas tend to be higher than those offered in rural and poorer urban areas.

▶ Work Environment

The work environment in hospitality operations can be quite good compared with other industries. First-class and luxury hotels are often considered fine places to work, with their opulent surroundings and clean environment. The idea of spending one's working hours in contact with wealthy and famous guests is appealing to many. In better properties, employees are typically provided with excellent meals, and some management employees may be permitted to eat in the dining rooms of the hotels. Further, some hospitality organizations provide exceptional work sites: Caribbean beaches; resort areas with pools, tennis courts, golf courses; and a host of other superior facilities.

On the other hand, conditions can be viewed as less than satisfactory in some older, poorly maintained hotels, and in a sizable number of individually owned restaurants. The front offices of some hotels are without air conditioning, which can be unpleasant in sultry summer months. Aging equipment that continually breaks down can present working conditions in some properties that would be considered unsatisfactory. Kitchens with poorly maintained equipment and improper ventilation can be uncomfortably hot and very difficult to work in.

▶ Hours and Days of Work

Because the industry caters to travelers who may seek hospitality services at any hour of the day or night, a vast number of hospitality operations are open when other businesses are closed. Except for some resort properties, hotels are open and staffed twenty-four hours a day, seven days a week, including holidays. New employees, including managers, are often required to work evenings and weekends. Employees typically have one or two days off each week, depending on the establishment. The days off are not likely to be Saturdays or Sundays for new employees; weekend days off are usually reserved for employees with seniority.

On the other hand, some consider working on weekends to be an advantage. It gives them time off during the week, when shopping malls and recreation facilities are often least crowded. By the same token, those who work evening shifts look forward to having daylight hours for activities that would be difficult or impossible at night (e.g., boating, golf, and tennis). In some cases, employees work according to a system known as alternating watches, where an individual may work a normal day shift for one or two weeks and then an evening shift for a similar period. This provides variety and satisfies the lifestyles of many. Those who are in the resort industry often work very hard during times when their friends are playing but are able to take vacations when others cannot—between vacation seasons, when those in some other industries cannot possibly get away from their desks. This also gives them opportunities to vacation when resort areas are least crowded and rates are lowest.

New managers in the hospitality industry are often asked to work longer hours than they would in other industries. A work week of fifty to sixty hours is not uncommon. Neither are workdays of ten to twelve hours. However, because much of a hospitality manager's workday involves talking to interesting guests, most who do this have no complaints about the length of the day.

It should be noted that the spouses and family members of some hospitality managers object to the specific hours, the long workdays, or the somewhat unusual days off that can be common in this industry. However, the family members of anyone aspiring to a successful career in management in any field must recognize that long hours are likely to be among the requirements. Hospitality is not unique in that respect.

▶ Travel Opportunities

One of the attractions of a career in the hospitality industry is the potential it offers for travel. A number of chain organizations in the hotel/motel segment of the industry customarily transfer management employees from one property to another every few years. Some restaurant chains do so as well. Both lodging and foodservice chains are more likely to transfer management employees during periods of expansion, when their expertise is needed in new units. Some transfer management-level employees at the time of promotion; others transfer managers periodically to reduce the risk of long-term managers becoming "stale."

Another advantage of a career in hospitality is that job opportunities are not restricted to particular cities or regions, as in some other industries. Hospitality businesses can be found in literally every region, city, and town, and individuals can find positions available wherever they choose to live, regardless of climate or geography. Hospitality is very much an international profession.

There are those who choose their careers in hospitality specifically because of the travel opportunities the industry provides. There are even some who plan to take advantage of the travel opportunities by taking winter jobs in warm resort areas such as Florida and summer jobs in the cooler resorts of New England and the north central or Rocky Mountain states. For those who enjoy travel, a career in hospitality can satisfy a need that might be difficult to meet in some other field.

There are others in the industry who truly dislike travel and may take all possible steps to avoid it. Many in the hospitality industry have families and find it very difficult to move, particularly if there are school-age children or elderly parents involved. Many are settled members of their communities and have close ties they are unwilling to break. A substantial number own homes, which they may be unwilling or unable to sell. Others merely prefer to stay in communities where they have lived for many years. Those who prefer not to move from one region to another must be more particular about the types of positions they seek or the organizations from which they seek employment. It is possible, after all, to work for an independent city, resort hotel, motel, or individual foodservice establishment for many years without having to face the prospect of moving to a new geographical area.

▶ Opportunities for Advancement

In a number of businesses, youth has traditionally been a barrier to rapid advancement: promotions in these businesses have been slow, and managers on the higher levels have normally been close to retirement age. In some businesses, it may be necessary to wait, sometimes for years, until openings occur within the company and advancement becomes possible. Generally, this has not been the case in the hospitality industry.

In hospitality, there is a long tradition of mobility. Employees at all levels have almost always found it possible to change jobs readily, and many have done so with great regularity. The transient nature of the industry has generally meant that opportunities for higher-paying jobs have continually been available to qualified individuals. Thus, if an individual working in a given hotel or restaurant decides she has little possibility of promotion, she can readily find another position—often a better one—-in another hotel or restaurant.

The hospitality industry has ample opportunities for people of all ages. It is not uncommon for restaurant managers, resident managers, marketing directors, food and beverage managers, executive housekeepers, and others in equally responsible positions to be in their mid to late twenties. At the same time, many of those in the hospitality industry are people who are in their second or third careers—people who discovered the appeal of a career in hospitality after a number of years in some other, possibly less interesting field. Except for the extremes, neither youth nor age is a disadvantage in this industry.

▶ A People-Oriented Profession

Because the hospitality industry serves the needs of the traveling public, the majority of people working in this industry—and virtually all of its managers—are in constant contact with guests and customers. Ours is a people-oriented profession. Individuals preparing for careers in hospitality must understand that their responsibilities are likely to include daily interaction with customers to meet their needs and to solve their problems. Social skills and the ability to communicate effectively with others are important assets for anyone planning such a career. Understanding the varying needs and views of peoples from the many and varied cultural, ethnic, racial, and religious backgrounds that make up our international mosaic is a clear asset. So, too, is an ability to communicate well in writing and in speech—to select and use words and phrases that do not offend those with backgrounds different from one's own. In addition, one should have an understanding of the fact that facial and other physical expressions have meaning and that the meaning one intends may not be the meaning conveyed to people of different backgrounds. It has been said that diversity is a major factor in American society today. Nowhere is this more true than in the hospitality industry.

If a number of your interests and preferences match those detailed in this chapter, you may find the hospitality industry a suitable choice for your career. If so, you are likely to find many exciting and rewarding career opportunities available to you. Reliability, dedication, willingness to work hard, and an interest in meeting customers' needs and solving their problems are the primary requisites for success in this field.

▶ Summary

In this chapter, the distinction between the manufacturing and service sectors of an economy is drawn, and the scope of the hospitality industry within the service sector is defined and described. The relationships between the hospitality industry and travel and tourism, travel agents, tour operators, transportation, and entertainment are explored. The elements that make the hospitality industry unique are identified, as are the characteristics that distinguish hospitality and other service enterprises from manufacturing. The terms *moment of truth, cycles of service,* and *empowerment* are defined and discussed, and their significance for the hospitality industry is described. *Total Quality Management* is cited as an important means for reducing negative *moments of truth.* Career opportunities available in the hospitality industry and both the advantages and disadvantages of hospitality industry employment are explored. Finally, a variety of skills and values are identified as important assets for those planning careers in hospitality management.

 Key Terms

Cycle of Service	Service Quality Management
Employee Empowerment	Travel
Hospitality	Travel Agent
Hospitality Industry	Tourism
Moments of Truth	Tour Operator
Package	Total Quality Management

 Questions

1. Distinguish between the manufacturing and service sectors in an economy.

2. Define the terms *hospitality* and *hospitality industry.*

3. Identify the two principal segments of the hospitality industry and list the major types of businesses in each.

4. What is the scope of the travel and tourism industry? What is the relationship of the hospitality industry to the travel and tourism industry?

5. Historically, what kinds of entertainment have hospitality enterprises provided for travelers?

6. Discuss the relationship and the importance of transportation to the hospitality industry.

7. Define the terms *travel agent* and *tour operator.*

8. List and discuss two distinctions between the hospitality industry and other services.

9. What special characteristics of the hospitality and other service industries distinguish them from manufacturing?

10. Define the terms *moment of truth* and *cycle of service* and discuss the significance of each for the hospitality industry.

11. Does the study of hospitality management appear to be more important or less important today than in the past? Why do you suppose that this is the case?

12. What is *Total Quality Management?* Of what significance is it to hospitality operations?

13. What advantages would you expect graduates of hospitality programs to have in applying for their first management training positions? Why?

14. List several jobs that a new graduate of a hospitality management program could reasonably expect to be offered as a first job in a thousand-room hotel? In a fifty-unit motel? In a quick-service restaurant?

15. List and explain the significance of six qualifications hospitality employers commonly look for in applicants for management trainee positions.

16. For you, personally, what are the positive, appealing aspects of a career in the hospitality industry? What are the negative, unappealing aspects?

17. Why are social and communications skills important for people working in the hospitality industry?

Moments of Truth

1. You are working as a server in the Collins Hotel. One entree on the dining room menu is sea scallops, which are breaded and then deep fried. A guest in the dining room asks the server if she can have the scallops broiled instead. You ask the chef, who informs you that he will not permit any changes to menu items. Discuss this in terms of *moments of truth, cycle of service,* and *empowerment.*

2. You are the morning desk clerk in a large motel just off an interstate highway. A guest has just come to the desk to check out. He is complaining that he could not sleep because of noises in the next

room that continued until after 3:00 A.M. He claims that repeated calls to the desk produced no result. What would you do to change these negative moments of truth into a positive outcome?

3. You are the desk clerk at a seaside hotel. Half the rooms and suites face the sea; the other half face inland. One guest who was checked in by a clerk on an earlier shift assigned the guest to a room with an inland view. The rate is $85. This guest is now at the desk stating that he had reserved a room with a view of the sea. The reservation record confirms his statement, but you have no sea view rooms available at $85. However, there are three suites with sea views available, but all have rates over $150. What would you do?

Part Two

Foundations

T W O

Hospitality Foundations I

Early Development of the Hospitality Industry

After reading and studying this chapter, you should be able to:

1 Explain the historical interrelationships between travel and the hospitality industry.

2 Identify the types of hospitality enterprises common in the Egyptian, Greek, and Roman empires and describe their principal characteristics.

3 Describe the hospitality services generally available to travelers in the period between the Fall of Rome and the Renaissance.

4 Discuss conditions faced by travelers in western Europe during the Renaissance period.

5 List and explain the principal political, economic, and social developments that led to improvements in travel and in the hospitality services available to travelers in the period A.D. 1600 to 1800.

6 Identify the principal changes in the hospitality industry that resulted from the development of rail travel.

7 Identify and describe the earliest types of hospitality establishments in America.

8 Identify the historic significance of each of the following hotels and restaurants: Coles Ordinary, Fraunces' Tavern, City Hotel, Tremont Hotel, San Francisco's Palace Hotel, Denver's Brown Palace, The Greenbrier, Ye Olde Union Oyster House, Delmonico's.

9 Discuss the impact of railroads on the development of both city hotels and resort hotels in the nineteenth century.

10 List and discuss the characteristics of nineteenth-century city hotels in the United States that made them unique in their time.

11 Describe the dimensions of the fire problem in city hotels in the nineteenth century.

12 List and discuss the economic and social conditions that fostered the growth of the foodservice industry in the nineteenth century.

13 Name six types of foodservice establishments common in major U.S. cities in the nineteenth century.

14 Identify the following individuals and describe the principal contributions of each to the development of the hospitality industry: Samuel Coles, Samuel Fraunces, Isaiah Rogers, Harvey Parker, Henry Flagler, and Fred Harvey.

▶ Introduction

Anyone planning a career in the hospitality industry should have some interest in both the present state of the industry and in its history—a rich history that explains a lot about today's hospitality industry. As an educated person, every hospitality manager should understand the industry; that is, she should know more about it than the relatively limited information necessary for doing her job each day. In our view, all managers should be able to discuss any aspect of our industry, current or historic, with coworkers, superiors, and subordinates.

This chapter and chapter 3 offer some hint of the industry's classic and historic roots. They do not constitute a complete and comprehensive history of the hospitality industry worldwide and in its many manifestations: such a history would require volumes. However, the material presented here will provide a suitable foundation for understanding the development of our industry and may impel some—those who find themselves intrigued by the historical information presented here—to study the history of our industry further at the undergraduate or the graduate level.

▶ An Overview

Those beginning to study the history of the hospitality industry soon recognize that the development of the industry is inexorably tied to the development of transportation and the economic growth of cities, regions, and even nations.

Transportation and economic progress are clearly interdependent: they tend to develop together. Historically, those nations that achieved high economic status in a given era had transportation networks that were more advanced than those of other nations at the time. Examples of economic prosperity and superior transportation abound: the Roman Empire of twenty-one centuries ago and the British Empire of the nineteenth century are excellent examples. By contrast, and in our own time, nations that are part of the so-called Third World offer typical examples of inadequate transportation networks and relative economic distress. To the student of hospitality history, it soon becomes quite clear that growth and development in our industry has tended to occur most commonly in those nations that

1. were the most economically successful at the time, and
2. had the most highly developed transportation networks.

From the earliest days of human history, much travel has been dependent on the existence of roads of one sort or another. Whether people traveled on foot, on the backs of animals, in vehicles pulled by

The Via Appia (Appian Way), one of the many systems of roads that were built during the era of the Roman Empire. A variety of hospitality services—inns, taverns, and escorted travel—arose as transportation networks were built throughout the Roman Empire, as well as in the empires of Egypt, Greece, and China.

animals, by train, or by automobile, roads were a key element in the development of travel and transportation systems. As we shall see, each segment of the hospitality industry changed and grew as roads improved.

▶ Beginnings

Human population has existed for hundreds of thousands of years in all parts of the world including Africa, the Americas, Asia, and elsewhere. For example, Cro-Magnon man was active in Europe and the Middle East at about 40,000 B.C. At about 20,000 B.C., early humans crossed the Bering land bridge from Asia to North America. At about 10,000 B.C., Jericho, the oldest known city, was built in the Middle East. However, there was relatively little travel as we know of it today and no known hospitality industry until relatively recently in human history.

▶ The Sumerians

The recorded history of the hospitality industry begins with the Sumerians, a group of people who inhabited an area known as Mesopotamia, near the Persian Gulf, by about 4000 B.C. Much of this area, covering part of the modern country of Iraq, was particularly fertile, making some of the Sumerians prosperous as well as skilled farmers and cattle breeders. Sumerian skill at farming enabled them to raise and harvest sufficient grain to support artisans and craftsmen who could devote their time and talent to other activities, such as tool making, building, and pottery making. The Sumerian farmers were eventually able to produce so much grain that they had a surplus available to trade. Sumerians are often credited with inventing money and writing, both critical elements in the evolution of business.

In addition to growing and trading grain, the Sumerians became skilled at converting it to alcoholic beverages—beers primarily. These became the most widely and commonly consumed beverages at all levels of Sumerian society. The Sumerian beers were probably safer to drink than their water.

Local Sumerian taverns were probably among the first hospitality businesses. These were drinking establishments, catering to people who lived in the immediate neighborhood. These taverns served various beers and provided a gathering place for local residents to discuss the issues of the day.

▶ Early Traders Need Hospitality Services

By 2000 B.C., a considerable amount of trade had developed among the peoples of the Middle East. Many were earning their living from trade and were following established routes to trade for exotic goods. They needed places to stay and places to eat on these long journeys, and enterprising individuals set up hospitality businesses to meet the needs of these travelers. Known as **caravanserai,** these businesses were early inns, providing food and shelter. Their reputations were similar to those of taverns of the period: dirty, bug-infested places that travelers preferred to avoid whenever possible.

▶ Empires: 3200 B.C. to A.D. 476

While several civilizations were thriving in the region around the Persian Gulf, there were other civilizations developing around the Mediterranean Sea. They developed during the years from 3200 B.C. to A.D. 476—a period known to historians as the *Empire Era.* During this time, three significant empires flourished around the Mediterranean: the Egyptian, the Greek, and the Roman.

We do not mean to suggest that these parts of the world were the only areas where civilization was developing. Nor are we implying that these were the only areas where trade, travel, and the conditions for the evolution of a hospitality industry could be found. History clearly indicates otherwise. There is evidence, for example, that a road system was built in China about the year 2300 B.C. and that there were small road systems in northern Europe as early as 4000 B.C. There are also clear indications of developing civilizations in India by 2400 B.C. These examples show that a number of civilizations were developing around the world during this period.

Because of the advanced levels of their civilizations, the wealth of information available about them, and the direct influence they had on the development of the hospitality industry in Europe, we will restrict our discussion of this era to the Mediterranean empires of Egypt, Greece, and Rome. Each of these built and improved transportation systems and developed hospitality services for increasing numbers of travelers. These developments reached their zenith during the Roman period, with the creation of a transportation network that surrounded the Mediterranean and extended to such distant points as England, France, and Germany.

The Great Sphinx and the Pyramid of
Chefren at Giza (ca. 2500 B.C.). Since their
construction, visitors have traveled to
marvel at the awesome majesty of these
monuments to the pharaohs. (Photo
courtesy of Egyptian Tourist Authority.)

▶ Egypt

The Egyptian Empire developed over a period of several thousand
years. By about 3200 B.C., various groups had been united under one
government. The Egyptians are considered the first people to have created a political entity we could recognize as a single nation rather than
a group of city states. They developed a government to rule a large
number of people in an organized manner, with a hierarchy of civil servants dividing responsibilities for various aspects of governing. The
government was headed by a pharaoh, their term for a king.

The famed pyramids were built as tombs for the pharaohs. These
were constructed as early as 2700 B.C. and became tourist attractions
that people traveled great distances to view. They may well have been
the first "man-made" tourist attractions!

Travel was not uncommon in ancient Egypt. In addition to traveling to see the pyramids, people traveled to see other sights, to trade
goods, to transact government business, and to attend religious festivals. There is evidence to suggest that the ancient Egyptians may have
been the first to organize festivals, religious and otherwise, and to see
that foodservice and lodging was provided for the crowds attending.
Thus, the ancient Egyptians may have been responsible for beginning
the activity we now call tourism.

▶ Greece

Ancient Greek civilization began to develop about 1100 B.C. It evolved in
the form of independent city states that tended to be fiercely competi-

tive. In the early years, major battles took place between the peoples of two of these, Sparta and Athens. No unified Greek nation developed until the middle of the third century B.C., when Philip of Macedon united the city states. His son, Alexander the Great, built an empire that surrounded the Mediterranean and extended as far east as India.

The Greeks were great travelers. By 356 B.C., their travels over land and sea had made them dominant in the Mediterranean region. They had established colonies that stretched their empire as far west as Spain and even to the north coast of the Black Sea. Travel to these distant colonies was risky, at best: common dangers at sea included shipwreck and piracy. On land, robbery was a constant threat. In spite of the danger, many Greeks traveled to great religious centers, particularly Delphi and Olympia, to take part in games and competitions and to consult their oracles.

While there were good restaurants located in major cities to serve the needs of travelers, the inns and taverns in Greece were reputed to be particularly dreadful places. The proprietors were considered among the lowest forms of human life. Innkeepers commonly adulterated drinks with water and engaged in various criminal activities. Some were particularly good at extortion and espionage. They were almost universally despised by citizens of wealth, status, and power, who would not enter inns and taverns under any circumstances. If a government employee visited one, he risked his colleagues' having nothing further to do with him.

The two most important contributions the Greeks made to the development of the hospitality industry were

1. their language, which became universally accepted as the language of international trade; and
2. their currencies, which were widely circulated, accepted, and trusted as the medium of exchange for monetary transactions.

The general acceptance of the Greek language and currencies throughout the empire made travel and trade comparatively easy and thus played an important role in increasing the volume of both. And as travel and trade increased, so did the demand for the hospitality services of food and lodging.

► Rome

The Roman Empire dates from the time peasant farmers from central Europe settled at approximately the site of present-day Rome. By about 500 B.C., the Romans had established a government that provided for the election of some officials by citizens. The Romans were ambitious and pursued international power by both military and nonmilitary means. They aggressively increased their territory, and as they did so, their influence grew. In 146 B.C., after many years of conflict, the Romans were finally victorious over the Greeks. Roman efforts at territorial expansion continued, and by the time Rome had conquered most of western Europe and the Middle East, inns and taverns were well established throughout the empire.

Travel within the empire was relatively safe and easy, compared with earlier times. Travel was much easier than it had been because

1. The traveler needed only one currency—Roman coins—to travel anywhere in the empire.
2. The excellent system of roads the Romans built throughout Europe made travel faster and easier.
3. The traveler needed to know only Latin or Greek, the languages of business and government, to communicate fairly easily in any part of the empire.

These factors contributed to the development of an economic prosperity in Rome that surpassed any previously known. Goods of all kinds were sent to Rome from every part of the known world—some because of conquest, most because of trade. As a result, many citizens of Rome became wealthy.

There were a few good inns reserved for military and government personnel and a very few fine resorts available only to the wealthiest of citizens, but the general quality of the taverns and inns available to the public was poor. Although there were many inns along the great Roman roads, the upper classes did not patronize them if they could find any conceivable alternative.

Roman food, by contrast, was often excellent. It was not consumed in their inns, however. The Romans, particularly the wealthy, had lavish meals at home and at banquet facilities adjacent to the public baths.

The Roman public restaurants of the day served ordinary food to the population. In the ruins at Pompeii, there are a number of small restaurants that remind one of present-day fast-food establishments. They share a single basic design and appear to have been set up to prepare and sell essentially the same, very limited menu. They may have been operated by one person or by one small group, much like a modern small chain. It is thus conceivable that these Romans should be credited with the establishment of the first restaurant chain!

By the late fifth century A.D., the Roman Empire was in serious decline. In A.D. 476, the last of the Roman emperors was deposed by the Byzantines, who ruled much of the area to the east and south of present-day Italy—lands that had once been part of the Greek, then the Roman empires. After the collapse of the Roman Empire, the Byzantine Empire became dominant in the eastern Mediterranean for the next thousand years.

▶ Decline and Revival: A.D. 476 to A.D. 1300

After the fall of the Roman Empire and the decline in international trade, fine foods disappeared from the western European diet. These were replaced by very basic foods grown at home. About 90 percent of the population returned to farming and other forms of agriculture. Cities began to crumble and some virtually disappeared. Trade nearly ceased, and the middle class disappeared. This period was marked by invasions into the areas of Europe that had once been the Roman Empire. The invaders were so-called barbaric tribes of north central Europe. Travel and tourism—whether for business or pleasure—virtually ceased. Travel was primarily for religious reasons: some brave souls made pilgrimages to Rome and to the Holy Land. Innkeeping nearly disappeared, except for local taverns and a few inns scattered throughout Europe. This was the age of **feudalism,** a system whereby land was given by a ruler in return for loyalty and service.

Throughout this period, the Roman Catholic Church was thriving, gaining both spiritual and political power over the life of Europe. The church, through its monasteries, filled the vacuum created by the demise of the commercial hospitality industry. In effect, the church took over the job of feeding and housing travelers. The monasteries of the church were self-sufficient enterprises. Members of the religious orders were skilled farmers, growing vegetables and herbs within the monastic walls, and members of the orders raised animals for meat and grew grapes for wine.

▶ Renaissance: A.D. 1350 to A.D. 1600

The term *Renaissance* describes the period of European history from the early fourteenth century to the late sixteenth century. It is derived from the French word for rebirth and originally referred to the revival of artistic values, especially in Italy. Later, the term came to mean a distinct historical period characterized by the rise of the individual, scientific inquiry, and growth of worldly values.

▶ Renewed Travel and Trade

By about A.D. 1350, some degree of safety had returned to the roads, and travel and trade increased. Travel and trade created the conditions that led to the rise of the middle class in the economic life of Europe. In this period, the monasteries continued to be the principal providers of hospitality services to travelers in all economic strata.

▶ Commercial Accommodations for Travelers

Gradually, some taverns, inns, and wine shops began to make accommodations available to middle-class travelers, and the church began to take the position that since the middle classes could afford to pay for the hospitality services available outside the monastery walls, it was proper to direct these travelers to such establishments. Thus, the church played a role in the development of the hospitality industry during this period.

The number of inns began to grow. They were very small by today's standards: an inn of twenty-five to thirty rooms was considered large. But the standards of comfort and cleanliness varied greatly from country to country and region to region.

▶ Tavern Signs

During this period—until the nineteenth century, in fact—most people could neither read nor write. Taverns and inns developed signs with distinctive pictures so that people could identify and direct other people to them. The signs varied, but were usually of animals or birds. A weary traveler would be directed to the sign of the bull, or the black swan, or the lion or duck. These signs survive today and are found on many taverns and inns, particularly in the United Kingdom.

▶ The Discomforts of Travel

Traveling was uncomfortable at best. Many roads of the period were more like trails, and travelers intending to go any distance would ride

For people who could not read, distinctive names and signs made it easier to find the local public house. The Cat & Fiddle Pub in Hinton Admiral, England, is a fine example. (Photo courtesy of British Tourist Authority, New York City.)

horses. Women normally did not travel because of the discomforts of the road and the dangers associated with travel. Therefore, inns did not have provisions for women. It was not unusual to find the bedroom of an inn furnished with one or more large beds, each of which would sleep five or six people. In such places, the traveler would go to bed fully dressed in street clothes and share the bed with several strangers. The realities of travel were so terrible that women avoided it until the late nineteenth century.

▶ Food Service during the Renaissance

During this period, there were no restaurants as we know them. No dining rooms offered meals to the public at large. In England, there were taverns, public houses (pubs), ale houses, and inns. None of these were primarily dining establishments; to the extent that they served food, the food was intended only for travelers who had no other place to eat. As in other times and places, they were ordinarily avoided by the wealthy upper classes, who dined and entertained in their homes.

▶ Innkeeping

The monasteries that had been housing travelers since the fall of Rome continued to do so. When they could find it, travelers preferred this free housing to local inns. Innkeepers resented this unfair competition, and as students of the Reformation know, at this time a number of church practices were considered offensive. In England in 1539, Parliament passed an act that suppressed the 608 religious houses. Under King Henry VIII, the monasteries were closed and the lands given to many of the king's supporters, which helped insure the unification of England under one strong government. One unintended consequence of this upheaval was that travelers could no longer find accommodations in monasteries. This greatly stimulated the innkeeping business and dramatically increased the number of inns in England.

▶ Tourism in the Sixteenth Century

The sixteenth century also saw the beginnings of an activity known as the **Grand Tour.** Wealthy English would send their sons to "finish their educations" on a tour of Europe that might last as long as three years. Because most of the activity of the Renaissance was centered there, the Italian peninsula was a principal destination. Young men might spend an entire year learning about the arts and humanities.

▶ Early Modern: A.D. 1600 to A.D. 1800

The period from A.D. 1600 to A.D. 1800 was a particularly important period in the development of the hospitality industry. One critical element was the development of roads, which facilitated the use of the stagecoach between cities. Roads built by the Romans before A.D. 500 had not been maintained after Rome fell, and thus they had decayed. Moreover, after the fall of Rome, there had been no comparable central governments in Europe to build or maintain road systems. At the beginning of this period, roads were likely to be little better than trails. With continued use, a trail would come to resemble some of the primitive dirt roads found in rural communities. However, because no government was responsible for roads, maintenance was left to the discretion of the owners of the land through which a road passed. Therefore, although it was possible to go from one place to another by stagecoach, it was usually difficult and dangerous because of the condition of the roads.

▶ Introduction of the Stagecoach

With the introduction of the stagecoach, regular stagecoach routes were established, and so-called **coaching inns** soon followed. At the coaching inns, tired horses were exchanged for fresh horses; and stagecoach passengers were fed and given opportunities to rest, frequently overnight. Travel was difficult, since the roads were often mud soaked and full of potholes. One can imagine how uncomfortable it was to ride in a stagecoach all day. By the 1700s, the inns in England were much safer and more comfortable, although the standards varied from one inn to another.

▶ Post-Houses

The mails were an important element in the development of the hospitality industry during this period. Until the late 1700s, the mail in England was carried on horseback by messengers known as post-boys, who were able to ride at about six miles per hour. Any letter usually took several days to go even one hundred miles. With the development of stagecoaches, mail carrying was gradually transferred to stagecoach lines. These had established routes and contracts that provided that mail be delivered within specific amounts of time. Because of these provisions, stagecoaches began to travel faster. Teams of horses were run at full speed for approximately ten miles, at which point the stage stopped at a **post-house** to change horses. A new team would be hitched to the stage, and the process would be repeated.

Post-houses were much like the coaching inns described earlier. They were equipped to feed drivers and passengers or to accommodate them overnight. Locating the inns along coach routes ensured that the inns would serve a steady supply of customers arriving by stagecoach. Even in the eighteenth century, location was an important element in the success of a hospitality enterprise.

▶ Food Service in Coffee Houses and Taverns

Until the late eighteenth century, no public restaurants existed as we know them today. In England, there were establishments known as coffee houses, where one could get light snacks, and there were taverns that served a daily **ordinary,** which was a main meal at a fixed price. Most people consumed their meals at home. The wealthy had their own cooks, and when they entertained, they usually did so in their own homes. Inns were primarily for travelers and did not normally serve meals to local residents.

▶ Restaurants

The food service element of the hospitality industry changed dramatically and forever in France in 1765. In that year, a man named Boulanger was a soup vendor in Paris, operating a small business selling soups and broths. These were known as *restaurants*, a French word meaning restoratives. Soups and broths have long been noted for their ability to fortify the weary or to restore energy, and Boulanger was one of many such sellers of soup and broth in Paris at the time.

For reasons that are unclear, Boulanger decided to add an item to his product line—a dish made of sheep's feet with a sauce. Perhaps some had requested it; perhaps he was merely trying to make his small business different from others. In any event, the *traiteurs*—members of a caterers' guild who prepared roasts and meats for consumption in private homes—objected on the grounds that he was preparing and selling a ragout, and that only *traiteurs* were permitted to sell ragouts and similar foods under existing French law. They took him to court.

After careful study of the *traiteurs'* position, the court decided that Boulanger had not violated any law. The case created much publicity and interest and led to a decree authorizing both *traiteurs* and restaurateurs to serve guests within their establishments. After a while, this resulted in the development of public dining rooms in which guests could be seated and served the food and drink of their choice.

Boulanger is usually credited with creating the first restaurant, which has come to mean an establishment with a dining room open to the public where varied foods may be purchased and consumed. Technically, however, he merely reinvented a form of foodservice enterprise that had existed many centuries earlier but that had disappeared during the Dark Ages. After all, the forerunners of Boulanger's "restaurant" had existed in ancient Greece and Rome.

In the late eighteenth century, the restaurant business took another leap forward. During the French Revolution, the common people of France revolted against the monarchy, taking control of the government and of the properties of wealthy aristocrats, many of whom were executed. Cooks and chefs who had been employed by the aristocrats were suddenly out of work. Unemployed cooks and chefs had to find ways to earn a living, and many opened foodservice establishments. After the French Revolution, the number of restaurants in Paris and in other parts of France began to grow dramatically.

Another type of foodservice establishment to develop in France at this time was the **cafe.** *Café* is the French word for coffee, and it is probable that these cafes were the French equivalents of the English coffee houses. At first they may have served only snacks, just as the English did. It is likely that the proprietors of these establishments soon began to use their highly developed culinary skills to prepare more elaborate items—certainly to the delight of their customers.

These developments in France in the late eighteenth century mark the beginnings of the modern restaurant industry, which embarked on a period of growth and development in the early nineteenth century that continues to this day.

▶ The Industrial Era: From 1800

The Industrial Revolution, which dates from the mid 1700s, started in England with the development of machines to do work that formerly had been done by hand. It was an age of invention. Machines and the developing concept of the factory were key elements that changed forever the way work would be accomplished. It was no longer necessary to depend on water and water wheels for power. With steam engines, power could be made available in locations that had no access to water transportation. This led to the development of mill towns—later, cities—in many new locations across England and Scotland. The greatest period of growth for these new communities and work sites followed the invention of the railroad in 1825. This started the development of a transportation network designed to move raw materials and finished goods from place to place.

▶ Rail Travel and the Hospitality Industry

The significance of the railroad in the development of the hospitality industry cannot be overemphasized. As soon as the railroad was invented, it quickly became apparent that railroads could transport people as well as goods, and could thus reduce traveling time. Passengers could reach their destinations quickly and in relative comfort. The trip from London to Bath, England, a distance of 110 miles requiring eleven hours to travel by stagecoach, took only two and a half hours by rail.

As the rail network grew, stagecoach operators began to lose much of their business. Government contracts to carry the mail were not renewed. New contracts were negotiated with the railroads, and it was not long before the principal postal routes were in the hands of the railroads. People soon abandoned stagecoach travel, as well. This led to the demise of most stagecoach lines in a very few years. As the coach lines disappeared, the coaching inns lost their traditional sources of business and were forced to find new markets or close.

The development of railroad networks—first in England, then in other nations—had a greater effect on the hospitality industry than had any other single development since the fall of the Roman Empire. Passenger traffic on the railroads led to the establishment of railroad stations, which became obvious locations for new hospitality businesses in England and in any other nations with rail networks. Inns, taverns, restaurants, and, later, hotels opened in or near railroad stations. In England, examples include the Charing Cross Hotel and the St. Pancras Hotel in London and the Queen's Hotel in Birmingham. In Scotland, there were St. Enoch's Hotel in Glasgow and the Station Hotel in Perth. Later, in the United States, the Biltmore Hotel and the Commodore Hotel were built in New York City near Grand Central Station.

▶ Public Dining

In the last years of the nineteenth century, some important changes began to appear in the European hospitality industry. Until then, eating meals away from home was done of necessity rather than by choice. Business travelers and people working in factories, shops, and offices ate meals away from home because they could not return home for meals during the working day. Whenever possible, people preferred to dine in the privacy of their homes.

Because public dining was not popular, many hotels were constructed without dining facilities. It was the normal custom for hotel guests to have meals in their rooms—room service, in today's terms. In

▶ Cesar Ritz (1850-1918) ◀

Cesar Ritz was born in 1850 in Switzerland, the thirteenth child in a large family. His early days in the hospitality industry did not suggest that his was to be a brilliant future: he was dismissed from his first two jobs, one as an apprentice wine waiter and the other as an assistant waiter. After this inauspicious beginning, Ritz drifted to Paris where he obtained and lost other jobs before taking a waiter's job in the most fashionable establishment in Paris at that time, the Voisin. He quickly learned that the wealthy in Paris wanted, demanded, and appreciated excellent service. Soon, the wealthiest and most famous of the Voisin's clientele were asking for him by name. His reputation grew, and he became a maître d'hôtel, then restaurant manager at the Grand Hotel at Nice. Because of his superior abilities to please the wealthy, he was always able to work in the finest properties, some of which were being used by Thomas Cook's organization to accommodate those on luxury tours of Europe.

Before long, he progressed to hotel manager, and in 1870, at the age of twenty-seven, Ritz was offered a job managing the Grand National Hotel in Lucerne, Switzerland. The hotel was not a profitable venture when he assumed the manager's job, but Ritz was able to turn it into one with his deft management skills. He inspired the staff and the chef with his own enthusiasm and principles of good service, and he organized luxurious and fabulous entertainment for his guests. Soon the hotel became one of the most popular in Europe, and Cesar Ritz became one of the most respected hoteliers in Europe.

The Ritz name has been carried on and today is a symbol of superior products and luxury hotels. The Ritz chain has hotels throughout the world and includes the Ritz Carlton in Boston, the Chicago Ritz, and the Ritz Carlton in Laguna Niguel, California. Other Ritz Hotels are located in Atlanta, Barcelona, Cleveland, Hong Kong, Houston,

the hotel dining rooms that did exist, the patrons were all men: it was not customary for women to dine in public.

By 1880, dining out had begun to gain acceptability and some small measure of popularity. One of first steps taken in that direction occurred in 1875, in the Albemarle Hotel, London, when a dining facil-

▶ Auguste Escoffier (1846-1935) ◀

Auguste Escoffier was four years older than Cesar Ritz. His career began in Paris, and he was soon employed at some of the finest properties of the time in France. Escoffier and Ritz had worked together at the Grand Hotel, Monte Carlo, before Ritz became manager of the Savoy in London. Recognizing the need for a superior chef to enliven a dull menu in this new luxury hotel, Ritz sent for Escoffier.

Escoffier is noted for his many contributions to the improvement of cuisine and service. He is the only chef ever to be given membership in the French Legion of Honor, a distinction bestowed on him by the president of France in 1920. His principal contributions include

1. simplifying classical cuisine;
2. simplifying menus;
3. reorganizing the kitchen staff into the classical brigade (he divided the kitchen staff into specialized departments on the basis of the types of foods prepared, in contrast to the earlier method, discarded by Escoffier, that had each chef prepare an entire meal from appetizer onwards);
4. revolutionizing banquet service by serving only one or two dishes at a time, rather than the older, established practice of serving a whole table full of dishes at once;
5. naming dishes after famous people (Melba toast, Peaches Melba, and Melba Sauce were named for the opera star Nellie Melba);
6. writing *Le Guide Culinaire* (a culinary text and collection of recipes used by several generations of chefs).

Following the success of the Savoy, a number of other luxury properties were opened in London, including the Waldorf, the Strand Palace, and Claridges, to name but a few. All of these survive to this day.

Auguste Escoffier is perhaps the most famous and the most respected chef of all time. He has had a greater impact on culinary arts than anyone else.

ity was opened for the "accommodation of both ladies and gentlemen." By this time, the term restaurant had come into common English use but referred to the dining room of a hotel.

In London, new luxurious hotels were built. Some of them were known both for the excellence of their guest accommodations and for the superiority of their food. One of the best known of these was the Savoy, opened by an entrepreneur named Richard d'Oyly Carte in 1889. In the Savoy, d'Oyly Carte employed two men who would become famous throughout the world: Cesar Ritz and Auguste Escoffier.

▶ Hospitality in America

The development of the hospitality industry in the United States has been unique, having no precise parallel in any other country. There appear to be a number of contributing reasons for this, including the vast size of the country, the multinational character of the people, the formation of the transportation system, and the unique political and economic systems operating in the United States. A number of factors, listed below, have set the American hospitality experience apart from that in the rest of the world.

1.   Since the time of the earliest settlements in the late sixteenth century, a larger proportion of the American people have traveled greater distances than have the people of other nations; consequently Americans have patronized hotels and restaurants in greater numbers.

2.   The U.S. political and economic systems have made it possible for financially successful people to build grand hotels as monuments to their success, even if the properties they built were unprofitable. These systems have also enabled ambitious, hard-working people of limited means and little education to become successful in hospitality businesses.

3.   In the United States, innkeeping has always been considered an honorable and respected profession. This is in stark contrast to the tradition of innkeeping in other nations, where innkeepers were commonly relegated to the lowest classes of society.

4.   American hotels have always been "public places"—establishments used by local residents as social centers and places for entertaining. In other nations, inns and hotels were used only by travelers—at least until the late nineteenth century. In these countries, the local populace frequented taverns, but not hotels.

5.   The multicultural nature of the American population has led to a greater diversity in the kinds of restaurants established, in contrast to those established in other countries.

6.   Although other nations have long relied on railroads as their major means of intercity travel and transportation, at the end of World War II, the United States began to rely heavily on automobiles and air-planes instead. Today, automobiles account for over 80 percent of all intercity travel in the United States, airplanes account for approxi-mately 17 percent, and railroads less than 2 percent. The major differ-ence between American modes of transportation and those used in other nations has caused American hospitality operations to develop very differently.

7.   Several unique hospitality concepts originated in the United States and were later imitated in other nations. These include
   a.   large grand hotels,
   b.   restaurant chains,
   c.   franchises, and
   d.   motels.

▶ Ordinaries, Taverns, and Inns in Early America

The earliest known example of an American hospitality enterprise existed in Jamestown, Virginia, in 1610. Because the Jamestown settle-ment did not survive, there is no reliable information about it. There-fore, the beginning of the American hospitality industry is usually said to be 1634, when Samuel Coles opened an establishment in Boston that was named Coles Ordinary. It was a tavern—the first tavern of record in the American colonies, and probably the first inn, as well. It was quite successful, lasting well over 125 years: when John Hancock became governor of Massachusetts in the eighteenth century, Coles Ordinary was still in business and was renamed Hancock's Tavern.

The terminology used in the colonial period to identify these estab-lishments may be confusing. Throughout the colonial period, the terms ordinary, tavern, and inn were all used to refer to the same basic institution—an enterprise established to provide food, drink, overnight accommodation, or some combination of these to travelers, local inhabitants, or both. Over time, tavern became the more common term from New England to New York; inn became favored in the Penn-sylvania region; and ordinary was more common in the South.

The word *ordinary* is an old term, used originally in England to describe a midday meal served at a fixed price in a tavern to the local inhabitants. The term also came to mean the tavern itself. The ordinary offered no menu and no choice: the tavern keeper served whatever he had decided to prepare for that day. Ordinaries in New England were under strict Puritan guardianship and were not allowed, at one point, to charge more than six pence for a meal and one penny for a quart of ale or beer.

Opening and closing hours were enforced by the Puritans, and men who drank too much were punished. The punishment could be severe: miscreants could be put in bilbos (long iron bars with shackles that slide back and forth), set in the stocks, and whipped. Records show that Robert Wright was fined twenty shillings and put in the stocks for an hour for being "twice distempered in drink." Robert Coles—no relation to Samuel Coles—was fined ten shillings and ordered to wear a sign on his back that read "DRUNKARD" in large letters. Unfortunately, this penalty did not cure him. A year later he was at it again, and that time the badge of disgrace was made permanent: he was ordered to wear a large *D* around his neck. Lists of names of drunkards such as Coles were given to taverns in other towns, and the proprietors were warned not to serve liquor to these people under penalty of losing their licenses.

The number of ordinaries in the New England colonies grew. They were considered important establishments, and sometimes the courts directed that ordinaries or public houses be opened in communities where they did not exist. In 1656, the General Court of Massachusetts made towns responsible for sustaining an ordinary. For example, Concord, Massachusetts was fined by the court for not having an ordinary and was directed to open one. In 1644, the colonial records of Connecticut ordered "one sufficient inhabitant in each town to keep an ordinary, since strangers were straitened for want of entertainment." It was recognized early in the colonial period that the traveler needed a place to eat, drink, and find accommodation. Inducements were offered to a person willing to keep an ordinary. These included exemption from church rates and school taxes, grants of land, or pasturage for the owner's cattle.

Early ordinaries existed not only to accommodate the traveler but also to serve as gathering places for the local townsfolk. They were important centers for the exchange of news and served as places where public questions could be debated or public opinion sampled. In addition, they were places for local residents to seek refreshments—ale, beer, and cider among them. In wintertime, taverns were particularly popular places. For example, during church services, people became very cold in the unheated churches and meeting houses while they sat listening to long sermons. After the services, the men flocked to a welcoming nearby tavern to warm up.

▶ Innkeeping in the Colonies

Unlike the innkeepers in England, American innkeepers have always been respected members of the community, and inns located in cities and towns were generally clean and well run. When one traveled into rural areas, however, the quality of the taverns and inns was less reliable, ranging from "very uncomfortable" to "quite nice." In these areas, anyone who could both build a log hut and supply liquor could put up a Tavern sign. Those who did would then go to the woods nearby, kill some game, and put it into a pot to cook. The result was used to feed the "guests," and was known as potluck.

The practice of sharing a bed with strangers had disappeared in Europe by the 1700s, but it persisted in America, particularly in the rural inns or taverns.

▶ The Oldest Continually Operating Tavern in America

New York City, one of America's oldest cities, has had its share of firsts. One of special interest to the student of hospitality history is Fraunces' Tavern, a tavern in the lower part of the island of Manhattan known as Wall Street, now New York's financial center. Located at the corner of Broad and Pearl streets, it has the honor of being the oldest continually operating tavern in the nation, and it has some interesting history associated with it.

The building was constructed in 1719 as a private residence, which it remained until about 1757, when the owner moved uptown to a better neighborhood, a practice that persisted in New York City for generations. In 1762, it was sold to a West Indian named Samuel Fraunces, who converted it to a tavern that he named the Queen's Head. After operating it for a short time, he leased it out for several years but returned to operate it in 1775 because he was unable to sell it. He continued to run it throughout the Revolutionary War, but it was not actually known as Fraunces' Tavern until 1783, after the war.

Fraunces' Tavern® Restaurant in New York City, the oldest continuously operating tavern in the United States. (Photo courtesy of Fraunces' Tavern® Restaurant.)

One of Fraunces' customers was George Washington, whom Fraunces served when the general met with his staff at the tavern to plan various war campaigns. When the British occupied New York City, Fraunces continued to operate the tavern. Although his customers were then British generals, Fraunces remained loyal to the revolutionary cause, serving as a spy for the American army. Fraunces frequently sent word about British plans to General Washington. In fact, Fraunces has sometimes been characterized as the first American intelligence agent!

▶ The First Hotel Building in the United States

In 1794, the first structure designed specifically as a hotel was constructed in New York City near Wall Street. Aptly named the City Hotel, it occupied a large site on the island of Manhattan, on the west side of lower Broadway near Trinity Church. The hotel had seventy-three guest rooms and was the largest hotel in New York until 1813. It was simply furnished, was spacious and comfortable, and offered room service to its guests. For $2, it offered a room and meals—breakfast at eight, dinner at three, tea at six, and supper at nine.

The City Hotel's two proprietors were men named Jennings and Willard. Willard served as host, room clerk, bookkeeper, and cashier, while Jennings supervised food preparation and the operation of the dining room. Both were said to be very good at remembering names and faces and were generally considered excellent proprietors. For a period of several years, the City Hotel was the social center of New York—the setting for many important banquets, dances, and political events. Although it survived until 1849, it had long since lost its early splendor.

There has always been an important difference between American hotels and those of Europe. From their earliest days, American hotels—the City Hotel, and its successors—were considered to be gathering places for the local community, whereas European hotels were not considered to be such until the twentieth century.

▶ The Hospitality Industry in the Nineteenth Century

The nineteenth century was a notable period for the hospitality industry in the United States. The expanding railroad network caused considerable travel and spawned the building of excellent city hotels and resort hotels. Many important restaurants were established. It can be said that the nineteenth century saw the travel and hospitality industry develop at a greater rate than at any prior time.

▶ City Hotels in the 1800s

From 1800 to approximately 1880, a large number of city residents lived in hotels or in rooming houses and boarding houses that closely resembled small hotels. Those who could not afford private homes had no other choice. There were no apartments as we know them today: the first apartments in America were constructed in New York City in 1880. Consequently, over 50 percent of the rooms in the typical city hotel were occupied by permanent residents. There were hotels available for people of various income levels, and virtually everyone in need of rooms could find something affordable. Some hotels appealed to those employed in the immediate area; others catered to those in particular professions or income strata. All were usually very busy. We know most about those that earned grand reputations as the finest available in their times and comparatively little about the others.

"Palaces of the Public"

Those famous American hotels of the past about which much information survives have been dubbed **"Palaces of the Public,"** a title that refers not only to the public nature of American hotels but also to their elegance. In many small cities, the local hotel was the finest, most splendid structure in the city. In larger cities, there were commonly several hotels competing to be the best by having the latest in modern conveniences installed and often becoming self-sufficient cities within cities. Many featured such amenities as barber shops, libraries, billiard rooms, hair salons, ticket offices, florists, and cigar stands. Some eventually provided dining service for over twenty hours a day.

It is particularly interesting that the palatial hotels of this nature—the so-called grand hotels—were found only in America until the later years of the nineteenth century. Grand hotels were clearly an American invention.

The Tremont Hotel, Boston. The first of the truly grand hotels in America was the Tremont Hotel, a purpose-built property that opened in Boston at the corner of Tremont and Beacon streets in October 1829. By every standard of the times, it was a luxurious enterprise. The designer of this remarkable property was a young man of twenty-seven named Isaiah Rogers. The Tremont was three stories high and boasted 170 guest rooms and a dozen public rooms. It was the first hotel to have

1. bellboys;
2. clerks whose responsibilities were limited to the front desk;
3. a carpeted lobby and a large, carpeted (200-seat) dining room, both with gaslighted chandeliers;
4. bathing rooms (eight)—probably steam baths—located in the building;
5. private rooms (both singles and doubles), all equipped with doors having locks and keys for guests;
6. French cuisine;
7. a washbowl and pitcher in each room with a free bar of soap;
8. the first inside toilets, called water closets, located in the basement of the building; and

The Revere House, Boston (top), built in 1847, and the St. Nicholas hotel, New York (bottom), built in 1853, were among the several grand hotels that were constructed in the large urban centers of mid-nineteenth-century America. This first wave of "palaces of the public" offered their guests the latest in modern conveniences. (Lithograph of the Revere House by S. W. Chandler & Company; lithograph of the St. Nicholas hotel by F. Oppenheimer, courtesy of the Museum of the City of New York. Both images courtesy of the New York Public Library Picture Collection.)

9. a mechanical device known as an annunciator in each room, which made it possible for a guest to signal the hotel front office merely by pushing a button.

The ceilings of the Tremont were exceptionally high, and any floors not carpeted were made of black and white marble. The furniture was native, carved walnut. Although the list of firsts above may not connote a very luxurious operation by today's standards, one must remember that we are describing a property that was constructed thirty years before the Civil War—long before the advent of electricity, modern plumbing, and telephones. The Tremont was an extraordinary, luxurious hotel for its time.

The Astor House, New York. John Jacob Astor, a well-known American business tycoon, watched the success of the Tremont with great interest and decided that if a luxury hotel could succeed in Boston, one could do so in New York. Moreover, Astor decided to build a hotel in New York that would exceed the luxury of the Tremont. He proceeded to plan the Astor House, which was completed in 1836.

To design his hotel, Astor employed Isaiah Rogers, who was rapidly becoming known as the premier hotel architect in America. Rogers designed a hotel that was "more grand" than his Tremont. In addition to all the features that had first appeared in the Tremont, the Astor House contained not eight but seventeen bathing rooms, larger public rooms, and two new devices known as showers, which were located in the basement. The guest rooms were furnished with black walnut, and the floors were covered with Brussels carpets. In addition, all rooms were provided with gaslight; in fact, the Astor House was the first hotel to be fully illuminated with gas.

The Astor House was a hotel of 309 rooms on five floors. One of the more interesting problems in operating the hotel involved the gaslights. Guests were not used to the gaslight, which was a new invention at the time. They were accustomed to candles, which were normally extinguished when people went to bed. Because guests were accustomed to extinguishing their candles by blowing them out, some guests took the same approach with the gas lighting fixtures, often with disastrous results. Those who did extinguish the gaslights failed to realize that raw gas was escaping from the unlighted fixtures, and substantial numbers died—some from asphyxiation, others from explosions that occurred when they lighted matches to reignite the gaslights.

Other Grand Hotels of the Era

The Tremont in Boston and the Astor in New York established models for more ostentatious American hotels. In Boston, grand hotels constructed included the Adams House in the latter 1840s, the Revere House in 1847, and the original Parker House in 1855. New Yorkers were awed by such properties as the Howard Hotel in 1839, the New York Hotel in 1844, the Metropolitan in 1852, and the St. Nicholas in 1853. The St. Nicholas was the first hotel costing more than a million dollars to build—nearly $2 million, actually—and became the largest in the city after an 1856 addition increased its size to five hundred rooms.

Similar growth and development was occurring in other cities as well. In New Orleans, both the St. Louis Hotel and the St. Charles Hotel opened in the late 1830s, soon after New York's Astor House.

Philadelphians witnessed the opening of the American House in 1844 and the Washington House in 1845. In Buffalo, there was the American Hotel, which opened in 1836, the same year as the Astor House. Further west, the citizens of St. Louis were justly proud of their Planters' Hotel, which opened in 1841.

In Boston, after its 1855 opening, the original Parker House became very popular and was considered far more modern than the Tremont Hotel. This perception was one of the factors that led to the decline and eventual closing of the famed Tremont. Charles Dickens, the famous British novelist and lecturer, spent several days in the Parker House when he was on a lecture tour of the United States in 1867. Local newspapers reported that he caused a sensation when people lined up at the hotel to obtain his autograph.

None of the grand hotels of the period, including those discussed above, was more than five stories high. There were two reasons for this. First, the hotels were built of wood, and wood construction is not suitable for tall buildings. Of equal importance was that the elevator had not yet been invented, so guests had to climb stairs to get to their rooms. This made the rooms located on the upper floors less popular and less expensive than those on the lower floors. The absence of elevators helps to explain the popularity of bellboys in the luxury hotels: guests no longer had to carry their own baggage up flights of stairs to their rooms. Years later, after the first elevator installations in hotels (about 1859), the industry would witness an eventual reversal in the rates for rooms: those on higher floors became more popular, and more expensive, than the rooms on lower floors.

Fire was a constant danger in these wood buildings. The situation was serious enough when rooms and corridors were lighted with candles, which could accidentally start fires if knocked over or if placed too close to flammable materials. The problems were considerably worse when the newly invented gaslight became the principal means of illumination. With candles, fire had been an obvious threat, and both guests and employees were vigilant; the introduction of gas brought the added threat of explosions, which might precede and precipitate devastating fires. During this period, before water was available above the first-floor level of buildings, hotels were regularly destroyed by raging fires in which many lives were lost. Seeing a hotel destroyed by fire, then watching it being rebuilt to open the following year was a normal experience for the citizens of large American cities.

It is important to understand that this period, between the opening of the Tremont (1829) and the start of the Civil War (1860), was one in which more new hotels were opened than at any time in U.S. history until the 1920s. This could not and would not have occurred unless there had been a dramatic increase in the number of people traveling. This increase was directly related to the development of a network of railroads that became the primary means of transportation for people seeking to go from one to another of the growing cities in the United States. As in England, locations near railroad stations were quickly seen to be ideal for hotels, and the race was on in every city and town with a railroad station to build hotels close by. Tired travelers, emerging from the stations after long journeys on trains, typically sought the nearest hotel to find food, shelter, and rest.

Chicago's Hotels. Perhaps the most important railroad center of the age was then developing in Chicago. As the city and the railroad industry grew, so did the hotel industry. In 1837, the entire population of Chicago was only 4,170. By 1860, the city had grown to over two hundred thousand and had a sufficient number of first-class hotels to be able to host the second Republican national convention. This was the convention that nominated Abraham Lincoln. The list of grand hotels in Chicago at that time included a new Tremont, opened in 1850 to replace a prior Tremont that had burned, and which, in turn, had been the replacement for yet another Tremont that had also burned! The new Tremont cost $750,000 to construct and was at first considered too palatial for Chicago. Nevertheless, it quickly became a grand success and was enlarged twice. By 1868, it had reached nearly three hundred rooms.

The Palmer House, Chicago. Another of Chicago's first luxury hotels was the original Palmer House, a 227-room property that opened in 1870. In 1871, a great fire swept through Chicago, destroying most of its hotels, including the Palmer House.

After the great Chicago fire, the city began to rebuild, and many new hotels appeared. Twenty-three new first-class hotels opened within two years, including the Palmer House, the Grand Pacific, the Tremont, and the Sherman, which collectively became known as the "Big Four." By then, Chicago had a population of over three hundred thousand people.

San Francisco's Hotels. The success of the hotel industry in Chicago was paralleled in San Francisco. In 1848, San Francisco was a small western town, still part of the Mexican Territory. The "hospitality industry" consisted of one small tavern, which was just one and a half stories high. In 1849, when gold was discovered in that part of California, the

California gold rush brought millions of people to California to make their fortunes. In the next twenty-five years, the population of San Francisco grew to one hundred sixty thousand. As the population grew, so did the hospitality industry. New hotels, restaurants, taverns (saloons, actually), and other enterprises, which could best be described in a book of this nature as entertainment centers, were opening almost daily.

One of the earliest hotels in San Francisco was another Parker House, built in 1849 by Robert Parker who, coincidentally, had come from Boston. San Francisco's Parker House was noted for its high prices, its gambling hall, and its large ballroom. It set the standard for prices: when other similar properties were built, they, too, charged very high prices. With "gold fever" in the air, people were not very concerned about high prices. It was reported that a cigar stand at the Union Hotel rented for $4,000 a month and that the operator of the cigar stand, even at that high rent, was still able to make a handsome profit.

By 1859, a number of other grand—even opulent—hotels had been built. The list of these included the Occidental (four hundred rooms) and the Cosmopolitan, both of which opened in 1859. Perhaps the most expensive hotel to be constructed in San Francisco during this period was the Grand Hotel, built in 1869 at a cost of more than $1 million for a property of just two hundred rooms!

Transcontinental railroad service began in 1869 with the joining of the Central Pacific and Union Pacific railroads. As one might expect, a number of fine hotels were constructed along this route to the West. By the end of the century, there were several very fine hotels in cities west of the Mississippi. In fact, a reporter for one of Chicago's newspapers, the *Century*, wrote that two of the three finest hotels in the country were then located in the West. One was the Palace Hotel in San Francisco; the other was the Brown Palace in Denver. Perhaps not surprisingly, as the third in this trio of best hotels in America, the reporter chose one in his native Chicago—the Auditorium.

The Palace Hotel, San Francisco. The Palace Hotel in San Francisco was completed in 1875 at a cost of almost $5 million. It contained 755 rooms and boasted of having the same elegant features offered by the best of the New York and Boston hotels—and a few that even New York and Boston lacked. It was said that the Palace was so large that some guests had difficulty finding their rooms. One writer offered advice for those who experienced this problem: the best plan was to "pretend you are full, let yourself loose, and cuss. Someone will come and guide you to your room."

The rooms in the Palace Hotel were twenty feet square—very large rooms, even by today's standards. The dining room was 155 feet by 55 feet, the largest in the world at the time. The hotel had a large number of private dining rooms, reading rooms, and parlors, and even had card rooms. The Palace was furnished with upholstered furniture made with native hardwood. Operations were not profitable for the first ten years because of the huge cost of constructing the hotel. However, over the years it became extremely successful. The Palace was the pride of San Francisco and was said to be earthquake proof, earthquakes having been a matter of some concern as early as the late nineteenth century. Although it did survive the historic earthquake that rocked San Francisco on April 18, 1906, it burned to the ground in the ensuing fire that leveled the city.

The Brown Palace, Denver. The Brown Palace in Denver had only 440 rooms, compared with 755 in the San Francisco Palace, but was as elegant as any hotel in the world when it opened in 1892. The immense lobby was eight stories high, with a stained-glass interior roof, onyx walls, and tile floors with elaborate Greek designs. The public rooms in the Brown Palace were dispersed throughout the building rather than all on one floor—the more usual practice in hotels built both before and after the Brown Palace. These public rooms were grandly decorated in Louis XVI style. The hotel featured five honeymoon suites, known as bridal chambers and described by hotel management as "too beautiful and delicate for use." The daily rates for these suites were outrageously high—as much as $100, the equivalent of more than one year's salary for many American workers at that time. The other bedrooms in the hotel, half of which had private baths and many of which had fireplaces, were decorated in fifty shades of yellow—from cream to gold.

The Waldorf-Astoria, New York. As a fitting climax to the nineteenth-century growth of the hotel industry in the American city, two hotels were built in New York City on Fifth Avenue between Thirty-third and Thirty-fourth Streets on the sites of mansions owned by feuding members of the Astor family. The first, opened in 1893, was the Waldorf, built on the site of William Waldorf Astor's mansion at the corner of Thirty-third Street; the second, opened in 1897, was the Astoria, built on the site of the mansion owned by Colonel John Jacob Astor at the corner of Thirty-fourth Street. Colonel Astor was the grandson of the John Jacob Astor who had been responsible for the original Astor House over sixty years earlier. The two properties were joined by a passage from the day the Astoria opened. In addition, their names were soon joined by a hyphen, and the Waldorf-Astoria quickly became one of America's finest and best-known hotels.

The Waldorf-Astoria occupied the Thirty-fourth Street site for over thirty years but closed in 1928 when the level of real estate taxes had rendered its operation unprofitable. The site was sold to a new corporation that planned to build the world's largest office building. That office building—the Empire State Building—occupies the site to this day. The Waldorf-Astoria was rebuilt in 1932 and is located on Park Avenue between Forty-ninth and Fiftieth Streets.

▶ Resort Hotels in the 1800s

In the nineteenth century, while the great developing network of American railroads was providing the means for the economic development of the many and growing regions, cities, and towns of America, it was also putting in place a mechanism that would make possible a new period of growth and development for a group of hospitality operations that came to be known as resort hotels.

Railroads and Resort Hotels

The resort hotel industry in the United States could not have developed without railroads. The reason for this is apparent when one considers the distance of many nineteenth-century resort hotels from population centers as well as their relative inaccessibility by any other means of transportation available in the nineteenth century. In this period, it was not uncommon for families of means to spend entire summers or winters at resort hotels. A mother and her children—sometimes with servants—would remain at the resort hotel from week to week. But the father would spend only weekends with his family, traveling by train from a city to the resort at the end of the work week and returning to the city on Sunday evening or Monday morning to earn the money to pay for it all.

Early Resort Hotels

By the beginning of the nineteenth century, the resort hotel industry had begun its earliest period of development in the East. By 1789, for example, weary city dwellers in New York were being advised in advertisements to seek relaxation at Deagle's Hotel, far from the noise and crowds of the city—Deagle's was located in a then-rural part of Manhattan Island near what is now One Hundred and Fifty-fifth Street and Amsterdam Avenue. Deagle's, the earliest-known resort hotel on Manhattan, offered harassed New Yorkers opportunities for quiet fishing as well as other ways to relax and ushered in a period of growth for this new form of American hotel enterprise.

The 1800s saw the opening of many of America's important resort hotels and resort areas. In Cape May, New Jersey, the Congress Hotel was in operation in 1812 and was known for its sweeping verandas, which made it possible for resort guests to enjoy the cooling ocean breezes in the summer. The Catskill Mountain region, located in an area between 70 and 130 miles northwest of New York City, traces its beginnings to the opening of the Catskill Mountain House in 1823. By the 1820s, White Sulphur Springs, in what later became West Virginia, had begun to develop its reputation as a spa.

The Homestead, Hot Springs. An early and very famous resort hotel was The Homestead, in Hot Springs, Virginia. The property was acquired in 1832 by Dr. Thomas Goode, who then planned and developed it and continually made improvements to the property. By 1850, The Homestead was said to have approximately 15,000 visitors annually. Even today, it continues to be one of America's premier resorts.

The Greenbrier, White Sulphur Springs. In White Sulphur Springs, located in Virginia until West Virginia became a state in 1863, the mineral waters were said to have wonderful curative powers. This attracted people to the area, including presidents of the United States as well as wealthy individuals with various illnesses. The growing popularity of the waters resulted in the eventual building of the original Greenbrier Hotel, called the Grand Central Hotel in 1857. Several of the buildings had been constructed many years earlier, including The Greenbrier Museum, which was built as a private home in 1816. Many wealthy and famous people who had heard of the mineral waters and their alleged healing powers rented rooms there. The Grand Central Hotel was seldom called by its given name. Guests usually referred to it as "The White," or "The Old White," either in reference to its white-colored exterior or to its location: White Sulphur Springs.

Guests of the Old White included such notables as President Martin Van Buren, Senator Henry Clay, the future King Edward VII, and General Robert E. Lee. It was renamed The Greenbrier in 1861, but was closed during much of the Civil War. Over the years, The Greenbrier has gone through several periods of financial difficulty and has

Founded in 1832 and still in operation, The Homestead in Hot Springs, Virginia (shown as it appeared in 1891), was one of the first resort-spas in the United States. Fostered by the spread of the railroad, resorts were opened on the New Jersey shore, in the Catskill Mountains, and in other areas previously considered remote. (Photo courtesy of The Homestead.)

been owned by a number of individuals and corporations. The original property has been entirely reconstructed. A new 250-room building was added in 1913 and was expanded to 580 rooms in 1930. The Greenbrier was one of the first resorts to be classified as a five-star property—a rating it has continued to earn every year since.

The Balsams, Dixville Notch. In New England, another interesting resort property was developed in northern New Hampshire near the Canadian border. Named The Balsams, it was built in 1866 and was under continuing development up to the beginning of World War I. For over one hundred years, The Balsams has been considered one of the finest resorts in New England. Although the majority of the grand summer resorts of New England have long since closed because of their inability to operate profitably as summer-only ventures, The Balsams was able to convert to year-round operation successfully and is still considered a premier resort. In addition to its summer activities, The Balsams has excellent winter sports and has gained a reputation for its outstanding cuisine.

The Grand Hotel, Mackinac Island. Further west, in Michigan, there is a beautiful resort, the Grand Hotel, located on Mackinac Island in Lake Huron. No automobiles are permitted on the island, which makes this a unique resort. Transportation is by horse and carriage or bicycle, only. The hotel, billed as the largest summer hotel in the world, was first opened for business in 1887. It was a retreat for wealthy and famous people from Chicago and other nearby areas. Mackinac Island is only three miles long by two miles wide, and the hotel is situated to

▶ Henry Flagler, Resort Developer ◀

For most of the resort hotels of the nineteenth century, the railroad was the principal means of access. The close relationship between railroads and resort hotels can perhaps best be illustrated by examining the business career of Henry Flagler.

Flagler, who was a partner in John D. Rockefeller's Standard Oil Company, became wealthy and retired at the age of fifty-three. He went to Florida to relax in 1883, but like so many successful entrepreneurs before and since, he could not leave business behind. He was enchanted by the Florida climate and by its unspoiled beauty and decided to investigate the possibilities for profitable real estate development. In 1885, he began construction of the Ponce de Leon Hotel in St. Augustine, on the Atlantic coast of Florida. He planned that the hotel would cater to the wealthy but soon realized that it would be very difficult to attract the clientele he wanted because of the poor transportation in the area. He started to buy the small railroads in the region and eventually controlled most railroad service in the state.

With his control of an excellent transportation network, Flagler was able to build a number of fine resort hotels throughout Florida, including such well-known properties as the Palm Beach Hotel, the Royal Poinciana, and the original Breakers in Palm Beach.

provide guests with spectacular views of the lake. The Grand Hotel is still in operation and is still quite popular.

Railroad Networks

By the end of the nineteenth century, entrepreneurs in the United States had developed a network of rail lines for both passengers and freight that was second to none in the world. Today, it may be difficult to comprehend the importance and complexity of the rail system, most of which has vanished. For example, the Mount Washington Hotel in New Hampshire's White Mountains was easily accessible by rail from all major cities in the Northeast. Guests typically checked in for all or part of the summer, arriving by train with trunks full of their summer wardrobes. Today, although the hotel is still in operation, the passenger trains no longer come, and guests arrive by automobile and bus.

The passenger rail networks serving our resort areas—the Catskill Mountains, the New Jersey shore, and many others—are gone now, and the names of the railroad companies, once household words, are nearly forgotten. The Hudson River Railroad; the Ulster and Delaware River Railroad; the New York, Ontario, and Western Railroad; the Delaware and Hudson Canal Company Railroad; the Delaware, Lackawanna, and Western; these, and hundreds of others, with thousands of miles of track, are now just names for historians. But they were once lifelines for the guests and employees who made America's resort hotels the great successes they were in the nineteenth century.

▶ Restaurants in the 1800s

Restaurants in the United States are generally considered to have their origins in the ordinaries, inns, and taverns of colonial America. These older terms persisted through the seventeenth and eighteenth centuries. By the beginning of the nineteenth century, *ordinary* had all but disappeared as a synonym for inn or tavern. However, by this time we begin to see instances of a comparatively new term of French origin, *restaurant*, that was to become dominant. By the beginning of the nineteenth century, inns, taverns, and restaurants had become common in the major American cities and were thoroughly integrated into the fabric of American society.

Factors Affecting Restaurant Development

The development of the restaurant business in urban America is closely linked to the Industrial Revolution. By the early nineteenth century, two factors were beginning to have significant impact on the development of restaurants:

1. Manufacturing industries were expanding, creating a growing need for labor in cities and towns.
2. Agricultural methods and technology were improving, resulting in increased farm production on the one hand and less need for farm labor on the other.

Those who left rural America to seek jobs in urban areas faced the problem of locating living quarters, which became increasingly difficult as the urban population grew. The first apartment buildings did not appear until about 1880. Until that time, people lived either in private homes, which were expensive, or in less expensive alternatives: rooms they rented in early hotels, in boarding houses; or in lodging houses. Boarding houses included meals in their rates. Some gave guests excellent meals, whereas others served food of very poor quality. Hotels and lodging (or rooming) houses did not provide meals, and residents typically had no access to cooking facilities. This led them to seek food in the various kinds of restaurants that developed in this period.

The Variety in City Restaurants

The vast majority of city restaurants tended to be very simple and plain, serving basic, inexpensive meals to those who needed them, such as factory and office workers, most of whom lived too far from their jobs to go home for their midday meals. Other regular customers were those who did not have facilities for meal preparation at home. After all, cooking stoves were first patented in America about 1815 and did not become common in home kitchens until about 1850.

In the last half of the nineteenth century, a wide variety of foodservice enterprises were to be found in America's growing cities: street vendors; lunch carts and lunch wagons; lunch rooms in office buildings; taverns, both common and elegant, offering "free lunch"; hotel dining rooms; ethnic restaurants in ethnic areas; sandwich shops; cheap restaurants, known as "five-cent houses," and others known as "fifteen-cent houses," which served a portion of hot meat with potatoes, pickles, bread and butter for that price—these and many others were common.

Oyster Houses. One of the most popular and inexpensive American foods of the period was the oyster, found in the Atlantic Ocean in large beds near the East Coast. Oysters appealed to people of all backgrounds and were as popular in their time as hamburgers have become in ours. They were very cheap, and the types of establishments that specialized in serving them were known by many names: oyster house, oyster cellar, oyster saloon, and oyster wagon were all common terms. People consumed them in vast numbers, to the extent that many of the oyster beds were depleted. As this occurred, the price of oysters rose, and they began to lose their popularity, except in a few superior establishments.

One of these was Ye Olde Original Oyster House in Boston, now known as Ye Olde Union Oyster House, which opened in 1826. It is one of the oldest continuously operating restaurants in America, with an

Ye Olde Union Oyster House, Boston, was established in 1826. Offering their patrons inexpensive fare, oyster houses were among the most popular restaurants on the East Coast in the 1800s. (Photo courtesy of Ye Olde Union Oyster House, Boston.)

extensive menu that includes a large number of seafood entrees in addition to the oysters for which it is named. The semiprivate stalls, or booths, and the oyster bar itself are reported to be original furnishings.

Changing Service Techniques

One particularly important development in the nineteenth century was a change in the techniques of service. Until about 1830, hotels and boarding houses were serving **table d'hôte** meals (a term meaning a complete meal for one price), just as inns and taverns had done for generations. Meals were included in the room rate, and each meal was served at an appointed hour. Guests were seated at long tables preset with all the foods constituting the meal. Guests helped themselves from platters, bowls, tureens, and other serving dishes. Competition among diners for the choicest foods could be fierce, and entire meals were frequently consumed in ten minutes or less.

In hotels, a later and more civilized approach was to divide the meals into courses, which were served by waiters. Meals were still served at appointed hours and guests were still seated at long tables, but the earlier every-man-for-himself approach was eliminated. Waiters moving with military precision would serve each course to one guest at a time. The foods would typically be placed on sideboards to which waiters would go to select the items requested by each guest.

Later, the **European Plan** was introduced. Meals were not included in the room rate. Printed menus were offered, giving diners opportunities to select their foods. With this development, both fixed hours for meals and long tables for guests began to disappear. Eventually, dining rooms were open for meals for periods of several hours, and guests would dine at hours they chose.

Cities Known for Numerous Fine Restaurants

By the last years of the nineteenth century, all of America's great cities were able to boast about the quality of the meals available in some of their restaurants. The cities with truly outstanding reputations for fine dining were San Francisco, New Orleans, and New York.

San Francisco. After the Gold Rush, the population of San Francisco grew dramatically, setting the conditions for equally dramatic growth in the restaurant industry. Within a very few years, San Francisco was noted for its variety of fine restaurants, including Lazzuro's (Italian), Manning's (oyster house), The Mint (southern), Zinkand's (German), and Jacques' (French).

New Orleans. In New Orleans, one of the fine old establishments is Antoine's, which opened in 1840. Known for its superior seafood specialties, Antoine's is owned and operated by the family of the original owner, Antoine Alciatore, an immigrant from Marseilles, France. Other popular establishments included Moreau's, Begue's, Les Quatre Saisons, and Le Pelerin.

New York. Perhaps the most important American city for fine dining throughout the nineteenth century was New York, which took pride in its many restaurants. The list was long and varied, and included such famous names as Taylor's, Sherry's, Rector's, and von Mehlbach's—an establishment opened in 1842 that changed its name to Luchow's in 1882. It operated under von Mehlbach's name until it was purchased by a young, industrious waiter named August Luchow, who had immigrated from Hanover, Germany, a few years earlier.

Delmonico's. Perhaps the most famous, and certainly the most interesting, of New York's restaurants was Delmonico's, originally located on William Street, in lower Manhattan, near Wall Street. Delmonico's opened as a simple coffee and pastry shop in 1827 and grew to be a vast restaurant and private catering establishment. Reportedly the best and most expensive restaurant in the country, it was operated for several generations by members of the Delmonico family. As the commercial center of the growing city continued to move, the owners of Delmonico's kept pace by changing the location of the restaurant. In 1897, Delmonico's made its last move, to Fifth Avenue and Forty-fourth Street, where it prospered for many years. Eventually, surviving members of the family grew tired of the restaurant business, and Delmonico's closed forever in 1923.

Delmonico's was the first restaurant to print its menu in both French and English. It boasted an unusually long menu: 327 items, each of which was available every day, assuming that the necessary supplies could be purchased. Delmonico's also played a role in the emancipation of women: it provided both rooms and food in an acceptable social setting for luncheon meetings of organizations of prominent women, thus enabling women to appear unescorted in a public restaurant for the first time.

The Earliest American Restaurant Chains

A particularly interesting chain of restaurants was started along the southwestern route of the Atchison, Topeka, and Santa Fe Railroad in 1876 by an immigrant from England named Fred Harvey. He had extensive experience in foodservice and as a railroad mail clerk. He had observed the poor food and terrible service provided for railroad passengers traveling to the west, and he devised a system to improve it.

Under contract with the railroad, he established restaurants at stations for passenger dining. Railroad personnel were trained to distribute menus to passengers, record their selections, and inform the restaurant staff of these selections before the train reached the station. This was accomplished by means of a complex system of whistle signals. Meals were cooked to order and were nearly ready for passengers when trains reached the stations. They were served quickly and efficiently by waitresses who became known as Harvey Girls. The delays resulting from passenger dining were kept to an absolute minimum. Harvey's standards were high, and the meals were considered excellent. They were also inexpensive—because Harvey was not charged by the Atchison, Topeka, and Santa Fe for shipping his food supplies by rail.

The first restaurant in the Harvey chain was opened in Topeka, Kansas in 1876. By 1883, he owned a total of seventeen restaurants and hotels. Among Harvey's contributions to the growth of chain restaurants were centrally developed menus, identical uniforms for all waitresses in the organization, a central commissary, and strict quality control.

Another interesting chain grew from a single restaurant in New York City operated by William and Samuel Childs, called Childs'

Restaurant. By 1898, the Childs brothers were successfully operating nine restaurants in the city. That year, they introduced a new concept in restaurant dining: the "cafeteria." Customers were able to select foods from long counters, place their selections on trays, and pay for the foods at the end of the counter. This was a great success, and was widely imitated by foodservice operators across the nation, including Horn & Hardart, Bickford's, and a number of others.

Restaurants in Hotels

Perhaps the most important restaurants in the United States during the 1800s were not the independent, individually owned establishments, but those restaurants located in the principal hotels of major American cities. Because these hotels could afford to hire the finest chefs from Europe and because they were the social centers of their cities, where the elite entertained, the food service available in these establishments eclipsed that available in most private restaurants. For example, the Parker House in Boston had an unsurpassed reputation for fine food. The owner, Harvey Parker, paid the chef $5,000 per year when a good chef could be hired for less than $500.

The Waldorf-Astoria was known internationally for its excellent cuisine. In fact, at one period in its history, the original Waldorf-Astoria was better known for its exceptional food than for its fine accommodations. Foodservice has been supervised by some of the best people in the field. The Waldorf-Astoria was the setting for Oscar Tschirky, known worldwide simply as Oscar of the Waldorf, to cater brilliantly for many years to the wealthy and famous personalities who frequented the hotel.

Another hotel noted as much for its haute cuisine as for its grandeur was the Palace Hotel in San Francisco. The Palace maintained a staff of 150 waiters, and management claimed that the Palace chefs could prepare the national dishes of any country in the world, without exception, in the manner of chefs of that country. And on many occasions, they proved that they could.

▶ Summary

In the first section of this chapter, the historical development of the hospitality industry is explored, from the earliest civilizations in the Middle East, through Egypt, Greece, Rome, and western Europe, with special attention to developments in England from the fifteenth to the late nineteenth centuries. Economic links between hospitality and several other industries are described, and improvements in methods of transportation and the economic development of population centers are illustrated. Various types of early hospitality enterprises are described, along with the principal characteristics of the establishments and their owners. The growth of the industry through the Fall of Rome, the role of the church in providing hospitality services during the Dark Ages, and the importance of several social and economic phenomena in the rebirth of the hospitality industry during the Renaissance are traced. Finally, various elements that fostered dynamic change in the industry during the early modern period are illustrated, including the development of road networks, stagecoaches, postal networks, the reinvention of the restaurant in eighteenth-century France, and the extension of English common law to the business of innkeeping. The growth of the hospitality business in the Industrial Era is described, and the invention of the steam engine, the development of railroad networks, and the acceptance of dining out by the public at large are cited as principal determinants of the industry's development.

In the second section of this chapter, the earliest types of hospitality establishments in America are identified and described. The impact of railroads and railroad travel in the nineteenth century on the hospitality industry in general and on city hotels and resort hotels in particular is examined in detail. Significant hotels of the nineteenth century are identified, and the characteristics that made them unique described. These include hotels that were erected in major cities, such as New York, Chicago, Boston, and San Fransisco, as well as major resort hotels in various locations in the East and Midwest. The ever-present problem of hotel fires is also discussed. Various economic and social conditions that fostered the growth of the foodservice industry are listed and described, and a variety of types of foodservice establishments common in the period are named. In addition, the following individuals are identified and their principal contributions to the hospitality industry enumerated: Samuel Coles; Samuel Fraunces; Isaiah Rogers; Harvey Parker; Henry Flagler; and Fred Harvey.

Key Terms

Caravanserai
Cafe
Coaching Inns
Empire Era
European Plan
Feudalism

Grand Tour
Ordinary
Palaces of the Public
Post-house
Table d'hôte
Traiteurs

1. The history of the hospitality industry is tied closely to the development of transportation. Explain.

2. What contributions did the Sumerians make to the development of the hospitality and travel industries?

3. What kinds of establishments were probably the first hospitality businesses?

4. What were the characteristics of a typical inn of the year 2000 B.C.?

5. Identify one important contribution of ancient Egypt to the development of the hospitality industry.

6. What were the two most important contributions of ancient Greece to the development of travel?

7. Were ancient Greek inns generally clean and well-run? How good were their restaurants?

8. Of what significance was the ancient Roman road system to the development of travel?

9. Some Roman inns were clean and offered excellent accommodations to one special group of travelers. Explain.

10. Why did the business of innkeeping virtually disappear during the period lasting from A.D. 476 to 1300? Where did travelers stay?

11. What was the "Grand Tour?"

12. What impact did an A.D. 1539 act of the English parliament have on the innkeeping business of that era?

13. During which period in European history did the stagecoach become a common method of transportation? What effect did this have on innkeeping development?

14. When and where did public restaurants first become common? What caused them to increase in numbers?

15. How did the invention of the railroad and the development of railroad networks affect the development of the hospitality industry?

16. Why did the Industrial Revolution increase the number of inns in Europe?

17. Define the term *ordinary.* What was the role of an ordinary in the life of a seventeenth-century community?

18. What difference was there between the status of the early American innkeeper and that of his counterpart in Europe?

19. Discuss the role of Samuel Fraunces and his tavern during the Revolutionary War.

20. Hotels in the United States have always been considered "Palaces of the Public." Explain.

21. What was the first purpose-built hotel structure in the United States? Where was it located and when was it built?

22. Name the property that is considered to be America's first luxury hotel. Where was it located? When was it built? List five features that made it an outstanding hotel for its time.

23. Name the New York hotel designed and built to rival the luxury of the Tremont. Who designed it? How was it illuminated?

24. Why were none of the hotels built in the early nineteenth century above five floors in height?

25. The period between 1830 and 1860 was one in which more new hotels were opened in America than at any other time until the 1920s. Why?

26. What characteristics of the hotels built before the Civil War made fire an ever-present danger?

27. What was the impact of railroad development on Chicago in the twenty-five year period between 1835 and 1860?

28. What characteristics of the Palace Hotel, San Francisco, and the Brown Palace, Denver, led to their being known as "grand" hotels?

29. Why were railroads important to the development of the resort hotel industry?

30. How does the career of Henry Flagler illustrate the close relationship that developed between railroads and the resort hotels in the nineteenth century?

31. Describe early nineteenth-century changes in agriculture and manufacturing that set the stage for significant growth in the restaurant industry.

32. Discuss the role of boarding houses and lodging houses in the development of the foodservice industry from 1800 to the start of the Civil War.

33. List six types of foodservice establishments found in major American cities in the period after the Civil War.

34. Which three American cities were reputed to have the best restaurants in the late nineteenth century? List the names of three restaurants in each city during this period.

35. Which restaurant had the reputation of being the finest restaurant in the United States in the late nineteenth century? Why?

36. What were the contributions of Fred Harvey to the development of the restaurant industry in America?

37. Why were the grand hotels in nineteenth-century America able to develop reputations for providing food and service of a quality exceeding that available elsewhere in major American cities at the time?

38. What distinguished the foodservice operation of San Francisco's Palace Hotel from that of other American hotels of the late nineteenth century?

Moments of Truth

1. You are assistant to the president of an international hotel chain. The president is interested in expanding its operations into more countries and is considering several of the less developed countries in Africa. You have been assigned the task of researching these countries and reporting to him on their potential for travel and tourism. Based on the knowledge you have gained from reading this chapter, what are the most important topics to research about any country you might consider?

2. You have been discussing career opportunities with a friend and have told him you are currently taking a course in hospitality that includes a sizable amount of history of the industry. He tells you that you are wasting your time studying history because it will be of no use to you in your career. How do you respond to this argument?

Hospitality Foundations II

The Hospitality Industry in the United States in the Twentieth Century

After reading and studying this chapter, you should be able to:

1 List the important inventions of the late nineteenth century and describe the impact of each on the hospitality industry.

2 Identify three major reasons for the growth in mass travel after World War II.

3 List the principal appealing features of a vacation cruise.

4 Discuss the importance of railroads to travel in the United States during the first half of the twentieth century.

5 Identify Amtrak and trace its development.

6 Discuss the early history of aviation and explain the importance of mail contracts to airline development.

7 List and discuss three results of the Airline Deregulation Act of 1978.

8 Describe in general terms the principal developments in the three major segments of the industry—restaurants, hotels, and resort hotels—in the period from 1900 onward.

9 Identify each of the following and describe their principal contributions to the development of the hospitality industry: Ellsworth M. Statler; Conrad Hilton; Howard Johnson; J. Willard Marriott; Kemmons Wilson; Ray Kroc.

▶ Introduction: An Overview

Following a golden age of invention in the late nineteenth century, there had been some dramatic changes in American life. Electricity, for example, was beginning to replace gas to illuminate homes and offices. Henry Ford and others were further developing the recently invented automobile, which promised new and improved methods of motor transport. Streets and roads were being paved and otherwise improved in cities, towns, and rural areas so that people could take full advantage of the new automobiles. The telephone was becoming common, making voice communication possible over long distances, just as the railroads had made rapid transit between cities and regions a reality. These and other important developments were moving America toward becoming the world's foremost economic power. This dramatic increase in economic development gave rise to more travel for Americans than they had ever known before, setting the stage for the major developments in America's hospitality industry.

The first half of the twentieth century was a time of rapid growth for American business. This growth produced an increase in travel, particularly business travel. Long-distance trips were still primarily by train, but use of the automobile was becoming increasingly common. New paved roads were constructed in the early part of the century, and more and more of the older unpaved roads were paved. By 1920, it was becoming possible in many parts of the country to drive an automobile from one city to another without using the dirt roads of earlier decades.

The first recorded journey across the United States by automobile was undertaken in 1903 by a physician from Vermont named Nelson Jackson. It took Dr. Jackson sixty-nine days—from May 23 to August 1—to drive from New York City to San Francisco. Many of those days were spent in hotels, waiting for the automobile to be fixed and for parts to be shipped. America's roads were not yet well suited to long-distance driving.

World War II marked a turning point in travel and hospitality. After 1945, the hospitality industry embarked on a period of dramatic change that was unequaled and unparalleled at any time in history. Travel, transportation, foodservice and lodging—literally every aspect of travel and hospitality—were affected.

In the nineteenth century and the first half of the twentieth, the average American did not engage in long-distance travel for pleasure. The only people to travel long distances frequently were businessmen and theatrical people (who could not earn their livings without traveling) and the wealthy, who had the time and money to travel for pleasure. The workweek for the average American was five and one half or six days, and very few Americans were able to take vacations. Those who were able to do so were not necessarily given vacations with pay. The cost of long-distance travel for vacations was quite beyond the financial ability of most Americans. For the majority, "travel" might mean an occasional trip to the seashore, a not-too-distant lake, or a short journey to visit relatives in a nearby community.

▶ Mass Travel

After World War II, great numbers of Americans began to travel. Of the many reasons for this, there were three of special significance for the hospitality industry.

1. Economic life was changing for many Americans. More industries were becoming unionized, and the contracts that resulted from collective bargaining provided for shorter workweeks, higher wages, and more fringe benefits. Vacations with pay became nearly universal for both unionized workers and for nonunionized white-collar workers who had held their jobs for the stipulated prerequisite periods (one year was a typical minimum). In general, Americans in all walks of life began to have more leisure time than ever before in history. This set the stage for increased travel.

2. Modes of transportation were changing. America's railroads were in decline, and the automobile became the primary means of private transportation for local and long-distance travel. The airplane was increasingly regarded as the major means of public transportation for long-distance travel. With increased volume and improved technology, travel also became more affordable. This led to the development of new travel destinations.

3. Major improvements were made in America's highways. With the decline of the railroads and growing reliance on motor vehicles—

both trucks and cars—the development of a national network of superior, limited-access highways became an important public concern. There had been major highways for a number of years in all regions of the country. There had never been, however, any coast-to-coast, border-to-border network of limited-access, interstate highways. Planning for this national system began during President Eisenhower's administration, and construction proceeded in the following years.

In the balance of this chapter, we will take a closer look at the various elements in the travel and hospitality mosaic to illustrate the more important changes that have taken place in the twentieth century—changes that have affected the industry in ways that are evident today.

▶ Travel and Transportation in the Twentieth Century

The decline of passenger ship and railroad travel, and the development of the automobile and airplane are major factors in the changing American life in the twentieth century. We begin with a look at the role of passenger ship transportation.

▶ Passenger Ships

Until the twentieth century, all travel and transportation between the United States and nations overseas was by ship. There was no other means for transporting people and goods between Europe and America, or between Asia and America. Ships dominated intercontinental travel and transportation in much the same way that railroads dominated domestic travel and transportation.

World War II brought a halt to most scheduled passenger shipping. Many passenger ships were used for troop transports, and some were sunk by enemy submarines. After the war, passenger service resumed. The luxurious SS *France* was built in 1961, and the *Queen Elizabeth II* went into service in 1968. Although the United States has never invested heavily in passenger ships, it did build the *United States*, a superliner, in 1952. At the time, this was the fastest liner afloat, capable of a speed of 35 knots. By this time, however, the days of transatlantic passenger ships were numbered, and the *United States* never carried the numbers of passengers that might have been possible some thirty years earlier. By the late 1960s, the *United States* had to be taken out of service for lack of passengers.

The beginning of the end of transatlantic passenger crossings came in 1957, the first year more people crossed the Atlantic by plane than by ship. Travelers no longer wanted to spend five to seven days traveling to Europe by ship when a plane would take them across the Atlantic in a matter of hours. The last ship to provide scheduled transatlantic service was the *Queen Elizabeth II*, and this was only during the summer months.

Today, most of the grand transoceanic liners are gone. The *Queen Mary* is permanently docked in Long Beach, California, as a tourist attraction. The original *Queen Elizabeth* sank in Hong Kong harbor. The *France* was sold to the Norwegian Caribbean Line, was refurbished, and is now sailing as the cruise ship *Norway*. The *Queen Elizabeth II* is used almost exclusively for long-distance vacation cruising.

Vacation Cruising

Vacation cruising goes back one hundred years to 1891 when the P&O line, the world's oldest cruise line, began to offer vacation cruises to distant parts of the world. For generations, taking a cruise meant boarding a ship in Boston, New York, Los Angeles, or some other city—then sailing to ports around the world.

The scheduled lines—those that provided scheduled transoceanic service—had specific year-round routes. However, sales always decreased in winter, which was never a good time to travel by ship. The seas were rough, the winds were fierce, and the temperatures could be frigid. In the mid 1930s, owners of lines that crossed the Atlantic Ocean started scheduling ships for winter vacation cruises to keep them going during the cold months when there was limited demand for transatlantic service. These ships carried passengers from cold-weather ports to warmer climates. New York City was the major port of embarkation. Ships that normally traveled from New York to Europe went on vacation cruises to the Caribbean, South America, and the Mediterranean.

Today, the large seagoing passenger vessels are used almost exclusively for vacation cruising. They are concentrated in the Mediterranean, Caribbean, and on the West Coast of the United States. The typical cruise is three, four, seven, or eight days long, although cruises of ten to fifteen days are not uncommon. Extended vacation cruises to distant ports of call are still available on ships such as the *Queen Elizabeth II*, but the greater demand is for short-term cruises that are within the budgets of the average working person.

Although the ages of vacation cruise passengers are younger and the length of the cruises is shorter, the appealing features of cruises have not changed over the years; they continue to be

1. food
2. activities and entertainment
3. weather
4. elegance and comfort

The level of service on many ships is as high as that in luxury hotels. Cabin stewards are available twenty-four hours a day and provide turndown service in the evening. Food and beverage service is commonly available day and night, and all sorts of recreational activities are available at any given time. Pursers are there to store valuables, cash checks, and convert currencies. Because of the high level of service, a cruise on one of these luxury liners can be an elegant and refreshing experience.

▶ Railroads

In the United States today, the railroad plays only a minor role in intercity passenger traffic, accounting for about 1 percent of long-distance trips. Nevertheless, the historical role of railroads in the expansion and development of many parts of the United States cannot be ignored. In the previous chapter, the importance of the railroads was discussed. Railroad stops were natural locations for hotels, and resort hotels were natural destinations for railroads. In some cases—Henry Flagler's hotels, for example—reaching existing hotels was the chief reason a railroad was built.

The number of miles of railroad track in the United States reached a peak in 1916. However, the railroads were still the primary means of long-distance public transportation for many years thereafter. All through the 1920s, the 1930s, and most of the 1940s, American railroads provided excellent passenger service. In fact, the railroad cars were generally considered more comfortable than other means of transportation, and the staff was efficient and polite. Trains generally ran on time, and food served in the dining cars of some trains was as good as that served in some fine restaurants. During the period of their greatest popularity, railroads accounted for as much as 70 percent of all intercity traffic.

The best intercity trains were named, just as cruise ships are named. In fact, the practice of naming trains continues with Amtrak. Some of the famous trains of the past include the following.

The Twentieth Century Limited. The deluxe train of the New York Central Railroad, this train provided service between New York City and Chicago. It was introduced in 1902 and made its last run in 1967.

The Broadway Limited. This train was inaugurated in 1902 by the Pennsylvania Railroad; it traveled between New York City and Chicago as competition for the *Twentieth Century Limited.* Amtrak retains a train with this name.

The Panama Limited. Started by the Illinois Central Railroad in 1912, this train ran between Chicago and New Orleans.

The Super Chief. This train was inaugurated in 1936 by the Santa Fe Railroad to provide service between Chicago and Los Angeles.

After World War II, competition from airlines and private automobiles led to a decrease in the number of railroad passengers. Passenger service has never been highly profitable, and decreased ridership caused the railroads to operate at a loss. As a result, passenger service began to deteriorate: service was perceived as less friendly; cars were not kept in the best condition; and food in dining cars was not up to previous standards. Roadbeds for the railroad track were not well maintained, and train travel was less comfortable than it had been.

The original Panama Limited was inaugurated in 1912 by the Illinois Central Railroad to provide rail service between Chicago and New Orleans. Pictured here is Amtrak's updated version of that famed train. (Photo courtesy of Amtrak.)

Railroads were required by law to maintain passenger service; but because it was not profitable, they spent less money on the service—with predictable results.

Creation of Amtrak

In an attempt to preserve long-distance train service, the federal government formed **Amtrak** in 1971. It is a national passenger train service but differs in organization from railroad service in other countries. Amtrak is a quasi-public corporation that is neither nationalized nor completely private. It is independent of the federal government, having its own board of directors and nongovernment employees. At the same time, it is financially dependent on the federal government, which regulates it.

Amtrak has never made a profit and has been subsidized each year by Congress. From its inception in 1971 Congress has given Amtrak between $500 million and $800 million each year. This has represented 35 percent to 50 percent of its total revenues. In an attempt to balance its budget, Amtrak has reduced service to locations with limited ridership. Amtrak management has predicted that it will eventually be able to operate without government financial support, but that has not happened to date. This attempt at a national rail passenger network continues to require subsidy from the federal government and operates under continuing financial threat.

▶ Airlines

The invention of the airplane and the development of commercial passenger airlines has had the greatest influence on long-distance travel since the invention of the railroad. It may be the most important transportation development in the history of mankind.

Lighter-than-Air Craft

The first airline, Deutsche Luftschiffahrts AG, was founded on November 16, 1909. It was more commonly known as Delag. Headquartered in Frankfurt, Germany, its purpose was to operate **zeppelin** airships. These were a particular type of lighter-than-air craft known as dirigibles. They were similar in appearance to blimps seen today in the skies over major sports and entertainment events advertising Goodyear and Met Life.

Lighter-than-air craft have been around for many years. The first successful one was constructed and flown as early as 1852 by Henri Giffard from Paris to Trappe.

The name *zeppelin* comes from Count Ferdinand von Zeppelin, who designed many successful lighter-than-air craft. These airships were constructed of a lightweight frame connected to gas cells that was covered by a thin exterior "skin" of aluminum and powered by internal combustion engines. Zeppelins were an important part of early aviation and transported many passengers throughout Europe and across the Atlantic. The popularity of the zeppelin reached a high point in commercial aviation in 1929, when the *Graf Zeppelin*, a large version of the original zeppelin, made a historic round-the-world flight in twenty-one days, seven hours, and thirty-one minutes. The *Graf Zeppelin* flew until 1940, when it was finally retired. Between 1928 and 1940 it completed 590 flights, including 140 Atlantic crossings, and carried 13,100 passengers.

Commercial Air Travel Service

The first scheduled air service on a commercial airplane was January 1, 1914, from St. Petersburg to Tampa, Florida. It was accomplished by the newly formed St. Petersburg–Tampa Airboat Line in a single-engine biplane (a plane with two sets of wings) that was open to the sky. It appeared to be a successful venture, but for unknown reasons, the airline continued operations only until the end of March of that year. During the period of its existence, it carried a total of 1,024 passengers.

The first international commercial flight was on January 10, 1919, from London to Paris. It was established by the British Royal Air Force primarily to provide transportation for government officials attending the Paris Peace Conference. Flights continued until September 1919. A total of 749 flights were made.

Another attempt at scheduled passenger service in the United States was made by Ryan Airlines in 1925. This was a West Coast airline that flew from Los Angeles to San Diego. That service lasted about a year.

Continual scheduled passenger service did not begin until 1927. It was started by Colonial Air Transport, an airline that had a contract to carry the mail from Boston to New York. It was one of the many airlines that had been carrying mail for the U.S. Postal Service since 1918. In 1926, Congress passed the **Kelly Act** which authorized long-term mail contracts for airlines. The passage of the Kelly Act led to the founding of many airline companies. All were competing for the contracts to carry U.S. mail; and many, like Colonial Air Transport, carried passengers as well. Many of these new airlines failed; some succeeded; and many of them merged. By 1931, these mergers had resulted in the establishment of such well-known airline carriers as American, Eastern, TWA, and United.

One very important airline in American aviation history is Pan American. It began regular mail service between Key West, Florida, and Havana, Cuba, on October 28, 1927. Passenger service on that route began in January 1928. Travelers were charged $50 for a one-way ticket. Over the next few years, Pan American expanded its routes to other Caribbean islands and into South America. By 1934, it was operating eighty-five aircraft and carrying over one hundred thousand passengers a year.

Martin M–130 China Clipper. In November 1935, Pan American inaugurated transpacific mail service with its new four-motor seaplane, the Martin M–130 China Clipper. It departed from Alameda, California, for Manila, in the Philippines, and arrived there almost sixty hours later. Paying passengers were allowed on this flight beginning October 21, 1936. Pan American's new long-distance seaplanes were named the China Clipper, the Philippine Clipper, and the Hawaii Clipper. They could carry forty-one passengers and had a cruising speed of 157 miles per hour. Pan American subsequently extended this service to Hong Kong.

Boeing 314—Yankee Clipper. Airline service over a portion of the Atlantic began on June 16, 1937, when Imperial Airways inaugurated service between Bermuda and New York. Pan American began its passenger service between New York and Southampton, England, on July 8, 1939, with the Yankee Clipper, another new long-distance plane. It was a Boeing 314, which carried seventeen passengers, each paying a fare of $375.

DC–3. Most of the planes used on domestic airline routes during the latter 1920s and the 1930s were small, accommodating eight to fifteen passengers. They cruised between 100 and 135 miles per hour. In 1934, Douglas Aircraft introduced its DC–2, a twin-engine plane that could travel at a cruising speed of 196 miles per hour. Douglas soon produced a larger version, the DC–3, with a cruising speed of 186 miles per hour. The DC–3 became the workhorse of civil and military passenger service for many years. It is said that the DC–3 was the first plane

One of Pan Am's "clippers," a Sikorsky flying boat, used to provide transoceanic service from the late 1930s to the early 1940s. (Photo courtesy of the New York Public Library Picture Collection.)

that could operate profitably without the benefit of a mail contract. There were a total of 10,655 DC–3s built, and several hundred of them are still flying today.

Commercial Jet Aircraft. An important development that had profound effect on the hospitality industry was the introduction of commercial jet aircraft in 1958. Because of their increased speed, flights between cities took less time, and this improved people's perceptions of travel: because it consumed less time, it was less arduous than ever before. More people began to travel by air, and as new—and later, larger— models of aircraft were introduced, the relative cost of long-distance travel began to decrease. Round-trip fares between cities became less than one-way fares had been when piston aircraft were used, and the time to travel between cities was cut by nearly half.

Perhaps one of the most important developments in air travel was the introduction of wide-bodied aircraft. The first of these was the giant Boeing 747, which went into service with Pan American World Airways on January 22, 1970. The aircraft had 58 seats in first class and 304 in economy class, and a maximum cruising altitude of forty-five thousand feet. More recent versions of the 747 accommodate as many as five hundred passengers.

The 747 is too big and costly to operate on short flights; however, it is designed for long-distance routes. Smaller and less costly wide-bodied aircraft were manufactured about the same time. These include the DC–10, which has a seating capacity of 270 passengers, and the Lockheed L1011, which can carry 330 coach passengers or 272 passengers in a mixed configuration. The DC–10 came into service on August 5, 1971, and the L1011 on April 26, 1972.

In June of 1995, the Boeing 777 was introduced. It is a very large two-motored aircraft that can carry 292 passengers. It was designed in cooperation with airline representatives and contains many new features for the comfort and safety of passengers. Each of its two motors is larger and generates more thrust than each of the motors on the 747. Other smaller aircraft have been introduced to serve short- to medium-range flights relatively inexpensively. These include the Boeing 737, 757, 767, and the McDonnell Douglas MD–80. These smaller planes are also now used for long-distance flights when there are a limited number of passengers. They feature fuel-efficient engines and many modern advances in airline technology.

The Concord. Perhaps the most interesting aircraft is the supersonic Concord, a joint development of Britain and France. It underwent many years of design and testing before it was put into service. It first flew on March 2, 1969, but was not put into service until January 1976. This remarkable plane cruises at an amazing 1,332 miles per hour. It is a slim delta-winged aircraft that accommodates relatively few passengers. It can fly from western Europe to New York, however, in about three hours, enabling it to arrive in New York at a local time earlier than its local time of departure in Europe. It is also very costly to operate; therefore, compared with fares on traditional jet aircraft, the Concord is very expensive.

Airline Regulation

The airline industry in the United States was highly regulated until 1978. The Civil Aeronautics Board (CAB) allocated routes, approved fares, and ruled on mergers. Relatively little competition existed among airlines; comparatively few were allowed to serve major routes. For example, direct service from New York to Los Angeles might be awarded to only two airlines, which would submit proposed fares to the Civil Aeronautics Board for approval. Knowing the number of potential passengers between New York and Los Angeles, they would submit fares that would guarantee a profit. In return for limited competition, airlines were required to serve cities with few potential passengers, where service was unprofitable.

The Airline Deregulation Act of 1978. The **Airline Deregulation Act of 1978** led to major changes in the airline industry. It eliminated the Civil Aeronautics Board and transferred its responsibilities to the Federal Aviation Administration (FAA) and the Department of Transportation (DOT). The act was designed to increase competition and to provide the airlines with more freedom to choose routes and set rates.

The Airline Deregulation Act of 1978 had major consequences. Major airlines eliminated unprofitable routes, and hundreds of small commuter airlines were born to fill the need for commuter service from smaller cities. Consolidation of airlines soon followed, and financially weak airlines went out of business.

Competition has driven the price of airline travel down, and more people are flying than ever before. Airline profits have all but disappeared. The industry is still evolving; it appears that there will be a few very large long-distance carriers that will dominate the industry. Smaller commuter airlines will be tied very closely with the larger airlines, many of them controlled or owned by the large carriers.

Frequent-Flyer Programs

In an effort to develop a loyal customer base, the airlines introduced **frequent-flyer programs.** These are incentive programs that award mileage for travel on their airlines and provide various rewards for accumulation of miles. The awards may include upgrades to first-class seats, free flights, free car rentals, and free hotel rooms. It has been estimated that airlines now owe more than three million free round-trip tickets, enough for flyers to travel at least 5.4 billion miles at no cost, as a result of these frequent-flyer programs.

Hub-and-Spoke Routing

In an effort to fill the maximum number of seats on each flight and to simplify scheduling, airlines have developed a system of routing commonly referred to as the **hub-and-spoke** method. Each airline has several major airports, that serve as hubs, providing meeting points for planes coming from outlying cities (spokes). Flight schedules are established so that many planes arrive at the hub at about the same time. Passengers then change planes and proceed to their final destinations. Delta, for example, has a major hub in Dallas. Many flights originating in Boston, New York, Philadelphia, Pittsburgh, Washington, Atlanta, and elsewhere fly directly to Dallas. They are scheduled to

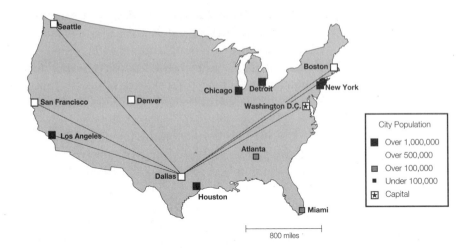

arrive in Dallas within approximately one half hour of each other. On arrival, passengers change planes and proceed to their final destinations. Not all flights on any airline are scheduled this way, of course. A number of them still operate as direct flights.

The hub-and-spoke method has advantages over direct routing. The major advantage to the airlines is that flights can be more fully booked. For example, suppose that on a given day, Delta has sold three hundred tickets on flights from Boston: one hundred for Los Angeles, one hundred for San Francisco, and one hundred for Seattle. If it scheduled three direct nonstop flights, one to each of the three cities, each plane would be only about one-half full. However, using the hub-and-spoke method, only one wide-bodied plane need be used. It could be scheduled to go, for example, to Los Angeles. The plane would stop first in Dallas where it would meet other planes coming from New York, Washington, and other cities. Those passengers continuing to Los Angeles would stay on board, whereas those for Seattle and San Francisco would transfer to other planes that had come from New York and Washington. The Los Angeles plane would be filled from passengers transferring from the New York and Washington flights.

From the viewpoint of the passenger, the advantage of the hub-and-spoke method is that one can fly to virtually any city in the Delta system with only one stop and a change of planes. The disadvantage is that the stop at the hub makes the time to fly from one city to another somewhat longer than it would be for a direct flight. For some flights, it is necessary to fly extra distance because it is necessary to go to a hub airport that may be inconveniently located for the passenger. In addition, for those passengers changing planes, there is an increased chance that baggage will be lost. And in the event that one incoming flight is delayed or canceled, passengers due to transfer to that flight will miss their connection and be delayed in Dallas until the next scheduled departure for their intended destination.

▶ Restaurants in the Twentieth Century

The early twentieth century saw the development of some new foodservice establishments, such as diners, drive-ins, hamburger restaurants, roadhouses, and ice-cream stands. These years also gave rise to trends that were to become increasingly important. The growing popularity of the automobile, for example, led to the development of different kinds of restaurants along the highways of America; Roadside diners and drive-ins were typical.

▶ Diners

Diners became common after 1897, when the cities of Boston, New York, and Philadelphia began to replace their old horse-drawn trolleys, called horsecars, with the new electric variety. Many of the horsecars were sold to dealers who refitted them with stoves and dishes, then resold them as lunch wagons. Later, after World War I, larger well-lighted, furnished, and fully equipped versions were manufactured especially for use as diners—restaurants that were seen by many as imitating for the middle class something of the glamour that had once graced the dining cars on the railroads. By 1930, dozens of manufacturers were building diners, which became typical features of the highways, cities, towns, and villages of America. They were everywhere.

▶ Drive-ins

Drive-in restaurants were an important development of the automobile age. J. G. Kirby of Dallas, Texas is credited with the idea for the drive-in restaurant. In 1921, he opened the first of a chain of these, calling it Pig Stand. These were small restaurants within large parking lots that featured food served to customers in their parked automobiles. The idea was widely copied. Orders were taken by young men and women, conveyed to the kitchen, and served when ready. The food was served on special trays that hooked onto the frame of the open automobile window, and customers could eat without leaving their cars. In some drive-ins, servers were equipped with roller skates to speed service. Drive-ins were very popular from the 1920s until nearly 1960.

▶ Other Types of Restaurants

Other establishments that developed during the period following World War I included those that were acceptable to unescorted women, typically shoppers: tea rooms, women's exchanges, and the restaurants found in department stores.

▶ White Castle: The First Fast-Food Hamburger Chain ◀

The origins of the hamburger restaurant chain can be traced to Wichita, Kansas and the opening of the first White Castle in 1921. This restaurant featured a portion of ground beef cooked on a grill and served between halves of a sliced roll with fresh onion. No one knows who originally invented the hamburger, or where, or in what year, but it is certain that Walter Anderson and E. W. (Billy) Ingram, the founders of the White Castle system, were responsible for the first fast-food hamburger restaurant chain.

White Castle had many imitators, the best known of which was the White Tower. White Castle considered the White Tower imitation flagrant and sought the assistance of the courts to stop it. White Castle sued White Tower in the Minnesota courts, and White Tower sued White Castle in the Michigan courts. At the request of White Castle, the case was transferred to federal court. Hearings, decisions, and appeals consumed several years. Finally, in 1937, the U.S. Court of Appeals affirmed a lower court decision in favor of White Castle, ordering White Tower to stop operating its business in such a manner as to confuse the public by making it difficult to distinguish between the identity of restaurants in the White Castle system and those of the White Tower system.

The first fast-food hamburger restaurant chain in the world, White Castle. Founded in 1921 by Walter Anderson and E. W. (Billy) Ingram, White Castle survived early legal battles with an imitator and still operates successfully today. (Photo courtesy of White Castle.)

▶ Prohibition

By the end of World War I, a long-standing political disagreement between two groups of American voters was about to be resolved—at least temporarily. The groups were the "drys" and the "wets"—those in favor of prohibiting the sale of all alcoholic beverages, and those opposed. By 1919, a sufficient number of states had ratified an amendment to the Constitution that made the manufacture, transportation, and sale of alcoholic beverages illegal. This amendment, the eighteenth, ushered in Prohibition, a period later known as the "Noble Experiment." Prohibition went into effect in 1920 and lasted until 1933. Its impact on the restaurant industry was profound.

Speakeasies

Prohibition led to the demise of a number of established restaurants. Unable to sell wine, spirits, and beer, some could not attract sufficient customers by serving food alone; others were not able to earn sufficient profit without selling drinks. Customers looking for drinks by the glass or alcoholic beverages by the bottle soon found them available in a new, illegal, and highly profitable type of establishment known as the **speakeasy.** The number of these grew very quickly. Soon millions drank in the speakeasies; millions more drank at cocktail parties in private homes. By 1929, the police commissioner of New York estimated that there were approximately 32,000 speakeasies in the city, about twice the number of licensed and unlicensed saloons before Prohibition. Some speakeasies survived both Prohibition and repeal, and have become particularly well known. These included two of New York's finest—the famed '21 Club and El Morocco.

The Road House

Prohibition led to the development of an establishment known as the **roadhouse**—a roadside restaurant that sold alcoholic beverages, alone or as accompaniments to meals, and that provided live or recorded music for dancing. These were formidable competitors for restaurateurs who chose not to break the law. After repeal, many of the roadhouses were able to continue in operation as legitimate restaurants.

Some of America's best-known restaurants opened in this period. In New York, these included Pavillon, the Stork Club, and the Rainbow Room; in New Orleans, Galatoire's, Arnaud's, and Brennan's; and in San Francisco, Taidsch Grill, Schroeder's, and Marchand's.

▶ Marriott and the Beginning of Restaurant Franchising

Another chain to develop in the 1920s had some units that were drive-ins and others in which the customers walked up to outdoor stands to order a specific product: root beer. Roy Allen and Frank Wright established the organization in California, and the root beer was called A & W, for Allen and Wright. They were very successful and soon developed the idea of selling franchises—contracts that permit others to use the name of the parent company and to sell its products or services under conditions defined in a contract.

In 1926, two young men became partners in the purchase of the A & W franchise for Washington, D.C. One was a young college graduate named J. Willard Marriott; his partner was Hugh Colton. They opened their first store in the summer of 1927. By fall, with the arrival of cooler weather, sales began to drop, and Marriott quickly decided to enlarge the product line. He removed the A & W logo and adopted the name Hot Shoppe, principally because of the spiced Mexican foods he was selling. From this simple beginning has come the Marriott Corporation, one of the world's leaders in the hospitality industry.

▶ Howard Johnson

The first entrepreneur to promote franchises aggressively was Howard Johnson, founder of the company that bore his name. The first franchised Howard Johnson restaurant opened in Massachusetts in 1935. Under the contract, it was owned and operated by the builder, Reginald Sprague, who was to purchase ice cream and other products from Johnson's firm. By 1940, there were over 130 Howard Johnson restaurants along the eastern seaboard.

World War II brought problems for the foodservice segment of our industry, and the Howard Johnson restaurants were hard hit. The federal government imposed gasoline and food rationing during the war. Food rationing limited the menu choices available to foodservice operators. Gas rationing restricted the distance that people could drive, which kept potential customers from many of the Howard Johnson restaurants located along highways. Many were closed for the duration of the war because of lack of business.

After the war, Americans resumed the practice of driving for pleasure, which they had been forced to curtail during the war. Many people were stopping at restaurants on these trips away from home. A substantial number were uncomfortable with the idea of eating in strange establishments and elected to stop at a familiar and trusted Howard Johnson restaurant, with its orange roof. Howard Johnson restaurants were reopened, heralding a period of great prosperity for the chain. The Howard Johnson name and reputation were already well established, and the organization was able to compete favorably for new locations on the developing interstate highway network and elsewhere.

Because of their standard physical features (including the orange roofs), their excellent ice cream, and their reputation for products of consistent quality, the Howard Johnson restaurants became a model organization for others.

▷ Changes in the Foodservice Industry

After the end of World War II in 1945, the foodservice industry entered a period of development that was linked to changes taking place both in American culture and in other segments of the hospitality industry. The most significant of these are the following.

1. *Women in the workforce.* This important change had its origins during World War II. When men were drafted into the armed forces, labor shortages occurred in business and industry. The only reasonable solution was to hire women to fill the jobs, so that, by war's end, millions of women were employed full time. Many of these women had never before been employed. A great many discovered that they enjoyed working, they liked earning money and the sense of independence it gave them, and they did not want to be full-time homemakers or housewives.

2. *Economic expansion.* After the war, men discharged from the armed forces returned home to resume their lives. Considerable economic disruption was expected but comparatively little took place. The economy expanded to meet the demand for consumer goods resulting from the end of the war. Gasoline, for example, had been rationed during the war, and automobiles had not been produced for the consumer market in 1943, 1944, and 1945. Demand in this area was very strong in the years immediately following the war, and the number of jobs for workers in automobile plants expanded considerably.

▶ The Restaurant Industry Grows

Gradually, the interaction of an expanding economy, higher levels of disposable income, increased leisure time, and greater numbers of automobiles on the road led to significant growth in the restaurant segment of the hospitality industry, in particular.

As automobile travel increased, the traveling public wanted more restaurants at which to stop. Local restaurants often were not convenient to travelers, and it was difficult for travelers to determine food quality and prices of restaurants they had not previously visited. This set the stage for nationally recognized images and price structures that the traveling public could rely on.

▶ New Chains Develop

In the 1940s and 1950s, a number of foodservice chains were developed, and they employed some of the same techniques used by Howard Johnson. Creating brand names—which came to represent in consumers' minds a particular product, price, level of quality, and perception of service—was one technique. Another was to build into each restaurant physical characteristics that made it instantly recognizable as one of the units in a particular chain. To be successful with these techniques, millions of dollars were spent on advertising—especially using the new national medium that had become commercially available in 1947, the television. Some of the organizations to do this were Kentucky Fried Chicken, Dairy Queen, Denny's, Dunkin' Donuts, Burger King, Jack-in-the-Box, and Googie's. With the establishment of this general operating pattern, the era of so-called fast food had begun.

McDonald's

Of all the fast-food companies to develop in the United States, the most clearly and consistently successful has been McDonald's. Interestingly, Ray Kroc, who is responsible for its ultimate success, was not its founder. The original idea and the early development of the chain was

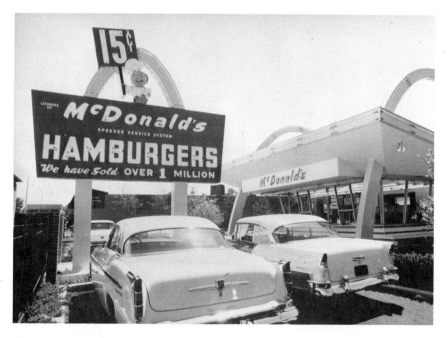

One of the first McDonald's, Des Plaines, Illinois (ca. 1955). Employing the assembly-line method to produce a limited menu, the McDonald brothers devised their formula for success. Later, under Ray Kroc's management and marketing strategies, McDonald's grew to become one of the most successful foodservice businesses in the world. (Photo courtesy of McDonald's Corporation.)

the work of two brothers born in Manchester, New Hampshire, after whom the company is named—Richard and Maurice McDonald.

The McDonald brothers had been in the restaurant business for some years by 1948, which was to become a particularly important year for our industry. By then they had become tired of the personnel problems common in the restaurant business and were looking for a new method of operation to free them of the burden. After considerable discussion and planning, they attempted an operating method that reduced their former dependence on highly-skilled staff members. Their method was similar to the assembly line used in the manufacturing industries. They devised an operation offering a limited menu of products prepared by unskilled workers who had been carefully trained to perform simple tasks in a repetitive manner. Each product was thus the result of a number of simple tasks performed by several workers. It became possible to hire people with limited educational backgrounds and no foodservice experience, and to train them quickly. Because of the assembly-line format, it was easy to respond to demand by producing large numbers of products quickly, and to do so at low labor cost. Because the jobs were unskilled, wages and labor costs were very low compared with competitors'.

The McDonald brothers were successful, and they were beginning to sell franchises when their success came to the attention of Ray Kroc.

Ray Kroc and McDonald's

Ray Kroc was one of the most influential restaurant operators in the history of our industry. He was fifty-two years old in 1956 when he noticed during a trip to San Bernardino, California that people were lining up to purchase hamburgers from a stand owned and operated by the McDonald brothers. He learned that they were selling franchises, and he bought a franchise that allowed him to open McDonald's restaurants anywhere in the state of Indiana. Over the next few years, Kroc opened a number of units but had numerous disagreements with the McDonald brothers over various policies and procedures. Eventually, Kroc offered to buy the business from the McDonalds, and they accepted his offer and retired from the business.

Under Kroc's management, McDonald's became extraordinarily successful, internationally as well as within the United States. His strengths were his ability to organize and standardize, and his marketing ability. He made franchising common in the restaurant business. Today, the company he founded accounts for a greater dollar volume of sales than any other restaurant company in the world.

The Growth of Additional Specialized Chains

By the third quarter of the twentieth century, the seeds had been sown for still more national foodservice chains, many of which grew by selling franchises. The chains typically offered limited menus of specialized, standardized items for consumption, either on the premises or for takeout, as the customer preferred. These organizations included Arthur Treacher's, Kentucky Fried Chicken, and Pizza Hut, among others. Some chains developed around particular themes (such as Victoria Station, the Magic Pan, Trader Vic's, and the Red Barn), whereas others were defined by the specialty foods they offered (such as Taco Bell, Red Lobster, Steak and Ale, and the Spaghetti Factory); another group catered to families (for example, Friendly's and Denny's). Some of these chains have not survived (Arthur Treacher's and Victoria Station), whereas others have continued to succeed.

▶ Changing Tastes in Dining Out

The variety of restaurants in the preceding discussion suggests that Americans have shown a broad taste in their restaurant selections in the years since World War II and that the industry has responded with many types of restaurants. Prior to 1940, dining out was reserved for special occasions for most Americans. As our standard of living has risen, dining out has become more common. For many people, dining out is now considered an everyday experience, part of a normal lifestyle. The term *dining out*, however, conveys varying images to people, and a dining-out experience that some might consider pleasant can induce horrified groans in others. The beauty of a dining-out experience, like beauty itself, is in the eye of the beholder.

The trend toward dining out has caused the restaurant industry to grow in size and scope, and to become one of the fastest growing industries in the United States. In the following chapter, we will discuss the lines along which the restaurant industry has developed as a result of the growth in demand for foodservice.

City Hotels in the Twentieth Century

The twentieth century has brought major changes to city hotels. The first half of the century was perhaps the most important in the history of the hotel industry in the United States. The last half has also seen major changes take place.

▶ From 1900 through World War II

The first half of the twentieth century was both an unprecedented period of growth and later, a period of economic depression that led to many hotel company failures. One hotel organization, founded by Ellsworth M. Statler, began, grew dramatically in the early years of the century, survived the economic downturn, and managed to prosper in the years that followed.

The Buffalo Statler

This three-hundred-room hotel opened on January 18, 1908 in Buffalo, New York. It was named the Buffalo Statler and is considered to be a milestone in the history of the hotel industry. This was one of the first modern commercial hotels to cater to the ever-growing number of traveling businessmen, and it offered them the following.

1. A private bath in every room
2. Circulating ice water in every bathroom
3. A telephone in every room
4. Full-sized, lighted closet in every room
5. Light switch on the wall just inside the door of each room[1]
6. Free newspaper delivered to every guest's room each morning[2]
7. A mail chute that ran from the top floor to the lobby, so that guests could post letters without leaving their floors

The advertising motto of the hotel was "A room with a bath for a dollar and a half," an incredible value for travelers at the time. The Buffalo Statler was very successful, and Statler began to open additional hotels bearing his name, thus creating a group of properties assigned the modern term *chain*. Eventually, he owned or operated properties in Cleveland, Detroit, New York, Boston, and most other major American cities. When he died in 1928, Statler controlled more hotels than anyone in the history of the industry.

The Plaza Hotel in New York

During the years when Statler was developing his Buffalo property and expanding his holdings, many individuals, partnerships, and corpora-

---

[1]Other hotels had a pull chain hanging from the light fixture, which guests had difficulty locating in the dark.

[2]Each guest-room door had a slot cut out at the bottom so the paper could be slipped through.

One of the most famous hotels in the world, the Plaza Hotel in New York City. Along with E. M. Statler's several luxurious hotel properties, the Plaza was among the most important hotels built in the United States before World War I. (Photo courtesy of the Plaza Hotel.)

tions were designing and building new hotels in cities all across America. In New York City, nearly a mile from the nearest railroad, a new hotel opened in 1907. Named the Plaza, it was actually the second hotel of that name to occupy the site. The first, erected only seventeen years earlier, was torn down so that the new eight-hundred-room Plaza could be built.

The world-famous Plaza is a particularly notable establishment, an excellent example of one of the great American "Palaces of the Public." Interestingly, it is one of the few successful hotels anywhere to operate without a sign. In addition, the Plaza has been continuously operated as a luxury hotel since 1907—an unusually long period. Managers of the hotel have been known to boast that those who would not recognize the Plaza without a sign clearly do not belong there. In the early years, up to 90 percent of the rooms and suites in the Plaza were occupied by permanent residents. This provided financial stability and helped to assure the hotel a prosperous future.

Other Well-Known Hotels

Other important hotels constructed in the period before World War I included the Copley Plaza (1912) in Boston; the McAlpin (1912) and the Biltmore (1916) in New York City; the Willard (1901) in Washington D. C.; and Statler properties in Cleveland (1912), Detroit (1915), and St. Louis (1918).

"The Golden Age of Hotels"

The decade of the 1920s—popularly known as the Roaring Twenties—was a particularly important period of hotel development. It has been characterized as the "golden age of hotels" because of the large number of hotels constructed, their size, and the very high occupancy rates they were able to maintain.

Occupancies during the 1920s were the highest the hotel industry had ever known. Annual guest-occupancy rates for many American hotels averaged above 80 percent during this period. New hotels were almost instant successes, and it seemed as though hotels could not be built quickly enough to satisfy the increasing demand for rooms. This high demand was one consequence of a booming economy that had led to great increases in travel for business purposes, and given the improvements in railroads, automobiles, and roads, long-distance travel was far easier than it had ever been in history.

The opening curtain went up with the opening of the Pennsylvania, a two thousand, two hundred-room hotel located just across the street from a major railroad terminal—New York's famed Pennsylvania Station. The Pennsylvania opened for business in January 1919 and was the world's largest hotel at the time. Although the building was owned by the Pennsylvania Railroad, it was operated by Ellsworth M. Statler. It was his first venture in New York City.

The Pennsylvania was a vast enterprise. When it opened, the chef's staff was reported to consist of "nine bakers, ten pastry bakers, four ice-cream chefs, nine butchers, twelve cold-meat cooks, nine roast cooks, twelve sauce cooks, nine fry cooks, six vegetable girls, four soup cooks, four banquet chefs, eight pot washers, four cleaners," and others too numerous to list. Many years later, it became a Hilton hotel—the Statler Hilton—when Statler's chain was purchased by Conrad Hilton in 1954.

Many important hotels were built during the 1920s, including the Ritz Carlton (1927) and the Statler (1927) in Boston; the Roosevelt (1924) and the New Yorker (1927), both in New York City; the Biltmore (1927) in Santa Barbara; the Mayflower (1925) in Washington D. C.; and both the Palmer House (1924) and the Stevens (1928) in Chicago. The Stevens, a 3,000 room property, was later purchased by Hilton and renamed the Conrad Hilton, after the founder of the company that symbolized the hotel industry for many Americans in the period from the 1930s through the 1960s. The Conrad Hilton long served as the headquarters of the Hilton organization and was the world's largest hotel for many years.

The Great Depression

The Great Depression began in October 1929 and continued for the next decade. During this period, banks failed and firms, large and

▶ Conrad Hilton (1887–1979) ◀

Hilton is one of the most recognized names in the history of the hospitality industry. The chain that bears this name was founded by Conrad Hilton, who had embarked on a successful career prior to going into the hotel business. He was a banker in New Mexico and purchased his first hotel—the Mobley, in Cisco, Texas—in 1919 with an investment of $5,000. This was a time when much oil was being discovered in Texas and the owner of the Mobley decided to try drilling for oil rather than staying in the hotel business. Hilton happened to be in Cisco on bank business at the time and discovered the hotel was for sale.

Hilton was very successful at operating the Mobley. He used some of the techniques employed by innkeepers over many centuries: he increased occupancy by renting each room to two, three, or even four persons every night. They were prospectors and oil field workers who did not know one another, but they were all desperate for sleeping accommodations, which were in short supply in the area. Hilton, who lived in the hotel, was even known to rent his own bed and sleep in a lobby chair on occasion. He was obviously able to achieve maximum revenue from the hotel under these circumstances.

Hilton acquired seven hotels in the area in a very short time, expanding as fast as his credit rating would permit. He knew the banking business well, and he had maintained contacts who would lend him the funds to make the necessary down payments on hotel properties. His business philosophy was to borrow as much as possible on each of his hotels in order to expand as rapidly as possible. This worked well as long as hotel occupancy rates were high. However, when occupancy rates dropped during the depression of the 1930s, Hilton was unable to meet the payments required by this heavy debt and lost several of his properties in bankruptcy proceedings.

small, went out of business. Because the government did not insure against bank failures back then, many people lost their life savings. Unemployment rose to alarming rates, and people were sometimes out of work for years. Nature compounded the economic problems in some parts of the country: prolonged drought was followed by dust storms, and land that had once been fertile could no longer be used for agriculture or to support livestock. Some limited recovery began in

1933, and slow progress continued. However, historians tend to agree that the Great Depression continued until the production demands of World War II reduced unemployment and brought the nation a measure of prosperity.

During the depression, the hotel industry experienced the same problem as other industries—sharply reduced sales volume. The hotel business closely follows business cycles and therefore is profitable when the economy is healthy and unprofitable during economic downturns. The explanation is fairly simple: profitability in the hotel business is closely linked to travel. During periods of prosperity, more people travel, for business and pleasure. During a recession or depression, individuals and businesses reduce the amounts they had formerly spent on travel and related expenses, including food, beverages, and lodging. As a consequence, hotel occupancy rates plunge. Occupancies for those hotels that were able to survive the depression were often below 50 percent, a level that is typically below the break-even point for most hotel operations.

One of the few hotels to open during the Great Depression was the world-famous Waldorf-Astoria, which opened in New York in 1932. The new location was 301 Park Avenue, between Forty-ninth and Fiftieth streets. Actually, it was the second hotel to use that name, the first one being located further downtown (see chap. 2).

The End of the Depression

World War II brought an end to the Great Depression. It also brought renewed prosperity to the hotel industry. Many of the hotels in major cities had higher rates of occupancy than ever before or since. Virtually all economic activity was being directed toward the war effort, and many products, including building materials, were unavailable for civilian use. Thus, no commercial hotel construction was taking place. At the same time, there was a dramatic increase in travel by civilians and by government personnel, including the military. Gasoline was rationed, so people relied increasingly on public transportation for long-distance travel.

Many hotels had failed during the depression, and a number of these hotel buildings had been converted to other uses. Consequently, there was an inadequate supply of hotel rooms available to meet the wartime demand. The existing hotels were busier than anyone had ever thought possible. Day after day, hotel desk clerks would spend eight hours facing unending lines of weary travelers wanting rooms. Travelers to many of the major cities—New York City and Washington, most notably—found it nearly impossible to get rooms. Many hotels failed to honor reservations; others would not even take reservations. It was a desperate time for travelers. National hotel occupancy percentages reached a record annual average well above 90 percent.

After World War II, the changes described earlier in this chapter—increased leisure time, improvements in the comfort of travel, reductions in the time it required, and greater economic prosperity—had a significant negative impact on hotels. The average number of nights a traveler would stay in a given city or resort hotel declined, and as the years passed, that number continued to decrease, with dramatic effect on the industry. There were many positive effects, as well: greater amounts of leisure time, ease of travel, and increased disposable income created a growing number of actual and potential customers for hospitality services.

The Development of Motels

By the early 1950s, the increasing numbers of Americans traveling by automobile and airplane found many of the grand old hotels located near major railroads stations no longer appealing or convenient. Those traveling by automobile sought accommodations in new, more convenient locations.

The new American traveler—both working class and middle class—was not accustomed to the formality of the traditional hotel. Nor was he willing to pay the prices and tip the great numbers of uniformed hotel employees found in the traditional establishments. Moreover, the traditional city hotel did not provide on-premises parking. This new traveler wanted a clean, comfortable room at an affordable price and ready access to his automobile. Business travelers, who had formerly used the train, were also becoming confirmed automobile travelers. They could carry more in the trunk of their cars than they ever could in a train. As a result, it was easier and cheaper to travel by car.

The demand for convenient accommodations for automobile travelers led, inevitably, to the development of the **motel.** There had been establishments providing roadside accommodations for motorists since the earliest uses of the automobile for long-distance travel in the 1920s. There were two types of these accommodations: groups of small individual cabins, known as **tourist courts,** which offered parking space near the cabins; and private homes, known as **guest houses,** in which spare bedrooms were rented to transient guests. Neither of these forerunners of the motel constituted a significant element in the lodging industry.

Early Motels. Early motels were usually built, owned, and operated by individuals or couples, not by chains. They were typically purpose-built, single structures, constructed all on one floor. Parking was free and convenient; the car was normally parked just outside the door of the rented unit.

The motel was a very informal place, such that the casually attired motorist did not feel out of place. One stopped at an office to check in, pay for the accommodations, and pick up the key; then one drove to the room, parked one's car, and carried one's own luggage. There was no one to tip. There were seldom any foodservice facilities as part of the motel, so the traveler had to walk or drive to a restaurant to eat. These motels were simple, and they were inexpensive compared to the price of hotels; but there were not many of them.

The best and most sought-after location for a motel at the beginning of the motel age was on a main highway close to a city or town. It was generally agreed that a motel should be located on the right-hand side of a road, because travelers driving to a city would be more inclined to turn right into a motel parking area than to turn left across oncoming traffic. As the interstate highway network was developed, the exits from these highways became the preferred locations for motels.

Kemmons Wilson and Holiday Inns. While driving with his wife and children on a family vacation in the early 1950s, a building contractor named Kemmons Wilson from Memphis, Tennessee, took special notice of the difficulty they had finding acceptable, reasonably priced places to spend the night. He conceived of an improved motel, which would offer many of the services of the traditional hotel but would be situated more conveniently for the increasing number of people who traveled by automobile. When he returned home, Wilson began to plan the construction of a motel that was to become the first Holiday Inn. It opened in 1952 in Memphis.

Kemmons Wilson's Holiday Inn was so successful that he constructed another nearby, and thus began the development of an organization that would eventually control more guest rooms than any other in the world. Wilson's special talent was in identifying sites for the location of successful motels. The growth of his chain kept pace with the development of the interstate highway system: wherever an exit was planned, Wilson would be one of the first to determine if that exit was an appropriate location for one of his Holiday Inns. In order to keep pace with the development of the highway system, it was necessary for Holiday Inn to franchise its operations.

An early Holiday Inn hotel (ca. 1955). Following World War II, the typical American traveler—either working or middle class and usually traveling by automobile—required affordable accommodations convenient to major highways. One of the first establishments to satisfy this need, Holiday Inn kept pace with the development of the interstate highway systems and at one time controlled more guest rooms than any other hospitality organization in the United States. (Photo courtesy of Holiday Inn.)

Franchising

Although **franchising** had existed in the restaurant industry for many years, as previously described, it was not an important phenomenon in the lodging industry until it was adopted by Holiday Inns. A franchise is a contract between two parties, a franchisor and franchisee, that allows the franchisee the right to use the franchisor's name, sell the franchisor's products, and participate in the franchisor's programs and services under set, specific conditions. In the lodging field, the franchisor may own and operate many of the establishments bearing the franchise's name. The franchisor will seek independent affiliates—franchisees—for two main reasons: (1) so that the franchisor can expand the network of establishments at a more rapid rate than would otherwise be possible, and (2) so that the franchisor can increase revenues through the fees collected from franchisees without actually owning additional properties. The fees generally include a percentage of sales, an advertising fee, a fee for access to the reservations network, and sometimes other fees.

The advantage to the franchisee is as follows: the franchisee's property is part of a chain that is known, the franchise has the ability to profit from regional or national advertising campaigns conducted by the franchisor, and the franchisee obtains access to professional management and management training (in most franchises) as well as to a national reservation network.

Older Hotels Begin to Change

While Wilson and others were building motels in the 1950s and 1960s, the established center-city hotels, many of them near the disused railroad terminals, were aging and becoming ever more costly to maintain. Some were indifferently maintained, and most were losing much of their business to the new booming motel industry.

A number of the older, decaying properties were finally forced to close; they simply could not compete. In other properties, management added staff to the sales departments and began to look for new ways to survive. Some hotels sought to lure long-term residents by advertising appealing weekly and monthly rates. Some attempted to compete directly with the new motels by merely changing their signs. Many—typically those that lacked meeting and banquet space but had access to parking—began to call themselves motor hotels and motor inns, to suggest that automobile travelers would be as satisfied in these accommodations as they were in a motel.

Many of the hotels that had served the individual commercial traveler attempted, often successfully, to develop tour business—groups of vacationers traveling together, typically by bus or airplane. At about this time, tour wholesalers started to reserve large numbers of rooms at these older hotels because they were able to negotiate comparatively low rates.

Hotels with adequate meeting and banquet space made efforts to attract special varieties of group business, such as conventions and business meetings. These ranged from sales meetings to trade shows, from fraternal to political meetings, and from alumni reunions to educational seminars. Center-city hotels became increasingly popular sites for all of these.

Finally, older center-city hotels attempting to survive would adopt any combination of techniques to fill the vacant rooms. It was not unusual to find a hotel sales staff aggressively competing for both convention and group business; while the banquet manager sold wedding parties, the front office manager sold rooms at weekly and monthly rates. Many of these hotels were very large, and great amounts of skill and imagination were required to produce adequate sales volume from the vast number of banquet, meeting, and sleeping rooms they contained.

Hotel Construction Begins Anew

Unfortunately for the older center-city hotels, their competition was not limited to the new motels being constructed around the perimeters of cities. A new and lively threat was developing much closer than the outskirts of the city: builders and developers had started a new era of hotel construction. For most cities, this new era saw the first hotel construction since the earliest days of the Great Depression thirty years before. In many American cities, new hotels were being built and opened at a record pace. In New York, for example, new properties constructed between 1960 and 1965 included the New York Hilton, the Americana, the Summit, the Regency, and the City Squire, all of which continue to thrive, although some have new names and new owners.

A number of the new center-city hotels constructed during this period were purpose-built, designed specifically to cater to large groups of people. They were truly convention hotels in every sense, with meeting rooms for hundreds of people and banquet rooms for thousands. For many of these, convention and other group business accounted for at least 80 percent of the sales.

International Operations

The introduction of commercial jet aircraft also made international travel for masses of people a practical possibility for the first time in history. Americans began to travel abroad in great numbers, and visitors from other countries began to come to America. This led to more business for the lodging properties in many cities—particularly, at first, for those on the East and West Coasts with international airports. Later, when international arrivals and departures became common at other airports, hotels in those cities were also able to benefit.

One of the outcomes of increased international air travel was the development of international hotel operations: American hotel chains that had formerly restricted themselves to domestic operations began to expand abroad. Until that time, only two major American hotel companies were operating abroad. Intercontinental Hotels, a subsidiary of Pan American had been international since 1947, when the United States government had suggested that the company construct hotels in

Central and South America as an aid to the economic development of those regions. Hilton Hotels had also become international in 1949 with the opening of the Caribe Hilton in San Juan, Puerto Rico.

Most hotel companies were focused on the burgeoning American market during the early 1950s and were slow to go into the international area. Today, most American hotel chains are international in scope. Some of the principal examples include Marriott, Hyatt, Hilton, Sheraton, Holiday Inns, Ramada, and Best Western. Today, these names are clearly visible on lodging signs around the world, and there is no evidence that the American hotel and motel industry will retreat from its international leadership role anytime in the years ahead.

Computers in the Lodging Industry

In the early 1980s, an additional important development began to take hold in the lodging industry: hotels and motels started to become fully computerized. Computers had been around for many years, and many hotels had tried them out; however, until the early 1980s, computers had not been successful in lodging properties because they were not yet reliable enough for lodging operations that were open twenty-four hours a day, seven days a week. Further, they were very expensive and very bulky. As early as the late 1960s, the New York Hilton hotel opened with a complete IBM computer operation. However, after only a short period, the system was scrapped and a traditional system put back in place. Other hotels ran traditional systems side-by-side with computers, because they were afraid that the computer system would crash and they could not check in or check out guests. Some of these problems are likely to have stemmed from the fact that hotel people had little computer expertise and computer people had little understanding of the hotel industry. It took some years to get past that initial hurdle.

By the early 1980s, computers became more reliable, less expensive, and more powerful. Furthermore, growing numbers of hotel operators had learned a great deal about how computers could improve operations, and many computer experts had acquired sufficient understanding of lodging operations to develop useful systems. Hotel and motel companies began to adopt various computer property management systems. Today, most properties with more than fifty rooms are computerized.

Market Segmentation

Until the 1980s, most lodging companies operated properties that appealed to one or two specific types of travelers. Some operated only

Some lodging companies have become multi-segmented, offering products under several brand names. Marriott is a good example, with the Fairfield Inns, Courtyards, Residence Inns, and Marriott Hotels and Suites. (Photos courtesy of Marriott Corporation.)

luxury hotels. Other companies specialized in economy motels, or budget motels. Still others restricted their operations to first-class hotels catering primarily to business travelers, vacationers, or tours.

In the early 1980s, lodging organizations began to change their approach: they began to make serious efforts to attract more than one part, or segment, of the travel market. Some companies built hotels and motels for specific segments of the market, recognizing that profits could be made by creating establishments designed to appeal to one or another of these segments. Over time, operators established a number of different types of properties to appeal to a large number of different segments that the industry had identified. **Market segments** became more clearly defined, and new types of properties were built. Examples include the development of all-suite hotels for guests who want separate living and sleeping accommodations with limited cooking facilities, and residence motels for guests who intend to stay more than one or two nights.

Some lodging companies became multisegmented, with various brand names for their products. One good example is Marriott. In addition to first-class and luxury Marriott hotels and resorts, Marriott has developed the following brands for various segments of the lodging market.

Courtyard—A midpriced chain of first-class hotels and motels
Marriott Suites—A chain of all-suite hotels
Residence Inns—A chain of first-class accommodations catering to travelers staying more than one or two nights
Fairfield Inns—A chain of limited-service budget motels

Recent Hotel Construction

In recent years, many new large hotels have been built throughout the United States. A number of these have been constructed in the larger American cities, many of which have new or renovated convention centers or exhibition halls. In Philadelphia, for example, Marriott has opened the largest hotel in the state of Pennsylvania, adjacent to the new Pennsylvania Convention Center. Hyatt has built the 2,000-room Hyatt Regency in Chicago, the home of McCormick Place, America's largest (and growing) exhibition center. A number of large new properties have been built in Las Vegas, Nevada, one of America's key resort and convention cities. At present, the world's largest hotel is in Las Vegas; it is the MGM Grand Hotel, with 5,005 rooms and suites. The MGM Grand is more than a hotel; it can perhaps best be described as a complete entertainment center that includes shops, stores, restaurants, lounges, pools, a health club, a casino, a thirty-three acre theme park, and a showroom.

▶ Resort Hotels in the Twentieth Century

By the early years of the twentieth century, several important factors were beginning to affect the quality of life for the American workforce, and these changes became significant for the operators of resort properties as the years wore on.

▶ Leisure Time in America

Early in the twentieth century, some Americans began to have measurable amounts of leisure time. Most had very little, but it was more than their parents had ever known. At the same time, some had enough disposable income to be able to make plans for their newly found leisure hours. For most, there was little time and little money, but they went about enjoying the little there was.

There were day trips to everywhere by train or by boat, and later, by car as well. The seashore, a park, a zoo, a historic site—Americans were visiting them all. These activities introduced new possibilities, including hotels, rooming houses, and boarding houses catering not to business travelers but to those with a day, a weekend, or a week of leisure time. Increasingly, those who could afford it began to stay awhile.

▶ Vacations

By 1915, growing numbers of white-collar and government workers were being given paid vacation time of one or two weeks a year, and many, with their families, began to take vacations—a nearly revolutionary concept in the industrialized world. As unionized industrial workers began to obtain increased benefits through collective bargaining, many began to pressure their union leaders for vacations with pay. Although it was not easy for the unions to win paid vacations at the bargaining table, they were making gradual progress in this area by 1929.

As time went by, those who could afford it began to travel somewhat farther away. In the New York area, for example, there were a number of possibilities: for those of limited means, a day at the beaches of Coney Island; for others with greater incomes, the extensive rail network offered opportunities for weekends or weeks at destinations in the nearby Catskill Mountains of southern New York and the Pocono Mountains of eastern Pennsylvania. By the mid 1920s, over two hundred resort properties in the Catskills alone catered to holiday seekers, principally from New York City.

There were other possibilities, as well. The beaches along the New Jersey coast were always very popular with New Yorkers and Philadelphians. President Grant said of Long Branch, one of the New Jersey resorts, "In all my travels I have never seen a place better suited for a summer residence." In the early twentieth century, packed trains from New York City arrived at the New Jersey resort towns on summer weekends at the rate of twelve or more each hour.

▶ The Grand Resorts

The resort hotels developed during this period were many and varied. Many of those enjoyed by white-collar and blue-collar workers have not survived. However, it is likely that they attempted to imitate elements of some of the grand resorts, described in the following sections, all of which continue to operate.

The Broadmoor Hotel

One of the premier resort properties in the United States is located in Colorado, near Pikes Peak. Near the bottom of this fourteen thousand foot mountain, in Colorado Springs, stands this classic example of the elegant resort hotels of the West. Named the Broadmoor Hotel, it was founded by Spencer Penrose, an entrepreneur who had attempted to purchase the Antlers, a hotel in downtown Colorado Springs. He had not been able to do so and had decided instead to purchase another property outside of town. This property had once been an established hotel operation, but it had burned down, had been rebuilt, had failed, and had been converted to a girls' school. Existing facilities were inadequate for the resort, so construction began in 1917, and the new resort hotel opened in 1918. It was one of Colorado's first nationally-known resorts. The architects were from the firm of Warren and Wetmore of New York City, designers of New York's Grand Central Station, Biltmore Hotel, and Ritz-Carlton Hotel, among other important buildings.

The Broadmoor quickly became a success. All through the 1920s, the Penroses entertained many wealthy and famous people, and their Broadmoor became a fashionable place for New York society. It is said that one of the reasons for this success was Penrose's preparation for Prohibition: the Broadmoor allegedly had on hand one of the largest liquor supplies in the United States when Prohibition began in 1920.

This period of success for the Broadmoor ended with the onset of the Great Depression. Occupancy rates and guest counts dropped sharply, and Penrose was forced to reduce operating costs. He cut the size of the staff drastically, and it is reported that bellstaff and waitstaff earned only their tips.

After World War II, improving economic conditions brought prosperity back to the hotel. New facilities and new rooms were added during the 1960s and 1970s, and today the Broadmoor is a five-star resort with 560 rooms.

The Arizona Biltmore

Another of America's grand, five-star resorts—the Arizona Biltmore—is located just eight hundred miles south of Colorado Springs, in Phoenix, Arizona. It was built in the style of America's best-known architect, Frank Lloyd Wright, who participated in its design. At the time the hotel was built, Phoenix was a very small community in a large valley, Paradise Valley, which was essentially desert. The Biltmore was situated on a large tract of barren land in the northeastern part of the city, near the foothills of the mountains that surround the valley.

The Biltmore was designed and constructed by Albert Chase McArthur, an architect and disciple of Wright. It opened in 1929 and was sold later that year to William Wrigley, Jr., the chewing gum manufacturer. Wrigley built a mansion for his personal use on a knoll overlooking the hotel. His home was visible for miles around; the resort hotel was not.

After World War II, the population of Phoenix began to increase dramatically. As the city grew, the Biltmore was eventually surrounded by newly constructed homes and businesses. In 1973, the Wrigley family sold the hotel to Talley Industries.

During the summer of 1973, while it was closed for the installation of a sprinkler system, a major fire damaged the property. Repairs were made promptly, and it reopened for the start of the guest season later that year.

Interestingly, the Arizona Biltmore was originally open only during the winter months. Phoenix is normally extremely hot during the sum-

The Arizona Biltmore, Phoenix, Arizona, as it appeared in 1936. Fostered in the early twentieth century by an increase in leisure time and the availability of paid vacations, the "grand resorts" of the United States provided their patrons with respite from the pressures of an industrialized society. Originally intended as a seasonal resort—open only during the winter months, serving primarily individual guests—the Arizona Biltmore now operates year-round, hosting groups and conventions as well. (Photo courtesy of Arizona Biltmore/Westin Resorts.)

mer months, and it is only the development of suitable air conditioning systems that has made it possible for resort hotels in the region to stay open year-round.

The Arizona Biltmore is typical of resorts that have found it increasingly difficult—in some cases, impossible—to survive solely on individual guest business; the vacation seasons are too short to generate the necessary sales volume. In order to remain open year-round, the Biltmore began booking conventions and other group business. The Biltmore, however, enjoys a reputation for restricting its group business to periods of the year when comparatively few individual reservations are booked.

The Boca Raton Hotel and Club

Another five-star hotel built during this period is the fabulous Boca Raton Hotel and Club, which was originally opened in 1926. It was envisioned as a palatial establishment by Addison Mizner, a successful architect who had become famous in Florida for designing many of the homes and other properties there. Mizner wanted to turn the seventeen thousand, five hundred acre site into "a happy combination of Venice and Heaven, Florence and Toledo, with a little Greco-Roman glory and grandeur thrown in." His grand plan included a castle with drawbridge in the middle of a man-made lagoon—for himself! He was not able to construct all he originally had in mind, but all that he did build used the best and most expensive materials available. One of his creations was a luxurious one hundred room hotel that cost $1.5 million to build—a fortune in those days for such a small establishment. He named it the Cloister Inn. He would use this name again later for a property he designed in Sea Island, Georgia.

The Cloister Inn was not financially successful. It was open for only three months before it was forced to close. It was then sold to Charles Dawes, a former vice president of the United States. It was sold again in 1928, to Clarence H. Geist of Philadelphia. Geist closed it and spent millions of dollars converting it to a private club by adding rooms, swimming pools, and other features to the original building. He brought the total number of rooms to four hundred and reopened the facility in 1930 under a new name: the Boca Raton Hotel and Club. During World War II, it was taken over by the United States army and used as a training facility.

In 1956, the Boca Raton Hotel and Club was purchased by Arthur Vining Davis, who set up a corporation to own and operate it. His corporation, Arvida, built a twenty-seven story tower, which added new guest rooms and a convention center. The property has been under continuous development since then, and it is now one of the larger resorts in the area, with one thousand rooms, twenty-nine meeting rooms, four outdoor swimming pools, seven dining rooms, an eighteen-hole golf course, twenty-two tennis courts, and a half mile of private beach.

▶ The Impact of Changing Transportation Modes on Resort Hotels

We have observed how the decline of the railroads and the increased use of automobiles began to affect traditional hotels in the cities and towns of America after World War II. These developments also had a significant and lasting impact on America's resort hotel industry. In New England, for example, the summer resort hotels historically had catered to guests who had arrived by rail and stayed for weeks and months. With changes in transportation, it became more difficult—eventually impossible—to reach these properties by rail, and more guests began to arrive by car, particularly as the quality of the roads improved. Because people in cars have greater mobility, guests tended to stay for shorter periods; they used their new-found mobility to visit other areas and see new sights.

Some of the New England ski areas, formerly accessible principally by train, were much easier to reach by car, particularly as the train service deteriorated. Guests with private cars also found that the car simplified the daily transit problem of getting from hotel to ski slope. As time went on, developers began to plan and construct hotels closer to the slopes and accessible only by car, which helped to sound the final death knell for rail travel in the ski areas. Later, the automobile gave impetus to the development of new ski areas that would clearly not have been built if rail travel had remained the primary means of access.

As people began to accept air transportation as a common means of travel, various changes took place in the resort hotel industry. Just as the acceptance of air travel occurred gradually, so did these changes.

1.   Nearby resort hotels accessible with reasonable ease by rail or by automobile—including many fashionable properties in the East—gradually lost their traditional business. Many of their former guests found new destinations easily reached by air. These included Caribbean islands, South Pacific beaches, and historic cities and sights of Europe.

2.   Resort hotels in remote locations—including many in the West—that had always been difficult to reach by ground transport were readily accessible by air. It became convenient for residents of the East Coast, for example, to fly to Colorado to ski for a short time. Previously, such trips took more time and were less comfortable. Those who made such trips tended to stay longer to justify the time and trouble the journey represented.

3.   Some resort areas that had remained small because of the time and cost incurred by travelers in reaching them began to grow as air travel made them more accessible and the cost of flights decreased. Some destinations—the Hawaiian Islands and Las Vegas, Nevada, for example—grew quickly. After the introduction of commercial jet aircraft in 1958, the number of visitors to Hawaii increased, reportedly by 500 percent between 1959 and 1967.

4.   Later, as remote areas became accessible, imaginative developers began to plan and construct resort hotels—and even new resort areas—in places where none had previously existed. Vail, Colorado is an excellent example of this; so are the island of Maui, in Hawaii, and Cancun, Mexico.

5.   Operators of chain hotels, recognizing the outstanding potential for growth in resort areas, gradually developed various types of properties in domestic and international locations. Privately developed resort hotels began to include the names Sheraton, Hilton, Marriott, and Hyatt. Many independent resorts were sold to the chains or were managed by them. Two properties in Phoenix, Arizona are excellent examples: the Camelback Inn, which was sold to Marriott Corporation, and the Biltmore Hotel, which was managed by Western International. Both of these are luxurious, five-star operations.

6.   In order to remain competitive, to retain their capable staffs, and to generate sufficient dollar volume to meet growing overhead costs, seasonal resort hotels—both the older, traditional properties and their newer competitors—increasingly began to remain open year-round.

7.   In order to generate volume in their off seasons, resort hotels began to move into markets that had formerly been the provinces of the large center-city hotels, such as conventions and other business meetings. To survive, many resort properties competed with commercial hotels for as much convention and meeting business as they could attract. Eventually, many resort operators found that they grossed more money on this kind of business than they did from their traditional customers—families and individual guests.

8.   An era of "instant" resort development began. Developers acquired large areas of land and created complete resorts with the typical amenities, all within a short period. Complete resort operations—the Dorado Beach Hotel built by Rock Resorts, for example, and such theme parks as Sea World and Disney World—became both popular and successful. Many of the earlier, more traditional resort hotels that had started as small operations expanded as their fame and success increased. By contrast, many of these new resorts are large operations when they open; they are grandly and imaginatively designed and constructed for instant and continuing success.

Two examples of new properties in the resort world will dramatically illustrate some of the differences between such traditional resorts

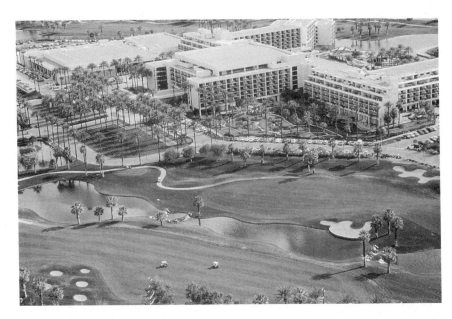

Marriott's Desert Springs, in California's Palm Springs area, is one of the exciting new players in today's resort industry. (Photo courtesy of Marriott Corporation.)

as the Broadmoor and the Arizona Biltmore, and the exciting new players in today's resort industry.

Marriott's Desert Springs

In the deserts of southern California, over one hundred miles from the Pacific coast, lies a resort area known as Palm Springs. The region has been popular with celebrities for a number of years, and various developers have built important golf resorts in the area. One of the more interesting of these is Marriott's Desert Springs, a beautiful four-diamond Palm Desert resort and spa created on desert land. There, with the aid of modern irrigation, Marriott has developed a lush, green resort property that includes a main hotel building of more than nine hundred rooms and a series of villas. Special features include thirty-six holes of golf, a twenty-court tennis complex, a twenty-seven-thousand square-foot European-style spa, and a number of elegant restaurants. One of the most interesting features is the unexpected series of lakes and waterways that offer incredible views and improbable possibilities for boating in the middle of the desert. In fact, the waterways extend into the main lobby of the hotel, which has a dock for launches that transport guests from the main building to two of the restaurants located across the lake.

Prince Resorts' Hapuna Beach Prince Hotel

In 1994, on the island of Hawaii, Prince Resorts created a new three hundred and fifty unit property in which all rooms and suites face the white sands of Hapuna Beach, considered America's best beach by many discriminating travelers. Special features include five restaurants, a golf course designed by Arnold Palmer, tennis courts, a swimming pool, and a health and fitness center.

Typical of many new resort properties, the designers included features and facilities to attract meeting and convention business. These include over fourteen thousand square feet of function space, an eight thousand, four hundred square foot grand ballroom, four smaller meeting rooms, and two executive board rooms. With the addition of facilities of this type, today's resort hotel operators need not depend exclusively on reservations from individual vacationers, as did the operators of resort properties in the past. Today, the operator of a modern resort hotel is prepared to compete for business with operators of any other kinds of hotel properties.

▶ Summary

In this chapter, late nineteenth-century inventions that helped change the hospitality industry are identified, and the impact of each is described. Ships and trains are identified as principal means of travel in the early years of the century, prior to the development of automobiles and planes. The development of the airline industry is discussed in detail. Its growth and importance to travel are examined, and the effects of deregulation are detailed. The significance of current methods of routing aircraft and frequent-flyer programs are explained.

Significant developments are discussed that occurred in three segments of the industry—restaurants, hotels, and resort hotels—from the turn of the century onward. Economic and social factors that led to increased travel by Americans in the period after 1945 are identified and discussed, as are the principal changes that took place in restaurants, hotels, and resort hotels in this same period. These include the impact of chain operations, the role of franchising and market segmentation, the importance of computers, and the impact of changing transportation modes. The contributions of several important figures—

including Ellsworth M. Statler, Conrad Hilton, Howard Johnson, J. Willard Marriott, Kemmons Wilson, and Ray Kroc—are also examined.

Key Terms

Amtrak
Airline Deregulation Act of 1978
Diner
Drive-in Restaurant
Franchising
Frequent-Flyer Program
Great Depression
Guest House
Hub-and-Spoke Routing

Kelly Act
Market Segmentation
Motel
Roadhouse
Speakeasy
Tourist Court
Vacation Cruising
Zeppelin

Questions

1. List three important inventions of the late nineteenth century and briefly describe the impact of each on the hospitality industry of the early twentieth century.

2. Identify the three major reasons cited in the text that explain the growth in mass travel after World War II.

3. Why are vacation cruises becoming increasingly popular?

4. List the four main attractions of vacationing on board cruise ships.

5. Why did the number of railroad passengers decline after World War II?

6. What is Amtrak? When and why was it created? Has it been profitable?

7. What is a zeppelin? In which decades of the twentieth century were they used for commercial passenger service?

8. Of what significance was the Kelly Act of 1926 to the development of passenger airlines?

9. When was Pan American's first international passenger flight? Its first Pacific passenger flight? Its first Atlantic passenger flight?

10. In what year was the Boeing 747 introduced into commercial service? What was the impact of this plane on air travel? Which airline was first to use it?

11. In what year was the Concord supersonic jet introduced into commercial service? Why was the introduction of this new plane significant? How fast does it fly?

12. List and explain three effects of airline deregulation.

13. What is the hub-and-spoke method of routing aircraft? What are the advantages and disadvantages of this method over direct routing of aircraft?

14. List and describe four types of restaurants that developed in the early twentieth century.

15. What was Prohibition? What was the impact of Prohibition on each of the following: taverns, fine restaurants, roadhouses?

16. Name the first fast-food hamburger chain. When was it started?

17. Who founded the Hot Shoppe restaurants? What circumstances led this individual to start the first of these establishments?

18. What were Howard Johnson's principal contributions to the restaurant industry?

19. After World War II, the interaction of several forces led to significant growth in the restaurant industry. List two.

20. Who founded McDonald's? Who first sold McDonald's franchises?

21. What were Ray Kroc's two principal contributions to the development and eventual success of McDonald's?

22. Identify four specialty food restaurant chains that developed after World War II.

23. What were Ellsworth M. Statler's principal contributions to the development of the hotel industry?

24. Name the property that is generally considered the first modern commercial hotel and describe five features that distinguished it from competitors. What was the advertising motto of the hotel?

25. Name the world-famous New York City hotel that has operated without an identifying exterior sign throughout its history.

26. List three reasons that the 1920s were considered the "golden age of hotels."

27. What effect did the Great Depression have on the hotel industry? What happened to levels of occupancy during this period?

28. Are hotels affected by recession, depression, prosperity, and other changes in the economy? Why?

29. What caused the high levels of hotel room occupancy during World War II?

30. Why did the motel segment of the lodging industry experience rapid growth in the period following World War II?

31. What contribution did Kemmons Wilson make to the development of the motel segment of the industry?

32. What is a franchise? What are the advantages of franchise arrangements for the franchisor? the franchisee?

33. Faced with declining business volume after 1950, older, center-city hotels devised ways to attract new business. List three.

34. Why did American hotel chains begin to move into international markets in the 1960s? Identify five chains that are engaged in international hotel operations today.

35. What factors made it possible for lodging companies to take advantage of computer systems in the 1980s?

36. What is market segmentation? Why did lodging companies begin to move towards multisegmentation?

37. In the early twentieth century, some American workers were beginning to have measurable amounts of leisure time. What kinds of activities does the text indicate were available to the American worker on his day off?

38. Name three five-star resort properties built and opened between 1900 and 1930.

39. The text identifies eight significant changes in the resort hotel industry that have occurred since 1945. List and discuss five of these.

40. What features of Marriott's Desert Springs property set it apart from older, more traditional resorts?

Moments of Truth

1. You have just been appointed assistant to the general manager of a 150-room motel with foodservice, bar, convention facilities for two hundred persons, swimming pool, and exercise room. The motel is an independent operation located on the outskirts of a midsize city. Occupancy and profit at the motel has not been good. One of the options to improve occupancy and profit is to become a franchisee for a well-known chain. The general manager has asked you to

investigate this option. How could this option help? Do you see any advantages to remaining independent rather than becoming a franchisee?

2. You intend to travel by air from Boston, Massachusetts to Seattle, Washington. Your airline tells you that there is no direct flight between these two points. You will have to fly to Dallas, Texas, change planes and then fly to Seattle. What benefits do you suppose that airlines gain from this arrangement? Do you see any benefits to travelers?

3. The president of a chain of high-priced first-class hotels knows that there are many travelers looking for first-class accommodations but unwilling to pay first-class prices. They are willing to give up some services and amenities in order to pay less for their rooms. What steps would you recommend she take to gain a share of this business?

Part Three

Food and Beverage Perspectives

Four

Dimensions of Food and Beverage

After reading and studying this chapter, you should be able to:

1 Cite the percentage of gross domestic product (GDP) attributable to food and beverage service.

2 Identify the importance of the food and beverage industry as an employer of women, minorities, and teenagers.

3 List and discuss the three principal reasons cited in the text for increased demand for foodservice.

4 Define *foodservice* and a foodservice enterprise.

5 List and discuss the five most important characteristics of a foodservice operation.

6 Describe each of the characteristic types of foodservice establishments identified in the chapter.

7 Define *beverage service* and a beverage-service operation.

8 List nine reasons for patronizing beverage-service establishments.

9 List and discuss the three terms used to describe the focus of beverage-service establishments.

10 Identify the major categories in the National Restaurant Association's classification system for reporting industry sales.

▶ Introduction

Immigrants from Europe recreated in America the eating and drinking establishments of their homelands in the seventeenth century. These establishments have always enjoyed a high degree of popularity in America. As we discussed in previous chapters, seventeenth- and eighteenth-century taverns sold alcoholic beverages of various types (beer, ale, wine, and rum among them), and most served food as well. Many served a midday meal, known in some parts of the country as an *ordinary*. Many were popular social centers in their communities.

In the nineteenth century, the number and variety of food and beverage operations grew at an amazing pace, and the foundations of the modern food and beverage industry were developed at that time. Restaurants and taverns of all sorts served meals relatively inexpensively. People who lived in lodging houses, where there were no cooking facilities, ate many of their meals in inexpensive restaurants. At the same time, there were also a number of hotels and restaurants providing the finest of food and wines in luxurious surroundings to the growing number of wealthy Americans.

By the beginning of the twentieth century, Americans had access to a number of different types of restaurants—diners, cafeterias, roadhouses, and hamburger stands, to name a few. The concept of dining out—making an important occasion out of the dining experience, with the finest of food and beverages served in a pleasant environment—began to play a growing role in American life.

▶ The Size of the Industry

The foodservice industry ranks as one of the largest in the United States. A recent publication of the **National Restaurant Association** (NRA), the industry's principal trade association, states that "eating and drinking places are first among all retailers in the number of establishments and the number of employees." Today, there are over seven hundred and seventy-three thousand eating and drinking establishments, employing over 9 million people. Information published by the NRA reveals that the foodservice industry employs more women, more teenagers, and more members of minority groups than any other industry in America. Approximately 57 percent of foodservice workers are female; 56 percent are under thirty years of age; almost two-thirds are high school graduates. The foodservice industry employs more minority managers than any other industry.

> ▶ **Trailblazers** ◀
> # More Women Are Gaining Entry into the Executive Ranks in the Foodservice Industry
>
> The National Restaurant Association reports that in 1994, 45.5 percent of all managers in foodservice and lodging operations were women. This is up from 39.4 percent in 1980. During the past fifteen years, many women have committed to careers in the foodservice business and are now valued members of unit management staff.
>
> Where are women making the most progress? Company rosters show that women have moved up in the ranks of human resources, marketing, finance, and training. Operations, the longtime bastion of men, is just starting to attract more women, and that interest in operations seems to be strongest among the twenty-something managers. According to Julie Thompson, vice president of training for a California restaurant chain, "In terms of unit manager classes, of nine trainees, four are usually women."
>
> *Adapted from an article in* F & B Business, *July/August 1995, Page 32.*

One out of every four retail outlets in the nation is an eating or drinking establishment. In one recent year, more than two out of three eating and drinking places had annual sales of less than $500,000. Approximately three out of four are single-unit operations. Four out of every ten are sole proprietorships, establishments owned by one individual.

On a typical day, foodservice establishments provide approximately 30 percent of American adults with lunch and nearly 25 percent with dinner. Of those patronizing these establishments, over 50 percent are men. On this typical day, over 55 percent of adult men eat out, compared with under 50 percent of adult women. Well over 70 percent of the adult population eats at a restaurant once a month. Younger adults eat out more frequently than older adults: on a typical day, over 65 percent of younger adults eat out, compared to under 35 percent of those over 65. Nearly 50 percent of all consumers visit a restaurant on their birthdays, and the most popular day for eating out is Saturday.

The growth of food and beverage sales has been continuous. In 1970, NRA figures placed foodservice sales at $42.8 billion. By 1975, sales volume had grown to $70.3 billion. By 1980, it had grown to approximately $120 billion, and the 1980 figure had nearly doubled by

1990. Although these figures are not adjusted for inflation, they point out the extraordinary growth in that ten-year period. Today, food and beverage sales account for over $312 billion. This is nearly 5 percent of the gross domestic product (GDP) of the United States—generally defined as the value of all goods and services sold. By any measure, this is indeed a major industry.

Although a great number of establishments in our industry offer both food and beverages to their customers, it is not a universal practice. The majority of foodservice operators do not sell alcoholic beverages. Because of this, and because there are significant differences between food operations and beverage operations, we will discuss the foodservice and beverage service segments of the industry separately in this chapter.

▶ Foodservice

As suggested by the statistics of the NRA, the demand for foodservice has grown at a very rapid pace in recent years. In today's world, even children are patronizing foodservice establishments at very early ages: young children have "happy meals" at McDonald's and then continue to patronize McDonald's and restaurants in general in their adult years. Today, many adults eat out several times each week—more than ever before in our history. Studies have shown that almost half of all adults are foodservice patrons on a typical day. Furthermore, the NRA reports that 44 percent of the money Americans spend on food is spent in foodservice establishments.

In addition, the frequency of eating out is increasing. Americans are consuming more meals away from home each year, and nationwide foodservice sales continue to increase dramatically. Experts have predicted that Americans will soon be eating half of all meals away from home.

Several reasons are commonly cited for America's increased demand for foodservice. These include

1. increased discretionary income,
2. smaller families, and
3. changing lifestyles.

▶ Increased Discretionary Income

The average American has more discretionary income than ever before. Individuals have more money to spend as they choose, and growing numbers are spending a substantial amount of it in foodservice establishments. For most Americans today, having a meal or a snack in one or another of the restaurants or other foodservice operations that we see everywhere is an unremarkable, everyday occurrence.

▶ Smaller Families

Another reason that Americans patronize foodservice operations more frequently is a decrease in the size of the family. One explanation for this is that more women are in the workforce and are choosing to postpone having children. In fact, many are choosing to have fewer children altogether. In two-earner households, with both adults tired at the end of the day, going out to eat or having a meal delivered has become an acceptable alternative to preparing the evening meal at home. Also, it is probably easier and certainly more affordable to go out to dinner with a small family than with a large one.

▶ Changing Lifestyles

The daily routines of families are considerably different from what they were thirty or more years ago. The term *two-earner household* implies that one individual no longer stays at home all day to take primary responsibility for food shopping, meal preparation, and cleaning up after a meal. As a result, Americans are less inclined to prepare evening meals at home.

Another change in lifestyle that affects the foodservice industry is the fact that neither young people attending school nor working adults carry their lunches from home to the same extent that they did in years past. Students and workers have foodservice readily available at very low cost at school, at work, or at any number of fast-food establishments nearby.

Similarly, each individual in today's family has a greater degree of independence than in the past. Each makes more personal decisions about his or her life than before. More family members have automobiles and can easily decide to go out for a quick meal with friends rather than eat at home. In some households, it would be difficult to identify an evening meal period at all: family members may come home at different times and either prepare their own meals or elect to go to a restaurant to eat. This would have been unusual a generation ago.

At the same time, the increase in the number of wage earners in America has led to a decrease in the number of family members trained in the art and science of food preparation. In many households, there is no longer anyone able to prepare an excellent meal. Thus, for holiday meals and other occasions for celebration, many are depending on restaurants.

Foodservice Defined

Foodservice can be defined as providing fully prepared foods for immediate consumption on or off premises. Foodservice establishments are those engaged in providing foodservice. These establishments include not only the obvious examples of restaurants and college dining halls but also the salad bars and sandwich counters in food markets and such "distant relations" as food vending machines.

Foodservice enterprises range from full-service restaurants to self-service buffets, from fine restaurants to takeout operations, and from company cafeterias to hamburger stands. Foodservice operations may be either **commercial**—those operated with the aim of earning a profit—or **noncommercial**—those operated primarily for the convenience or welfare of those served rather than primarily for profit. In the sections that follow, we will examine in more detail the various kinds of foodservice establishments and the kinds of service they offer.

Variations among Foodservice Establishments

Anyone who has observed the variety of foodservice establishments will agree that there are significant differences from one to another. These differences are the result of decisions made by owners and managers about the five most important characteristics of a foodservice operation.

1. Menu items
2. Food quality
3. Menu prices
4. Service
5. Ambiance

▶ Menu Items

Perhaps the most important difference among foodservice enterprises can be found in the menu items offered. Some establishments present the customer with a menu consisting of several pages, listing many kinds of dishes. This is common in establishments open for long hours daily and serving a varied group of customers. By contrast, other foodservice operations offer a very limited menu, such as a few luncheon or dinner items—two appetizers, three entrees, and two desserts, for example.

Some establishments specialize in particular menu items, such as **ethnic** or **regional** dishes. Ethnic dishes are those associated with a particular culture—Chinese or Mexican, for example; regional dishes are those characteristic of a particular geographic area—New England or the South, for example. Regional establishments sometimes cater to the tastes of those living in the region in which they are located: a menu for a restaurant in the South might feature catfish, black-eyed peas, and hush puppies. These items would not normally be found in the North, except in establishments specializing in regional southern dishes. Similarly, a substantial number of restaurants on the coast of New England sell Maine lobster, New England clam chowder, and New England boiled dinner—items one would not commonly find on menus in the South.

Some establishments restrict their menus to **specialty foods.** Specialty foods are those belonging to a particular food family, such as vegetables, seafood, or pasta. Others do not specialize but instead offer menus that appeal to a broader range of customers. School and college foodservice operations typically take this approach. They try to serve foods that appeal to many different groups of students.

▶ Food Quality

Food quality is defined as the degree of excellence in food products. Food quality can vary greatly from one foodservice establishment to another. In the final analysis, variations in quality result from decisions made by management to establish a given level of quality. In general, the level of quality is determined by the interplay of three elements:

1. The quality of the food ingredients used
2. The professional skill of those preparing the food
3. The time and effort expended on food preparation

The quality of the food products prepared is determined largely by the quality of the ingredients used. For example, no one can prepare an appealing tossed green salad using wilted lettuce and unripened tomatoes or an excellent fisherman's platter using fish caught several days before and refrigerated improperly. In addition, a foodservice operator must know that many fresh foods are graded for quality and that items of a given quality may be entirely unsuited for use in certain dishes. For example, oranges used for freshly squeezed juice may be entirely unsuited to displaying on a buffet or using in fruit baskets delivered to guests' rooms in a hotel.

Another important element in determining food quality is the professional skill of those preparing the food. Some food preparers are trained in one of the excellent colleges and institutes offering culinary degrees and diplomas or in one of the splendid apprenticeship programs in Europe. Others have learned on the job from mentors willing to train them. Some claiming to be professionals have never really learned very much about food preparation, but only pretend to know. Still others lack the intelligence, the ability, or the will to excel at food preparation.

Each foodservice operator must determine the amount of time and effort that should be devoted to preparing food for customers. As a general rule, food that is prepared on premises from fresh ingredients should be better than food purchased in a frozen, canned, or other pre-prepared state. The latter is known as **convenience food,** a term used to refer to food products that have been processed prior to purchase, thus reducing in-house preparation time.

The reasons for not preparing all food products from fresh ingredients vary. In some establishments, the kitchen staff lacks the professional skill to prepare products equal to the convenience items. In others, hiring skilled personnel would make the cost of labor too high and cause menu prices to be more than customers would pay. For many, convenience items are of acceptable quality. In fact, sometimes the convenience foods are of better quality than those available fresh. And for many chain operations, in which management wants products of uniform quality used throughout its chain, convenience foods provide the most reasonable means of achieving uniformity.

▶ Menu Prices

Menu prices can vary greatly from one foodservice operation to another. On one hand, some charge low prices and attempt to be successful by making a small profit on each of a large number of sales. Others charge low prices for very different reasons: they are providing a service for a specific group of people—club members or hospital patients, for example—and no attempt is being made to earn a profit. On the other hand, some charge high prices knowing that they will attract fewer customers. Each sale, however, normally results in a comparatively high profit, enabling the operator to prosper with fewer customers than the lower-priced establishment. Other reasons for variations in menu prices relate to differences in operating costs, numbers of customers required for profitability, and the image the operator intends to project for the establishment.

▶ Service

Foodservice operators may provide a number of different service arrangements for their customers. Establishments are often differentiated from one another on the basis of these service arrangements, which include table service, counter service, room service, self-service, and takeout or delivery service.

Table Service

For table service, servers normally take customers' orders selected from menus or their equivalent, then deliver the foods to the customers seated at their tables. There are many variations on this basic procedure as well as several specific forms of service, including those known as American, Russian, French, and English. These will be described in greater detail in chapter 6.

Counter Service

For counter service, customers are served food across a level surface called a counter. They may be either seated at the counter or standing, and they may consume the food at the counter or at some other location within the establishment.

Room Service

For room service, customers are situated away from a normal dining area, typically in a hotel room or a hospital room. Food is transported to the individual's room and "served."

Self-Service

For self-service, customers select foods from an array of displayed items; then they carry the items, with or without a tray, to some location in the establishment to consume them. Cafeterias, buffets, and salad bars are three common examples of self-service arrangements.

Takeout or Delivery Service

Takeout or delivery service differs markedly from the others: the menu items are expected to be consumed off premises and are packaged accordingly. With takeout, the customer collects the food on premises and carries it out before consuming it. With delivery service, the customer places an order by telephone or fax, then waits for the food to be delivered. Some establishments offer takeout service only; others offer only delivery; and others offer both.

There are no general rules about the types of service offered by foodservice establishments. Some offer only one type—table service, for example. Others provide more than one type—possibly table service and counter service. Still others may employ all of these in their efforts to please the greatest number of customers.

▶ Ambiance

In the foodservice industry, ambiance is a term used to refer to the aesthetic or emotional impact of an establishment on its customers. It has any number of elements, including furnishings, lighting, sound, decorations, themes, table settings, and employees' appearances and atti-

A restaurant's ambiance is one of the most important elements of the dining experience. Beneath its stained-glass dome, the Garden Court of San Francisco's Sheraton Palace Hotel has elegantly served dignitaries from all over the world. (Photo courtesy of San Francisco Convention and Visitor's Bureau.)

tudes, all of which are aspects of the establishment's environment. In a professionally designed restaurant, the ambiance is never left to chance; it is carefully crafted to achieve a particular impact. One of the reasons that the units in a chain operation are the same is that this helps insure that all will have the same ambiance.

The elements of ambiance vary greatly from one establishment to another. Some—often family restaurants—are typically bright, cheerful, and informal. Others are far more formal, featuring subdued lighting, crisp white linen, fine china and glassware, highly polished silver, and a professionally trained staff. Still other establishments—those that cater to college students, for example—are more likely to be lively, noisily informal, and feature current, popular music. Those attempting to create romantic settings may be dimly lighted and provide soft background music.

▶ Characteristic Types of Foodservice Establishments

Because of the large number of variables in foodservice establishments, most attempts at classifying them are not very successful. The classifications are either too simple to be of any value—"with or without parking," for example—or too complex to be useful, with categories based on the many possible variations in menu, food quality, prices, service, atmosphere, and so on.

However, because people discuss foodservice establishments, describing them and comparing one to another, some terms have become commonly accepted. Those that follow are characteristically regarded as describing types of foodservice establishments. One must remember, nevertheless, that they do not constitute any real system of foodservice classification because they are not mutually exclusive: to describe a single foodservice operation, it is commonly necessary to use more than one of these terms.

Fast Food

Fast-food establishments are those that serve foods for which there is little or no waiting. Many people in the industry are beginning to identify these as fast service or quick service restaurants[1] in recognition of the fact that the service is fast, not the food.

---

[1]As stated in chapter 1, all three terms will be used interchangeably in this text.

In fast-food restaurants, customers wait in line for access to a counter at which they order food from a very limited menu. Often the food is prepared and packaged ahead of time, and the customer's choices need only be picked up by a server and delivered to the customer—on a tray or in a bag, depending on whether the customer intends to consume the food on or off premises. Fast-service operations are relatively low priced. Examples of fast-service restaurants include McDonald's, Burger King, Dunkin' Donuts, Kentucky Fried Chicken, Wendy's, Roy Rogers, Nathan's, and a relative newcommer— Boston Market.

So that the concept works, a high degree of standardization is required: management typically sets rigid standards for procedures, portion sizes, and packaging. Procedures are methods for doing work; portion sizes are the quantities of specific menu items that are to be served each time a given item is ordered; packaging is the particular container or wrapping in which a single portion of a given menu item is to be served.

Other prerequisites to successful operation of a fast-food restaurant typically include an almost inflexible menu, specialized equipment for preparing the foods on the menu quickly, and a staff properly trained to use the equipment efficiently and serve a large number of customers in a short time. A fast-service restaurant is a very well-organized enterprise designed to operate with staff that can be trained quickly and easily.

Table Service

A table-service establishment is one in which customers are seated and served at tables. Individuals may be escorted to their tables by an employee known by a title, such as host or hostess, or may select their own tables. They may be given printed menus from which to select foods, or foods may be selected from an equivalent device, such as a sign or a chalkboard.

At the customer's table, an employee may suggest particular menu items and will normally make note of the item or items selected. The selections are conveyed to the kitchen, where the food is prepared. Selections are served to customers when prepared, with the delivery suitably timed if several items have been ordered by one individual. The individual doing the serving (waiter, waitress, or server) is typically the one who has taken the customer's order.

In most table-service restaurants, the customer is presented with a bill at the conclusion of service. The bill is commonly called a guest

Even though most restaurants have a pasta specialty or two, Italian restaurants are gaining in popularity. Piero Selvaggio, owner of Valentino in Santa Monica, California explains why: "The cuisine has more than 25 centuries of history. It has so much to offer." Customer demand has turned Italian food and restaurants into big business. Imported and domestic products that once seemed exotic are now available and familiar. Nancy Barocci, a Chicago restaurateur points out, "sundried tomatoes, pesto, polenta, and balsamic vinegar have become part of our food culture in just a few years."

Adapted from an article in Restaurants USA, *January 1995, Page 13.*

check, and the customer is expected to pay, charge, sign, or otherwise attend to the bill at that moment. In some establishments, the bill is settled directly with the server; in others, it is settled with a cashier, who is typically stationed near the exit. Exceptions occur in operations that include meals with room prices.

Ethnic

An ethnic foodservice operation is one that specializes in foods associated with a particular culture. Among the most common of these are restaurants offering Chinese, Mexican, Greek, Japanese, German, Italian, Spanish, Thai, and Indian cuisines.

Ethnic restaurants vary considerably in menu, food quality, menu prices, service, and ambiance, even within a specific ethnic grouping. Chinese restaurants, for example, may serve foods from one or more of four regional cuisines—Peking, Szechuan, Canton, and Shanghai—each of which differs from the others. Some Chinese restaurants offer table service; others offer counter service or takeout. Some ethnic restaurants use high-quality ingredients and prepare the finest of foods; others use food of lower quality in order to keep menu prices low.

Specialty

A specialty foodservice enterprise is one that features foods of a particular type, such as seafood, pancakes, chicken, vegetables, steaks,

A specialty foodservice enterprise is one that features foods of a particular type, such as seafood, chicken, or steak. Long John Silver's, pictured here, specializes in seafood. (Photo courtesy of Long John Silver's Restaurants, Inc.)

doughnuts, omelettes, or sandwiches. The possibilities for specialties are many and varied, as are the establishments that feature them. Some limit their menus almost exclusively to the specialty while others use the specialty item as the focal point of the menu but add other items to broaden the establishment's appeal and attract additional customers.

Specialty restaurants can vary considerably in menu items, food quality, menu prices, service, and ambiance, and this can be true even within one specialty. For example, some seafood operations may specialize in shellfish; others feature a more varied assortment of fish and shellfish on one menu. Some have extensive menus, limited only by the availability of particular items in the markets; others may restrict their menus to a very few items that are always available.

Some operators will insist on purchasing fresh seafood daily for their establishments, and others will use frozen products. In some parts of the country, one or another item may be readily available and very popular with diners, while that item may be rare or virtually unsalable in another geographic area. Equivalent differences can be easily observed in relation to menu prices, service, and ambiance from one specialty establishment to another.

Fine Dining

Establishments in this category are those that emphasize high-quality foods, expertly prepared and professionally served. Few convenience foods are used, and most foods are prepared from fresh ingredients.

▶ 20,000 Leagues under Los Angeles ◀
Famous Movie Director Moonlights as a Restaurateur

Steven Spielberg, academy award winning director, has opened a new specialty restaurant featuring gourmet sub sandwiches. The restaurant is named Dive; it looks like a submarine and has twenty different sub sandwiches including a Chinese chicken salad sub, a Tuscan steak sub, and a soft-shell crab sub. Additional items include sourdough bread stuffed with beef stew, chicken pot pie, or tuna burgers. However, the food is not the complete story. Every forty-five minutes, lights flash, sirens blare, bubbles rush past porthole windows, and video monitors flash footage of an undersea voyage.

The restaurant is a definite success. It serves two thousand, five hundred customers a day, and annual sales are projected between $13 million and $15 million.

Such restaurants are typically among the most formal and are often among the most expensive.

Service is a particularly important element in the fine dining experience, but the type of service may vary from one restaurant to another. Some may offer elegant French service, and others Russian or American.

The term *fine dining* gives no indication of the nature of the foods served. The menus may be ethnic, such as Swiss or northern Italian;

Differences between foodservice operations are the result of decisions about their five most important characteristics: menu items, food quality, menu prices, service, and ambiance. In The Manor (West Orange, New Jersey), the owner's decisions about these five have been the key to developing one of the best fine-dining establishments in the region. (Photo courtesy of The Manor.)

they may feature specialties, such as seafood; they may rely on the skill of a chef to prepare dishes unique to the restaurant. Other possible variations among fine-dining establishments include the number of items on the menu: many offer extensive menus with a few special creations that change frequently, whereas some others—often among the finest restaurants in an area—offer only one or two entrees that change daily. In some (which typically require reservations), customers may be given no choice at all: they are served the several courses that constitute the dining experience planned by the chef.

Limited Menu

An establishment that offers a limited menu is one in which management has made a conscious decision to restrict the number of items on the menu. This may be a small but varying number, or it may be a specific, unchanging number—as in a steakhouse that offers only three entrees, all of which are sirloin steaks of varying weights. Sometimes there may be only one basic menu item, such as pizza or hamburgers, for which a large number of variations are available (often in the form of toppings). Other kinds of restaurants with limited menus may feature chicken, hot dogs, lobster, omelettes, or roast beef, among other possibilities.

   The quality of limited-menu establishments can vary considerably. A steakhouse may offer the finest aged beef in the state, or the steaks may be of a quality such that miniature hacksaws are required to cut them. Menu prices in limited-menu establishments may vary as well, from the minimum common in hot dog stands to some extraordinarily high prices in some of the finest steakhouses. Ambiance can vary as dramatically as can menu price, from one to another—from the hot dog stand to the steakhouse.

Chain Restaurants

Chain restaurants are those that are linked in some way. For some, ownership provides the link: two or more establishments that may or may not resemble each other in any way have common ownership. For others, the links are provided by common name, appearance, and products, or some combination of these. For those in the well-known national chains—Wendy's, Pizza Hut, and Kentucky Fried Chicken, for example—all three apply. In some instances, all units in a given chain are under common ownership; more frequently, groups of units in one geographical area may be commonly owned by some entity other than

Some chain restaurants are linked by name, appearance, and product line. The restaurants in the Pizza Hut chain are linked this way. (Photo courtesy of Pizza Hut.)

the national organization. For example, Burger King owns some, but not all, of the restaurants bearing that name; groups of Burger King restaurants are owned by other companies, and some are owned by individuals.

Chain restaurants vary considerably in their other characteristics, as well as in their identification as chains. Their menu items range from pizza to steaks and from hamburgers to seafood. Some, such as McDonald's, are relatively inexpensive; others, such as Red Lobster or Houlihan's, are more expensive. Food quality and service vary as well. Some offer table service; others, only counter service. Some feature takeout; others do not. Nevertheless, the ambiance in chain restaurants affiliated by product is typically the same from one unit to another.

Theme Restaurants

A theme restaurant is a restaurant designed around a particular theme such that the theme is used or reflected in every element of the establishment's ambiance. For example, if the circus were selected as the theme, the interior of the restaurant might be decorated to resemble some idealized version of the interior of a circus tent, complete with trapeze; the servers might be costumed as circus performers; the menu might be printed to look like a circus program; and the menu items might be named for circus acts—a hamburger special described possibly as the "Lion, King of the Burger Jungle." Other possibilities for themes are railroad cars or stations, antique automobiles, colonial

America, the old West, Medieval dining, World War II, kitchenware—the number is endless, limited only by human imagination.

Theme restaurants are naturally different from one another in ambiance: any developer of a theme restaurant or chain clearly makes every effort to avoid resemblance to any other foodservice establishment. Menu items and service are typically closely linked to the theme and the atmosphere. Food quality and menu prices vary considerably from one theme establishment or chain to another.

"Tops"

"Tops" is a shorthand term used by some to refer to food and beverage operations located on the top floors of hotels or other tall buildings, usually located in some part of a major city where there is an interesting or spectacular view. Some "tops" restaurants have been specially constructed so that either the floor or the entire room turns, revolving to give customers panoramic and ever-changing views of the city as they dine.

"Tops" vary as greatly as other foodservice operations. Some offer foods and service of excellent quality, while others may not purchase the finest ingredients and hire the most talented professionals to prepare and serve their food. Similarly, one may present the appearance of a very formal atmosphere and select menu items accordingly, while another strives for a high degree of informality in atmosphere and menu to attract larger numbers of younger customers.

Menu prices vary among "tops" restaurants, but as a group, their prices tend to be higher than those in similar restaurants that are not located at the top of a building. Menu prices in "tops" reflect the higher costs of construction and operation, as well as the premium one would expect to be charged for the privilege of dining at an establishment that may represent not only the pinnacle of a building but also the very essence of business or social success.

Family Restaurant

A family restaurant is one that caters to family groups—parents with children and other contemporary family groupings. In order to appeal to families, operators must make a number of important decisions with respect to menu, food quality, menu prices, service, and ambiance.

Family restaurants usually include a sufficiently broad range of items on the menu so that there is something for everyone from child to grandparent. Some have special menus for children under a given age. These menus may be separate from the regular menu or may be in one section of it.

Family restaurant menu items are typically low to moderate in price, in tacit recognition that the American family faces difficult collective financial burdens and is either unwilling or unable to spend large amounts of the family's limited disposable income on restaurant meals. Menu prices reflect food quality, and owners usually attempt to match food quality to their customers' perceptions of quality. The atmosphere in family restaurants tends to be informal: at their best they are cheerfully decorated, bright and well lighted, and radiate a sense of welcome to their customers.

Cafeteria

A cafeteria is a foodservice establishment that permits the customer to see the foods available and to make selections from among those displayed. In many cases this makes it possible for the customer to select the actual portion he or she will consume.

Cafeterias impose a greater degree of self-service on their customers than most other establishments. Food portions are individually plated and priced, and the customer is typically expected to take a tray through an area where foods are displayed, make selections, place them on the tray, and take the tray to a station where the prices are totaled. In some establishments, the customer pays for the food at that point; in others, the customer is given a bill that must be paid at the exit. In either case, the tray is then carried to another part of the establishment, where the food is either consumed or packed for takeout.

Buffet

A buffet is a type of service characterized by a long table or counter on which a selection of varied foods are attractively displayed on platters, in bowls, and in other suitable vessels. Typically, each diner carries a plate, determines selections, places desired quantities of selected foods on the plate, then takes the plate to a table. A set price is usually charged for each person, regardless of particular foods or quantities selected, and diners are commonly permitted unlimited access to the buffet. This is to encourage diners to take smaller portions and revisit the buffet as desired.

Catering

Catering is preparing and serving food to groups of people gathered for a specific purpose, such as a meeting or a wedding. Some caterers prepare and serve food only in their own halls; others prepare food in their own kitchens but serve only on premises provided by their clients. Some will both prepare and serve on premises provided by the client. Some will agree to any of these arrangements. Those in the catering business are normally very flexible and are willing to meet any reasonable requests for particular foods. Most caterers are prepared to offer the client preplanned menus at various price levels for various types of functions, and most will adjust any of these to meet the client's particular needs or desires.

Catering has several advantages over normal restaurant operations. Functions are always booked in advance, so management knows the number of people to expect and can easily determine the proper quantity of food to serve. Staffing and food purchasing, therefore, can be planned precisely, making it possible to estimate costs accurately in advance and thus plan a predetermined profit on each function.

A large number of restaurants are simultaneously in the catering business. Some restaurants have separate rooms used primarily for catering, and others are able to close off part of the public dining area to accommodate groups. The food for these groups is typically prepared in the restaurant's single kitchen: there is no special kitchen set aside for catering.

Many city hotels are in the catering business. These hotels often have both special kitchens and dining facilities for catering. In the hotel business, catering is done by what is commonly known as the **banquet department.** This represents one part of the hotel food and beverage operation that is typically quite profitable. Some hotels staff their banquet operations with part-time or full-time employees who work only in this area.

Institutional Foodservice

Institution is a term used to refer to a wide variety of service organizations, public and private, that attend to one or another of many possible public needs. Schools, colleges, hospitals, nursing homes, and prisons are some common examples of institutions. An institutional foodservice operation is one whose principal purpose is preparing food for those associated with a particular institution. Students in grade schools, patients in hospitals, and inmates in prisons are all examples of those served by institutional foodservice operations.

Institutional foodservice operations are established primarily to meet the needs of the institutions in which they operate by providing food to those working in or using the services of the institution, willingly or otherwise. In some instances, those being served are confined to the institutions and must be provided with foodservice, as in hospitals, nursing homes, and prisons. In others, because of institutional decisions or public policy, foodservice is made available for those who want it, as in schools, colleges, and similar settings.

Institutional foodservice operations may be run on either a profit or not-for-profit basis and may be managed either by the institution or by some outside foodservice contractor.

Institutional foodservice operations are similar to several other types of foodservice operations—business and industry foodservice and airline catering are two examples. None of these are operated primarily for public dining; they are intended to provide foodservice for a particular group, such as children in a school, passengers on an airplane, or employees of a corporation.

Business and Industry Foodservice

Business and industry foodservice operations are those that provide food during working hours for employees of particular firms in their offices or factories. As in the case of institutional foodservice, they may be operated on either a profit or not-for-profit basis and may be managed by the firm whose employees they serve or by some outside foodservice contractor.

In large firms, it is not uncommon to find several foodservice operations at one site preparing foods at several levels of quality, service, and price for different groups of employees. For example, within a specific building, one might find a cafeteria serving adequate foods at moderate prices for workers earning modest salaries, a table-service restaurant with more elaborate meals at higher prices for midlevel managers, and a fine-dining facility for the executive staff.

Airline Catering

Airline catering is the business of providing food prepared and packaged for service by an airplane crew during a flight. The food is prepared by an airline catering organization at a central facility, called a **commissary,** where it is suitably packaged in serving containers. It is transported to planes in storage units that will keep food warm or cold, as required, until it is served. The storage units are stowed in specially designed units on the plane and served by flight attendants at appropriate times.

An airline catering operation may be owned by the airline it serves, by another airline, or by one of a number of hospitality firms, large and small, that have gone into this specialized business. Marriott, Sky Chefs, Dobbs, and Trust House Forte are some of the leading names in this field.

Club Foodservice

Club foodservice operations are those that provide foodservice in membership establishments known as clubs. Many types of clubs— golf, tennis, athletic, luncheon, college alumni, fraternal, social, to name a few—are organized to appeal to people with some common interest.

Foodservice operations in clubs range from very simple and inexpensive to those that provide some of the finest food and service available—from hot dog stands near a swimming pool to spectacular dining rooms with fine linen, china, glassware, and elegant professional service. Private clubs restrict service to members and their guests; some clubs, however, are open to the general public.

Stand

A stand is a stationary, open-air foodservice establishment without a dining room facility. Customers walk to a counter to order and obtain foods, then consume the foods at the counter or elsewhere, as they prefer. Examples include hot dog stands at beaches and roadside stands selling ice cream, hamburgers, or cider, among other possibilities.

Coffee Shops

Traditionally, a coffee shop was an establishment with a limited menu to which customers typically would go to order coffee and some other item such as a donut, a sandwich, or a slice of pie. They did not provide full meals. Coffee shops tended to be small, usually offering seating on stools at a counter. Some provided a limited number of tables or booths. Today, many have more extensive menus resembling those of diners, as described below.

Diner

A diner is normally a moderately priced, full-service restaurant, typically open very long hours—sometimes twenty-four hours a day—and serving breakfast, lunch, and dinner from a single, multipage menu. In most diners, the customer can order any meal at any hour—breakfast at 11 P.M., for example.

The Tick Tock Diner, located in Clifton, New Jersey, is a good example of a modern diner—a moderately priced, full-service restaurant open very long hours and serving breakfast, lunch, and dinner from a single multi-page menu. (Photo courtesy of Tick Tock Diner, Clifton, New Jersey.)

The modern diner is a direct descendant of the establishments discussed in chapter 3. The exterior design has evolved from trolleys and railroad dining cars of an earlier period, but only older diners display any of the characteristics of the diners of earlier times. There is little physical similarity between today's diner and one built sixty years ago.

Neighborhood Restaurant

A neighborhood restaurant is one that caters to the needs, tastes, and preferences of those who live or work nearby. In general, they reflect the character of the neighborhoods in which they are found. Some are inexpensive, some are medium priced, and some are actually quite expensive, depending on the neighborhood.

More than any other type of establishment, the neighborhood restaurant depends for survival on repeat business from people in the area. Thus, owners of neighborhood restaurants must pay particularly close attention to their customers' likes and dislikes. Failure to do so will have a greater negative impact with more immediate consequences than would be the case in other types of establishments.

Drive-Through

A drive-through is an operation at which a customer can drive a vehicle to a window to obtain and pay for food without ever leaving the vehicle. Having received the food, the customer drives away to consume the food elsewhere. In effect, these can be considered the descendents of the drive-in restaurants of the 1950s and 1960s.

The process limits the kinds of foods that can be sold. They tend to be preportioned items prepared in advance and easily packaged for takeout—in other words, the typical products of the fast-service restaurants. In fact, a number of the chain restaurants specializing in fast-service products have been very successful in providing drive-through service for their customers.

Takeout

A takeout is an operation that prepares foods for consumption off premises. Foods for takeout may either be fully prepared in advance and packaged when ordered by a customer, or they may be prepared when ordered; takeout merely means that food leaves the premises where it is sold. The food may be picked up and transported by the purchaser or delivered, depending on the nature of the operation. Some do both. Most pizza establishments deliver; those offering hamburgers or chicken typically do not.

Some takeout establishments have no facilities for on-premises consumption; they operate exclusively as takeouts. Some are parts of other foodservice operations that provide seating for customers.

These are some of the terms used in general conversation to identify or describe various kinds of foodservice establishments. However, one can readily see that no single term will fully describe a given establishment. For example, the term *fast service* suggests that a customer should be able to obtain food quickly in such an establishment, but it does not provide information about the kind of food served or the extent of its menu. To describe the establishment more completely and usefully, we would have to say, for example, that it is a fast-service restaurant with a limited menu, specializing in chicken. Similarly, to describe a particular restaurant as one dedicated to fine dining is to imply that it features foods of high quality, that it is probably expensive, and that it offers table service. But the term fine dining tells us nothing about the kind of food served, the type of service, or the ambiance. And because the quality of ethnic, specialty, and all other restaurants can vary so greatly, simply stating that a particular establishment is "Italian" tells us next to nothing about it. We would need to know a great deal more to describe it fully.

▶ Beverage Service

Society has not always viewed the consumption of alcoholic beverages favorably. On the whole, however, American society has generally tolerated "drinking" and has even encouraged it under some circumstances, provided it is not done to excess. Today, many believe that alcoholic beverages have therapeutic value when consumed in moderation. Everyone recognizes the dangerous and debilitating effects of alcohol when consumed in excess.

As discussed in the previous chapter, the sale of alcoholic beverages was illegal in the 1920s under the provisions of the Volstead Act. Nonetheless, this did not stop Americans from drinking. Drinking establishments called speakeasies were very popular. Making alcoholic beverages at home—the so-called bathtub gin, for example—was a hobby for many Americans, and illegally transporting and selling alcoholic beverages—bootlegging, in the vernacular of the period—made rich men of many underworld characters.

After the repeal of the Volstead Act in 1933, the authority to regulate the sale and consumption of alcoholic beverages was returned to state and local governments. Laws passed in the years since 1933 have resulted in great variations from one state to another, and even from one community to another within a state. The extent of these variations is so great that it is quite beyond the scope of any introductory text. A few examples will illustrate.

All states and almost all local communities allow properly licensed establishments to serve alcoholic beverages in one form or another— by the glass or by the bottle, or both of these. In a few communities, the sale of alcoholic beverages in any form remains illegal. In some of these, however, a customer can bring his own alcoholic beverages, and the establishment will provide the glassware, ice, mixer, or whatever combination of these the customer requires. In some states, customers cannot be served alcoholic beverages unless they are seated. In others, customers are not permitted to order drinks at a bar and then carry their own drinks from the bar to a table: they must be served by an employee. In some, it is illegal to have more than one drink in front of a customer at any given time. In others, a customer can carry a drink to his table, but only one. If the customer wants a drink for a companion, he cannot have it; the companion must get his own.

All states now prohibit the purchase of alcoholic beverages by anyone under the age of twenty-one years. This was the result of a decision by the federal government to withhold federal highway funds from any state that did not raise the drinking age to twenty-one.

▶ Beverage Service Defined

There are several possible ways to define **beverage service.** In this text, we will define beverage service as providing alcoholic and other related beverages for consumption on premises. The term beverage includes all alcoholic beverages and any nonalcoholic beverages typically prepared by bartenders. A beverage service establishment is one that provides beverage service for its customers. In many cases, beverage service establishments provide customers with food as well, and food sales may even constitute the major source of sales revenue.

▶ Reasons for Patronizing Beverage Service Establishments

There are a number of reasons commonly cited for patronizing beverage service establishments. These include

1. Dining
2. Seeking entertainment
3. Socializing
4. Discussing business
5. Meeting new people
6. Getting away from home
7. Killing time
8. Relaxing
9. Drinking

These are some of the many possible reasons for going to beverage service establishments. For most of the people who patronize these establishments, drinking would appear to be a secondary consideration. In fact, data reveal that sales of alcoholic beverages have actually decreased in recent years, whereas sales of nonalcoholic drinks have increased a great deal. This may indicate that patrons of beverage-service establishments are switching from alcoholic to nonalcoholic beverages because they never had been drawn to these establishments in the first place to consume alcoholic drinks.

There are doubtless reasonable numbers who patronize these establishments primarily to purchase and consume alcoholic beverages. They appear to be a minority, however. To the extent that they abuse alcohol, the social pressures to modify their behavior continue to grow, particularly for those who drive.

▷ The Focus of Beverage Service Establishments

Because customers patronize beverage service establishments for different reasons, those who operate such businesses attempt to appeal to their potential customers by featuring or emphasizing those elements that they hope will attract customers. These elements can be grouped into three catagories, each of which we will characterize as a focal point for operations.

Beverage service establishments can be distinguished from one another on the basis of this focus. Each beverage service operator will have established one of the following as primary:

1. Food
2. Entertainment
3. Beverages

▶ Food

Many establishments that provide beverage service place primary emphasis on their food. These tend to be foodservice establishments

A beverage service establishment, such as the hotel lounge shown above, may have a variety of focuses on food, entertainment, or beverages in order to attract potential customers. (Photo courtesy of Stouffer Harborplace Hotel, Baltimore, Maryland.)

that provide beverages as accompaniments to food. Many of the characteristic types of foodservice establishments described earlier in the chapter—ethnic, theme, family, fine dining, "tops," neighborhood, and others—have this focus. They make beverages available before, during, and after meals: customers may order cocktails before dinner, wines with the meal, and any of various after-dinner drinks, such as liqueurs or dessert wines. To many customers of these establishments, beverages are integral parts of the dining experience. Many would probably not return if the establishment no longer offered beverages with the food.

These businesses may be regarded as both foodservice and beverage-service establishments. They serve beverages to satisfy the expectations of their customers and because drink sales are profitable. But their emphasis, their principal business focus, tends to be the food, which normally provides greater revenue than the beverages.

Some of these establishments may also offer entertainment—live piano music during dinner, for example—but only as a secondary element. The principal focus is food.

▶ Entertainment

In other establishments, primary emphasis is placed on entertainment. *Entertainment* is a very broad term, encompassing any number of possibilities. It can range from sports events on television to professional musicians, from coin-operated games to horse races at a track, or from professional team sports to theatrical companies. Such establishments as night clubs, gambling casinos, theaters, piano bars, racetracks, and sports arenas provide beverage service to those who have come for the entertainment features of these establishments. For many customers, the beverages are an indispensable element of the entertainment.

In some of these establishments, there is no charge for the entertainment. The cost to management may be so low that there is no need to recover any of that cost from customers. This would be the case if the entertainment consisted of sports events on television. However, professional entertainers can be very costly, and the owner of an establishment featuring professional groups might attempt to recover the cost of the entertainment by selling tickets or by imposing either a cover charge or a minimum. A cover charge is an amount per person added to the total bill incurred for food and drink. A minimum is the least amount each customer is permitted to spend; those spending less are charged the minimum.

Many of these establishments also offer food—excellent food, in some cases. For example, some dinner theaters feature professional performances of musical productions. They offer food and beverages as well, but their principal focus is clearly the entertainment.

▶ Beverages

In a vast number of beverage-service establishments, the primary emphasis is clearly and conspicuously on the beverages themselves. Some may give away simple salty foods to stimulate beverage sales. Others may provide entertainment in the form of background music from a radio. The focus of these establishments is clear and simple: they sell beverages and have little or no interest in any other possibilities. Many neighborhood bars are of this type. Closely related to these are the typical bars at airports or railroad stations that cater to those waiting to board planes or trains.

Some beverage service establishments, although focusing primarily on beverages, make some attempt to broaden their appeal. They may, for example, provide a wider range of foods than salty snacks—sandwiches, hamburgers, or a few hot foods in a steam table located near the bar. But the food even in these is typically of secondary importance. Some attempt to provide a limited kind of entertainment for their customers—coin-operated games, for example. In all of these, however, the principal focus is on neither the food nor the entertainment: it is on the beverages.

There are several terms used to identify those establishments in which beverages are the primary focus, including tavern, inn, saloon, cocktail lounge, and bar. Historically, the distinctions among these were well known and generally accepted. That is no longer the case. It is perfectly possible today to see an establishment identified by its owner as a tavern, then to find another nearby, virtually a duplicate of the first, called a cocktail lounge. Such terms are not readily distinguished from one another any longer.

Strange as it may seem, no one ever speaks of a beverage-service industry. In our industry, beverage service is treated as part of foodservice, and the data related to establishments selling beverages and to beverage sales are commonly reported with foodservice data. Thus, when an individual mentions the foodservice industry, it is unlikely that he means foodservice alone: he is probably referring to the combined industries known by the single term *foodservice industry*.

▶ National Restaurant Association Classification

A number of years ago, the NRA developed a classification system for the foodservice industry, primarily to report information about the industry's total sales. Table 4.1 illustrates the NRA's classification system and provides some interesting data about total food and drink sales for the years shown.

Note that all food and beverage enterprises are divided into three groups.

Group I is the largest, representing the majority of both food and beverage establishments and sales. It encompasses those establishments whose primary business is foodservice, beverage service, or some combination of both. All are profit oriented. This does not mean that every one of them actually earns a profit but that they are being operated with the intention of profitability.

Within Group I, the largest category is Eating Places. This includes establishments operated primarily as foodservice businesses, not those that are part of other businesses. There is no attempt to differentiate among them on the basis of size, type of food served, or food quality. Eating Places are divided into several types, including full-menu restaurants, limited-menu restaurants, cafeterias, caterers, and ice-cream stands. Bars and taverns are separately listed in this category.

The second category in Group I is Food Contractors. These are commercial firms that provide foodservice in other establishments (commercial and noncommercial), such as banks and other financial service operations, office buildings, factories, hospitals, colleges, primary and secondary schools, transportation services, and recreation and sports centers.

The third category in Group I is foodservice operations in Lodging Places.

The final category in Group I is a collection of commercial foodservice operations that do not belong in other categories, including restaurants in drugstores, food stores, and recreation centers, as well as mobile caterers and vending machines.

Group II is for foodservice establishments operated by organizations whose primary focus is in some other field. Foodservice is not their primary business: they choose to operate their own foodservices for the convenience of employees, students, patients, or customers rather than have firms from Group I run them. Some are operated for profit; others are not. This group includes school, college, and university foodservice, and foodservice provided by hospitals and nursing homes, providing they operate their own foodservice.

Table 4.1 **Foodservice Industry Food-and-Drink Sales Projected Through 1996**

	1993 Estimated F&D Sales ($000)	1995 Projected F&D Sales ($000)	1996 Projected F&D Sales ($000)	1995-1996 Percent Change	1995-1996 Percent Real Growth Change	1993-1996 Compound Annual Growth Rate
Group 1—Commercial Foodservice[1]						
Eating Places						
Full-service restaurants[2]	$87,011,439	$95,701,837	$100,008,420	4.5%	2.0%	4.7%
Limited-service (fast-food) restaurants[3]	82,061,346	93,864,066	100,152,958	6.7	4.2	6.9
Commercial cafeterias	3,631,929	3,793,128	3,910,715	3.1	0.6	2.5
Social caterers	2,450,184	2,724,531	2,868,931	5.3	2.8	5.4
Ice-cream, frozen-custard, yogurt stands[4]	2,314,365	2,505,370	2,588,047	3.3	0.8	3.8
TOTAL EATING PLACES	**$177,469,263**	**$198,588,932**	**$209,529,071**	**5.5%**	**3.0%**	**5.7%**
Bars & tavern	10,161,726	10,864,460	11,201,258	3.1	0.3	3.3
TOTAL EATING & DRINKING PLACES	**$187,630,989**	**$209,453,392**	**$220,730,320[5]**	**5.4%**	**2.9%**	**5.6%**
Food Contractors						
Manufacturing & industrial plants	$4,152,768	$4,513,253	$4,716,349	4.5%	2.0%	4.3%
Commercial & office buildings	1,356,484	1,453,013	1,490,791	2.6	0.1	3.2
Hospitals & nursing homes	1,811,249	1,951,519	2,013,968	3.2	1.6	3.6
Colleges & universities	3,454,792	3,892,777	4,157,486	6.8	3.6	6.4
Primary & secondary schools	1,460,874	1,658,516	1,769,636	6.7	3.5	6.6
In-transit foodservice (airlines)	1,547,813	1,841,119	1,856,768	0.8	-1.7	6.2
Recreation & sports centers	2,167,118	2,345,467	2,486,195	6.0	3.5	4.7
TOTAL FOOD CONTRACTORS	**$15,951,098**	**$17,655,664**	**$18,491,193**	**4.7%**	**2.1%**	**5.0%**
Lodging Places						
Hotel restaurants	$14,253,057	$15,713,981	$16,436,824	4.6%	2.1%	4.9%
Motor-hotel restaurants	529,410	562,741	577,935	2.7	0.2	3.0
Motel restaurants	782,598	818,436	832,586	1.7	-0.8	2.1
TOTAL LODGING PLACES	**$15,565,065**	**$17,095,158**	**$17,847,345**	**4.4%**	**1.9%**	**4.7%**
Retail-host restaurants[6]	$11,220,440	$12,406,873	$13,014,810	4.9%	2.4%	5.1%
Recreation & sports[7]	3,185,131	3,453,447	3,617,354	4.7	2.2	4.3
Mobile caterers	876,743	970,295	1,017,839	4.9	2.4	5.1
Vending & nonstore retailers[8]	5,989,836	6,447,484	6,705,383	4.0	1.5	3.8
TOTAL GROUP 1	**$240,419,302**	**$267,482,313**	**$281,424,253**	**5.2%**	**2.7%**	**5.4%**

Table 4.1   (continued)

	1993 Estimated F&D Sales ($000)	1995 Projected F&D Sales ($000)	1996 Projected F&D Sales ($000)	1995-1996 Percent Change	1995-1996 Percent Real Growth Change	1993-1996 Compound Annual Growth Rate
Group II—Institutional Foodservice—Business, educational, governmental, or institutional organizations that operate their own foodservice						
Employee foodservice[9]	$1,727,526	$1,731,012	$1,729,594	-0.1%	-2.5%	0.0%
Public & parochial elementary, secondary schools	4,183,108	4,528,445	4,739,047	4.6	1.4	4.2
Colleges & universities	4,514,277	4,610,730	4,652,147	0.9	-2.3	1.0
Transportation	1,378,068	931,662	931,776	0.0	-2.5	-12.2
Hospitals[10]	9,207,584	9,557,475	9,702,188	1.5	-0.1	1.8
Nursing homes, homes for the aged, blind, orphans, and the mentally & physically disabled[11]	4,167,096	4,524,479	4,709,983	4.1	2.5	4.2
Clubs, sporting & recreational camps	2,273,128	2,489,215	2,611,080	4.9	2.6	4.7
Community centers	958,162	1,156,214	1,271,835	10.0	6.8	9.9
TOTAL GROUP II	$28,408,949	$29,529,232	$30,347,650	2.8%	0.5%	2.2%
TOTAL GROUPS I & II	$268,828,251	$297,011,545	$311,771,903	5.0%	2.5%	5.1%
Group III—Military Foodservice[12]						
Officers' & NCO clubs ("Open Mess")	$738,184	$761,935	$778,698	2.2%	-0.3	1.8%
Foodservice—military exchanges	368,450	378,541	386,112	2.0	-0.5	1.6
TOTAL GROUP III	$1,106,634	$1,140,476	$1,164,810	2.1%	-0.4%	1.7%
GRAND TOTAL	$269,934,885	$298,152,021	$312,936,713	5.0%	2.4%	5.0%

1   Data are given only for establishments with payroll
2   Waiter/waitress service is provided, and the order is taken while the patron is seated. Patrons pay after they eat. Formerly restaurants, lunchrooms
3   Patrons generally order at a cash register or select items from a food bar and pay before they eat. Formerly limited-menu restaurants
4   Formerly ice-cream, frozen-custard stands
5   Food-and-drink sales for nonpayroll establishments will total $4,042,918,000 for eating places and $1,302,239,000 for drinking places in 1996.
6   Includes drug- and proprietary-store restaurants, general-merchandise-store restaurants, variety-store restaurants, food-store restaurants, grocery-store restaurants (including a portion of delis and all salad bars), gasoline-service station restaurants and miscellaneous retailers
7   Includes movies, bowling lanes, and recreation and sports centers
8   Includes sales of hot food, sandwiches, pastries, coffee, and other hot beverages
9   Includes industrial and commercial organizations, seagoing and inland-waterway vessels
10 Includes voluntary and proprietary hospitals; long-term general, TB, mental hospitals, and sales or commercial equivalent to employees in state and local short-term hospitals and federal hospitals
11 Sales (commercial equivalent) calculated for nursing homes and homes for the aged only. All others in this grouping make no charge for food served either in cash or in kind.
12 Continental United States only

Source: *Restaurants USA,* December 1995.

Group III is military foodservice, a relatively small part of the industry. It includes only those military foodservice enterprises where people pay for food—officers' clubs, noncommissioned officer (NCO) clubs, and the like. Because those in military service do not purchase their meals, the vast number of meals prepared daily for those in the military are not reflected.

Note that some operations listed in Group I appear at first glance to be duplicated in Group II. For example, colleges and universities are listed in both Group I and Group II. The colleges and universities listing in Group I includes foodservices operated by an outside profit-oriented food contractor, such as Saga, Canteen, or some other. Listings in Group II, however, are for colleges and universities that operate their own foodservice establishments.

The principal reason for developing the NRA system was to provide a means for reporting quantitative data about industry size and dollar sales. Establishments are divided into specific categories, and information about each establishment is classified accordingly.

Because this system is not and cannot be concerned with the very real and significant qualitative differences evident between establishments in our industry, we must use other terms to take these into account—family restaurant, offering table service, moderate prices, and ethnic Italian food, for example; or cocktail lounge focusing on entertainment, featuring live piano music. We must use the kinds of terms discussed earlier in the chapter to make meaningful distinctions between the various types of foodservice and beverage-service operations. Both approaches are useful. The first enables professionals and the public at large to distinguish one operation from another, and the second facilitates the collection and reporting of statistical information about a vast and important industry.

▶ Summary

In this chapter, the size of the food and beverage industry is illustrated. Three explanations for the increase in public demand for foodservice are offered and discussed. A definition is provided for the term *food-service*, and five important elements of foodservice operations that differentiate one from another are discussed in detail. An extensive list of characteristic types of foodservice establishments is provided, and each is described in detail. *Beverage service* is defined, and the principal reasons for patronizing beverage-service establishments are listed. A rationale is presented for distinguishing one beverage service establishment from another on the basis of focus. Finally, the classification system used by the National Restaurant Association to collect and report statistical information is presented and explained.

Airline Catering
Banquet Department
Beverage Service
Buffet
Business and Industry Foodservice
Cafeteria
Catering
Chain Restaurant
Club Foodservice
Coffee Shop
Commercial Foodservice Operation
Commissary
Convenience Foods
Counter Service
Diner
Drive-Through
Ethnic Restaurant
Ethnic Foods
Family Restaurant

Fast Food
Fine Dining Establishment
Foodservice
Institutional Foodservice
Limited Menu Restaurant
National Restaurant Association
Neighborhood Restaurant
Noncommercial Foodservice Operation
Regional Foods
Room Service
Self-Service
Specialty Foods
Specialty Restaurant
Stand
Table Service Restaurant
Takeout
Takeout and Delivery Service
Theme Restaurant
"Tops" Restaurant

1. What percentage of gross domestic product has been attributable to food and beverage sales in recent years?

2. What is the rank of the foodservice industry as an employer of women? of teenagers? of members of minority groups?

3. Approximately what percentage of America's retail outlets are eating or drinking establishments?

4. What are the three reasons commonly cited for America's increased demand for foodservice in recent years?

5. Define *foodservice*. What is a foodservice enterprise?

6. What are the five most important characteristics of a foodservice enterprise? Illustrate by example how changes in each can affect the character of a foodservice enterprise.

7. Define each of the following characteristic types of foodservice establishments and cite one example of each: fast service; table

service; ethnic; specialty; fine dining; limited menu; chain restaurant; theme restaurant; "tops"; family restaurant; cafeteria; buffet; catering; institutional foodservice; business and industry foodservice; airline catering; club foodservice; stand; coffee shop; diner; neighborhood restaurant; drive-through; takeout.

8. Cite a particular foodservice establishment in your area, an adequate description of which requires the use of four of the terms in question number 7.

9. Define *beverage service.* What is a beverage-service enterprise?

10. List nine common reasons for patronizing beverage-service establishments.

11. Identify three beverage-service establishments that attract customers by featuring or emphasizing entertainment.

12. Identify three beverage-service establishments that attract customers without featuring either food or entertainment. Do these provide any kind of food? What kind?

13. Distinguish between a commercial and a noncommercial foodservice operation.

14. Which of the three major groups in the National Restaurant Association's foodservice classification system accounts for the greatest dollar sales annually? Which accounts for the least? What is the principal difference between the establishments in Group I and those in Group II?

Moments of Truth

1. Imagine you are a regular customer of a restaurant near your home. The restaurant caters primarily to your community, has an extensive and varied menu of items appealing to both adults and children, is moderately priced, is informal, offers both table service and take-out service, is well lighted, and uses some convenience foods to make food preparation easier. Using the terms for restaurants described in this chapter, characterize the restaurant.

2. Identify three beverage-service establishments in your area that attract customers by featuring or emphasizing food. Indicate how each differs from the other two with respect to menu items, food quality, menu prices, service, and ambiance—the five most important elements of a foodservice operation.

3. Your friend wants to open a restaurant and has enough money to do so. She is unsure of the type of restaurant she should open but has found an available location at a busy intersection on the outskirts of a midsize city with a population made up primarily of middle-class families. There is plenty of space for a large parking area. Assuming that there would not be extensive competition from other restaurants, what characteristic types of restaurants would you suggest?

Five

Food and Beverage Facilities

After reading and studying this chapter, you should be able to:

1 Define the term *concept* and describe its significance in food and beverage layout and design.

2 Discuss the need for owners and managers of food and beverage facilities to have some knowledge of the laws and regulations affecting their operations.

3 Define the term *product line* and identify the elements in the service product line offered by food and beverage operations.

4 List and discuss six principal considerations in the layout and design of food and beverage facilities.

5 List and discuss the major activities that commonly take place in the food area of a food and beverage facility.

6 List and discuss the major activities that commonly take place in the beverage area of a food and beverage facility.

7 Identify the three types of bars.

8 List and describe the three principal parts of a front bar.

▸ Introduction

The previous chapter was devoted to examining the size and scope of the food and beverage industry and to imparting some sense of its great importance in American life. With that objective accomplished, we will now turn to a discussion of food and beverage facilities, a subject that will introduce the remaining chapter in this section. The purpose of this chapter is to identify and describe the work areas that tend to be common to all food and beverage facilities and to explain the interrelationships between them. The following chapter will discuss operational aspects of food and beverage facilities.

Prior to discussing food and beverage facilities, it is necessary to address three key topics that are fundamental to the layout and design of food and beverage facilities.

1. Concept
2. Legal requirements (local, state, and national)
3. Product line

▸ Concept

Every food and beverage operation is—or should be—established around a **concept**—an imaginative and unifying idea of the operation that serves to focus the type of operation, its potential customers, and its location. This concept originates with the owner or with some other individual or firm commissioned to create it.

Type of Operation

A number of possible types of operations were discussed in chapter 4, including fast-service operations, fine-dining establishments, family restaurants, cafeterias, ethnic restaurants, specialty restaurants, bars, taverns, and cocktail lounges, among many others. Determining the type of operation is a key element in developing the concept of an establishment.

Potential Customers

Each type of operation can attract specific customers. Ethnic restaurants, for example, attract those who seek the particular foods characteristic of a given ethnic group, such as Chinese, Italian, Greek, or

▶ In the Fun House ◀
A New Concept in Restaurant Dining

In Orlando, Florida, there is an entertainment center that combines restaurants and entertainment in one interesting complex. Several food, beverage, and entertainment options, each with a different theme, are located within the same complex. Customers come to enjoy the food, atmosphere, and entertainment and have their choice of several different environments.

One of these is a western entertainment restaurant known as Wild Bill's Wild West Dinner Extravaganza. It features a nightly show that includes cowboys, saloon hall dancing girls, and Native Americans, all demonstrating knife throwing, arrow shooting, and lasso skills throughout a four-course, two-hour dinner show.

Another is King Henry's Feast, which recreates an English castle, complete with a moat and a tower. The customers are entertained with a nightly show featuring King Henry VIII's quest for a new wife. Throughout dinner, strolling magicians and wandering minstrels invite guests to join in the show.

Multiunit restaurant and entertainment complexes such as this are becoming popular throughout the United States. Other locations where similar centers can be found include Phoenix, Arizona; Sacramento and San Jose, California; Cincinnati, Ohio; Norfolk, Virginia; and Bloomington, Minnesota.

Adapted from an article in F & B Business, *July/August 1995, Page 40.*

Indian foods, among many other possibilities. Fine-dining establishments typically attract those who have the financial means and the desire for high-quality foods and elegant service offered. Specialty restaurants attract customers looking for the specialties offered, such as steak, seafood, pasta, pancakes, or some other type of food. Some food-service operations, such as those in schools, colleges, nursing homes, and hospitals, typically serve those who have little or no choice of place to eat. Similarly, neighborhood taverns and bars tend to attract customers who live nearby, and airport bars typically attract transient customers who are waiting for planes to arrive or depart. Each establishment attracts customers because of the food, beverages, service, atmosphere, location, or some combination of these and because customers are willing to pay the prices charged by the operator.

Location

In order for a food and beverage operation to be successful, there must be an adequate number of potential customers within reasonable distance who will be willing to patronize it. Some locations would not provide sufficient numbers of potential customers to support particular types of establishments. For example, fine-dining establishments are normally unsuccessful in working-class communities, principally because those living in the community cannot afford to pay the prices such establishments must charge to be profitable. In addition, residents of the community sometimes dislike the food such restaurants offer and the service they provide. Similarly, some ethnic restaurants fail to succeed in certain locations because the type of food they offer does not appeal to a large enough segment of the population. By the same token, bars and taverns are typically unsuccessful in communities where the consumption of alcoholic beverages is discouraged by social or religious custom.

To assess the potential for successfully operating a particular type of food or beverage establishment in a specific location, it is advisable to obtain such relevant information as: the number of potential customers for the type of food, beverages, and service planned; the extent to which there are competitive establishments; the cost of constructing the necessary facility; the availability of a suitable labor pool; the dollar amounts potential customers would be likely to spend; and the potential for profitable operation at the projected level of revenue and expense. All the relevant considerations should be included in a **feasibility study,** the name given to an investigation of a given project's likelihood for success. Location, then, is a key element in determining whether or not a given type of establishment will succeed and is an important part of the initial concept.

▶ Legal Requirements

A potential operator must become familiar with a number of laws and regulations affecting food and beverage operations. Any applicable laws and regulations—federal, state, or local—must be taken into account. Health codes, fire codes, building codes, zoning regulations, and licensing requirements are among the most common. Each of these provides specific direction for what an owner can and cannot do in creating and operating a food and beverage enterprise.

Legal requirements vary considerably from one state to another and even from city to city within a given state. For example, health codes in some states require that operators provide the staff with lavatories other than those intended for customers. A facility built without staff lavatories would probably require costly reconstruction before it would be permitted to open. This is just one example of the many possibilities. Before proceeding to open a facility, individuals lacking full knowledge of the laws and regulations that apply in given locales must seek professional advice from lawyers, architects, food and beverage consultants, and others with the necessary expertise. Failure to do so can lead to costly errors.

For purposes of the present chapter, we will assume that the individual establishing a food and beverage operation has developed a concept that has the potential to be successful, has constructed or purchased a facility that works as a restaurant, and has become familiar with the various local, county, state, and national laws that will affect the enterprise. Having attended to all these necessary prerequisites, the next step is to direct attention to the products that will be offered to customers of the establishment.

▶ Product Line

Product line is a term used in marketing and retailing to refer to a group of products having similar characteristics. Some common examples of product lines are shoes, luggage, and jewelry. Foodservice has borrowed the term from retailing and uses it to mean the group of service products that a hospitality enterprise offers, based on the concept developed for the establishment.

The product line of a food and beverage operation is more than just the foods or beverages it offers for sale. It also includes the services and the ambiance of the facility. This is because most customers are attracted to a specific food or beverage establishment for more than one reason. For purposes of the following discussion, the product line of a food or beverage operation has three components:

1. Food and beverages
2. Services
3. Ambiance

Food and Beverages

Every foodservice operation has a group of potential menu items that includes all the food products the operator intends to offer at present and into the future. Some, such as Kentucky Fried Chicken or Red Lobster, specialize in one type of food—chicken, fish, or some other—and offer additional items that serve as accompaniments to those featured. Any number of specialized food products are key elements in food operations today. Sandwiches, pasta, pizza, hamburgers, crepes, ice cream, and hot dogs are all good examples. Other food-service operations have a more generalized list of potential menu items, such as a family restaurant.

Bars and taverns specialize in beverage products. This is an entirely different product list, consisting of beverages rather than food. In some establishments, both food products and beverage products are available to customers. In a restaurant devoted to fine dining, for example, the operator typically offers both beverage products and food products. Similarly, some taverns offer meals to their customers.

Whatever constitutes the food and beverage component of the product line to be offered by a particular operation, it is desirable that all elements be identified and defined in advance, because the equipment to be purchased and the layout of the facility will be based on it. The specific food products will be the basis for the menu that will be offered to customers, and detailed information about these items will determine the proper kitchen equipment and layout. The question of whether or not a given piece of equipment should be purchased can best be answered by referring to that list. If it is needed to prepare items appearing on the list of food products, it should be purchased; if there are no menu selections requiring its use, it should not be purchased unless a specific future need can be predicted. For example, an establishment that serves only pizza obviously needs kitchen equipment that is very different from that required in a luncheonette serving only soups and sandwiches, and an ethnic restaurant serving Chinese food prepared in woks needs very different kitchen equipment from that of a neighborhood restaurant offering an Italian menu. Similarly, a restaurant specializing in deep-fried and broiled menu items needs different equipment from that of one offering convenience foods heated in microwave ovens. Kitchen equipment, once purchased and installed, limits the possibilities for adding new items to the list of food products. Great care must be exercised in determining the selections that will be offered on both the original menu and future variations. Therefore, establishing the list of food products is clearly the first key component of a food and beverage facility. This list will be much larger than the menu offered to customers on any given day. Menus change, and the list of items that constitute the menu for a particular day should be drawn from the predetermined list.

It is important to recognize that the lists of items that constitute the food and beverage components of the product line never reach a state in which they can be considered final or complete. Change is constant and continuous in hospitality operations: dishes are added to and removed from the list of food products; new drinks and brands are added to the list of beverage products while others are eliminated; any number of changes may be made that will affect the service and the ambiance. It is critical, however, to develop preliminary lists of the particular items that will constitute the product line at opening because of their central role in the facility.

In establishing the list of food products for a particular operation and the subsequent menu that will be offered, the operator should have knowledge of the following:

1. Food and service preferences of customers
2. Prices acceptable to customers
3. Skills required to prepare selected items
4. Availability of labor with the necessary skills at suitable wage rates

The success of a foodservice operation is determined by the willingness of potential customers to patronize the establishment. If the

▶ Niche Brewing: A Beer for Each Season ◀

Beer sales are strongest in summer, when baseball, the beach, and backyard barbecues call for six-packs of something light, refreshing, and cold. Increasingly, microbreweries and brew pubs that make specialty beers are trying to capitalize on summer's thirst by brewing specialty beers that are light in color, flavorful, and thirst quenching. For example, Steve Hindy, an owner of Brooklyn Brewery, made two thousand barrels of a new lemony East India Pale Ale. In an interview at his microbrewery, he stated, "Seasonal beers are real winners for the microbrewers because they satisfy the seemingly bottomless thirst of the microbrewer's drinker for variety, for something new." It's an interesting example of changing product lines that are seasonal in nature.

Adapted from an article in the New York Times.

foods on the product line are not those that the potential customers want, or if the prices of the menu items are too high, the establishment will not attract sufficient numbers of customers to be successful.

Additionally, the product line must be prepared by employees with sufficient skill to meet the standards of the establishment, and thus the operator must know what skills are required to prepare each item. If the operator is unwilling or unable to pay sufficient wages to attract employees with the necessary skills, or if employees with necessary skills are not available, the quality of the products produced will not be acceptable to customers.

Over the long term, many food and beverage operations elect to change the original product line, adding and deleting a few items or even making far more radical changes. This may be much harder to do than one might imagine. A change in the product line may make it necessary to teach the staff new skills so that they can prepare new menu items; major changes may make it necessary to purchase new equipment or even to redesign some parts of the facility.

Once the product line has been established, it is possible to determine which of the items in the product line will be listed on a menu for a given day or meal. There is no more important selling device in any foodservice operation than its menu. A good menu requires considerable time and effort to produce but is well worth it. Menu development is an interesting combination of art and science, and it is clearly one of the keys to successful foodservice operation. Discussion of menu development will be deferred to the next chapter.

Services

Another important component of any food or beverage service product line is the range of services associated with the specific food and beverage products. This second component includes all the services the operator intends to offer to customers, now and into the future. The more obvious services are the styles of service adopted for dining rooms—American, French, or some other, as well as variations on the basic styles, such as weekly buffets, possible use of dessert carts, or occasional use of table-side cooking. (Styles of service is a complex topic that is addressed in detail in the next chapter.) Other services include food preparation in the kitchen, friendliness on the part of the staff, dishwashing, valet parking, attended coat rooms, background music, special attention to birthday celebrants, complimentary photographs of customers, even entertainment, such as musicians, clowns, or magicians.

Ambiance

The third component of the hospitality service product line in food and beverage operations is perhaps best identified as the ambiance of the establishment. This includes those essential details—some tangible, some intangible—that give a specific food and beverage operation its distinctive character. These essential details include theme, lighting, uniforms, furnishings, cleanliness, fixtures, decorations, table settings, and any other related features that customers see or sense and that contribute to the total atmosphere of the establishment.

These components—food, beverages, services, and ambiance—are offered by any food and beverage operation. Some choose to add such other product lines as retail foods, gifts, or souvenirs. In this text, we will limit our discussion to the primary service product line cited above and treat all others as being outside the normal scope of food and beverage operations.

To comprehend the discussion of food and beverage facilities that occupies the balance of this chapter, the student may find it useful to refer to particular food and beverage operations. To meet that need, case studies 5.1, 5.2, and 5.3 are provided below. These describe three food and beverage operations that, at first glance, differ markedly from one another. The three illustrations help make the point that these three seemingly different operations—and any others the student may know from firsthand work experience—have much in common with one another. The first of these, The Steak Shack, is an independently owned specialty restaurant with a limited menu. The second is an employee foodservice facility operated for a bank by Marecki Foods, an independent-business foodservice company. The third, Frog's Pub, is an English-style pub specializing in imported beers and ales, and offering very limited foodservice.

Case Study 5.1

The Steak Shack is a family owned and operated restaurant located in a middle-class suburb twenty-three miles from a city of two hundred and fifty thousand. It is open six days for dinner only and closed all day Sunday. The goals of the Steak Shack include meeting the dining needs of those local residents seeking steaks and a limited number of related items, moderately priced, with efficient, friendly service.

The restaurant is the sole tenant in a purpose-built, stand-alone building surrounded by parking for up to fifty cars. The interior consists of a dining room; a cocktail lounge and bar; a production area consisting of food preparation, dishwashing, and storage areas; offices; dressing rooms and lavatories for staff; and men's and women's restrooms for customers. The dining room seats one hundred at tables for two, four, or six people, and the tables can be combined when necessary for larger groups. The cocktail lounge, adjacent to the dining room, offers seating for thirty at tables for two or four and is used principally by customers having predinner drinks. In this cocktail lounge, there is a bar seating twelve. During busy periods, two bartenders at this bar prepare all drinks for the bar, the cocktail lounge, and dining room.

The production area includes facilities for receiving, storing, and issuing foods and beverages. In addition, this area has facilities used to prepare food for cooking, such as ranges and other equipment for cooking, and counters for dispensing finished food products to servers. The production area also includes facilities and equipment for dishwashing, pot washing, and waste disposal.

Office space is limited. The manager and bookkeeper share one office, where the computer is located. The other office is used by the chef, who manages kitchen operations and does all purchasing except for beverages, which are purchased by the manager.

The menu consists of six appetizers, three soups, a salad bar, and ten entrees—five steak, two poultry, one roast beef, and two seafood. In addition, the chef prepares three special entrees each night. Customers are given a choice of french fried or baked potatoes and either of the two vegetables of the day. Desserts include three pies, one layer cake, cheesecake, and eight flavors of ice cream. Coffee, tea, and milk are available. The customary selection of beers, wines, and spirits and mixers is available at the bar.

Figure 5.1 is a floor plan of the Steak Shack showing the food area, the dining area, and the beverage area.

Case Study 5.2

The Mountain Bank staff dining room is a foodservice facility located in the corporate headquarters of the Mountain Bank and Trust Company in a large city in the West. In compliance with various laws, smoking is not permitted in the staff dining room. The facility is not open to the public; it is provided by the bank as a service for the staff. One of the bank's goals is to provide staff members with good food at very reasonable prices during working hours so that they do not have

Figure 5-1

Floor plan of the Steak Shack

to leave the premises for meals. Another is to provide efficient service so that staff members can eat within the allotted time. The service is operated by Marecki Foods, a regional company specializing in business and industry foodservice. Marecki has a contract to provide the service for a set fee per month.

The facility is located on the second floor of the bank's new headquarters building, constructed just four years ago. The dining, kitchen, and storage facilities are all attractive and modern, and the bank insists that they be properly cleaned and maintained by the foodservice contractor.

The facility is open from 7 A.M. to 3 P.M. and limits service to breakfast and lunch. Menu selections are limited. Breakfast items include juices, cold cereals, muffins, pastries, eggs, bacon, sausage, and the usual breakfast beverages. Daily lunch items include a choice of three sandwiches, an extensive salad bar, two hot entrees, several desserts, and a choice of beverages.

Employees pay as they enter. At breakfast, they pay $1.25 for cold selections with beverage and $2.50 for full breakfast. At lunch, they pay $4, regardless of their selections. At the end of each month, the foodservice contractor bills the bank for the difference between revenues and expenses, plus the monthly fee.

Employees take trays, flatware, and napkins at the entrance to the facility. Foods are attractively displayed on several buffet islands. Employees make their selections and carry these to tables in the dining room, which seats 120 persons at tables for two and four. Employees bus their own trays, but there are two foodservice employees in the dining room to clean tables.

Figure 5.2 is a floor plan of the facility operated by Marecki Foods for the Mountain Bank, showing the food area and the dining area. This operation has no beverage area.

Case Study 5.3

Frog's Pub is an American version of an English pub, located in a prosperous and growing city of two hundred and fifty thousand people in the Midwest. It is in the downtown area on a street known locally as "Restaurant Row;" and it attracts large numbers of customers at lunch, after work, and throughout the evening hours. The owner's goals include providing an eating and drinking place for those seeking something out of the ordinary. Another is to provide a casual atmosphere in which customers can relax and feel at home.

Figure 5-2

Floor plan of the staff dining room at the Mountain Bank and Trust Company

Frog's Pub occupies rented premises in a four story brick building. Customers enter a large room that gives the appearance of an authentic English pub, with a long bar along one side of the room. The bar has stools to seat thirty customers. Seventy-five additional customers can be seated at tables.

At the bar, two bartenders prepare drinks for customers at the bar as well as for those seated at tables. Table service is provided by three servers, aided by one individual who clears and cleans tables. Food is prepared in a small kitchen at the rear of the establishment by a chef who has one assistant. There is a small dishwashing machine operated by a third individual. All food and beverages are stored in the basement. Dressing rooms for the staff and a small office for the manager are also located in the basement.

Frog's Pub is different from any other establishment in the region: it offers thirty-six imported beers and ales, many of them English. While spirits and some wines are available, the vast majority of customers order the specialty beers and ales, in spite of relatively high prices per glass or bottle. Food accounts for a comparatively small percentage of dollar sales, and the food menu is restricted: it includes eight items that serve as accompaniments to drinks or as appetizers. The remainder of the menu includes several sandwiches and three hot items that are changed daily. Limited desserts and both coffee and tea are available. All menu items have names that sound British.

Figure 5.3 is a floor plan of Frog's Pub showing the combined food and beverage area.

▶ Facility Layout and Design

Once the product line has been established, it becomes feasible to design an appropriate facility, to select the specific kinds of equipment required and the number of pieces of each, and to plan suitable equipment layout for each area of the facility.

For the present discussion, we will assume that food and beverage facilities have three main areas. The first of these is a food area, where the food products are prepared. This includes the kitchen and such related facilities as food storerooms, refrigerators, and freezers. The second is a dining area where customers may consume food, or food and beverages. The third is a beverage area, where the beverage products are prepared. This includes at least one bar and at least one storage facility for liquor, beer, and wine.

Figure 5-3
Floor plan of Frog's Pub

The layout and design of an efficient food and beverage facility, one that contributes to smooth day-to-day operation, is critical. Efficient layout and design takes into account six considerations, although some of these are of less significance in the dining and beverage areas.

1. Space
2. Equipment
3. Lighting
4. Ventilation
5. Materials flow
6. Traffic flow

In the following pages, we will focus on each of the three main areas—food, dining, and beverage—and discuss applying the most significant of these six considerations to each area.

▶ The Food Area

The food area is that part of the facility where food products are prepared. In most foodservice operations, the following activities take place within the food area.

Purchasing

This normally takes place in an office with a desk for working, a file cabinet for keeping records, a computer workstation, and space for meeting quietly with the sales representatives of vendors.

Receiving

This activity is conducted in an area that contains equipment used to verify that the goods received conform to the orders placed. Quantity, quality, and price must all be checked. To do this properly, it is necessary to plan an area that is easily accessible to delivery drivers and large enough to hold an entire normal delivery.

Storing and Issuing

These activities require three types of facilities for storing foods: dry, refrigerated, and frozen. A dry storage facility, typically called a storeroom, is maintained at normal room temperature. It is used to keep a

Some foods are stored at room temperature, while others require refrigeration or freezing. Pictured here is a walk-in refrigerator of the type used for fruits, vegetables, and dairy products. (Photo courtesy of InterMetro Industries Corporation.)

reasonable supply of bags, bottles, boxes, and jars of food that need not be refrigerated or frozen. This storeroom must be large enough so that shelves can be constructed and foods can be stored in an orderly manner. Refrigerated facilities—reach-in or walk-in refrigerators—are used to store meats, fish, vegetables, dairy products, and any other foods that will spoil if not kept cold. Freezers—reach-in or walk-in types—are required to store those items that are purchased in a frozen state.

Chefs preparing the raw ingredients and basic preparations for the day's service. The challenge is to prepare only as much as is needed for the day or meal period, based on sales histories and production sheets. (Photo courtesy of Cryovac.)

Producing

In a foodservice operation, food production takes place in the kitchen. Most kitchens require two production areas: one for advance preparation and another for the final preparation of foods immediately before they are ready to be served. The advance preparation area is for basic preparation of foods that will later be transferred to another area for final preparation. The final preparation, or finishing area, is for making foods ready for service.

Serving

This activity is defined as the transfer of finished products from preparation staff to servers. This even occurs in self-service operations—cafeterias and buffets among them—where the customers are also the servers.

▸ Layout and Design Considerations in a Food Area

Space

If the facility is to run efficiently, adequate space should be provided for the activities associated with the food area of the facility. The amount of space allocated for the food area will vary from one establishment to another, depending on such considerations as products, type of service, type and amount of equipment, and number of personnel required to work in the area. For example, the Steak Shack is a full-service restaurant with relatively greater space devoted to food preparation than is the case in Frog's Pub, which offers a very limited menu. While it may be possible to plan sufficient space for every kitchen need in a new facility, older facilities being converted to foodservice use may lack the ideal amount of space for a specific activity. In such circumstances, compromise may be necessary.

Equipment

There are many considerations that determine the equipment required in a food area. The two most important are product line and preparation methods.

Product Line. Product line is a key determinant in equipment selection. If the product line is to include Chinese food, the equipment needs will be very different from those in operations featuring French or Italian food. Similarly, specialty restaurants serving pizza require different equipment from those serving hamburgers. In contrast, family restaurants with varied menus require more varieties of equipment than do specialty restaurants.

Preparation Methods. The equipment in food areas varies considerably from one establishment to another. In some, such as the Steak Shack, one sees stock pots, kettles, mixers, steamers, and the other heavy equipment characteristic of kitchens preparing food from raw, primary ingredients. This equipment may include broilers, ranges, conventional ovens, microwave ovens, deep-fat fryers, and a number of other possibilities. In other establishments, the equipment may be limited to a few counters used to arrange food on small platters just before they are microwaved. In Frog's Pub, the kitchen equipment is simple and basic because the menu is limited. Needs vary from one operation to another, and the choice of equipment should be based on the food products prepared.

Many food items can be prepared a number of different ways, and it is important to establish the preparation method for each food item before purchasing equipment. Chicken, for example, can be fried,

Kitchen equipment varies considerably from one establishment to another. Broilers, ranges, grills, ovens, and deep-fat fryers are among the most common in American commercial kitchens. (Photo courtesy of Vulcan Hart.)

sautéed, deep fried, baked, roasted, boiled, or broiled. If an operation establishes deep frying as the proper preparation method for a particular chicken entree, then a deep fryer—or more than one—should be on the list of equipment to purchase. Similarly, if soups are to be prepared from stocks made in the establishment, as is the case in the Steak Shack and the Mountain Bank staff dining room, then suitable equipment to produce the stocks—stock pots, or steam kettles, depending largely on volume—should be on the list. If the product list includes a large number of frozen convenience foods, it would be necessary to purchase a larger freezer than would be required if the restaurant were to use mostly raw, fresh ingredients. The number of examples illustrating this point are endless.

The arrangement of equipment in each part of the food area is influenced by the extent of the work to be done in the area and the number of staff members available to do it. A large establishment may set up a specific station for broiling, another for frying, and yet another for sautéing, and provide each of these with appropriate equipment. Smaller establishments, not having the volume of work to justify a specific station and staff, may combine these three in a single station. That station would clearly have less equipment of any one type than each of the three stations in the larger establishment.

It is important to recognize that once equipment decisions have been made and the equipment has been purchased and installed, it may be extremely difficult to change the product line in any significant way. For example, some specialty restaurants have found it impossible to enlarge or change their menus because they have neither the appropriate equipment nor the space in the kitchen to add that equipment.

Lighting

For employees to work efficiently, they must have sufficient light. Light is required so that employees can attend to the detailed work required for the elegant presentation of foods. It is also required so that employees can read portion scales and be certain that they are providing the correct number of ounces or grams in a portion.

There are many considerations to take into account when making decisions about the lighting for a work area. The amount of light reaching a particular workstation will be considerably less than the amount available at the lighting source itself. Also, the color of the walls and ceiling will influence the amount of light available at a workstation. More light will be available if wall and ceiling surfaces are light colors: light colors reflect light; dark colors absorb it. The amount of light on a surface, such as a worktable, is measured in **lumens** per square foot, or **foot-candles.** A foot-candle of light is the amount of light that can be measured at a distance of one foot from an ordinary candle. One lumen per square foot is equal to one foot-candle, a term whose origin precedes the invention of electric lights. Lighting experts suggest that employees need at least 60 foot-candles of light for ordinary work and about 110 foot-candles of light for detailed work, such as cake decorating.

Ventilation

Adequate ventilation is another basic requirement for work areas. The air that foodservice employees breathe should be clean—free from smoke and other pollutants. The climate should be at a temperature at which staff can work in reasonable comfort.

Because kitchens produce smoke and odors, the air must be replaced continually. If not, air quality will deteriorate as levels of smoke and odors rise. In addition, temperatures in the kitchen will rise quickly from stoves, ovens, and other heat-producing equipment in use, and the air may become unhealthy. The proper rate of air exchange in a kitchen is determined by the type of cooking, the type and amount of equipment used, and the height of the ceiling. In heavily used kitchens, the rate of air exchange may be as high as fifty times per hour. Fresh air may come from any of three different sources: other rooms in the facility, outside, or a ventilation system in the establishment.

Materials Flow

Work areas and equipment should be arranged so that foods can proceed smoothly and logically from the receiving area to the storing and issuing area. From there, foods should move smoothly to the producing area for advance preparation and final preparation, and from there to the serving area.

To facilitate this smooth and even flow, the receiving area and all equipment required for receiving is typically located near a rear entrance to a foodservice facility. The storing and issuing area and the attendant equipment and facilities—storeroom, refrigerators, and freezers—should be located close to the receiving area. The producing area and its equipment should be located close enough to the storing and issuing area that advance preparation and final preparation can be accomplished expeditiously. The serving area should be close to the finishing area so that foods can be served as quickly as possible once they are ready. Note the arrangement of the equipment on the floor plan of the Steak Shack, found in figure 5.1. Food deliveries come to receiving at the rear of the building, then move to one of the storage facilities nearby, from which they are transferred to the food preparation area as needed. The preparation and finishing areas are very close to one another to facilitate quick service of the finished product to guests in the dining room.

Dishwashing equipment has traditionally been placed in a part of the kitchen near the entrance to the dining room, so that servers returning to the kitchen with soiled china, glassware, and flatware can place these things in a convenient spot before proceeding to pick up food. However, because the noise associated with the handling of dishes can often be heard in the dining room, some establishments have installed conveyor systems. This is the approach taken in the Steak Shack. With these systems, dishwashing areas can be located some distance from the kitchen entrance with soiled items moved to the dishwashing area by the conveyor belt.

Traffic Flow

People working in food areas must be able to move around without interfering with the work of others. They are all working in aisles, real or potential. In general, there are two kinds of aisles: traffic aisles and working aisles. These two should not coincide: employees moving about the food area in traffic aisles should not interfere with those storing, issuing, or preparing food, for example, in working aisles. Traffic aisles should be wide enough to permit the passage of personnel and equipment. Working aisles should be wide enough to give employees sufficient space to move with reasonable freedom as they work. Note the wide aisles in the kitchen facility at the Mountain Bank staff dining room, illustrated in figure 5.2. In a serving area, for example, space is required to accommodate both personnel returning soiled china and linens from a dining room and those picking up foods to be served in the dining room; there must be adequate space for the anticipated number of personnel to go about their work without crowding.

In planning a food area, then, adequate space and suitable equipment must be provided for purchasing, receiving, storing, issuing, producing, and serving food. Similarly, adequate lighting and ventilation must be provided in all parts of the food area. Finally, the food area should be arranged to facilitate efficient movement of personnel and materials.

▶ The Dining Area

The dining area is that part of the facility where food and beverage products are consumed by customers. It normally includes tables, counters, or similar surfaces on which the products are placed, and chairs, stools, benches, or other seating arrangements for customers to use as they consume the products. It may also include such items as salad bars, buffet tables, and other similar items designed for customer self-service.

▶ Layout and Design Considerations in a Dining Area

Space

The amount of space devoted to seating in the dining area will be determined by the type of service, the variety and mix of table sizes, and decisions about space between tables.

The dining area is that part of a restaurant facility where food and beverage products are consumed by customers. Above, just before opening time, the tables, chairs, and place settings in the Hyatt Regency St. Louis at Union Station are ready to provide an attractive welcome to customers. (Photo courtesy of Hyatt Regency St. Louis at Union Station.)

Type of Service. Some types of service require more space than others. French service (discussed the the next chapter), for example, requires considerable space between tables so that the gueridons characteristic of French service can be moved table-side. American service (discussed in the next chapter), on the other hand, requires comparatively little space between tables—just enough for servers to walk quickly carrying plates or trays. In the Mountain Bank staff dining room, where self-service is the rule, aisles in the dining area can be much narrower than would be the case in the Steak Shack. There, servers require considerable space to move large trays of hot foods quickly from kitchen to customers.

Variety and Mix of Table Sizes. Table sizes and the mix of table sizes in the dining area will also influence the amount of space required to accommodate a given number of diners. Tables for two, four, six, or eight customers require varying amounts of floor space. Round tables require different amounts of space than square or rectangular tables. Knowledge of the number of tables of each shape and size will help determine the total number that can be accommodated in a dining area of a given size. Round tables, for example, require slightly more space than squares. It takes only one half the space to seat eight persons at one table as it does to seat the same eight persons at four separate tables accommodating two persons each. Tables intended to seat two persons can be purchased in various standard sizes ranging from 24″ × 24″ to 30″ × 36″. An establishment catering to families will have a greater number of tables accommodating larger parties than one that caters to couples. Establishments offering luxurious evening dining will require larger tables than those offering only breakfast or lunch. In Frog's Pub, there is no real need for large tables because customers do not ordinarily order full meals. Consequently, the tables are smaller, and are selected because they provide enough table area for beverage products rather than food products, which tend to be secondary in Frog's Pub. The tables in the Steak Shack are somewhat larger because customers normally order full meals. In a sense, beverage sales are secondary in the dining room of the Steak Shack.

Decisions About Space Between Tables. The distance between tables will influence the number of customers who can be accommodated in a given area. Many managers see no difficulty in having customers seated very close to one another. Others prefer to seat customers at greater distances from one another and to preserve the privacy of their conversations. In the former, a greater number of customers will be seated; in the latter, fewer can be seated.

Equipment

The equipment required in the dining area will be determined by the type of service and other decisions of management as to the need for specific pieces of equipment, such as buffet stands, serving stands, and coat-racks. In the Mountain Bank staff dining room, considerable space is devoted to three buffet islands, pieces of equipment not found in Frog's Pub. The Steak Shack has one similar piece of equipment, a salad bar.

Lighting

There are two primary considerations in dining area lighting: the amount of lighting and the type. The decision to have a well-lighted dining area as opposed to one dimly lighted is based on the atmosphere management is attempting to create. Some establishments—Frog's Pub, for example—keep lighting levels low to create an intimate atmosphere. In some, the lighting level is so low that older customers may have difficulty reading a menu. By contrast, other establishments, both the Mountain Bank staff dining room and the Steak Shack among them, are brightly lighted. Sometimes this is because they are family establishments; other times it may be because they feature an interesting or unique theme.

There are two basic types of lighting—direct and indirect. The bulbs providing direct lighting can be seen, and the light shines directly into a room. For indirect lighting, bulbs are not visible. Indirect light shines toward the ceiling and walls and is reflected back into the room. Direct lighting produces shadows, but less light is required to achieve a given degree of brightness. Indirect lighting is softer and produces no shadows, but more indirect lighting is required to reach a particular level of illumination than would be required with direct lighting.

Ventilation

Adequate ventilation is another basic requirement for a dining area. The air in a dining area should be at a temperature at which people can dine in reasonable comfort. Today, with the growing tendency to provide smoke-free areas for diners—especially when required to do so by local laws—ventilation has assumed greater importance than in previous years.

If smoking is permitted, air quality will deteriorate as levels of smoke and odors rise. Therefore, the owners of the Steak Shack provide a separate smoking area along with equipment to insure that smoke from the smoking area is vented outside. This is not a consideration in the Mountain Bank staff dining room, where smoking is not permitted. However, temperatures in a dining area will rise quickly without adequate ventilation, and the air will become unhealthy. Fresh air may come from any of three different sources: other rooms in the facility, outside, or a ventilation system in the establishment.

It is important to note that the air pressure in the dining room and other rooms should be higher than in the kitchen. When such is the case, air will flow from the dining room to the kitchen, not the other way around. If air pressure were higher in the kitchen, the smoke and odors from the kitchen would soon flow into the dining room, making that facility uncomfortable for diners.

Traffic Flow

Traffic in a dining area must move smoothly. Traffic patterns should be planned to avoid cross traffic between customers and service personnel and among the service personnel. Service personnel must be able to move freely and conveniently within the facility. In some places, this means, for example, that servers must be able to move into and out of a serving area to pick up food orders and to deposit soiled china and flatware for washing. In other kinds of establishments, it may mean that employees must be able to move about the dining area to clean tables and get rid of disposable paper and plastic food packaging.

The measures taken to facilitate free movement vary from one type of operation to another. In table-service restaurants, for example, the servers' exit from the dining area to the kitchen is typically located some distance away from the street entrance used by customers. In establishments that do not provide table service, the area where customers order or select foods is typically near the street entrance. In part, this is to facilitate freedom of movement for customers carrying foods to their tables.

If servers are required to pick up plates of food in a kitchen, it is important to have two doors between the kitchen and dining areas—one for traffic going into the kitchen, and the other for traffic coming out. This is illustrated in figure 5.1, which shows the floor plan of the Steak Shack. If only one door were provided, accidents could result from service staff coming and going into the kitchen at the same time. In addition, the farther apart these two doors are placed, the better the traffic flow.

Similarly, lavatories should be installed in locations such that traffic to and from these facilities will not interfere directly with servers or other customers. Note their locations in the Steak Shack and in the Mountain Bank staff dining room (figs. 5.1 and 5.2).

In planning a dining area, then, adequate space and suitable equipment must be provided for efficient and orderly service of food and beverage products to customers. Knowledge of the type of service, the variety and mix of table sizes, and management decisions about space between tables is critical to determining space requirements. As with a food area, adequate lighting and ventilation must be provided in all parts of the dining area. Finally, the dining area should be arranged to facilitate efficient movement of personnel and materials. Throughout, one must bear in mind that the ambiance, or atmosphere—a critical factor in overall success—is determined largely by the layout and design of the dining area.

▶ The Beverage Area

The beverage area is that part of the facility where beverage products are prepared and served. The following activities take place within the beverage area.

The bar pictured at right provides an elegant focus for the beverage area in the Cite Grill. (Photo courtesy of The New York Restaurant Group, Inc.)

Purchasing

Beverage purchasing requires making decisions about the quantities and kinds of beverages to be purchased. Orders for beverages are often placed from the purchasing area by telephone or by direct contact with sales persons, if that is consistent with state law and the policies established by management for beverage purchasing.

Receiving

Receiving beverages requires verifying that beverages delivered conform to the orders placed. In many small establishments, the beverage receiving area is the bar; in larger establishments offering both food products and beverage products, one receiving area is likely to exist for both.

Storing and Issuing

Beverage storing and issuing activities vary greatly from one establishment to another. The variations stem from differing needs based on the size of the establishment, the number of customers served in a given period, and the complexity of the beverage product list. In a small neighborhood bar, the storing and issuing facility may be only a small closet located near the bar; in a large hotel or restaurant doing high-volume business and offering a complex array of beverage products, at least two separate areas will be used for storing and issuing beverages. One of these will be a locked storeroom, maintained at normal room temperature, which will be used for storing liquors and may be used for storing mixers and any alcoholic beverages that are not refrigerated. Another will be a locked, refrigerated room for the storage of beers, ales, and those wines that require chilling.

Those restaurants that offer their guests choices from wine lists must keep reasonable supplies of bottled wine on hand. Some of the finer restaurants maintain wine inventories worth thousands of dollars. These are typically kept under secure conditions in climate-controlled storerooms known as **wine cellars.**

Wine cellars should be maintained in an organized manner, so that particular wines can be located quickly when ordered by customers. To accomplish this, wines are normally classified by type, and each individual wine is given a number. The still wines and sparkling wines are stored on their sides in special racks or bins designed for storing wines. The number assigned to each wine is both printed in the wine list and posted on the bin or rack where the corresponding wine is stored. This makes it easier to find any wine ordered by a customer.

Producing

Beverage production activities typically take place at bars, where drinks are produced by bartenders. There are three types of bars: **front bars, service bars,** and **special purpose bars.** An understanding of beverage facilities requires that one know about these three and comprehend their differences.

Front Bar. A front bar is a fixed counter for beverage service that is open for business on a regularly scheduled basis and is directly accessible to customers. Front bars are permanently fixed in particular locations within establishments. Many of these establishments are open long hours daily, but the days and hours of operation are determined by owners within the parameters of state and local laws.

There are three specific parts of a front bar: **bar, back bar,** and **under bar.**

The term **bar** is normally used to refer to that physical device in a barroom or taproom that fulfills several purposes: it is a counter where bartenders can serve drinks to customers; it is a convenient surface used by customers who consume drinks; it is a surface on which bartenders may prepare drinks; and it is a serving station where servers may pick up drinks for consumption elsewhere.

A back bar is a storage and display facility located behind the bartender. The top surface is used to hold shelves on which are displayed bottles of some or all of the wines and liquors available at the bar. Glassware may be displayed here as well. The compartments underneath are used for storage of bar supplies, which may include beers, wines, liquors, mixers, paper supplies, or any other item used at the bar. If the facility is refrigerated, it may be used to store bottled beers and such food supplies used in beverage production as milk, cream, lemons, limes, and various fruit juices.

An under bar is a work area under the bar surface, containing equipment and supplies used by bartenders. The work area will have stations—one for each bartender. The number of stations will govern the number of bartenders who can conveniently work at the bar at any one time. A station consists of one steel sink for ice surrounded by wells to hold bottles of frequently used liquors and mixers. In addition to these stations, the under bar has sinks or a machine for washing glassware and a sink for disposing of liquids and washing bar equipment. There may also be work space for preparing drinks, for storing supplies and equipment, and for additional refrigeration facilities.

Front bars are the most common of the three types of bars. At the typical front bar, customers walk to the bar, where they are greeted by a bartender who takes their orders and prepares and serves their drinks. This is the type of bar found in the Frog's Pub, illustrated in figure 5.3. Beyond the point at which the drink is served, there are many possible variations. Customers may or may not consume their drinks at the bar. In some establishments, customers can remain at the bar, sitting on stools or standing as they drink. In others, customers can carry their drinks elsewhere. Sometimes the bartender acts as a cashier, collecting for each drink as it is served. Sometimes the bartender records a given customer's drinks on a paper form called a **guest check,** which the customer settles before leaving. Occasionally, there is a cashier at the bar who does not act as a bartender but who serves as cashier for the establishment.

Service Bar. A service bar is a counter at which a bartender prepares drinks but does not serve them directly to customers. Drink orders are given to the bartender by servers who take the orders from customers and serve the drinks when ready.

Service bars are frequently located in kitchens and similar areas that are neither visible nor accessible to customers. In other instances, a service bar may be visible but not accessible: some service areas are too small for customer access to be feasible; others are behind glass walls; some are in establishments in which the level and extent of service is such that any appearance of self-service would be unseemly.

Some service bars are permanently located in fixed positions. Others are mobile—bars on wheels that can be moved from one location to another as needs dictate. Still others are temporary—folding tables set up quickly, possibly draped or otherwise covered, then dismantled when no longer needed. What differentiates service bars from others is not the degree of permanence but the fact that customers are not permitted access to them. Customer access is not a characteristic of a service bar.

Special-Purpose Bar. A special-purpose bar is one that, although directly accessible to customers, is open only for a defined period to accommodate a special need. Special-purpose bars are most commonly used in banquet or catering businesses to accommodate guests at special functions—parties, dances, or the receptions preceding special events. At special-purpose bars, customers have direct access to a bartender: they order and receive drinks just as at a front bar. But although a front bar is open on a regularly scheduled basis, the special-purpose bar is open only to accommodate the beverage service requirements of those present at the event. When the event is over, the special-purpose bar is closed. Thus, special-purpose bars are open for varying periods—some long, others short, depending on the length of the event.

Special-purpose bars can be permanent, mobile, or temporary. Some are permanent and are built into the physical structure of a banquet room. Others are mobile, such as bars on wheels that can be moved from one location to another. Still others are merely tables or counters, folding or otherwise, that are fitted out to be used as bars when required.

Bars can be built in various shapes and in any desired size. The layout and design of a bar will be determined by the use that management plans for the bar. If the bar is to be used only as a service bar, it probably will be compact—no larger than required to prepare and serve a projected number of drinks in a given time period, with some space allocated for storage. In contrast, if it is to be a front bar used in a cocktail lounge that also serves as a holding area for customers waiting to be seated in a dining area, it probably will be considerably larger, providing work space for several bartenders and counter space to accommodate a substantial number of customers seated at the bar. The sizes of special-purpose bars vary with the number of customers to be served.

Serving

This activity involves transferring finished beverage products from the bartender to servers, to customers, or to both of these. These transfers take place at one of the three types of bars just discussed and described earlier in this chapter: front bars, service bars, and special-purpose bars.

▶ Layout and Design Considerations in a Beverage Area

Space

If the facility is to run efficiently, adequate space should be provided for the activities associated with this important area of the facility. The amount of space allocated for the beverage area will vary from one establishment to another, depending on such considerations as product line, type of service, type and amount of equipment, and number of personnel required to work in the area. For example, an up-scale cock-tail lounge advertising the ability of its bartenders to make any drink requested by any patron is likely to require more preparation space than a neighborhood tavern offering nothing other than five brands of bottled beer. While it may be possible to plan sufficient space for every need in a new facility, older facilities being converted to bar use may lack the ideal amount of space for a specific use. In such circum-stances, compromise may be necessary.

Equipment

There are many considerations that determine the equipment required in a beverage area. The two most important are product line and preparation methods.

Product Line. Product line is a key determinant in equipment selection. If the line is to include mixed drinks, the equipment needs will be very different from those in operations featuring imported beers on tap. Similarly, operations offering drinks requiring shaved ice require dif-ferent equipment from those offering straight shots of blended rye. In the Steak Shack, for example, an ice machine is an important piece of bar equipment. At Frog's Pub, there is an ice machine in the kitchen, but none at the bar: most of the beverage orders are for the featured imported beers and ales, and the bartender has little need for ice.

Preparation Methods. The equipment in beverage areas varies consider-ably from one establishment to another. In some, one might find **pour-ers**—measuring devices that hold a precise amount of liquor each time a drink is poured. In others—those with automated equipment for measuring drink quantities—there may be few bottles in view and no pourers at all. Needs vary from one operation to another, and the choice of equipment should be based on the beverage products pre-pared.

Lighting

The primary consideration in beverage area lighting is the atmosphere management intends to create. Lighting is a critical element in this area. Some establishments—Frog's Pub, for example—keep lighting levels low to create an intimate atmosphere. By contrast, the bar in the Steak Shack has a higher level of lighting.

In designing a beverage area, the planner must include adequate and suitable equipment for those purchasing, receiving, storing, issuing, producing, and serving activities associated with the beverage product list. Just as in the food area, adequate lighting and ventilation must be provided in all parts of the beverage area. Finally, the beverage area should be arranged to facilitate efficient movement of personnel and materials.

The key factors in food and beverage facilities discussed in this chapter—concept, legal requirements, product line, and layout and design—are major elements that lie at the heart of food and beverage operations. There are obviously many other aspects to planning and operating a food and beverage enterprise. There are a number of other topics requiring close attention, including menu, organization plan, marketing plan, and budget. These will be topics for discussion in the next chapter.

▶ Summary

In this chapter, concept, legal requirements, and product line are introduced as fundamental to the layout and design of food and beverage facilities. Product line is described as having three components: food and beverages, services, and ambiance. Case studies describing three different foodservice facilities—Steak Shack, Mountain Bank staff dining room, and Frog's Pub—were presented as aids to understanding facilities' layout and design. Six key considerations in food and beverage facilities layout and design are identified as space, equipment, lighting, ventilation, materials flow, and traffic flow. These considerations are discussed as applicable to the three main areas of a food and beverage facility, identified as a food area, a dining area, and a beverage area. Front bars, service bars, and special-purpose bars are identified as three types of bars that may be found in beverage facilities. Finally, the three specific parts of a front bar are identified as bar, back bar, and under bar.

 Key Terms

Back Bar	Producing
Bar	Product Line
Concept	Purchasing
Feasibility Study	Receiving
Foot-Candle	Service Bar
Front Bar	Serving

Guest Check	Special-Purpose Bar
Issuing	Storing
Lumens	Under Bar
Pourers	Wine Cellar

1. The authors state that every food and beverage operation begins with a concept. In this context, define the term *concept* and describe its purpose.

2. Owners and managers of food and beverage facilities are said to require some knowledge of various laws and regulations. What types of laws and regulations should they know about?

3. Define the term *product line* as it is used in food and beverage operations.

4. What are the three elements in the hospitality service product line offered by food and beverage operations?

5. Identify the three main areas in a food and beverage facility, describing the principal activities that take place in each.

6. List the six considerations that should be taken into account in the layout and design of food and beverage facilities. Describe the importance and significance of each to efficient day-to-day operation.

7. What is a lumen? a foot-candle? How many foot-candles do experts suggest for normal kitchen work? for detailed work?

8. Distinguish between traffic aisles and working aisles.

9. Explain the importance of space, traffic flow, and lighting in the layout and design of a dining area.

10. In what ways do the arrangement and size of tables in a dining room influence the amount of space required for a given number of customers?

11. Distinguish between direct lighting and indirect lighting. Why might food and beverage operators choose to use one or the other?

12. Why is it necessary that air pressure in a dining room and in other rooms adjoining the kitchen be greater than that in the kitchen itself?

13. Three types of bars are described in the chapter. Identify these three and discuss their differences.

14. List and describe the three principal parts of a front bar.

1. Describe a restaurant that you have recently visited. Can you identify the concept of the establishment?

2. For the restaurant identified in number 1 above, describe its product line as completely as you can. Include in your description a summary of the foods and beverages offered, the services offered, and the ambiance of the establishment.

3. Does the layout and design of the restaurant identified in numbers 1 and 2 above follow the principles described in this text? If not, where does it differ?

S i x

Food and Beverage Operations

After reading and studying this chapter, you should be able to:

1 List and describe the seven basic steps common to food and beverage operations of all types.

2 List and explain the four critical issues that purchasing procedures must address.

3 Distinguish between perishables and nonperishables.

4 List the three primary goals of receiving procedure and explain the importance of each.

5 Identify the four goals of storing procedure.

6 Describe the two goals of issuing procedure.

7 Name the four goals of food or beverage production procedures.

8 Identify the purposes of each of the following: sales histories, production sheets, standard recipes.

9 Compare the goals of sales procedures in profit-oriented operations with those in not-for-profit operations.

10 List and describe three common means used to help sell food and beverage products.

11 List and describe eight styles of foodservice.

12 Identify three types of wines.

13 Discuss the interdependence of the seven steps common to all food and beverage operations.

▶ Introduction

The previous chapter was devoted to examining the common components of food and beverage facilities. With that objective accomplished, we will now turn to a subject that is typically of the greatest interest to those preparing for careers in the foodservice industry: food and beverage operations.

Given the array of types of food and beverage establishments discussed in chapter 4, it should be apparent that the operational details differ greatly from one type to another. The operational details relating to a hot dog stand at the beach or a hamburger stand at a county fair will differ greatly from those relating to a sophisticated city restaurant dedicated to fine dining. Similarly, the operational details for a college cafeteria serving students will differ from those for a neighborhood restaurant serving ethnic fare to a family clientele. The differences from one to another are apparent upon detailed consideration of the five most important characteristics of any foodservice enterprise, and these are identified in chapter 4 as menu items, food quality, menu prices, service, and ambiance. Similarly, operational differences are apparent from one type of beverage enterprise to another: the neighborhood bar focused on beverages differs from the fine restaurant focused on food.

In the authors' view, it is not generally useful in an introductory course to attempt detailed descriptions of the great many operational differences evident in the food and beverage industry. They tend to be confusing and to get in the way of understanding the general principles of a food and beverage operation. To those who lack experience in the field, some of the differences from one to another, insignificant as they may be to more experienced professionals, tend to obscure the basic similarities. Discussions of most such differences are best deferred to reasonably advanced courses. We will focus our attention, instead, on similarities—the many steps of food and beverage operations that are really much the same from one enterprise to another. We believe strongly that it becomes much easier to understand the differences from one operation to another if one first comprehends their underlying similarities, that is, the basic operational activities and principles that are common to all.

The purpose of this chapter, then, will be to identify some important points of similarity from one establishment to another. We will identify and describe a number of basic steps that all food and beverage enterprises tend to have in common.

▶ Basic Elements of Food and Beverage Operations

All food or beverage operations have the following basic steps in common.

Purchasing
Receiving
Storing
Issuing
Producing
Selling
Serving

Many will recognize these basic steps, largely because they seem much the same as the parts of a food and beverage facility that were discussed in the previous chapter.

These basic steps are essential for all food or beverage operations—from college cafeterias to national fast food outlets, from neighborhood taverns to hotel cocktail lounges, from nursing home foodservices to catering halls. They are the sequential steps that are necessary for preparing and serving portions of food or beverages. Each of these will be described in detail, and we will explore their interrelationships.

▶ Purchasing

The first of the basic steps of a food and beverage operation is purchasing, a necessary first step in any production process. All food or beverage enterprises must establish procedures for purchasing. The primary objective of purchasing foods or beverages for production is to ensure the availability of suitable materials for preparing food or beverage products and for other related uses. These materials must be available when needed; they should be in sufficient but not excessive quantities and of appropriate quality; and they should be purchased at suitable prices.

Four critical issues that any purchasing procedure must address are

1. quantity,
2. quality,
3. price, and
4. space.

Quantity

Food and beverage operators cannot ask customers to wait for deliveries. When a customer reading the menu in Frog's Pub requests a glass of Bass ale or an order of shepherd's pie, the owner is expected to have the item on hand. The purchasing procedure must be designed to ensure that foods, beverages, and other necessary materials are available when needed so that menu items can be produced on demand. One means for accomplishing this is to establish daily routines for evaluating existing supplies of raw materials, assessing needs for the upcoming period, and placing orders as required.

For the Steak Shack, it is obviously important to maintain adequate supplies of steak. This can be accomplished by establishing daily routines for evaluating existing supplies and by placing regular orders with a supplier. Assuming that the supplier delivers only on Tuesdays, it is necessary to order a sufficient quantity to last for one week. Purchasing food can be the job of any one of several people in a foodservice operation. Some restaurant managers do their own food purchasing. In other restaurants, the chef does it, and in some larger operations, the purchasing is done by a purchasing steward. At the Steak Shack, the chef purchases all food for the establishment. The individual responsible for ordering must know the quantity used in a normal week and know when larger or smaller amounts than normal may be needed. A good purchasing procedure is designed to help determine proper quantities for purchase.

Quality

Product quality is another critical issue. The food and beverages must be of a quality acceptable to customers and should be consistent. There are degrees of quality, and products need not always be of the highest quality obtainable, but they should be of the quality that meets customers' needs and preferences. Some would add that the quality should always match the image the establishment attempts to convey. If, for example, the Mountain Bank is attempting to convey to its employees the image of a caring employer, foods available to them in the dining facility—even the simplest foods—should be of consistently good quality. The purchasing procedure should be designed to ensure the purchase of products of consistent quality each time the food and beverages are ordered.

The quality of any item purchased should also be appropriate for its intended use. For example, when the steward in the Mountain Bank staff dining room buys oranges for fresh orange juice, she buys Valencias or Temples, which are juice oranges, rather than California navels, which are eating oranges. The latter are more expensive and yield less juice. If someone were mistakenly to purchase the Californias, the bank's operating costs would be higher than necessary, and the quality of the orange juice would be lower than desired.

Any procedure designed for food purchasing must take into account the two different categories into which all food purchases are divided: **perishables** and **nonperishables.**

Perishables are those foods that will keep for only short periods of time before they begin to lose their quality. These foods spoil and become unusable. Such foods are typically fresh foods, such as meat, fish, fruit, and vegetables. Fresh vegetables will retain sufficient freshness for several days; fresh fish, by comparison, will not, and it must be used much sooner. Perishables must be ordered frequently, sometimes each day. The quantity ordered is limited to anticipated demand.

Nonperishables are those foods that will keep for extended periods before spoiling. They typically come in cans, jars, bags, bottles, and boxes. Some are dried or frozen. Nonperishables are ordered infrequently and in larger quantities because they have longer shelf life than perishables.

The terms perishable and nonperishable are not normally used in beverage purchasing. This does not mean, however, that shelf life for beverage products is unlimited. Some beverages, such as draft beers, for example, have a very limited shelf life and must be kept refrigerated. For bottled beer, shelf life is considerably longer—but not unlimited. By contrast, spirits can be kept indefinitely.

Questions of quality should not be left to chance. Beef tenderloin, the commercial cut of beef used in the Steak Shack to prepare special steaks called filet mignons, is available at several levels of quality, known as grades. Someone must determine which grade is appropriate for intended use in a given establishment. In addition, if customers ordering filet mignon are to receive steaks of the same quality on each visit to the establishment, then provision must be made for ordering the same grade each time beef tenderloins are purchased.

One means for ensuring consistency in the quality of items is to prepare a carefully considered written description of each item to be purchased. This could include such information as grade, size, count, color, type and size of container, degree of freshness, and other characteristics that vary with the product to be purchased. These descriptions are known as **standard purchase specifications** and are commonly used to one extent or another in most well-managed food or beverage operations. In the Steak Shack, all beef is purchased to match carefully written standard purchase specifications.

Price

Price is always a critical issue in food and beverage purchasing. The higher the purchase price for raw materials of a given level of quality, the higher the cost of the food and beverage products an establishment offers its customers. The purchasing procedure should facilitate the purchase of the needed quantity of an item at the most favorable price for the quality selected. For example, while the Mountain Bank may be willing to subsidize the cost of its employees' meals, it is certainly unwilling to spend money wastefully.

There are several methods that purchasers use to determine the best price for the desired quality. Most commonly, purchasers obtain several quotations for desired products and then select the dealer offering the best price. A good purchasing procedure makes provision for comparing the prices offered by various dealers for a given item and selecting the best price. Before purchasing meats for the Steak Shack, the buyer obtains price quotations from three dealers, each of whom has a copy of the standard purchase specifications.

Storage Space

The final critical issue that the purchasing procedure must take into account is storage space. Storage space is always limited, and decisions must be made as to amounts to be allocated to particular uses. Marecki Foods must determine the maximum quantity of each food item used in the Mountain Bank staff dining room facility that can be stored in the limited space available. When storage space is severely limited, it clearly becomes necessary to place orders for some items more frequently than would be necessary otherwise. Thus, storage space can affect the timing of purchases. Quantities of any item purchased should never be greater than the storage space available for that item.

As we shall see, if an establishment lacks proper quantities of food or beverage ingredients to produce for customer demand, or if the food or beverage ingredients are of improper quality because the purchasing procedure malfunctions, other parts of the operation will not be able to function properly. The entire operation may be unable to achieve its goals.

▶ Receiving

The second important step in food or beverage operations is receiving. The procedure for receiving has three primary goals. It must be designed to verify

1. that the quantity delivered is the same as the quantity ordered;
2. that the quality of the items delivered conforms to the quality specified in the order placed; and
3. that the price on the invoice is the same as the price quoted by the dealer when the order was placed.

Food and beverage orders must be received by someone with sufficient knowledge to check carefully and accurately for quantity, quality,

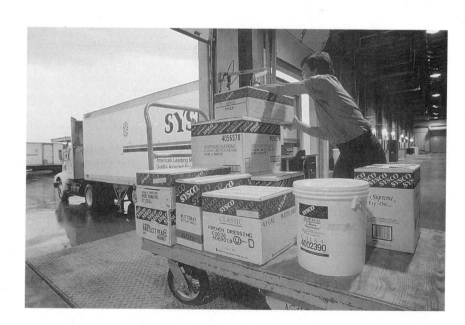

Receiving clerks in many hotels and restaurants regularly receive deliveries from Sysco, one of America's leading foodservice suppliers. Here, food products for a major hotel are about to be loaded for shipment. (Photo courtesy of Sysco Corporation.)

and price. Each delivery must be counted or weighed, and the quality and price of each item must be verified. Finally, after the verification process is completed, the food is sent to the appropriate storage facility—dry storage, refrigerator, or freezer.

For example, assume the Steak Shack has placed an order for fifteen beef tenderloins, U.S. prime grade, weighing approximately eight pounds each, at a price of $9.60 per pound. When the delivery is received, it is necessary to verify that the beef is prime quality, that the invoice indicates a price of $9.60 per pound, and that the total weight for all fifteen pieces equals the weight shown on the invoice. Experienced receivers would also be certain to check other attributes listed in the purchase specifications, such as packaging, freshness, and thickness of fat cover, for example. If the delivered beef conforms to the order, it would be moved to refrigerated storage.

Should the delivery fail to conform to the order placed, there are likely to be problems in other parts of the operation that could have a negative impact on the success of the overall operation. For example, if the Steak Shack receives only twelve pieces of beef tenderloin, some customers may not be able to have filet mignon. Or if the beef is of a lower grade, the steaks will be less acceptable to customers, and the reputation of the restaurant may be negatively affected. If the invoice price is higher than quoted, the profit of the restaurant will be somewhat lower than anticipated.

The receiving procedure must be able to determine that items ordered are received at the quoted prices, and it must provide for ways to make the necessary adjustments when incorrect items have been sent to the restaurant.

▶ Storing

The third important step in food and beverage operations is storage of purchased items. The procedure for storing must satisfy four primary goals:

1. Ensuring the security of purchased materials
2. Preserving the quality of those materials
3. Providing ready access to available materials
4. Facilitating the determination of quantities on hand

All purchases are stored in one of three places: food or beverage items that can be stored at room temperature should be placed in dry storage areas; those items that require chilling should be placed in refrigerators; and frozen foods should be stored in freezers. All storage areas should be locked to prevent **pilferage**—an industry term for theft—and it is essential that the storing procedure make provision for safeguarding all food and beverage supplies. Pilferage is a major cause of unwarranted costs and must be prevented.

The storage procedure must also ensure that the quality of supplies is maintained. Therefore, to preserve quality, rooms used for dry storage should be maintained at reasonable levels of temperature and humidity; if either or both become excessive, the shelf life of all foods and some beverages will be negatively affected. Refrigerators must operate at the proper temperatures—33 to 40 degrees Fahrenheit for chilled foods and slightly higher (45 degrees Fahrenheit) for draft beers. Frozen foods belong in freezers that maintain temperatures of 10 degrees below zero Fahrenheit.

Another consideration in preserving the quality of food items is the potential for odors and flavors from some food products to affect other foods stored nearby, particularly if foods are improperly wrapped or covered. In the Mountain Bank staff dining room, employees of Marecki Foods store eggs and other dairy products in a different refrigerator from that used for fish, because these products would take on the odors of the fish very quickly.

One final consideration in preserving the quality of food in storage is taking all necessary steps to see that foods in dry storage are secure from contamination by rodents and other vermin. The manager of the Steak Shack, for example, must be careful to see that any items in bags

The third important step in food and beverage operations is storing purchased items. Milk and other dairy products are commonly stored in walk-in refrigerators such as the one pictured here. (Photo courtesy of InterMetro Industries.)

and boxes are carefully protected from invasion by these perennial pests.

Providing ready access to stored food and beverage supplies is another key aim of the procedure for storing. When a food or beverage item is needed from storage, it is clearly important that the storage facility be organized so that items can be obtained quickly and easily.

In most establishments, items are stored by category. In a food storage facility, canned fruits are stored together; so are meats. In beverage storage, spirits are stored together: the scotch whiskeys, for example, are separated from the ryes and the bourbons. Each item has a predetermined location, and supplies are placed in these locations after they have been properly received. When an item is needed, an employee familiar with the storage facility goes to the location of the needed item and gets the desired quantity. Thus, the owner of the Frog's Pub can quickly and easily obtain a bottle of dry gin to replace one that has just been emptied at the bar.

When all stored items are kept in predetermined locations, it is easier to assess the quantity on hand of any food or beverage item and to make a judgment about whether to place an order for an additional quantity on any given day. Thus, the procedure for purchasing is closely linked to that for storing: it is necessary to obtain accurate data from the storage procedure concerning quantity on hand if the purchasing procedure is to function properly.

▶ Issuing

The fourth important step in food and beverage operations is issuing. The procedures for issuing are designed to insure that materials for production are released to authorized personnel (a) in the correct quantities, and (b) at suitable times. These goals can be accomplished in any of several ways. For example, the owner of the Steak Shack may limit access to food storage to the chef, who would then be the only individual with keys. Another possibility is to have one employee whose workstation is the food storage area and who gives supplies only to those requesting them on special forms bearing the chef's signature.

If accurate records of issues are maintained by employees of Marecki Foods (on paper forms or by some other means), these records may provide data that can be useful in other parts of the operation. With data from both the receiving procedure about goods received and from the issuing procedure about goods issued, methods can readily be devised for maintaining perpetual inventories of goods. The value of the inventory at any given time, the cost of the foods or beverages issued, and considerable additional information can also be determined.

► Producing

The fifth important step in food and beverage operations is producing, or production, as it is better known. Production has four primary goals for producing food products and beverage products: these goals are that the products are produced

1. in suitable quantities,
2. of appropriate quality,
3. in a timely manner, and
4. with minimal waste.

The production of a menu of food or beverage products is a complex business. Some items are very simple to prepare—merely placing bottles of beer in a refrigerator to chill or arranging portion-packs of breakfast cereals on a breakfast buffet. Others are equally simple, but most require additional preparation and sometimes quite extensive preparation. The extent of this varies from item to item and from one establishment to another.

Every establishment does some daily preparation before opening for business. For example, the owner/operator of a simple hamburger

The production of a menu of food products is a complex task. The last step, pictured here, is plating the finished product to delight the eye and palate of the customer. (Photo courtesy of Four Seasons.)

stand must do some basic work before he can produce hamburgers: he moves several boxes of frozen hamburger patties from a freezer to a convenient location next to the grill and then places a corresponding number of packaged sliced rolls nearby. Both hamburger patties and rolls must be handy when the stand opens and customers begin to order hamburgers. He may even open several packages of rolls and place a few open rolls on plates just before opening. If this basic work is not done, service will be very slow, and both sales levels and revenues are likely to be lower than desired.

In the Steak Shack, prime ribs of beef and baked potatoes must be cooked ahead of time because of the length of time the cooking process requires. The steaks must be portioned in advance because these items should be ready for broiling when customers' orders reach the kitchen. Similarly, the chef in the Mountain Bank staff dining room prepares the tuna salad for sandwiches before the lunch hour begins. At Frog's Pub, the bartender cuts pieces of lemon peel and sections of lime as garnishes for drinks, then fills several bar containers with ice from the kitchen and places opened bottles of various spirits and mixers in predetermined, easy-to-reach wells located under the bar. Employees producing food or beverage products do such work in advance so that guests may be served quickly and efficiently.

Many food and beverage employees commonly describe this as preparing their ***mise en place,*** a French culinary term that means having everything in place. Thus, with the *mise en place* ready, the bartender in Frog's Pub and the chef in the Mountain Bank staff dining room are ready to serve customers the foods and drinks of their choice without any unnecessary delay.

A significant problem with many food items is determining the quantities to prepare in advance. The proper quantity of any item is that amount that will enable the establishment to serve the item to each customer who orders it without delay and without leftovers at the close of business. Ideally, the last portion of any item prepared for any given day will be served just as the establishment is about to close for the day.

At best, this is very difficult. Most would say it is next to impossible. Chefs normally do not know the precise number of customers who will order a given menu item. Without a precise number, they are likely to prepare too much or too little. If too little is prepared, some potential customers will be disappointed, and sales revenues may be less than would otherwise have been possible. If too much is prepared, unsold quantities may be unusable for their originally intended purposes. For example, the chef in the Steak Shack must prepare roast prime ribs of beef in advance. If too much is cooked, it is difficult to use the remaining amount the next day, and if too little is cooked, some customers will be disappointed when told that none is left. Unless the chef can find some suitable alternative use for the leftover beef, it may go unused, then spoil, and be discarded.

Because of their need to set production targets in advance, many foodservice operators have incorporated into their production procedures some useful devices adapted from the manufacturing sector. These are **sales histories** and **production sheets.**

Sales Histories

As the name implies, sales histories are records of the number of customers served during past periods and the number of portions sold of each menu item. Some establishments maintain records of portion sales by day of the week, whereas others find alternative approaches preferable. The data may be obtained from a cash register that keeps track of items sold, a computerized management program, or by manual means.

A sales history should include additional important information, such as inclement weather and out-of-the-ordinary events such as holidays, strikes, special sales in nearby stores, or nearby road construction. Any data that will shed light on the sales records for a given meal, day, or other period should be included.

It has often been said that the best indicator of future human behavior is past human behavior. Thus, the sales history for a given establishment will provide the foodservice operator with some rational basis for predicting the total number of customers likely to patronize the establishment on a given day and for making some reasonable assumptions about which menu items they are likely to order. The collection of such assumptions for a given day becomes the basis for judgments about the quantities of particular menu items to prepare for the day.

Production Sheets

A production sheet is a list of menu items that will be prepared for a specific day or meal period, along with the amount of each item for production personnel to prepare. Some production sheets will also indicate particular recipes to be used in preparation.

The initial entries on a production sheet are normally made by a foodservice manager after the sales history has been reviewed and evaluated. When completed, the form is given to the kitchen staff as a work plan for the day. It provides cooks with essential information for them to do their work.

In both food production and beverage production, product quality and cost are established by means of the recipes selected for cooks and bartenders to use in preparing food and drinks. The recipes are normally selected with great care, after comparing a number of similar recipes. The recipe selected for the preparation of any food or beverage is that which management believes will produce a desirable product at a satisfactory cost. It must be of suitable quality and be acceptable to customers. The recipe finally selected for producing a given menu item is known as a **standard recipe.**

Standard Recipes

The standard recipe is a recipe that has been established as the correct recipe to use each time a given item is prepared. This is a very important element in production procedure. Standard recipes insure that menu items will be prepared the same way each time, using the same ingredients, proportions, and methods. This provides consistent quality and does so at a cost that can be planned in advance.

Many menu items for food or beverages can be prepared several different ways. Each variation results in a product of different quality, taste, and cost. Yet each of these products could be listed on a menu by the same name. For example, a seafood Newburg can be prepared using many expensive ingredients, such as lobster, shrimp, and scallops, or it can be done cheaply, using inexpensive fish with very little of the more expensive ingredients. In the first instance, the cost and quality will obviously be higher than will the latter. It is very important for managers to determine which shall be the standard recipe for each item produced. In establishments that use standard recipes, customers can reasonably expect the same quality food and drinks, which taste the same every time they come to the establishment.

▶ Selling

The sixth important step in a food and beverage operation is selling, or sales, as it is better known. One of the principal aims of selling food and beverage products is maximizing customer satisfaction. In such not-for-profit establishments as the Mountain Bank staff dining room, this is likely to be the sole purpose of selling menu items. In the Steak

Shack, Frog's Pub, and other profit-oriented enterprises, selling has a second goal: to maximize revenue.

The difference between the goals of the selling in these two types of establishments has to do with the difference between the noncommercial goals of one type of enterprise and the commercial goals of the other. Therefore, two possible goals of selling are to maximize customer satisfaction and revenues.

To help sell food and beverage products, food and beverage operators often use

A. sales-oriented menus,
B. visual sales materials, and
C. personal selling.

▶ A. Sales-Oriented Menus

A **menu** is a list of the items offered for sale in a food or beverage enterprise. Food menus normally list these items by category and in the same sequence in which they are customarily ordered. A dinner menu for a restaurant such as the Steak Shack would list appetizers first, followed by soups, salads, entrees, vegetables, desserts, and the usual nonalcoholic beverage accompaniments for meals: coffee, tea, and milk. By contrast, beverage menus normally list contents by category alone. Typical categories include aperitifs, cocktails, spirits, wines, beers and ales, cordials, and dessert wines.

A good menu, however, is much more than a simple list of food or beverage items for sale. It is a sales tool that will influence customers' orders and the dollar amounts they spend. Menus are carefully designed to be attractive and are written in language intended to promote sales. Some menus give special emphasis to the items that yield the greatest profit per sale.

Developing successful menus is a complex process. Many food and beverage operators use professional consultants, whose many years of experience are of invaluable assistance in preparing this important sales aid. Some of the important considerations in menu making are

1. selecting which food/beverage items to include,
2. determining the best location for each category/item,
3. writing sales-oriented item descriptions, and
4. making numerous art and design decisions.

Appetizers

CHEESE CRISP!
Fried tortilla covered with melted cheese.
3.75

DELUXE QUESADILLA
Two flour tortillas filled with melted cheese and topped with tomatoes, onions, guacamole and sour cream.
5.50

GUACAMOLE DIP
With chips.
3.75

MEXICAN PIZZA
Fried flour tortilla topped with beans, beef, cheese, tomatoes, onions, guacamole and sour cream.
5.50

NACHOS
Chips covered with Cheddar cheese.
3.95

SUPER NACHOS
Chips with Cheddar cheese, beans, beef or chicken, tomatoes, onions, guacamole and sour cream.
5.50

Las Tostadas

A tostada is a deep-fried corn tortilla topped with beans and meat, lettuce, cheese and tomato.

REFRIED BEAN TOSTADA
3.75

REFRIED BEAN & BEEF TOSTADA
4.00

WHOLE PINTO BEAN TOSTADA
(No fat.)
3.75

REFRIED BEAN & CHICKEN TOSTADA
4.25

REFRIED BEAN & PICADILLO TOSTADA
4.25

For Avocado-Style (sour cream and avocado slices), add 1.25.

For Deluxe (sour cream and guacamole), add 1.25.

Las Ensaladas

Our taco salad is prepared in a bowl-shaped, deep-fried tortilla. It consists of your choice of meat, lettuce, cheese and tomato.

GROUND BEEF TACO SALAD
4.50

CHICKEN TACO SALAD
4.65

PICADILLO TACO SALAD
4.65
For Deluxe (sour cream and guacamole), add 1.25.

RIO BRAVO PETITE CALORIE SALAD
Whole pinto beans, lettuce, green peppers, onions, tomato and your choice of pico de gallo salsa or low-cal dressing.
4.25

With broiled chicken pieces, add 1.00.

Sopa
(Soup)

ALBONDIGAS
A delicious Mexican soup made with pork meatballs, vegetables and mint. Served with your choice of flour or corn tortillas.
Bowl 4.50   Cup 2.00

Las Enchiladas

An enchilada consists of a soft corn tortilla that is stuffed with cheese, beans or meat, rolled and smothered in a thick tomato sauce and topped with melted cheese.

DELUXE CHEESE ENCHILADA
4.15

DELUXE REFRIED BEAN ENCHILADA
4.15

DELUXE WHOLE PINTO BEAN ENCHILADA
(No fat.)
4.15

DELUXE GROUND BEEF ENCHILADA
4.15

DELUXE CHICKEN OR PICADILLO ENCHILADA
4.55

With rice, add .95.

Dinner Combinations

All combinations come with rice, beans and a filling choice of cheese, beef, chicken or picadillo.

SMALL 6.95		LARGE 7.95
1. One Enchilada and One Taco	8. One Deluxe Tostada with Guacamole and Sour Cream	15. Two Burritos (your choice of beans, beef, pork, chorizo, chicken or picadillo)
2. One Meat-Filled Chile Relleno with Guacamole and Two Tortillas	9. Three Huevos Rancheros and Two Tortillas	16. One Enchilada and One Chalupa
3. One Enchilada and One Tostada	10. One Enchilada and One Meat-Filled Chile Relleno	17. One Enchilada, One Taco and One Meat-Filled Chile Relleno
4. One Burrito (your choice of beans, beef, pork, chorizo, chicken or picadillo).	11. Chorizo con Huevos and Two Tortillas	18. One Enchilada, One Taco and One Tamale
5. One Chalupa	12. Two Enchiladas	19. One Enchilada and One Avocado Tostada with Sliced Avocado and Sour Cream
6. One Chimi-changa with Guacamole and Sour Cream	13. Two Tacos	20. One Enchilada, One Tamale and One Meat-Filled Chile Relleno
7. One Avocado Tostada with Sliced Avocado and Sour Cream	14. One Enchilada and One Tamale	21. Two Tacos and One Enchilada
		22. One Enchilada, One Taco and One Tostada
		23. One Burrito and One Enchilada

Los Burritos

A burrito is a soft flour tortilla stuffed with beans or meat that is smothered in a clear red tomato sauce.

WHOLE PINTO BEAN BURRITO
(No fat.)
3.25

REFRIED BEAN BURRITO
3.25

GROUND BEEF BURRITO
4.50

CHORIZO BURRITO
4.50

CHICKEN BURRITO
4.50

PORK BURRITO
4.50

COLORADO BURRITO
4.50

DELUXE BURRITO
Filled with your choice of meat, rice or beans, then topped with guacamole, tomatoes, onions, Parmesan cheese, and our special sauce.
5.95

AZADA BURRITO AL PANCHO
A soft flour tortilla stuffed with thin sliced flank steak, beans, onions and tomatoes, then brushed with guacamole and sour cream and dusted with Parmesan cheese.
7.25

A good menu is much more than a simple list of food or beverage items for sale. It is a sales tool that will influence customers' orders and the dollar amounts they spend.

Customers tend to read menus from top to bottom and from left to right. Thus, a one-page menu should list appetizers at the top and desserts and beverages near the bottom. Two-page menus tend to list appetizers at the top of the first page, followed by soups, salads, entrees, and any other items in sequence, carrying over to the second page.

Since the menu is a critical factor in any food and beverage operation, it will be useful to present and discuss seven principal considerations in menu development. These are

1. Product suitability
2. Product variety
3. Ingredient availability
4. Staff time and capability
5. Equipment capacity
6. Product salability
7. Item profitability

Product Suitability

This consideration refers to the need to see that each item on a menu is suitable for the clientele, the time of day, and the season of the year. One assumes, of course, that a feasibility study and other preliminary work has established an acceptable concept for an intended market and that the question of product suitability has thus been addressed. Beyond that, it is necessary to refine the list of items offered, according to time of day and season. Breakfast items, after all, are normally quite different from dinner items. Less obviously, such items as hearty beef stew and warm apple pie are likely to be more popular on winter rather than summer menus.

Product Variety

To obtain the broadest appeal, menus should include a sufficient variety of items to attract the greatest possible number of customers. The extent of the variety required to do this will vary from establishment to establishment. Even a specialty restaurant will usually have some variety within its specialty. It will also have some items on its menu outside of the specialty, so that those who do not care for the specialty items will have alternatives. Even units in the nationwide hamburger chains, which formerly sold only hamburgers, now have such other items as chicken, pizza, fish, and salad.

Ingredient Availability

All restaurants must limit their menu items to those that are available in the marketplace. It is true that most menu items are available year round, but during parts of the year, some fresh vegetables and fruits either are not available, are available in limited quantities or at very high prices, or are of inferior quality. For example, in New England, fresh corn is unavailable in January, and during that month, blueberries are available only at very high market prices because they must be imported from other countries. During some periods, the only tomatoes available at reasonable prices come from hothouses, and their quality is inferior to those available during the normal growing season.

Staff Time and Capability

Because of the high cost of skilled labor, many restaurants employ cooks whose training and skill are limited. In such instances, management would be wise to avoid offering menu items requiring special skills to prepare. Management must be careful to choose items that the kitchen personnel can prepare within the limits of their skill. Similarly, if staff members have the requisite skills but cannot prepare a given item within the space of time available, it is best to leave it off the menu.

Equipment Capability

Although establishing the food product list makes it possible to select the equipment for an establishment, the equipment selected serves to limit the items that can be included on a menu (see chap. 5). In fact, available equipment often determines which of the specific items from the complete list will actually be offered at any one time. For example, a kitchen with one deep-fat fryer would be unable to produce french fries, deep-fried chicken, and deep-fried fish during the course of one meal. The reason for this is that the fat will transfer odors and flavors from one item to another, thus affecting the taste of all products cooked in it. Similarly, a kitchen having limited broiler space or oven space must be careful not to offer too many menu items at once that require the use of these pieces of equipment.

Product Salability

The location of items on a menu will greatly influence their sales appeal. Studies show that consumers who have not come to restaurants with particular menu items in mind tend to select the items that first catch their eye. Because of this, foodservice operators often emphasize menu items in such a way as to capture the customer's attention quickly and to sell the featured item. One way is to print these items in larger or bolder type. Another is to enclose the item in a box on the menu and position it in a place that customers will see first. On a one-page menu, this is typically in the upper center, where customers' eyes usually focus first.

Other studies have shown that customers tend to purchase items appearing at the top of a list more than those near the bottom. Thus, managers commonly list their most profitable items first or nearly first on the list of entrees, and they list those that are least profitable near the bottom.

Another useful sales technique employed by the operators of many chain restaurants is to display pictures of items on the menu. These may be either photographs or artists' renderings. Colorful and appealing, they tend to increase sales of the items pictured.

Most managers agree that as much time should be devoted to writing menu descriptions as might be spent writing an expensive advertisement to place in a newspaper or a magazine. Each item description should be thought of as an advertisement; if the description makes the item sound appetizing, it will increase sales. After all, it is more probable that a customer will order a "U.S. Prime filet mignon: eight ounces of America's finest beef, broiled to perfection the way you want it done, then topped with a giant mushroom cap and served sizzling on one of our hot steak platters" over a simple menu listing of "broiled steak." Menu descriptions should always be honest and accurate and include information about method of cooking, major ingredients, and presentation. Menus are designed to tempt the appetite, and a customer should be able to visualize an item just by reading the menu description.

Item Profitability

In foodservice, one measure of profitability is the difference between the selling price of an item and its food cost—the cost of the ingredients in that item. The resulting figure can be called **item gross profit.** The item gross profits from all item sales in a given period go toward meeting other costs of operation for that period, including labor costs, rent, and insurance. If the sum of the item gross profits for a period are greater than these other costs, the operation has earned a profit for that period. If the costs are greater, a loss results.

▶ **The Ten Commandments for Menu Success** ◀

A recent article by Allen H. Kelson, a prominent consultant and restaurant critic, suggests ten commandments for menu success.

1. Speak Plainly—Don't go overboard with obscure terminology.
2. Say What's Important—If the dish has strong flavors, say so. If the dish is fried, or the soup is creamed, say so.
3. Describe It Completely—Don't just say what it is, describe it.
4. Remember: "Less Is More"—Don't itemize every ingredient. Speak only of those ingredients whose presence is significant to flavor and value.
5. Don't Be Afraid to Be Descriptive—Use appealing modifiers like *crispy, crunchy, drizzled, scented,* and others.
6. Maintain a Sense of Perspective—A menu that recommends everything recommends nothing. Don't try to give every item preferential treatment.
7. Say It Correctly—If it contains sweet and sour onions, don't call it "onion marmalade."
8. Spell It Properly—Customers might ask, if you can't spell it properly, how can you make it correctly?
9. Punctuate Intelligently—Hyphenate compound words properly: hot-pepper soup, not hot pepper soup. Use commas properly.
10. Follow Rules of Good Typography—Don't gimmick-up your menu with too many typefaces. Choose ink and paper sizes that allow good legibility. Don't isolate prices on the right margin; that makes them too obvious. Group ingredients sensibly; the menu that reads,"wood burning oven roasted whole fish baked with lemon and thyme" is not as good as, "wood-roasted whole fish with lemon and thyme."

Adapted from Restaurant Hospitality, *July 1994, Pages 103–105.*

In general, it is advisable to price menu offerings at levels that will ensure suitable item gross profits. By doing so, managers ensure the profitability of each individual item. Then, provided the establishment sells a sufficient number of portions of each item, management may achieve its financial goal for the period. In commercial operations, the financial goal is usually profit; in not-for-profit operations, it is more likely to be simply meeting all expenses for the period. If it is not possible to price a menu item accordingly and still sell an acceptable quantity of it, the item should probably be removed from the menu.

There is no more important selling device in any foodservice operation than its menu. A good menu requires considerable time and effort to produce but is well worth it. Menu development is an interesting combination of art and science and clearly one of the keys to successful foodservice operation.

▶ B. Visual Sales Materials

In addition to the menu, there are other visual means for increasing food and beverage sales. Small signs, colorful pictures, tent cards, and other printed items for tables or counters can make customers aware of menu items that they might not otherwise have considered. Posters on walls or windows, visual displays of desserts on a cart, lobsters in tanks, or racks of wine bottles provide similar suggestions to customers.

Another useful approach is to use service techniques that draw the attention of customers to items being artistically prepared or served. In some very fine restaurants, the preparation at table side of such foods as Caesar salad, veal piccata, or cherries jubilee by thoroughly professional servers may provide visual suggestions to other diners. Similarly, sales can be influenced by skilled servers trained to carry attractive plates of food so that they are easily viewed by customers.

▶ C. Personal Selling

Personal selling requires that servers be trained to do more than simply take orders for food and beverage products. In turn, servers in a food or beverage enterprise are the sales force of the establishment and have the potential to influence the number of sales and the particular items sold. In the Steak Shack, servers who are properly trained can often sell appetizers, soups, wines, or desserts to customers who might otherwise order entrees alone. In addition, servers can influence customer choices by suggesting those items that provide higher profit.

Servers adept at personal selling are usually those who provide greater customer satisfaction. And satisfied customers who have enjoyed the food and beverages suggested by their servers typically leave larger tips—partially because they are satisfied and partially because their checks are higher. After all, tips are commonly calculated as percentages of customers' total checks.

▶ Serving

The seventh important step in a food and beverage operation is serving, or service, as it is better known. The goal of service is to deliver portions of food or drink to customers in a manner consistent with the objectives of the establishment. For some restaurant operators, the primary objective of service is to perform it as quickly as possible. Servers appear at the table promply to take orders, deliver the food to customers quickly after the order has been placed, and clear the table and present the check as soon as customers are finished with their meals. For fine restaurants, service objectives are considerably more complicated. Servers are expected to know the ingredients of menu items and how they are prepared. Service techniques are very important, and professionalism is a key element.

▶ Styles of Foodservice

There are a number of specific styles of service that professional foodservice managers should know. Each has specific characteristics, and each is more suited to achieve some goals than others. An operator must determine which one, if any, will best achieve the goals of the food or beverage facility. One can choose to adopt one of the styles of service identified below or to develop some hybrid based on these.

1. American service
2. Russian service
3. French service
4. English service
5. Cafeteria service
6. Buffet service
7. Takeout/delivery service
8. Room service

American Service

American service is characterized by food portioned and plated in the kitchen and carried by servers to diners. Virtually everyone has experienced some form of American service. In too many cases, it has come to mean simply transporting plated food from the kitchen to the dining room and placing the plates in front of diners in any manner that suits the server. Sometimes the food is served from the right, sometimes from the left, and occasionally from across the table. In some establishments, plates of food are even passed from one diner to another until they reach the individuals who have ordered them.

In the authors' view, none of these methods of delivering food should really be called American service. These are simply ways of transporting food expeditiously; it is similar to placing cartons of goods on a warehouse conveyor belt, and just about as inviting. True American service involves a great deal more than that.

In proper American service, plates of food are placed before diners from the left. To do this correctly, servers use their left hands. Beverages are served from the right with the right hand. Plates and glassware are removed from the right. When a course is removed, the flatware for that course is also removed, even if it has not been used. At the conclusion of the main meal, prior to coffee and dessert, all plates, glassware, and salt and pepper shakers are removed and the table is crumbed. Appropriate silver is served with dessert.

American service has the advantage of being relatively simple, and comparatively little training is required for servers to achieve proficiency.

Russian Service

Russian service is characterized by food arranged on serving platters in the kitchen for maximum eye appeal, then carried to a serving stand near the table. The server uses the right hand to place empty warm plates in front of each diner from the diner's right. The platter of food is shown to those at the table for visual effect, then transferred from serving platter to diners' plates. To do this, the server balances the platter on the left hand, then uses fork and spoon with the right hand to serve the food—which is done from the diner's left. Beverages are served from the right. All dishes, glassware, and flatware are removed from the right.

Russian service, sometimes mistakenly called French service, is used in many of the finer restaurants of Europe. It is elegant: food arrives at the table beautifully arranged on silver serving platters and is presented to diners prior to being transferred to their plates. It also has the advantage of facilitating the delivery of food at the correct serving temperature—a common problem with American service. The serving

Restaurants adopt one or another of several specific styles of service, some of which are quite complex. Pictured is service in the Russian style, courtesy of The Manor in West Orange, New Jersey, one of the finest restaurants in the New York metropolitan area. (Photo courtesy of The Manor, West Orange, New Jersey.)

platters are very warm, and the plates set in front of diners are also warm. Both contribute to maintaining the proper temperature for the food ordered. Russian service is particularly well suited for serving soups, which come to the table in hot tureens and are served into warm bowls.

A variation on Russian service is often used at large banquets. Servers wearing white gloves will carry large silver serving trays, each of which will be used for a single menu item—filet mignon, for example. A server will proceed around a table placing single portions of meat before diners on plates previously set in place. That server will be followed by others who have food to accompany the meat—potatoes and vegetables, most commonly. In this fashion, large numbers of people can be served very quickly with both elegance and grace.

French Service

The most expensive and most elegant service used in restaurants is **French service.** It is sometimes called **gueridon** service, named after the specially equipped cart or trolley on which food is transported from kitchen to dining room. A gueridon is equipped with a gas burner for table-side cooking.

French service usually requires a staff of four.

The *chef de rang* is in charge of the service staff. A *chef de rang* takes diners' orders, supervises the service, finishes the preparation of some foods on the gueridon at table side, and attends to any carving, slicing, or boning of meat, fish, or poultry.

The *demi chef de rang*, who assists the *chef de rang*, takes drink orders, and serves food under the *chef de rang*'s direction.

The *commis de rang* is a waiter in training who will serve some items, clear the tables, and perform other duties as directed.

The *commis de suite* takes orders to the kitchen and brings food from the kitchen on the gueridon. She assists in clearing tables and performs other duties as needed.

In French service, the gueridon is wheeled to a position close to the diners' table and is used by the *chef de rang* to complete the cooking of food. He expertly carves or slices the meat, fish, or poultry, then places the food on plates. It is served from the diners' right. Beverages are also served from the right, and all plates and glassware are removed from the right. One can appreciate the great expense, skill, and time required to perform this kind of service. For that reason, it is used only in the most expensive restaurants.

Additionally, French service requires more square feet of floor space per seat than other types of dining room service. Aisles must be wider than normal to accommodate the gueridon, and tables must be placed farther apart than normal to provide room for the *chef de rang* to finish the preparation of the food.

French service takes a considerable amount of time compared with other forms of service. For that reason, establishments that use it must charge high prices to compensate for the relatively fewer number of customers they can serve in the course of a meal period.

English Service

English service is seldom if ever used in restaurants. It would only be used in those few private homes that employ a staff of servants, or in one of a select few catering establishments. English service is often thought of as "host" service, because the main entree—a roast of beef or lamb, or a turkey, for example—is placed in front of the host, who carves and plates it at the head of the table. A server then takes each plate and sets it in front of the diner from the diner's right. Beverages are also served from the right. Vegetables, potatoes, and other foods are either put on plates from a side stand prior to service or passed from one diner to the next in bowls—family style. All dishes and glassware are removed from the right. As with American service, the table is cleared of flatware, glassware, and salt and pepper, and the table is crumbed prior to dessert.

Cafeteria Service

Cafeteria service is characterized by prepared foods displayed so that customers can view the array of offerings prior to making selections. Hot foods are in warmers and cold foods are packed in ice or stored in reach-through refrigerators. Many foods are preplated for the convenience of diners selecting those items. Diners typically have trays and proceed to the area where the kinds of foods they want are displayed. If a customer wants a sandwich, she goes to the area where the prepared and wrapped sandwiches are displayed and takes one. If a customer wants a hot entree, she goes to the area where hot entrees are displayed, and a server plates the item selected by the customer. Each item is usually priced separately. After the customer finishes making selections, she proceeds to a cashier who adds and totals the prices of all items selected. The customer pays the cashier and takes the tray to a table.

Variations of this procedure are common. In some cafeterias, customers receive a bill at the cashier's station but do not pay until they exit the restaurant. In others, employees may carry customers' trays to tables.

There are several types of cafeteria service. They are

1. Straight line
2. By-pass line
3. Shopping center

Straight Line. As the name suggests, in straight line service, customers follow one another along a long line of displayed foods. Each customer reaches the cashier in turn, at the end of the display. This form of service is perhaps the easiest to set up but has the disadvantage of providing the slowest service. The speed of the line matches that of the slowest customer.

By-Pass Line. To speed up service, many cafeterias have established by-pass lines. These enable customers to skip a section of the cafeteria line and proceed to the section where the foods they wish to buy are displayed. For example, many cafeterias have separate sections for salads and hot items. Customers who want only salads go to that section of the display, select their salads, and get back in line at a point beyond the hot food section. Those seeking hot foods go to the hot food section, make their selections, then proceed to the cashier.

There are several variations on the by-pass line. One variation resembles the teeth in a saw, with foods displayed on counters that are at angles to one another. Another variation has recessed sections in the line, so that individuals who do not want any foods in the recessed section pass it by, proceeding to another part of the line.

Shopping Center. The shopping center approach is to arrange foods by type at islands—freestanding stations. It eliminates the appearance of a single line. Customers take trays to the specific stations containing the foods they wish to buy, make their selections, then proceed to a cashier to pay. This approach is becoming increasingly popular, particularly in establishments where many customers arrive at one time.

Cafeteria service has several advantages over table service. Customers can obtain their food selections quickly and consume their meals in a very short time. Large numbers of people can be served very quickly in a cafeteria setting. Customers can select whatever they wish—anything from a full meal to a cup of coffee. There is no pressure to take a great amount of food, although the better cafeterias have very attractive displays, and frequently customers will take more food than they intended because it looks so appealing. Since customers serve themselves, they typically do not have to tip servers.

Cafeterias also make it possible for people with limited incomes to eat out more frequently. They are particularly popular in the southern part of the United States, where a large number of retired people are on limited budgets, and in schools where large numbers of students must be served at one time.

Buffet Service

Buffet service differs from cafeteria service in several ways. Trays are not used: customers take plates and proceed to select and place on their plates foods displayed on the buffet. Items on the buffet are not individually priced: there is one fixed price for the meal regardless of the items selected or the quantities of food taken by customers.

Restaurants often use buffet service, either for such functions as wedding receptions or for specific meals—breakfast or Sunday brunch, for example. Buffet service is sometimes used in restaurants as the primary means of serving food. This type of service has the advantage of minimizing the service staff required and offering faster service. Because diners do not have to study menus, wait for a server to take the order, and wait for food to be prepared and delivered, it can be much faster than table service. Patrons merely go to the buffet when they are ready, make their selections, and return to their tables to eat the food selected. One disadvantage is that management has less control over the amount of food consumed. Typically, customers help themselves and can normally go back to the buffet as many times as they like.

Many hotels and restaurants schedule buffets frequently to use up excess food. After all, buffets typically do not have set menus, except for a few specific items, and this allows the chef considerable latitude to prepare many different items and to use up leftovers.

Takeout and Delivery Services

Takeout and delivery services are becoming increasingly popular. These forms of service are characterized by food being consumed off premises. In many establishments, customers are given a choice of coming to the establishment to pick up food or of having it delivered to their homes or offices. Many restaurants offer takeout or delivery services, or both of these, in addition to their regular table service. Although there may be some extra cost to the establishment associated with packaging foods for consumption off premises, takeout and delivery services effectively increase the sales capacity of the establishment without necessitating an increase in its physical size.

Perhaps the most popular types of takeout and delivery establishments are those associated with common ethnic foods, such as Chinese food and pizza. Many of the foodservice establishments featuring these foods do not even have seating for customers. Because of this, they find it possible to operate in relatively small quarters and thus keep their operating costs to a minimum.

Room Service

Although **room service** is most commonly associated with hotels, hospitals also provide room service for their patients. This type of service differs from others in one major way: food is moved to and served in the room of the guest or patient.

Room service is not classified as takeout or delivery service. The food does not leave the premises, and it is served in a guest's or patient's room rather than in a traditional dining facility. This type of service is particularly labor intensive, typically requiring a greater number of servers per meal than other forms of service. In hotels offering room service on a twenty-four hour schedule, both kitchen and service staff must be on hand to prepare room service orders when the dining room is normally closed. Hotels charge higher prices for items on the room service menu than for equivalent items served in traditional dining rooms. Although they charge higher menu prices, however, hotels often lose money on room service, offering it merely as an accommodation to guests. The higher labor costs associated with room service commonly make it unprofitable.

▶ Styles of Beverage Service

The term *beverage* has previously been defined as those alcoholic and nonalcoholic drinks typically prepared by bartenders rather than the items listed as beverages on food menus—coffee, tea, and milk, among them. As indicated in the previous chapter, three types of bars are used in beverage operations: front bars, service bars, and special-purpose bars.

At front bars, drinks are normally served to customers seated at the bar by a bartender. If there are tables or booths for customers in the bar area, there are three common approaches to service. One is to employ a server and to have a service bar, which may be one small section of the front bar, commonly at the end of the bar. A second is to require the bartender to act as a server, going to the tables to take orders and serve drinks. The third is to require customers to place drink orders at the front bar, then to carry their own drinks to the tables. By contrast, service bars, as the term implies, provide servers with the equipment necessary to take drink orders and serve drinks. At special-purpose bars, customers act as servers, placing drink orders with bartenders and carrying their drinks from the bar.

In planning beverage service, it is necessary to consider what purpose a bar or bars will serve in the establishment. In some establishments, managers consciously decide to restrict beverage service to a service bar located in the kitchen. Some do this because they do not like the physical appearance of a front bar in the establishment. Others do it to reduce the noise level in an establishment: bars are typically noisy. Still others do it to discourage patronage by those who would be interested only in sitting at a front bar. In contrast, some restaurant operators elect to have both front bars and service bars. This arrangement makes it possible to provide beverage service in the dining room without placing unreasonable demands on the front bar and also to use the front bar as a holding area for customers who are waiting to be seated. Many of these establishments provide tables in the front bar area to facilitate its use as both cocktail lounge and waiting area for diners. Other establishments having side rooms that can be used to accommodate groups for functions often use special-purpose bars to serve the guests attending these functions. Some, in fact, have a front bar, a service bar, and special-purpose bars, the number of which is limited only by the number of functions that can be accommodated at one time.

It is important to note that laws regarding service of alcoholic beverages vary from state to state. In several states, for example, drinks must be served to customers by servers, which makes it illegal for customers to carry drinks from front bars to their tables. In these states, it is clearly illegal to set up special-purpose bars where customers or guests can place drink orders and carry drinks elsewhere to consume.

Another consideration in planning beverage service is the type of service that will be used for wines served to guests in a dining room. Essentially, wines are the fermented juices of fruits—grapes, principally, although there are some exceptions. There are three types of wines: sparkling, still, and fortified.

Still wines are those that do not continue to ferment after the wine is bottled. Cabernet sauvignon and Chablis are two of the better-known still wines. **Sparkling wines** are those in which the fermentation process continues after bottling. This produces the carbon dioxide that gives sparkling wines their characteristic "fizziness." Champagne is the best known of the sparkling wines. **Fortified wines** are still wines to which brandy has been added, thus increasing the alcoholic content. Sherry is among the best-known fortified wines.

Proper planning for beverage service requires knowledge of the techniques for serving wines. These are described as follows.

Still Wines

Still wines may be sold by the glass or by the bottle. The finer the wine, the more likely it is to be sold by the bottle. When wine is sold by the bottle, the following is a commonly used serving procedure.

After taking the order, the server brings the wine to the table and presents it for approval to the guest who placed the order. The server holds the bottle in a manner that facilitates inspection of the label. When approved, the bottle is opened, which normally entails removing the cork with a corkscrew. The cork is inspected by the server to be sure that it is moist and that its odor indicates a good wine—one that has not gone bad. The cork is then presented to the guest for inspection. Next, a small amount of the wine is poured in the guest's glass to be examined for clarity, color, and aroma. If these are satisfactory, the guest sips the wine. If the taste is satisfactory, the guest approves the wine and the server pours for those at the table who will be drinking it. If the bottle is not empty, the server leaves it on or near the table for refilling glasses later in the meal.

Sparkling Wines

Sparkling wines are not normally sold by the glass because opened bottles lose their effervescent character. When they are sold by the bottle, service technique is essentially the same as that for still wines. The major exception is in the removal of the cork, which never entails the use of a corkscrew: the corks in bottles of sparkling wine are removed by hand, very carefully, to prevent the cork from being projected some distance by the pressure in the bottle. As the cork is removed, it produces the "pop" that is characteristic of sparkling wines.

Fortified Wines

Fortified wines are not normally sold by the bottle. They are sold by the glass and poured at the bar by a bartender.

As you learned in chapter 5, it is important in planning food or beverage operations to determine in advance the type of foodservice and beverage service that will be offered so that equipment and space needs can be factored into the planning.

Because the goals of the Steak Shack, the Mountain Bank staff dining room, and Frog's Pub are quite different from one another, they have established different procedures for serving customers.

Service in the Steak Shack is typical of that found in many American restaurants. At the Steak Shack, once customers are seated, servers appear promptly to suggest drinks and distribute menus. Dinner orders are taken when drinks are served, with appetizers, soups, and dinner wines being suggested by the servers. After the entrees, servers present dessert menus and suggest after-dinner drinks. Dishes are cleared by the server, who takes them to the kitchen. Checks are placed on tables as soon as the last items are served, and customers are asked to pay the cashier as they leave.

By contrast, employees of the Mountain Bank pay as they enter the staff dining room and then serve themselves by selecting from the array of food displayed. One person is employed to clean the tables. Marecki Foods has chosen this method of serving to meet the bank's objective of quick, efficient service within the planned meal periods.

In Frog's Pub, the primary emphasis is on beverages rather than food. Customers choosing tables can either obtain their own drinks quickly from a bartender and carry the drinks to tables or wait to order from a server. Customers at tables order food from servers; those seated at the bar order food and drinks from a bartender. At lunch, extra servers are on duty to provide very fast foodservice. The servers are responsible for clearing all tables.

In all three establishments, washing dishes, glasses, and flatware is an important adjunct to the serving procedure. Dirty dishes, glasses, and utensils are returned to the kitchen, separated into appropriate racks, then sent through a dishwashing machine. When clean, they are placed where needed to serve additional customers: clean dishes in the food preparation areas, glasses at the bar, and flatware in the dining room.

The Interdependence of Food and Beverage Elements

All steps of a food or beverage operation must work well together if the goals of the operation are to be achieved. When preparing and serving portions of any food or beverage product, purchasing and receiving must work together to provide the necessary materials. If they do not, unfortunate consequences may result. For example, the kitchen might be unable to prepare the proper quantity of food or beverage products or to prepare products of the proper quality. This, in turn, could result in customer dissatisfaction, loss of revenue, or both. Similarly, if spoilage and theft are not prevented while materials are in storage, there could be problems. In production, for example, this could result in an inability to produce the required products because of inadequate supply of the necessary ingredients. If production does not turn out the necessary menu items at appropriate levels of quality and cost, sales goals may not be met and profits will suffer. If sales volume is lower than planned, materials purchased in quantities suitable for the planned higher levels of sales may spoil, leading to unanticipated costs. For the basic steps to work together in some coordinated way, effective management is necessary.

While management of the basic operational steps discussed in this chapter is clearly one requirement of successful operation, there are many other requirements as well, such as promoting sales in the establishment through advertising and other means, preparing and following budgets, and training members of staff to do their jobs correctly. These will be addressed in chapter 10.

▶ Summary

In this chapter, food and beverage operations are examined in detail. The steps of food and beverage operations—purchasing, receiving, storing, issuing, producing, selling, and serving—are identified, and the necessary procedures for preparing and serving portions of food and beverages are examined. Procedures for each of these food and beverage steps are illustrated in terms of the three case studies introduced in chapter 5: the Steak Shack, the Mountain Bank staff dining room, and Frog's Pub. Finally, the way in which these steps are interrelated is emphasized and offered as a basis for understanding the complexity of food and beverage operations.

American Service	Perishables
Beverage	Pilferage
Buffet Service	Production Sheet
Cafeteria Service	Room Service
English Service	Russian Service
Fortified Wine	Sales History
French Service	Sparkling Wine
Gueridon	Standard Purchase Specifications
Item Gross Profit	Standard Recipe
Menu	Still Wine
Mise en place	Takeout/Delivery Service
Nonperishables	

1. Define each of the following terms:
   a. *procedure*
   b. *perishable*
   c. *nonperishable*
   d. *sales history*
   e. *production sheet*

      f. *standard recipe*

      g. *beverage*

2. Identify the seven basic steps that all foodservice operations have in common.

3. Identify the four critical issues that any purchasing procedure must address and describe the significance of each.

4. List the three primary goals of the receiving procedure and explain their importance.

5. Identify the four goals of storing procedures for foods and beverages.

6. Describe the two goals of issuing procedures for foods or beverages.

7. Name the four goals of procedures for producing portions of food and beverage products.

8. Compare the goals of procedures for selling portions of food or beverage products in profit-orientated operations with those in operations that are not profit oriented.

9. List and describe three common means used to help sell food and beverage products.

10. Identify the goal of service in food and beverage operations.

11. List the eight styles of service described in the chapter and identify the distinguishing features of each.

12. Name and describe the three types of cafeteria service identified in the chapter.

13. List and describe the three types of wines identified in the chapter.

14. Describe the interdependence of the seven steps common to all food and beverage operations.

1. Visit some food or beverage operation that you are completely unfamiliar with; have the seven basic elements of foodservice clearly in mind when you do so. Identify the procedures used in the operations to deal with as many of the elements as you can. State the goals of these procedures from your point of view. Are the procedures achieving these goals? Why, or why not?

2. You have been appointed assistant manager of a new cafeteria scheduled to open in a busy ski area. You expect that there will be a

rush of business over the lunch hours and have been asked by the manager to suggest the best service arrangement for the cafeteria. Which of the types of cafeteria service described in this chapter do you suggest to accommodate the greatest number of people in the shortest time? State your reasons for selecting that type of the service.

3. You are the assistant manager in a family restaurant. There is a variety of equipment in the kitchen to produce the food items on the menu, including two ovens, one deep-fat fryer, and two broilers. The manager wants to offer more deep-fat fried foods and has suggested adding to the menu five more items requiring deep-fat frying. Five current items prepared in the ovens would be dropped from the menu. Given the type of restaurant and the kitchen equipment available, what do you think about making these menu changes?

Part Four

Lodging Perspectives

Seven

Dimensions of Lodging

After reading and studying this chapter, you should be able to:

1 Define the term *lodging property* and identify several types of properties covered by the definition.

2 Discuss the size and scope of the commercial lodging industry in terms of numbers and types of properties of various sizes.

3 Identify the approximate number of persons employed in commercial lodging and the annual sales volume generated.

4 Describe the characteristics commonly associated with each of the following: *inn, hotel, motel, lodge, tourist home/guest house, bed and breakfast, hostel, condominium, hospital, motor inn, transient hotel, residential hotel, resort hotel, traditional resort, all-inclusive resort, resort condominium, resort motel, guest ranch, commercial hotel, convention hotel, all-suite hotel, extended-stay hotel, conference center, casino hotel, health spa, boarding house, lodging house, dormitory,* and *nursing home.*

5 Identify ten lodging operations that are directly or indirectly associated with transportation.

6 List and discuss the five key elements that differentiate one lodging establishment from another.

7 Name and describe the four rate plans that include food and the one rate plan that does not.

8 List three methods used to classify commercial lodging establishments.

9 Identify the two national organizations that rate commercial lodging establishments and list a minimum of five factors used by each in making their ratings judgments.

▶ **Introduction**

Previous chapters have described the historical development of the lodging industry, but a recap here will be useful. Clearly of ancient origins, the lodging industry dates back to the beginnings of trade nearly five thousand years ago. Its development has paralleled the development of trade, travel, and transportation throughout civilization.

The modern age of travel and trade can be traced to the Industrial Revolution in the mid eighteenth century. The development of railroads and the increasing prosperity brought by industrial growth contributed greatly to making travel more common. The comparatively small coaching inns of an earlier era were replaced by larger properties—hotels—which were typically located near railroad stations.

Innkeeping in the United States developed in a manner similar to the way in which it developed in western Europe. However, unlike their European counterparts, American innkeepers have always been respected members of the community. Although many rural American inns of the seventeenth and eighteenth centuries were uncomfortable and somewhat primitive by modern standards, those located in cities and towns were generally better. Laws and societal values in many communities regulated eating and drinking in taverns.

In America, as in Europe, the Industrial Revolution was responsible for a period of unprecedented growth in the number of people traveling and in the distances they traveled. By the early 1800s, grand "palaces of the public" were being constructed in the developing cities. Unlike those in Europe, American hotels were community centers for local parties, dinners, receptions, and political events. They were often the most elegant and impressive structures in these cities. By the third quarter of the century, cities across the country were linked to one another by a network of railroads, and many of these cities were boasting of the quality of their luxury hotels.

In the twentieth century, mass production of automobiles and a developing system of paved roads began to make travel easy for all Americans. Eventually, the national government sponsored the development of a coast-to-coast network of roads, which facilitated the transportation of goods around the country. With the resulting economic growth, the United States grew strong in the world economy, and Americans became prosperous. Many American businessmen found it necessary to travel in the course of their work, and some Americans had sufficient disposable income to travel for pleasure. This increase in travel for business and for pleasure led to an expansion of the lodging industry that continued until the Great Depression of 1929, the most severe shock in history to the nation's economic system. During the depression, the number of people traveling declined dramatically, leading to numerous bankruptcies and general economic hardship for the lodging industry.

In the early 1940s, business and military travel associated with World War II brought renewed demand for lodging services, and the industry experienced a period of great prosperity. After the war, new directions for the industry were charted by Kemmons Wilson with his Holiday Inn concept. During the 1960s, new large hotels were constructed by growing organizations with names such as Hilton, Sheraton, and Marriott. And although the automobile had become America's favorite vehicle for travel, the airplane had replaced the railroad as the primary means of public transportation for long-distance travel. By the time commercial jet aircraft were introduced in 1958, airports were becoming favorable locations for lodging establishments.

The lodging industry continues to evolve, seeking new customers by offering new and different kinds of lodging establishments each year. Increasing amounts of travel continue to create opportunities for imaginative lodging developers.

▶ Lodging Properties Defined

A **lodging property** may be defined as an establishment that charges fees for providing furnished sleeping accommodations to persons who are temporarily away from home or who consider these accommodations their temporary or permanent homes. Many of these establishments also provide food, beverages, cleaning services, and a range of other services normally associated with travel and commonly sought by travelers.

This definition of a lodging property covers transient and residential hotels, motels, and inns as well as resorts, college dormitories, hostels, boarding houses, condominium rentals, and other related establishments. It even covers the accommodations aspect of such medically-oriented operations as hospitals and nursing homes. Identifying and distinguishing between various characteristic types of lodging operations is a major objective that will be addressed later in this chapter.

Many lodging properties provide accommodations to both travelers and nontravelers. The Plaza Hotel in New York City is an excellent example: at one time shortly after it opened, up to 80 percent of those staying in the Plaza considered it their permanent home. There are many properties that cater almost exclusively to permanent guests, providing them with many of the same services that other properties offer to travelers and temporary guests.

The Size of the Lodging Industry

Taken as a whole, the lodging industry is a vast but fragmented industry. There is reliable statistical data gathered by the American Hotel & Motel Association for the best-known segment of the industry, the commercial lodging segment, a group of profit-oriented lodging properties that includes hotels, motels, inns, and similar establishments that provide transient accommodations and operate as businesses.

The American Hotel & Motel Association reports that the **commercial lodging industry** in the United States consists of approximately forty-four thousand, eight hundred properties, ranging in size from small inns with fewer than ten rooms to giant hotels with over three thousand rooms. About 67 percent of the properties have fewer than seventy-five rooms. These small establishments account for approximately 21 percent of the 3.2 million rooms available in commercial lodging establishments in the United States. At the other extreme, only about 3.2 percent of the properties have more than three hundred rooms, but these establishments account for 22.9 percent of the total number of rooms available. The remaining 28.7 percent of the properties range in size from seventy-five to three hundred rooms and account for 57.3 percent of the rooms available. It is apparent that typical commercial lodging establishments are quite small and tend to be owned by individuals, partnerships, or small corporations. Many of these small properties are managed by their owners.

In total, the commercial lodging industry in the United States generates about $59.5 billion in sales, representing about 1 percent of the gross domestic product. The industry employs 1.52 million people, full time and part time.

The American Hotel & Motel Association reports that 17 percent of today's lodging customers are traveling for business purposes, 23 percent are attending conferences, and 47 percent are vacationing. Another 13 percent are traveling for any of a number of personal reasons.

Similar data can be obtained for such other segments of the lodging industry as hospitals, nursing homes, and college dormitories. However, because the general thrust of this text is aimed at the commercial lodging segment, that data is not presented here.

▶ Characteristic Types of Lodging Establishments

Owners and operators of lodging establishments select terms to identify their establishments for the public. A lodging property that is about to open in a community may be described in local newspapers by such terms as motel, lodge, or inn. Because the public tends to associate different characteristics with the various terms used and to select or avoid lodging establishments on the basis of their interpretation of the terms, it is useful to list and discuss the most common terms. This list does not constitute any real system of lodging classification because the terms do not represent mutually exclusive categories. Many lodging operations can be described by two or more of these terms.

Most people have heard the names used to identify lodging establishments—hotel, motel, inn, motor inn, resort hotel or motel, condominium, lodging house, residential hotel, tourist home, guest house, bed and breakfast, guest ranch, hostel, hospital, and dormitory among them. Each of these conveys an impression. No one believes that a hotel is the same as a dormitory, for example. These are clearly very different from one another, and someone opening a hotel would be making a terrible mistake to identify it as a dormitory; it would not appeal to those seeking traditional hotel accommodations. The following is an examination of the characteristics commonly associated with lodging establishments identified by each of these terms.

▶ Inn

The term **inn** was brought to the United States from England in the early seventeenth century. Originally, the term meant an establishment that provided rooms, food, and entertainment to both travelers and residents of the local community. Over the years, the term came to be used to describe any one of three different types of hospitality enterprises.

1. A small, typically rural, lodging establishment that may or may not serve food
2. A larger property—or one that may have once been known as a hotel—that wishes to convey an image of smallness and caring for its customers
3. A restaurant or bar that has no sleeping accommodations available

▶ Hotel

The term **hotel** was used traditionally to identify a lodging facility of two stories or more that provided sleeping accommodations and other services for its guests. In the United States, there has been a tendency to build hotels in or near the business centers of cities, towns, and villages and to regard them as centers of social and political activity.

Hotels have commonly offered housekeeping services and luggage-carrying assistance, as well as food, beverages, telephone, and other services. The extent of these services varies from property to property. Some hotels provide the full range: restaurants; bars; cocktail lounges; room service; hairstylists; exercise salons; computer, photocopy, and fax facilities; laundry; dry cleaners; gift shops; check cashing and other financial services; newsstands; travel agencies; drugstores, and others. Other hotels provide nothing beyond the basics: sleeping accommodations and housekeeping services.

▶ Motel

The term **motel** traditionally described a special variety of lodging establishment that catered to travelers with automobiles and provided self-service parking on premises.

The original motels built in the 1950s were single-story properties providing basic sleeping accommodations to overnight travelers. They were inexpensive, offering free parking and housekeeping service, but little else. Staff was kept to a minimum to keep costs down. There were none of the services normally associated with hotels—room service, bellmen, restaurants, and the like. Motels were located on the outskirts of cities and towns and catered to those who did not want the expense and formality of a hotel. Later, many had adequate land to expand and to add swimming pools, which helped to differentiate motels from hotels, and to attract new customers.

Over the years, many motels evolved into properties that so resemble hotels that it is impossible to identify any differences. Many are multistoried, provide full services, and are located in the centers of cities. They continue to characterize themselves as motels for a variety of reasons, the most common being to suggest that they are not expensive.

▶ Lodge

The term **lodge** was traditionally used to describe a lodging establishment associated with a particular type of outdoor activity, such as ski lodge or hunting lodge. This type of lodge was a smaller establishment, typically in a rural setting, that provided food and housekeeping services to guests who came to be with others engaging in the same activity.

Many lodging proprietors have used this term instead of the term *inn* in order to make clear that the primary emphasis of the establishment is providing transient accommodations for those engaging in some specific activity. As suggested above, the term *inn* can be confusing.

A substantial number of properties are known as **motor lodges.** For all practical purposes this is merely another name for a motel.

▶ Tourist Home/Guest House

Tourist home and **guest house** are terms that evolved to describe private homes in which the owners rented spare bedrooms to transient guests. There are very few remaining in operation today. In these establishments, no meals were served to guests. They were not normally run as business ventures in the usual sense; they were more often sources of extra income for those whose primary income was derived from some other source. Tourist homes and guest houses have largely been replaced by bed and breakfast establishments, as described on the next page.

▶ Bed and Breakfast

Bed and breakfast establishments have long been popular in Europe. In recent years, they have become very popular in the United States. They are close relatives of the tourist homes and guest houses that they have tended to replace: owners of private homes rent rooms to overnight guests. However, a substantial number are very much more professional than their ancestors. In fact, some rival luxury hotels for style, elegance, and comfort. They tend to differ from the more traditional commercial lodging properties in one important respect: a full breakfast is included in the rate. Some travelers prefer to stay in bed and breakfast establishments because they are smaller, more intimate, and less expensive than hotels and motels and because the proprietors of many offer a degree of hospitality seldom equaled in commercial properties.

▶ Hostel

Hostels are very inexpensive lodging establishments that typically cater to younger transient customers. They provide little or no service, and many offer very little privacy. The typical hostel provides a bed for the night and offers no frills. Some provide a community kitchen, in which guests may prepare their own meals. Everyone staying in a hostel is expected to participate in keeping it clean. There is usually a limit to the number of nights an individual is allowed to stay.

▶ Condominium

Condominium is a term that identifies a furnished housing unit with kitchen area, living room area, sleeping area, and bath. Condominiums are distinguished from other types of lodging establishments by their ownership characteristics: each condominium unit in a complex is independently owned, but the management of the complex provides maintenance for the outside and the common inside areas of the facility for a monthly fee. In addition, the grounds and other facilities are usually owned jointly by all of the condominium owners.

Many owners rent their units to permanent or transient guests. Those located in resort areas are called *resort condominiums*. Major corporations—Marriot, for example—have built large condominium developments in recent years, sold the individual units, and retained the management of the condominium development.

Condominiums take many forms. They can be freestanding single units, individual units among several built as a single structure, sections or segments of hotel facilities, or units in a residential apartment facility.

▶ Hospital

In many respects, a **hospital** can be regarded as a specialized lodging facility. Hospitals provide sleeping accommodations and many of the same services provided by hotels—including housekeeping, room service, a telephone, a television, and a pharmacy—and often such additional services as hairstylists, gift shops, and lending libraries. A principal difference is in the clientele: hospital guests are known as patients and are normally resident in the facility for medical reasons.

▶ Motor Inn

Motor inn is a term that came into use as an alternative to the term *motel* and originally described a motel property whose proprietors wished to convey the concept of free parking and the traditions of an inn—a kind of modern inn. During the 1950s and 1960s, when older hotels were no longer in favor because of competition from motels, many hotel properties that had parking facilities on premises or nearby changed their names from hotel to motor inn in order to compete with motels.

▶ Transient Hotel

A **transient hotel** is one that is designed to cater to temporary guests—people who have need of accommodations for a comparatively few nights. The guests may be business people, groups of sightseers, government employees, members of the armed forces, students, or any persons seeking temporary lodging.

▶ Residential Hotel

In contrast to transient hotels, some hotels have traditionally provided accommodations for long-term guests—individuals who consider the

▶ The Fairmont Hotel—Chicago ◀

The Fairmont Hotel is a landmark hotel in Chicago, Illinois. Located on North Columbus Drive, across from Grant Park, this forty-five-story hotel contains 692 guest rooms, each having goose-down pillows, terry cloth bathrobes, and hand-milled soaps for its guests. Twenty-four-hour room service is available.

The hotel has two restaurants with cuisines ranging from continental to classic Italian served by singing waitstaff performing opera and Broadway tunes. It has four lounges, two of which feature live music.

For groups, the Fairmont has twelve meeting rooms and is capable of handling up to two thousand, two hundred people.

Adapted from an advertisement in The Hotel and Travel Index, *Winter 1995–96, Page 871*

The Fairmont Hotel, one of Chicago's landmarks. This forty-five story property is a full-service hotel with 692 guest rooms offering luxurious accommodations and fine cuisine to American and international visitors to Chicago. (Photo courtesy of the Fairmont Hotel in Chicago.)

hotel their temporary or permanent home. Establishments that offer traditional hotel services—food and beverages, laundry and dry cleaning, telephone, and the like for those who choose to live permanently in hotels—are known as **residential hotels.** A considerable number of people stay for long periods in these hotels, and some stay for many years. They enjoy and are willing to pay for daily maid service and other services that a particular hotel may offer.

Some transient hotels emulate residential hotels. They set aside a number of rooms or suites for permanent guests. Many well-known hotels have permanent guests and some have whole sections of the hotel building set aside for resident guests. Perhaps the most famous of these is New York's Waldorf-Astoria. One section of the hotel, known as the Towers, caters to permanent guests. The Towers has a separate entrance for its guests and provides a full range of the finest hotel services for them.

▶ Resort Hotel

The term **resort hotel** is commonly used to describe lodging establishments that feature recreational activities for their guests. These activities may be strictly for enjoyment, health purposes, or both. Swimming, tennis, and golf are among the most common activities, although many others are possible. Some resorts have all the necessary facilities for these activities on premises. Others have only limited recreational facilities on premises and provide their guests access to other facilities nearby.

Resorts have traditionally catered to customers who stay for several days or several weeks. In past generations, many resorts had guests who would stay for an entire season. While this is no longer common, because transportation to the resorts has improved so dramatically, some resorts still have guests who stay for extended periods.

As discussed in previous chapters, the United States had a tradition of developing resort accommodations in rural areas. Today, many resort properties that were once in rural settings find themselves situated in suburban or urban areas. Older resort hotels in Miami Beach, Phoenix, and San Diego, for example, are actually located in or near city centers because metropolitan centers have grown up around the resort properties.

Many resort hotels that once catered exclusively to vacationers now cater to those attending meetings and conventions. Thus, it is becoming increasingly difficult to distinguish between resort hotels and other kinds of hotels.

Various types of resort properties exist. These include the following.

The Ihilani resort and spa on the Hawaiian Island of Oahu is a prime example of a modern resort hotel, offering a wide range of recreational activities, including a championship eighteen-hole golf course. (Photo of the Ihilani resort and spa courtesy of Sheila Donnelly & Associates, Honolulu, Hawaii.)

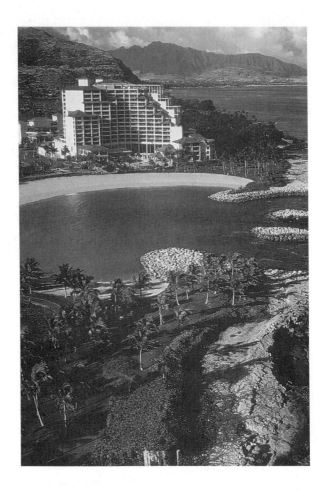

Traditional Resort

A **traditional resort** is one with recreational facilities on its premises. The rates include some or all of the meals. Entertainment is usually free, but liquor, gratuities, and many recreational activities are extra. Rates are charged on a daily or weekly basis.

All-Inclusive Resort

An **all-inclusive resort** is one that includes everything in one weekly rate—airfare to the resort, sleeping accommodations, all meals, liquor, gratuities, entertainment, and activities. The best known of these is Club Med.

▶ **Ihilani Resort and Spa** ◀

L ocated on the Hawaiian Island of Oahu, this 387-unit resort and spa is a brief twenty-five minute drive from Honolulu International Airport. It is situated on a 640-acre resort and offers almost all the amenities one would want. It features a thirty-five-thousand-square-foot state-of-the-art spa and fitness center that offers a variety of massage methods, including Thalasso therapies, with seawater and seaweed.

An eighteen-hole championship golf course and extensive private beach is available to guests. The resort has three different restaurants, which offer European, American, and Asian cuisine. Guest rooms average 680 square feet in size and feature lanais, deep-soaking European tubs, and custom designed furniture.

For meetings and conferences, the Ihilani has a 5,530-square-foot grand ballroom and six meeting rooms.

Adapted from an advertisement in The Hotel and Travel Index, *Winter 1995–96, Page 789*

Resort Condominium

A **resort condominium** is one that is located in a resort area or on a resort property. Some resort hotels have resort condominiums on their properties. The condominium units differ from regular guest rooms: they have kitchen and living room facilities, as well as the traditional sleeping accommodations. Customers may prepare their own meals in the condominium kitchen or dine in one of the restaurants operated by the resort. In addition, guests have access to all the recreational facilities of the resort.

Many older resort hotels that were lacking business have been transformed into resort condominiums. This is done when hotel rooms are sold to investors and the funds obtained are used to develop the property.

Resort Motel

Resort motels are simply motels located in resort areas. Many of them serve food and most of them have limited recreation facilities.

Guest Ranch

Guest ranches are resort properties that emphasize horseback riding and related activities. They are typically small properties of fewer than one hundred rooms that provide housekeeping services, food, and other seasonal recreational facilities such as a swimming pool, tennis courts, and hunting. Guest ranches are typically very informal and attempt to suggest the rough and ready, informal democratic spirit that we have come to believe was characteristic of the old West.

▶ Commercial Hotel

Commercial hotel is a term that used to refer to a specialized property, that is, one that caters to business travelers such as executives and sales personnel in need of transient lodgings. The term dates from the early twentieth century, when a number of newly constructed hotels—Statler's Buffalo property among them—were designed to accommodate single business travelers, providing the types of rooms and services that would appeal to these anticipated guests.

In recent years, as the mix of travelers has changed, the term has come to have less significance. Today, there are probably no hotels that accommodate only "commercial" guests; most cater to a more varied clientele.

▶ Convention Hotel

The term **convention hotel** refers to a very specialized type of hotel, that is, one that focuses on conventions as the primary source of business. A **convention** is a gathering of people sharing some business, professional, social, or avocational interest and is characterized by meetings, exhibits, and related activities regarding that interest.

Some convention hotels were specifically designed to accommodate convention business; others set their sights on conventions only after newer properties—motels, for example—began to capture their regular transient business.

The principal difference between convention hotels and other hotels is in specific facilities available for convention groups. These include at least one large ballroom or similar meeting room and a reasonable number of other meeting rooms nearby. Convention hotels also have the capacity to prepare and serve food and beverages to large numbers of people in their ballrooms and meeting rooms as well as in several public dining rooms and bars. Convention hotels normally do not limit their business to convention groups; they routinely accommodate individual reservations to maintain the highest possible level of occupancy.

▶ All-Suite Hotel

Suite is a term commonly used in lodging operations to describe an accommodation consisting of two or more rooms, one of which is a living room—sometimes called a parlor—plus one or more than one bedroom and bathroom. Many have some type of kitchen facility. Some properties offer suites that have several bedrooms and baths. Sometimes the term is used to describe a one-room accommodation with a living room area and a bedroom area rather than separate rooms.

All-suite hotels do not offer the traditional bedroom and bath accommodations provided by most hotels. They offer only suites. These often include facilities for limited cooking. Many all-suite hotels do not have traditional restaurants, bars, or public meeting rooms. By contrast, some provide foodservice or beverage service, or both. Free breakfast buffets in the lobby, food vending machines in designated areas, and in-room bars are also possibilities. For many, the elimination of restaurants, bars, and public meeting rooms reduces construction and operating costs and enables their owners to offer guests larger, more desirable accommodations at competitive rates.

▶ Sheraton Suites—Dallas, Texas ◀

Sheraton Suites hotel is an excellent example of a hotel that offers only suites. It contains 253 suites, each with a separate living area and bedroom. Suites contain a work table, refrigerator, wet bar, iron and ironing board, two telephones, and two color televisions.

The hotel provides a complimentary newspaper each morning along with the free breakfast. It has an indoor/outdoor pool, meeting facilities, and a restaurant on premises.

Adapted from an advertisement in OAG Business Travel Planner, *Summer 1994, Page 243*

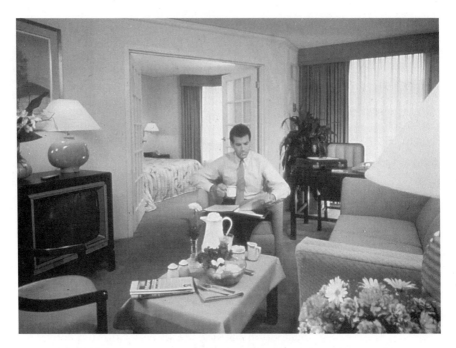

An accommodation in an all-suite hotel includes at least one bedroom and bath, as well as a living room. Some include kitchenettes. The accommodation pictured above shows a spacious living room and a bedroom in the background. (Photo courtesy of Sheraton Suites Country Club Plaza, Kansas City, Missouri.)

▶ Extended-Stay Hotel

A relatively new term, **extended-stay hotel,** is used to describe a property that caters to those who intend to stay longer than typical transient guests and who seek accommodations other than the traditional hotel accommodation of bedroom and bath. The typical extended-stay hotel provides a home-like environment and attempts to minimize the resemblance to other commercial lodging facilities.

Accommodations in extended-stay hotels tend to resemble those in a fine garden apartment complex, and a suite typically includes a kitchen, a living room, a bedroom, and bath and recreational facilities for swimming and other forms of exercise. Suites in extended-stay hotels commonly feature exterior entrances with parking by the door.

▶ Conference Center

Conference centers are facilities designed especially to accommodate meeting and conference business. They are typically located in suburban and rural areas and are designed to provide a setting that is comparatively free of distractions. Thus, conference centers tend to be conducive to concentration and learning and are selected by groups that require such settings for productive work.

Conference centers typically accept only group business. Given high operating costs in some regions of the country, however, some conference centers accept individual reservations during slack periods in order to maximize revenues.

▶ Casino Hotel

Casino hotel is a term used to refer to transient hotels that house gaming casinos. These hotels have allocated major amounts of space to casino gaming, which includes games of chance—blackjack, roulette, and poker, for example—and slot machines. Casino gaming, illegal in most parts of the United States, is a major attraction for many Americans, and casino hotels are very popular with vacationers and conventioneers. Casino hotel operators also provide lavish entertainment—nationally known artists and professionally staged shows—as added attractions.

The MGM Grand Hotel is the world's largest hotel, with over 5,005 guest rooms and suites. It cost over $1 billion to construct and includes four casinos and a thirty-two-acre theme park. (Photo courtesy of MGM Grand.)

▶ MGM Grand Hotel, Casino, and Theme Park ◀

The MGM Grand Hotel is the world's largest hotel, containing 5,005 guest rooms and suites. It cost over $1 billion to construct and includes four casinos and a thirty-two-acre theme park. Also included is a fifteen thousand, two hundred seat event center that can handle anything from a major concert to major league sports. It has one of the most spectacular showrooms in Las Vegas. The hotel contains shops and stores, restaurants, lounges, pools, and a health club.

Las Vegas has long been known as the most important city in the United States for casino gaming. Additionally, it has spectacular shows, very fine recreation facilities, and excellent restaurants. The MGM Grand is a key property in this city of entertainment.

Adapted from an advertisement in The Hotel and Travel Index, *Winter 1995–96, Page 1111*

Until recently, casino hotels in the United States were limited to the state of Nevada and the city of Atlantic City, in New Jersey. Now, however, casino gaming has spread far and wide to several jurisdictions in Colorado, Mississippi, and South Dakota; to riverboats licensed by the states of Illinois, Iowa, Louisiana, Mississippi, and others; and to growing numbers of Native American reservations. Newspapers across the country carry stories daily about consideration being given by state legislatures to the legalization of gambling within their borders. With an increase in the number of legal sites for casino gaming, it is likely that casino hotels will be constructed in other states in the near future.

Because casino gaming is very profitable, casino hotels can be very desirable properties to own. In successful casino hotels, the major share of revenues and profits comes from gambling operations rather than from lodging or from food and beverage. Casino hotels commonly offer free lodging, food, and drinks to guests who routinely wager large amounts of money—the so-called high rollers. Obviously, this is done to attract their continuing patronage.

▶ Health Spa

Health spa is a general term given to lodging establishments that focus on providing some form of beneficial, health-related services.

They tend to specialize—some in weight reduction, others in cosmetic therapy or drug or alcohol rehabilitation, among many others.

For obvious reasons, health spas typically do not accept guests other than those seeking the health-related services in which they specialize. Some even restrict admission to those referred by physicians.

▶ Boarding House

A **boarding house** is a residential facility that provides lodging and meals for guests who normally consider the facility their home, whether temporarily or permanently. The services they offer are typically restricted to limited housekeeping and meals; these characteristics tend to distinguish boarding houses from residential hotels. They are inexpensive compared to residential and other hotels. In the past, boarding houses were much more common than they are today.

A boarding house may be as small as a private home, or it may be a larger facility resembling a small hotel. Rates are commonly charged on a weekly or monthly basis. Housekeeping services in a boarding house are typically very limited: daily maid service is unlikely, and cleaning services may be restricted to once a week. In some, guests clean their own rooms and exchange soiled for clean linens in an office on the main floor. Foodservice is typically two or three meals a day served at specified hours or during specified time periods.

▶ Lodging House

Essentially, a **lodging house** is a boarding house that does not provide meals. The weekly or monthly rate is for the lodging alone. Lodging houses, also known as rooming houses, were more common in the past. Some lodging houses offer kitchen privileges—free use of a common kitchen—provided the user leaves the facility clean after each use.

▶ Dormitory

Typically, the term **dormitory** is used to refer to a lodging facility affiliated with some educational or other institution that provides sleeping accommodations for those in residence. It is this institutional affiliation that differentiates a dormitory from a lodging house.

The characteristics of dormitories are extremely varied. Some have daily maid service; others have none. Some have private rooms with private baths; others have rooms shared by several people and bathrooms shared by all residents of one floor. Some have kitchen facilities; others prohibit cooking. In most, foodservice is available, often in a separate facility. If food is available, it may be provided only to those who pay extra for it. In some instances, the fee charged includes both room and board—in which case, residents usually eat in a foodservice facility.

▶ Nursing Home

A **nursing home** is a residential facility that provides lodging and foodservice for people requiring nursing or related care. Those residing in nursing homes tend to be temporarily or permanently infirm, physically or mentally.

Some nursing homes cater to the elderly; others assist patients recovering from major surgery. Some specialize in the care of chronically ill children; others, called **hospices,** deal with the terminally ill. The services provided vary from one establishment to another and are closely linked to the needs of the residents.

▶ Other Lodging Operations

There is one entire collection of lodging operations that are loosely related to one another by their direct or indirect association with transportation—water, rail, air, or highway. These include cruise ships; freighters that accept passengers; riverboats; overnight passenger ferries; specialized commercial sailboats, or windjammers; railroad sleeping cars; planes with sleeping accommodations for passengers on long international flights; specially-fitted charter buses used for golf tours and similar purposes; completely furnished and outfitted motor homes, campers, trailers, boats, or barges rented on a daily or weekly basis; and lodging facilities known as *boatels,* located at marina developments. None of these constitutes a major segment of the overall lodging industry.

Variations among Lodging Establishments

Major metropolitan centers tend to have numerous lodging properties of widely varying types. These range from limited service to full service;

from simply-furnished small rooms to luxuriously-furnished large rooms; from the simplest to the most ornate decor; from very cheap to extraordinarily expensive; and from those targeting bus travelers to those catering to corporate executives and show business personalities. Smaller communities also have variety, of course, but tend to have less of it.

Any keen observer of the variety of lodging establishments is certain to note significant differences from one to another. These differences are a result of decisions made by owners and managers about five key elements in a lodging operation.

1. Services
2. Accommodations
3. Decor
4. Rates
5. Target clientele

These elements are generally used to define and differentiate among lodging establishments. Each will be discussed in the sections that follow.

▶ Services

The range of services offered to guests varies considerably from one lodging establishment to another. At one end of the scale are guest houses that offer little more than a bed in a room and bathroom facilities down the hall. At the other end of the scale are luxury properties that offer a complete range of services. These include twenty-four-hour room service, valet and laundry service, secretarial service, hairstylists, health clubs, pay-per-view sporting events and films, in-room bars stocked with a selection of beverages, in-room safe boxes, concierge service, and extensive maid service that incorporates placing fresh towels twice a day, turndown service at night, and wake-up coffee or tea in bed in the morning. In between these two extremes are most lodging operations that provide full or limited food and beverage service, color television, telephone, and private bath. Many motels limit their services to a private room with bath, telephone, and television. Ice and snacks may be available in a vending machine located in the hallway.

▶ Accommodations

The types and sizes of accommodations also differ from one lodging property to another. The types of rooms vary from the bunk room with bath down the hall, provided by some inexpensive ski lodges, to the elegant suite with bedroom, private bath, living room, dining area, and small kitchen offered by many luxury hotels. The most common type of accommodation is a bedroom with private bath. The room contains one or two beds, each of which is designed for one or two people. Other furnishings will depend on the nature of the property and the size of the room.

Room sizes for the typical bedroom and private bath vary considerably from one establishment to another. In the United States and Europe, the smallest may have 150 square feet or less. These properties are designed to operate profitably at rates that are even lower than those of the lower-priced motels. The minimum number of square feet for lower-priced motels ranges from about 175 to 250 square feet; mid-priced hotels generally allocate 250 to 325 square feet; and fine hotels may allow 450 square feet or more.

Many properties provide accommodations other than the typical unit of bedroom and bath. The sizes of these also vary—both with the type of property and the nature of the accommodation. It is quite possible, for example, for a unit with two bedrooms, two baths, and a living room in an inexpensive hotel to contain fewer square feet than a unit with one bedroom, one bath, and living room in a luxury property.

▶ Decor

The decor of a lodging establishment refers to the style and layout of its interior furnishings. It is the decor that determines its atmosphere. The higher the quality of the furnishings, the higher the degree of luxury the establishment will be perceived to offer. At one end of the spectrum are lodging establishments with simple, plain decor and inexpensive furnishings. At the other, there are the elegant luxury accommodations, where highly skilled interior decorators are hired to plan the decor and to select each item with great care, from fine period furniture to the simplest ash tray.

Lodging establishments belonging to a given chain are often noted for a particular style and type of decor. They may feature the same color scheme and style of furnishings in all their properties, so that customers in these properties may not be able to distinguish between the rooms in the chain's Boston unit and those in its Los Angeles unit.

▶ Rates

The fees charged by lodging operations for the sleeping accommodations they provide are commonly known as **rates.** In hotels and motels, one speaks of room rates, for example, as the fees charged guests who rent rooms. Rates for rooms vary from one locale to another and from one property to another, as do the charges for the various additional services a lodging facility may offer.

Generally, room rates are much higher in major cities than in suburban locations because of the higher costs of construction and operation. Some cities are well known for their high room rates. New York, for example, has traditionally been the most expensive city in the United States for hotel rooms, and London, Paris, and Tokyo are very expensive cities for lodging accommodations in their respective countries.

▶ Target Clientele

Throughout history, people opening lodging establishments have always attempted to attract particular types of customers. Four thousand years ago, lodging operators had caravans of traders in mind and set up their establishments on trade routes. In seventeenth-century England, lodging operators had stagecoach passengers in mind when opening their coaching houses. More recently, American companies opening hotels in major cities near railroad terminals were targeting railroad travelers. Today, we see lodging operators building properties along highways and at airports for much the same reason.

Targeting particular groups of potential customers has become a sophisticated endeavor. Properties are being designed and built to accommodate travelers at a number of different price levels, from low to high. Others are designed and built to accommodate the needs of a particular clientele—ski lodges, for example.

Taken together, the five elements we have just discussed—services, accommodations, decor, fees, and target clientele—determine the nature of the lodging property.

Meal Service in Lodging Establishments

As indicated above, a number of lodging establishments provide foodservice to guests. Some offer very limited foodservice—vending machines, for example—while others provide room service and several public restaurants. Some hotels quote room rates that include food-service; some do not include foodservice with the room rates; and others offer their guests a choice. The following are the accepted terms used to describe the various arrangements.

American Plan (AP)

American Plan rates include three meals daily: breakfast, lunch, and dinner. In some properties, these meals may include a full choice of the menu; in others, choices may be restricted to certain menu items with other, more expensive items available at an extra charge. In some, it can mean unlimited quantities of unlimited selections—anything the guest chooses from the menu. More commonly, it means a choice of one item in each menu category: one appetizer, one entree, and so on. In years past, many resort hotels offered American Plan rates. In recent years, the popularity of the American Plan has decreased markedly, except in those hotels in which alternative foodservice is not readily available.

Modified American Plan (MAP)

Modified American Plan rates include breakfast and dinner; lunch is available, but for an extra charge. This plan has become popular at resort operations. It was devised to satisfy those guests who objected to being charged for lunchs they did not eat, either because they were sight-seeing and found it inconvenient to return to the dining room for lunch or because they finished breakfast late in the morning and were not hungry at lunchtime. Other guests were weight conscious, and did not want to consume three hearty meals in any one day. Resort owners responded by offering rates that did not include lunch.

Breakfast Plan (BP)

The **Breakfast Plan,** sometimes called the **Bermuda Plan,** includes a full breakfast with the quoted room rate. Although this particular term has not always been used, this plan has been common and popular in many parts of Europe for years. However, rising operating costs have made it necessary for many European hotels to impose a charge for a full breakfast. In the United States, the Breakfast Plan survives as the standard in bed and breakfast establishments and a few other properties. Many all-suite hotels serve full breakfast; some impose the extra charge, just as in the European hotels.

Continental Breakfast Plan (CBP)

The **Continental Breakfast Plan** includes a light breakfast with the room rate. The composition of the light breakfast varies from one establishment to another. In some, it is limited to juice, Danish pastry (also known as sweet rolls in some parts of the country), and a choice of coffee or tea. In others, it can include an array of juices, fruits, pastries, croissants, rolls, bagels, doughnuts, and a choice of regular or decaffeinated coffee or tea.

A number of hotels and motels offer this plan to attract business travelers and other guests accustomed to having very light breakfasts—possibly just juice and coffee. When some operators in an area have done this, others have had to do it also in order to remain competitive: continental breakfasts are very popular.

European Plan (EP)

Rates quoted under the **European Plan** include no meals. Ironically, the European Plan has become the standard in most American transient hotels; this was not the case through most of the nineteenth century.

Although many hotel guests choose to dine in the restaurants operated by hotels, many do not. Hotel keepers have found that guests staying for two nights will commonly have one evening meal in the hotel restaurant and the other away from the hotel, depending on their sense of security about the area in which the property is located.

The weather often plays an important part in helping a guest decide whether or not to patronize the hotel's restaurant. If the weather is poor—rain or snow, for example—guests will stay in; if the weather conditions are good, they are more likely to go out.

Some resort hotels with long traditions of offering American Plan rates alone are now giving their guests a choice of American Plan, Modified American Plan, Breakfast Plan, or European Plan. Guests who select any of the latter three can still order other meals in the hotel restaurant. However, they must order from the menu and pay separately for meals not included in the plan they have selected. Prices for these meals are normally somewhat higher than for the same meals taken as part of a meal plan.

▶ Classification of Lodging Establishments

As in the case of food establishments, the number of possible variables in lodging establishments makes attempts at classifying them very difficult. Most classification systems are either too simple—urban, suburban, and rural, for example—or too complex to be useful. It can take dozens of categories to account for the variations from one operation to another in services, accommodations, decor, rates, and target clientele.

It is important to recognize that many of the transient lodging establishments listed and discussed above cater to more than one type of business. In major cities, many accommodate residential guests with weekly or monthly rates because they are not able to maintain a sufficiently high level of occupancy with transient trade alone. In contrast, some transient hotels do not accommodate residential guests but maintain high levels of occupancy by attracting several types of transients: business travelers, vacationers, and those attending conventions, for example. It is quite common to find a single hotel property that has characteristics of two or more of the many types that one encounters in this dynamic industry. This has been a major difficulty to those attempting to develop useful classification systems for lodging properties.

Many attempts have been made to classify lodging properties. Some have classified them by location; other have attempted various other approaches including size:

Under 75 rooms
From 75 to 149 rooms
From 150 to 299 rooms
Over 300 rooms

One classification system of interest is that used by the Bureau of the Census, a branch of the United States Department of Commerce. Because this is the system used by the government to report industry statistics, others have adopted it. This system separates properties into four categories:

Full-service
Economy
All-suite
Resort

The following quotation accompanies a table in which lodging properties are divided into these categories.

An economy property is defined as one that offers clean, standard-sized, fully furnished modern rooms at usually $10.00 to $20.00 per night below the rate of typical full-service motor hotels. Their customers do not need food facilities, banquet rooms or meeting facilities, indoor recreation areas, or entertainment. An all-suite hotel doesn't have rooms, only suites. A suite differs from a hotel room by several characteristics. Generally, there is a separate bedroom, and guest amenities often include "extras," such as a wet bar or microwave and in some cases a full kitchen. A resort hotel is a lodging facility providing an environment conducive to leisure and recreation and an ambiance of isolation/destination while providing a full range of leisure-oriented amenities.[1]

This system is intended to be used for reporting data obtained from surveys—rates, averages, and similar variations—of some characteristic types of lodging properties. Some lodging properties are not included—bed and breakfast establishments, hostels, and others.

▶ Travel Research Firms

Travel research firms categorize lodging operations according to the purposes of their research. For example, Smith Travel Research[2] categorizes lodging establishments according to prices charged in 162 separate market areas in the United States. Within each market area, lodging properties are classified as

Luxury—top 15 percent in the market area
Upscale—next 15 percent in the market area
Midprice—middle 30 percent in the market area
Economy—next 20 percent in the market area
Budget—bottom 20 percent in the market area

---

[1]Bureau of the Census, *Statistical Abstract of the United States* (Washington, D.C.: United States Department of Commerce, Bureau of the Census, 1990), p.786.
[2]*Lodging Magazine*, April 1995, p. 55.

The purpose of this approach is to record changes in price levels over time. In the Smith Travel Research classification system, it is possible for hotels of the same quality to be listed in more than one category if they are located in different market areas. Other research firms have very different approaches to classification—approaches that suit the purposes of their research.

In light of the foregoing discussion, a person attempting to learn about the lodging industry will find no single classification system for lodging properties that is both useful and all-inclusive. Some are useful but leave out large numbers of properties; others include all properties, but are not particularly useful; still others are useful, but only for specific purposes.

▶ Ratings of Lodging Establishments

Another method of differentiating one lodging property from another is to consult a guide that rates hotels and motels.

Because quality of lodging operations varies from one establishment to another, in some parts of the world, including some European countries, lodging establishments are rated for quality by government agencies. In the United States, no government agency performs any similar service for the traveler. There are, however, two well-known private organizations that judge the quality of lodging operations and publish rating guides based on these judgments. The first of these is the Mobil Corporation, which, in collaboration with the trade division of Prentice Hall, publishes the *Mobil Travel Guide*. The second is the American Automobile Association (AAA), which publishes the *Tour Book*. The *Mobil Travel Guide* is sold through many commercial outlets and may be purchased by anyone; the *Tour Book* is distributed only to members of the American Automobile Association.

Neither of these guides lists all lodging establishments. The publisher of each reserves the right to determine which to include. All properties listed are recommended by the rating organization. Unlisted properties are merely unlisted: they may be superior, equal, or inferior to a listed property. In every region of the country, one can identify numerous small properties with fine accommodations, food, and service that are not listed in the rating guides.

The following is the rating scale used in the Mobil Travel Guide.

*   Good; better than average
**   Very Good

***	Excellent
****	Outstanding—worth a special trip
*****	One of the best in the country

The principal areas evaluated by Mobil include quality of physical structure, furnishings, maintenance, housekeeping, and overall service. Each property listed in the Mobil guide must undergo an annual review, so no rating is ever final.

The five-star rating is awarded by Mobil to a comparatively small number of properties that represent the finest in the United States. This top rating is extremely difficult to achieve: cities with many excellent hotels may have only one with the five-star rating, and most cities have no five-star properties.

The tour books published by the American Automobile Association use a rating scale indicated by diamonds rather than stars. Rated establishments can be awarded as many as five diamonds according to the following criteria.

◇   Provides good but unpretentious accommodations. Establishments are functional, emphasizing clean and comfortable rooms; they must meet the basic needs of comfort, privacy, cleanliness, and safety.

◇◇   Maintains the attributes offered at the ◇ level while showing noticeable enhancements in decor and/or quality of furnishings. They may be recently constructed or older properties, both of which cater more to the needs of a budget-oriented traveler.

◇◇◇   Offers a degree of sophistication. Additional amenities, services, and facilities may be offered. There is a marked upgrade in services and comfort.

◇◇◇◇   Excellent properties displaying a high level of service and hospitality. Properties offer a wide variety of amenities and upscale facilities inside the room, on the grounds, and in the common areas.

◇◇◇◇◇ Exhibit an exceptionally high degree of service; striking, luxurious facilities with many extra amenities. Guest services are executed and presented in a flawless manner. The guest will be pampered by a very professional, attentive staff. The facilities, service, and operation of the property help set the standards in hospitality and service.

The American Automobile Association publishes the following list of factors taken into account when rating lodging establishments.

Exterior
Management and staff
Housekeeping
Room decor
Maintenance
Room furnishings
Security
Bathrooms
Parking
Guest services and facilities
Soundproofing

As with the Mobil guide, the top rating is very difficult to earn, although the American Automobile Association typically awards more top ratings than Mobil. Interestingly, the guides often differ in their judgments about specific properties. As with Mobil, no American Automobile Association rating is ever final: field representatives annually reinspect all properties listed in the *Tour Book*.

▶ Summary

In this chapter, the term *lodging property* is defined. Data are provided to illustrate the size and scope of the commercial lodging industry, including number of properties, number of employees, and total annual sales. Five key elements of lodging operations that differentiate one lodging establishment from another are listed and discussed. Numerous characteristic types of lodging establishments are described—both commercial and noncommercial, as well as both generic and specialized. Three classification methods for commercial lodging properties are identified, including one used by the Bureau of the Census and another used by a travel research firm. Various rate plans are identified—several that include food with room rates and one that does not. Finally, the two national organizations that rate the quality of lodging operations for consumers are identified and their rating scales illustrated.

Key Terms

All-Inclusive Resort	Hospital
All-Suite Hotel	Hostel

American Plan (A.P.)	Hotel
Boarding House	Inn
Bed and Breakfast Establishment	Lodge
Breakfast Plan (B.P.)	Lodging Properties
Bermuda Plan	Lodging House
Casino Hotel	Motel
Commercial Hotel	Modified American Plan (M.A.P)
Commercial Lodging Industry	Motor Inn
Condominium	Motor Lodge
Conference Center	Nursing Home
Continental Breakfast Plan (C.B.P.)	Rates
Convention	Residential Hotel
Convention Hotel	Resort Condominium
Dormitory	Resort Hotel
European Plan (E.P.)	Resort Motel
Extended-Stay Hotel	Suite
Guest House	Tourist Home
Guest Ranch	Traditional Resort
Health Spa	Transient Hotel
Hospice	

1. Define the term *lodging property* and list ten types of lodging properties that fit the definition.

2. Briefly describe the size and scope of the commercial lodging industry. Include data in your response to indicate number of properties, number of persons employed, and approximate gross sales annually.

3. What percentage of guests in commercial lodging establishments are
   a. traveling for business purposes?
   b. attending conferences?
   c. vacationing?
   d. traveling for personal reasons?

4. Describe the impressions lodging property owners tend to convey to the public by selecting the following terms to identify properties:
   a. *inn*
   b. *hotel*
   c. *motel*
   d. *lodge*
   e. *guest house*
   f. *bed and breakfast*

g. *hostel*

h. *condominium*

i. *hospital*

5. Identify the principal characteristics of each of the following:
   a. motor inn
   b. transient motel
   c. residential hotel
   d. resort hotel
   e. traditional resort
   f. all-inclusive resort
   g. resort condominium
   h. resort motel
   i. guest ranch
   j. commercial hotel
   k. convention hotel
   l. all-suite hotel
   m. extended-stay hotel
   n. conference center
   o. casino hotel
   p. health spa
   q. boarding house
   r. lodging house
   s. dormitory
   t. nursing home

6. In the chapter, the authors discuss a number of lodging operations that are thought of more commonly as modes of transportation. Cruise ships are one example; name ten others.

7. List five key elements that differentiate one lodging establishment from another.

8. Define each of the following:
   a. European Plan
   b. American Plan
   c. Modified American Plan
   d. Breakfast Plan
   e. Continental Breakfast Plan

9. Identify the specific categories used to classify commercial lodging properties by:
   a. number of rooms, and
   b. types of properties.

10. Identify the inadequacies inherent in each of the classification systems identified in number 9.

11. Given a two-hundred-room commercial hotel in the business center of one of America's ten largest cities, which of the five plans identified in number 8 would be appropriate to offer transient guests? Why?

12. Given a 350-room beachfront resort property located in Miami Beach, Florida, which of the five plans identified in number 8 would be appropriate to offer transient guests? Why?

13. Identify the two national organizations that publish widely recognized ratings of commercial lodging establishments. List a minimum of five factors used by each for determining these ratings.

1. The Wellington, a lodging operation just outside Midland City, is two stories tall and has three hundred guest rooms, each with a bath. It also has a restaurant, a swimming pool, an exercise room, meeting space for four hundred persons, and a large parking lot. Which of the terms presented in this chapter to describe characteristic types of lodging establishments could be used to describe the Wellington?

2. The Hotel Astor is situated in the center of Centerville, a city of one hundred thousand. It is rated by the American Automobile Association with four diamonds. The hotel has 350 rooms, two fine dining restaurants, a coffee shop, extensive convention facilities, a ballroom, a separate banquet kitchen, and various shops such as a barber shop, a beauty salon, a newsstand, and a travel agency. Which of the terms presented in this chapter to describe characteristic types of lodging establishments could be used to describe the Hotel Astor?

3. Imagine that you work as assistant food and beverage manager at the Welton, a resort property. The Welton has traditionally offered American Plan rates. In recent years, several fine restaurants have opened in the immediate area, and last year the resort added a golf course to the recreational activities available to guests. Many guests enjoy the new golf course, and many have dined at the new restaurants. However, those who have missed meals when they went to one of the restaurants or were on the golf course have been charged the full American Plan rate, even though they did not consume some of the meals. Many have begun to complain to management about paying for meals they did not have. What, if anything, do you think management should do?

Eight

Lodging Facilities

After reading and studying this chapter, you should be able to:

1 Define the term *product line* as used in lodging operations.

2 List and discuss the three elements in the service product line of a lodging enterprise.

3 Name the activities common to all front office operations that must be taken into account in their layout and design.

4 Identify by name and size eight types of beds commonly used in lodging properties.

5 Provide the size range in square feet for each of the following: sub-budget motel room; budget motel room; commercial hotel/motel room; luxury motel room; hotel junior suite; hotel standard suite; suite in an all-suite property.

6 Compare and contrast the size and furnishings of a budget motel room with those of a luxury hotel.

7 List and discuss ten engineering systems found in lodging facilities.

8 Distinguish between centralized and decentralized air conditioning systems.

9 List four possible sources of water for lodging operations having no access to a public water supply.

10 Identify the principal components of a fire safety system.

11 List and describe four common types of energy control systems.

▶ Introduction

The previous chapter was devoted to examining the size and scope of the lodging industry. We identified characteristic types of lodging establishments and discussed three classification systems. In addition, we identified several rate plans that include food and described two rating systems used for lodging properties. With that as background, we now turn to the subject of lodging facilities.

As indicated in the previous chapter, lodging establishments may offer any number of different services to guests. Some lodging operations offer very few—simple guest houses having only rooms with a bath down the hall, for example. Others present a full range—elegant luxury hotels, for example, offering twenty-four-hour service, laundry and valet services, concierge service, twenty-four-hour maid service, secretarial services, hairstylists, and many other services.

Lodging establishments also vary greatly in size and in target clientele. The simple guest house may have only one or two rooms to rent, whereas the large, complex hotel may have over three thousand rooms. Similarly, some lodging operations cater to business travelers while others specialize in convention business. Still others offer permanent accommodations to those who consider the hotel their home while some provide temporary accommodations to people on vacation.

It should be apparent from the broad range of possibilities for service, size, and target clientele that lodging facilities differ considerably from one another. For example, compare a resort property to a city hotel. The resort is likely to provide recreational activities—golf, tennis, and swimming, for example—requiring specialized facilities and equipment. In contrast, the city hotel might offer specialized services to appeal to high-level business executives—in-room computers and fax machines on each floor, possibly—requiring different kinds of specialized facilities and equipment. While there are obvious differences between these two—and between any two different types of lodging properties—there are a number of important similarities. All lodging properties provide accommodations for guests, and all provide some services, although the services may be very limited in some properties.

As we will see, however, the points of similarity are of far greater importance than the many apparent differences.

As we proceed with a discussion of lodging facilities, it is important to remember that the typical lodging facility is likely to be far more complex than the typical food and beverage facility. In addition, the amount of money and the length of time required to plan and open a food and beverage operation is far less than that needed to plan and open a lodging operation. These realities clearly help to explain why comparatively few people develop their own commercial lodging operations. Most are planned and developed by corporations.

Prior to a discussion of lodging facilities, it is necessary to address three key topics that are fundamental to the layout and design of a lodging facility.

1. Concept
2. Legal requirements (local, state, and national)
3. Product line

These are the same key topics that were addressed before the discussion of foodservice facilities in chapter 5. However, while the topic areas are the same, the details differ considerably.

▶ Concept

Every lodging operation is (or should be) established around a **concept**—an imaginative, unifying idea of the operation that serves as the focus for the people, energies, and other resources required to convert the idea into reality. This concept originates with the person or company that will own the property, or with some other person or firm that develops the property on commission.

We will begin with one fairly obvious element of this concept: the type of lodging operation to be developed. The person or company responsible for the concept has in mind some idea of the type or types of lodging operations that might be developed—motel, convention hotel, resort hotel, or some other. A new property is likely to resemble one of the various characteristic types discussed in chapter 7 or some combination of those.

Those responsible for the concept must clearly understand the nature of the hospitality service products to be offered in the lodging operation they are developing.

▷ Legal Requirements

The laws and regulations—federal, state, and local—that an owner faces in operating a lodging facility must be taken into account. Building codes, fire codes, health codes, zoning regulations, environmental regulations, and licensing requirements are among the most common. Each of these provides specific direction for an owner in planning, designing, and operating a lodging enterprise.

Laws and regulations vary considerably from one state to another and even from city to city within a given state. For example, zoning regulations in some areas limit the height of new buildings constructed in the area. Plans for a facility that fail to comply with these regulations will not receive approval from local authorities. Consequently, it would be impossible to obtain a building permit until architects and engineers had redesigned the building to comply with the regulations. This is just one example of the many possibilities.

Before proceeding with plans for lodging facilities, owners lacking full knowledge of the laws and regulations that apply in given locales must have advice from lawyers, architects, engineers, professional lodging consultants, and others with the necessary expertise. Failure to take these details into account can lead to costly errors.

▷ Product Line

As indicated in chapter 5, the term *product line* is used in marketing to refer to a group of products with similar characteristics. We will borrow the term from marketing once again and use it to mean the service products that a lodging operator intends to offer based on the concept developed for the establishment. For example, if one intends to operate a budget motel, the service products will be significantly different from those offered by a developer who intends to operate a luxury resort. Each lodging establishment offers its own distinct product line.

The hospitality service product line offered by lodging operations has three elements.

1. Accommodations
2. Services
3. Ambiance

Accommodations

Lodging establishments offer **accommodations**—the most basic element in their service product line. This accommodations element consists of all the accommodations that will be offered to the public. The accommodations are the specific rooms, suites, or other facilities to which guests are assigned. All of these, taken together, are defined as the accommodations element in the service product line.

Many lodging operations offer specialized accommodations. Some, for example, feature only one type, such as suites. Any number of specialized accommodations can be found in the lodging industry today. Two of the characteristic types of properties discussed in the previous chapter offer good examples: budget motels and residential hotels. In contrast, other lodging operations offer a broader range of accommodations, which may consist of both rooms and suites of varying sizes and types.

Services

The second basic element in the hospitality service product line offered in a lodging enterprise is the **service** available to guests. This element is defined as all the services the operator intends to offer. Again, the type of establishment will strongly influence the nature and extent of the services offered. Housekeeping service is the basic service offered by transient hotels, motels, and similar lodging enterprises. Other common services include security, parking, valet and laundry, and bell services. Additional services may include information about goods and services available in the geographic area and assistance in making reservations at affiliated properties in distant locations for future dates.

Many operators offer such additional services as entertainment and recreational facilities—common hospitality-related services that are central to specific types of lodging operations and expected by guests in these operations. Again, the characteristic type of lodging facility established strongly influences the nature and extent of any additional services offered. Thus, entertainment and recreational facilities are central to resort hotel operations.

Ambiance

The third basic element in the hospitality service product line in lodging operations is **ambiance.** This element includes a vast number of tangible and intangible features that give a specific lodging operation its special and distinctive character. These include theme, lighting, uniforms, furnishings, cleanliness, wall coverings, fixtures, fabrics, decorations, and any other related features, tangible or intangible, that customers see or sense and that help to form their impressions of the establishment. For example, when an arriving guest walks through the front door of a lodging facility, he gets an impression of the property from the lighting, furniture, carpet, wall coverings, works of art, and any of the other coordinated elements that make up the lobby area. Similarly, after being assigned to a particular accommodation, the guest gets additional impressions from the elevator, the elevator foyer on her floor, the general appearance of the corridor leading from the elevator foyer to her room, and so on. To a guest, the sum of these and many other tangible and intangible features constitutes the property's ambiance, or atmosphere.

The discussion above does not take into account that many lodging operations also offer food and beverage products. Some would say that the lodging enterprise that offers food and beverages is offering a second product line. Others would disagree, arguing that if food and beverages are offered because of guests' expectations, the food and beverage operations should be thought of as additional services, akin to the recreational facilities discussed above. One can agree or disagree with either point of view.

Accommodations, service, and ambiance are the three basic elements in a lodging product line. The ambiance of the lobby pictured right immediately conveys a sense of this hotel's special and distinctive character. (Photo courtesy of the Four Seasons Hotel.)

In summary, the service product line offered by a lodging establishment consists of three basic elements—accommodations, services, and ambiance. Some operators choose to add one or more of an array of other possible product lines by including boutiques, jewelry shops, gift shops, souvenir stands, and other retail shops on premises. Although these are interesting and often desirable additions to a property, they are not essential to the basic lodging enterprise. Therefore, we will limit the following discussion to the facilities required for the basic service product line of a lodging enterprise. (Appropriate discussion of food and beverage facilities appears in chapter 5.) In the present chapter, we will assume that the owner has attended to the necessary preliminaries and decided to proceed. At this point, we will turn our attention to the specifics of lodging facilities.

The student reading about lodging facilities may find it useful to refer to particular lodging properties. Therefore, in order to describe the various facilities and to point out some of the differences from one property to another, we will refer to the three distinctly different types of lodging properties described in case studies 8.1, 8.2, and 8.3. The first of these is a limited-service budget motel catering to economy-minded transient travelers. The second is a full-service, upscale resort hotel that provides accommodations and services primarily for vacationers. The third is a luxury hotel located in a major cosmopolitan city offering the services associated with that type of property.

Case Study 8.1

The Value Lodge is a fifty-room property located in a small midwestern town adjacent to an exit on Interstate 80. It is owned and operated by a couple name Roger and Janet Goodson. It is part of a chain called Value Lodges. Roger and Janet were both executives for major companies for many years. Eventually they both began to dislike their work and felt they were wasting their lives, so they decided to open their own business. They had always been fascinated by innkeeping and felt they had the talent for it. Because they had no formal training in the business, they decided to work with a chain to receive the necessary training and to reduce risk. The Goodsons sold their home and as many other assets as they could. Because they had limited funds, they could only afford a relatively small property. They answered an advertisement in the *Wall Street Journal* placed by the Value Lodge Company. After thorough investigation, they agreed to an arrangement giving them a motel in an excellent location, a Value Lodge sign, a large mortgage, and an obligation to pay various fees to the chain.

The Value Lodge is a fairly simple fifty-room operation. Roger and Janet, as owner-managers, live in quarters connected to the office where guests check in and out. The fifty units are modern and comfortable—pleasantly decorated, yet simply furnished. Each unit contains two queen-size beds, a private bath, a color television, two lounge chairs, a dresser with mirror, and a telephone, among other items. The motel has no restaurant, no meeting rooms, no swimming pool, and no recreational facilities. It does have a small dining area with tables, chairs, and vending machines from which guests can obtain ice, beverages, sandwiches, and snacks. The motel caters almost exclusively to motorists from Interstate 80 looking for clean, comfortable overnight accommodations. Most guests check in by late afternoon and are back on the road again early the following morning.

There is a fast-food restaurant located across the road and a family restaurant nearby. The Value Lodge Co. has a central system that takes reservations for all units in the chain. Roger and Janet receive about 25 percent of their business from the reservation system.

Roger and Janet take turns in the office during the day. Roger is usually there during morning hours, doing the bookkeeping and ordering supplies, while Janet supervises the housekeeping. During the afternoon, Roger sees to the maintenance of the grounds and rooms while Janet takes her turn in the office. In the evening, neither stays in the office, but the door to their quarters is open, so they can attend to any needs of the guests or to any check-ins.

Case Study 8.2

The Mountain Inn is a four hundred room, three-star resort hotel located in a major ski area in Colorado. It is owned by the Mountain Inn Corporation, a company formed by the group of investors that built the property. They have hired the Preferred Management Company to run it. The agreement calls for Preferred Mangement to receive 3 percent of gross room sales and 10 percent of profits.

The Mountain Inn is a seasonal resort hotel. During the winter months—early November to mid April—the hotel is a ski resort, catering to vacationers who come for winter sports. During the summer months—from June 1 to September 30—it is a summer resort catering to individuals and groups that come for summer recreational activities and meetings. The hotel closes during the months of October and May.

This four hundred room hotel has two dining rooms—one for individual guests and families and the other for groups. It has one large meeting room that can be divided into several smaller ones, as well as a coffee shop, pharmacy, hairstylist, several boutiques, an indoor pool and exercise room, two racquetball courts, and four outdoor tennis courts.

The hotel is located at the base of a ski slope within one mile of an excellent golf course. Mountain Inn guests receive special consideration at the golf course. There is an excellent stable nearby for horseback riding. Additional services offered guests include room service from 7:00 A.M. to midnight as well as tennis and swimming instruction.

Case Study 8.3

The Kensington is a 350-room, four-star luxury hotel located in the center of a major eastern city. It is a classical hotel, owned and operated by a nationally-known chain, but the name of the chain is not used on any signs, linen, literature, or other item that would be noticed by guests. Management decided that the image of the property would not be improved by being linked with this particular chain.

All 350 guest rooms are furnished with reproductions of antique furniture. There is a doorman on duty at the front door at all times to welcome guests, take charge of their cars, and obtain transportation for them. The lobby is finished in marble and brass. Each elevator is operated by an attendant, even though they can be operated automatically.

The Kensington has a large ballroom with its own kitchen and a separate entrance from the street for guests attending weddings and similar formal functions. The hotel does not have the number of meeting rooms that one would find in a convention hotel. It does have three small meeting rooms that can be used by guests—usually business executives—for small meetings.

Other services offered to guests include twenty-four-hour room service, concierge service, secretarial service, a hairstylist, gourmet dining in the Empire Room, cocktails in the Kensington Lounge, a pharmacy, an indoor pool and exercise room, and extensive housekeeping service that includes the service of early morning tea or coffee, fresh towels twice each day, and turndown service in the evening.

Seventy-five of The Kensington's 350 rooms are presently occupied by permanent guests. The remaining rooms are available for transient business. Guests are served by a staff of five hundred employees, half of whom have worked in the hotel for over ten years. The Kensington emphasizes personal service. All staff members—desk clerks, elevator operators, bellmen, and doormen, among others—make special efforts to know guests by name. Staff members are expected to be friendly and courteous at all times, and to attend quickly to all reasonable requests made by guests.

These three lodging properties, although they appear at first glance to be very different from one another, really have much in common. In fact, they have the same basic facilities that any property must have to be called a lodging facility.

1. An area for activities and records associated with guest reservations, check-in, and check-out: the front office
2. The accommodations themselves: guest rooms
3. An area for attending to housekeeping activities, including the storage of linens, uniforms, and cleaning supplies and equipment: housekeeping

In the following discussion, we will focus our attention on the layout and design of these three basic elements found in all lodging facilities.

▶ Facility Layout and Design

Because these three areas are so different from one another, the layout and design of each will be addressed separately.

▶ Front Office Layout and Design

Front office layout and design tends to be determined by the size of the lodging establishment. In smaller properties, for example, front office areas tend to be smaller, simpler, and more compact because there is no need to have more than one clerk on duty for each shift. By contrast, larger properties tend to have larger front offices because they need more people on duty at any one time to deal with the larger numbers of guests.

A lodging enterprise needs a facility to handle **front office** activities, which have traditionally been separated into several categories of work known by the terms **reservations, check-in, information,** and **check-out.** These four terms require some simple explanation.

Reservations is a term used to refer to a process for holding accommodations for future guests.

In a lodging facility, the front office is the area for activities and records associated with guest reservations, check-in, and check-out. To guests, pictured right checking in, the front desk is the front office. (Photo courtesy of Radisson Hospitality Worldwide.)

Check-in is the process by which people become guests.

Information refers to providing guests with advice and directions relating to shopping, dining, entertainment, local transportation, and a range of other possibilities.

Check-out is the process by which guests terminate their status as guests.

Further discussion of front office work will be deferred to the following chapter on lodging operations.

The facilities in which front office activities take place vary greatly from one property to another. In a fifty-room motel, such as the Value Lodge described above, a front office facility is normally quite small. Figure 8.1 is a diagram of the front office of the Value Lodge.

In a larger property, such as the 350-room Kensington hotel, the amount of work and the number of employees make a larger front office facility necessary. Figure 8.2 is a diagram of the front office of the Kensington.

Note that both facilities are designed to deal with the same activities—those associated with reservations, check-in, information, and check-out. As previously noted, these are the activities common to all front office operations, and every lodging establishment has some form of front office designed to accommodate the level of activity anticipated in each of those four areas. To that extent, the front offices of the Value Lodge and the Kensington hotel are the same. There are obvious differences, however, between the two front offices, and these

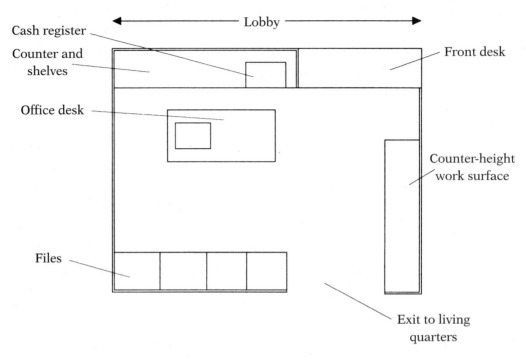

Figure 8.1

Layout of the front
office of the Value
Lodge

differences reveal much about the differences between the two properties. The principal differences are listed here.

Size

In the Value Lodge, the volume of work involving front office activities
can be handled by one individual in a single small area. The entire
front office area, including the front desk, is only 54 square feet: 6′ ×
9′. By contrast, the front office area in the Kensington is quite large,
encompassing 540 square feet: 18′ × 30′.

Space Allocation

The Value Lodge has one single area in which all front office activities
take place, and the volume of each is such that all can be handled by
one person. In the Kensington, however, some of the front office activities occur in sufficient volume to require that some employees dedi-
cate their time to specialized work. For example, the volume of financial activities—updating guest accounts, processing guest check-outs,
cashing checks, and making change—make it desirable to assign specialists (cashiers) to the work and to allocate one specific area for their
work. The same is true for the specialist employees assigned to deal

hold for
Jill Cohen

8/30/01

Fia-

Lobby

Front desk

8   8

2   3

5

4

8   8

7

8

Key:

1 Cashier's area
2 Information area
3 Room clerk's area
4 Wall of mailboxes for keys, mail, and messages
5 Counter-height bank of safe deposit boxes
6 Office for front office manager
7 Reservations office
8 Locations of computer terminals and printers

with reservations, information, and check-ins. In the Kensington, the front office staff is large enough to require supervision by a front office manager, for whom a separate office area has been allocated.

It should be noted that a number of larger lodging operations do not follow the Kensington's system for functional division of front office work. In many lodging operations with front offices similar to that of the Kensington, the three front office computer terminals could be used interchangeably for check-in and check-out. During evening hours, when the number of arrivals in commercial hotels tends to be higher, all terminals may be used to handle check-ins. By contrast, in the morning, when the number of departures are higher, all terminals can be used to process check-outs.

Equipment

In the Value Lodge, the front office requires some simple manual equipment: a room rack that also holds room keys and guests' bills, a cash register, a telephone, and a file cabinet for reservations records and for storage of various forms and records. In the Kensington, the front office has an integrated computer system with terminals in each area. For example, the reservations office has a workstation with a terminal in which all reservations are input. A telephone and a fax machine are within reach, as are file cabinets and other storage facilities for reservations and related forms.

▶ Rooms Layout and Design

To a great extent, the layout and design of guest accommodations in a given establishment are determined by the type of establishment. In economy motels, for example, guest rooms tend to be smaller, simpler, and more compact than in traditional luxury hotels.

Because beds, the principal furnishings in most guest accommodations, vary considerably in size, it is useful to know the dimensions of beds most commonly found in lodging establishments (see table 8.1).

Most beds are 75″ long. Some guests however, prefer longer beds, and these are readily available to lodging operators who choose to buy

Table 8.1 **Dimensions of Beds in Lodging Establishments**

Bed Type	Width
Rollaway/cot	30″
Studio	33″
Single	36″
Twin	39″
Three-quarters	48″
Double	54″
Queen	60″
King	78″

Table 8.2 **Typical Size Ranges of Lodging Accommodations**

Type of Lodging Accommodation	Common Sizes of Guest Accommodations (In Square Feet)
Sub-budget motel room	175–200
Budget motel room	225–250
Commercial hotel/motel room	250–325
Luxury hotel/motel room	350–450
Hotel junior suite	400–475
Hotel standard suite	450–550
Suite in an all-suite property	450–700

them. Some are 78″ long; others may be 80″ or 82″. The latter are often called California lengths.

Table 8.2 indicates typical sizes of guest accommodations in seven types of lodging operations. Note that the number of square feet in each accommodation includes bedroom, parlor or living room (if any), bathroom, and entry area, as well as any closets and other hallways.

Figure 8.3 illustrates typical floor plans for guest accommodations in the seven common types of lodging establishments listed in table 8.2.

The layout and design of guest rooms in the Value Lodge closely resembles that for the budget motel room in figure 8.3. Each unit has a private bath, two queen-size beds, a color television, two lounge chairs, and a dresser with mirror, among other items. Units in this property are of uniform size: 236 square feet.

Guest rooms in the Kensington more closely resemble those for the luxury hotel room in figure 8.3. Some, like that in the diagram, have a private bath, a king-size bed, two night stands, a desk/dresser with mirror, and a lounge area consisting of corner table, loveseat, lounge chair, and coffee table. Units in the Kensington hotel are of differing sizes but average approximately four hundred square feet. That illustrated is among the largest the property offers.

Note that both guest rooms are designed for the same basic purpose—to provide accommodations for travelers. Every lodging establishment has guest rooms designed to accommodate the needs and desires of the kinds of travelers management intends to attract to the establishment. To that extent, the guest rooms in the Value Lodge and the Kensington hotel have the same general purposes. There are, however, obvious differences between the two guest rooms illustrated, and these differences reveal much about the differences between the two properties. The principal differences are listed here.

Commercial hotel/motel room
312 sq ft

Suite in an all-suite property
690 sq ft

Hotel standard suite
546 sq ft

Budget motel room
243 sq ft

Hotel junior suite
450 sq ft

Sub-budget motel room
196 sq ft

Luxury hotel/motel room
442 sq ft

Figure 8-3

Typical floor plans for guest accommodations in lodging establishments

Size

The typical room in the Value Lodge is approximately 150 square feet smaller than that in the Kensington.

Space Allocation

In the Kensington, some of the additional space has been allocated to some additional furnishings not found in the Value Lodge. In addition, the Kensington hotel room appears to be more open and uncluttered. Some of the extra space is used, quite simply, as space, affecting the ambiance of the lodging product.

Furnishings

In the Value Lodge, the furnishings are better suited to those staying overnight than to those remaining for longer periods. They are not quite as attractive and comfortable as those in the Kensington, which features reproductions of classic antiques. However, the Kensington caters to guests who are seeking attractive furnishings and who are both willing and able to pay higher rates for more luxurious accommodations.

Today's work environment is changing. Many business travelers are carrying laptop computers so they can work on long airline flights and in hotel rooms. Marriott offers business travelers the "Room That Works," pictured right. (Photo courtesy of The Philadelphia Marriott.)

▶ Let Them Have Workspace ◀

Today's work environment is changing. Because of advances in technology, more people each year are doing work away from the traditional office. They are working at home during the day, in the evening, or on weekends. They are also taking their work with them on business trips, carrying laptop computers so they can work in hotel rooms.

Lodging operators have always provided for the basic needs of business travelers, offering desks, telephones, and message service. Today, however, many business travelers need more than yesterday's basics in their hotel rooms. Marriott understands this, and has begun a company-wide effort to provide the "Room That Works," which features

- ▶ A large console and mobile writing desk
- ▶ Two power outlets and a PC modem jack mounted in the console top
- ▶ A movable task light
- ▶ Fully adjustable ergonomic chair

This concept was introduced recently at the one thousand, two hundred room Philadelphia Marriott, a new property built adjacent to Philadelphia's Pennsylvania Convention Center. Marriott management announced that it expected to complete the process of converting 20 percent of its full-service guest rooms to "Rooms That Work" within two years.

Adapted from Lodging, *June, 1995.*

▶ Housekeeping Layout and Design

As in front office and guest accommodations layouts, the layout and design of a **housekeeping** area in a lodging establishment is determined, to a great extent, by the type of establishment. In economy motels, for example, housekeeping areas tend to be smaller, simpler, and more compact than in traditional luxury hotels found in the more affluent areas of major cities. The housekeeping area in the Value Lodge, for example, is quite small and compact. In the Kensington, by contrast, housekeeping requires considerable space because of the luxury nature of the Kensington and the comparatively large number of employees required to maintain such a property.

The layout of the housekeeping area in the Value Lodge is illustrated in figure 8.4. Note that the facility is comparatively simple, having storage space for laundered bed and bath linens and cleaning supplies, and providing floor space for the overnight storage of three mobile carts used by the housekeeping staff during working hours.

Figure 8.5 illustrates the layout of the main housekeeping facility in the Kensington. The housekeeping area in the Kensington includes an office for an executive housekeeper as well as considerable space for storing bed linens, bath linens, and cleaning supplies. A separate room is set aside for soiled linens. Here, soiled linens are separated and counted before being sent out to a commercial laundry to be washed and folded or ironed.

Caring for bed and bath linen is one of the major responsibilities of any housekeeping department in any lodging operation. Without adequate supplies of linen, it is impossible to operate a lodging facility properly. Essentially, one can adopt either of two approaches to laundering bed and bath linen: either send it out to a commercial laundry or install a laundry facility on premises. If the latter approach is adopted, considerable space must be set aside for the laundry facility, and considerable funds must be allocated to equip it. Additional discussion of this topic will be deferred to the chapter on lodging operations.

Note that housekeeping areas in both the Value Lodge and the Kensington are designed for the same basic purpose—to facilitate housekeeping services for guests. Every lodging establishment has a

Figure 8-4

Layout of the housekeeping facility in the Value Lodge

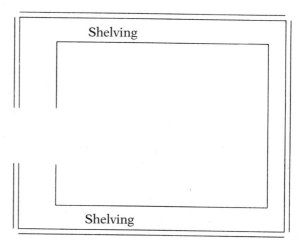

Figure 8-5

Layout of the
housekeeping
facility in the
Kensington

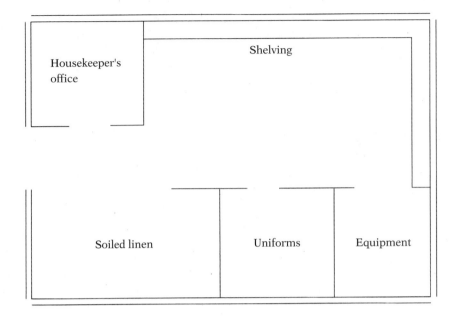

similar area designed to provide the kind and level of housekeeping services preferred by the travelers patronizing the establishment. To that extent, the housekeeping areas in the Value Lodge and the Kensington have the same general purposes. However, there are obvious dissimilarities between the two areas illustrated, which suggest some of the dissimilarities between the two properties. The principal differences are described here.

Size

Two major factors account for the differences in size between the housekeeping areas in the two properties. The first of these has to do with the number of rooms to be serviced—50 in the Value Lodge versus 350 in the Kensington. Thus, the Kensington must have at least seven times the amount of bed and bath linen. The second reason has to do with the need to store uniforms in the housekeeping area of the Kensington, a need that does not exist in the Value Lodge.

The diagram of the housekeeping area of the Kensington does not show the additional housekeeping storage facilities that are located throughout the hotel. Each floor has a housekeeping closet used for storing small amounts of cleaning supplies, guest room supplies, and linens, and for housing mobile carts when not in use by the housekeeping staff.

Space Allocation

Besides the space allocated for an office in the housekeeping area of the Kensington, there is also space for storing uniforms for all hotel employees required to wear them. This is not necessary in the Value Lodge, as we have noted. Because the Kensington is an older property, some of the side rooms now used for storage were once used by housekeeping employees with job titles no longer found in most hotels: upholsterers and seamstresses, for example. Work formerly done by people in these job classifications is now typically done outside the hotel by independent contractors, making it possible to allocate this space for additional storage.

Equipment

Because it is a luxury property with a large lobby and considerable public space, the Kensington has some heavy, specialized cleaning equipment used to maintain these areas. Because the Value Lodge has no comparable space, it has no such equipment.

In addition, the Kensington, as a luxury enterprise, makes available to its guests various kinds of equipment not offered to guests in the Value Lodge. Guests in the Kensington can telephone the housekeeping office to obtain such common items as steam irons and ironing boards, and guests visiting from other parts of the world can borrow conversion devices that enable them to use their electrical appliances.

From the foregoing discussion, it should be apparent that lodging facilities are relatively complex physical structures. Because of this, those studying lodging management need some basic knowledge of the complex physical systems required to make them operational. These are the systems designed to provide the basic requirements that make it possible for people to inhabit buildings in reasonable comfort and safety. These are commonly referred to as engineering systems.

▶ Engineering Systems

The following are brief descriptions of the basic engineering systems common to most lodging properties. These brief discussions will serve to suggest the degree of complexity inherent in the layout and design of a building constructed for use as a hotel, motel, or similar lodging enterprise.

The engineering systems in a building may include all of the following:

1. Heating
2. Air conditioning
3. Ventilation
4. Electrical
5. Water
6. Transportation
7. Waste
8. Fire safety
9. Energy control
10. Communications

Heating

In the United States, lodging facilities have **heating systems** to raise the temperature of air and water in the building, thus providing warm rooms and hot water. Heating systems accomplish this by converting energy resources to heat. Common energy resources include oil, gas, electricity, steam, coal, and solar energy. The selection of one of these over another depends on availability, relative cost, and particular preferences of the owner/operators of the facility.

Air Conditioning

Technically, **air conditioning** is any treatment of the air in a building that changes that air in any way. Thus, heating, cooling, humidifying, dehumidifying, and filtering are all air conditioning processes. However, the term *air conditioning* is commonly taken to mean improving the comfort level in a facility by reducing the temperature of air, by controlling the level of humidity in the air, or by doing both of these. There are two types of air conditioning systems used in lodging facilities.

Centralized. A central system services a number of guest rooms and other facilities, treating the air in one large unit and distributing the treated air through ducts.

Decentralized. A decentralized system relies on individual units in each room or part of the facility to treat the air. In some properties, these are built into the walls of the rooms they serve; in others, they are installed in windows.

Ventilation

Ventilation systems provide fresh or recirculated air and control the volume of air. They ensure an adequate supply of air with sufficient oxygen for human activity. Some ventilation systems also filter the air to remove dust and other particles as well as cigarette smoke and cooking odors. Lodging facilities in the centers of major cities commonly install air filtration equipment to remove the pollutants from automobile, truck, and bus traffic.

Ventilation systems are designed to remove and replace all the air in a given space or room a number of times each hour. That number may vary from a very few times per hour—possibly six, for example, in a large hotel ballroom—to a great many times per hour—up to fifty in a large hotel kitchen—according to one authority. Ventilation systems are typically linked to heating systems, air conditioning systems, or both.

Electrical

Electrical systems are designed to provide for the availability of electric power wherever it may be needed as an energy source in the building. Electrical systems consist of wires of various sizes as well as circuit breakers or fuses, switches, and outlets that facilitate the safe use of electric power. Electricity is used for three primary purposes in lodging facilities: lighting, heating, and operating specific equipment requiring electric power.

Because of their public nature, many lodging establishments are required to maintain emergency systems to use in the event of a power failure. The nature and extent of the emergency systems vary, depending on state and local regulations. Some are simple battery systems that provide emergency lighting in corridors and other public areas for limited periods; others are complex systems that may include gasoline-powered generators to provide sufficient electricity for lighting and limited elevator service. Many operators install emergency systems that will also provide power for refrigerators, freezers, and computer systems until the regular flow of power resumes.

Water

A **water system** consists of those parts of the plumbing system that provide fresh water to various parts of the lodging establishment, including guest rooms, food and beverage facilities, laundry facilities, and public bathrooms, among others.

In many localities, the source of fresh water is a public water supply with water pipes running under the streets. In many remote, rural areas, however, absence of a public water system makes it necessary for lodging operators to use some alternative means to obtain fresh water. Most commonly, this means drilling a well. Another possibility is pumping the water directly from a nearby lake or river. Others, although rare, include collecting it from rainwater and processing saltwater from the sea.

Sometimes incoming fresh water is processed before being distributed throughout a building so that its properties may be changed before use. There are various reasons for doing this. One is that the water is too *hard*, a term used to describe water containing excessive amounts of calcium and magnesium salts. Another is that the water may contain other minerals or impurities that must be filtered out. Still another is that the water may require the addition of chlorine to make it safe for human use.

Some fresh water—the cold water—is distributed directly to the areas in which it is used. The rest—the hot water—is diverted to the heating system, where its temperature is raised before distribution.

One of the significant engineering challenges in a multistory lodging operation is to design a water system that will provide

1. adequate water pressure on all floors during periods of peak use—if this is not addressed, guests in rooms on high floors may not be able to obtain adequate water at particular times;
2. an adequate supply of both hot and cold water, so that each water user can maintain the temperature he or she selects for any given purpose—failure to provide for this may result, for example, in sudden changes in shower water temperatures from comfortable to excessively hot or cold, either of which may be unpleasant or dangerous.

Transportation

The **transportation system** in a lodging establishment consists of those facilities used to move guests, employees, equipment, and supplies from one level of the building to another. Its most common components are elevators and escalators.

Wherever feasible, planners of lodging facilities provide for an adequate number of elevators so that those used by guests need not be used for other purposes. Elevators used for other purposes are often called service elevators and are usually located some distance from the guest elevators. They are used for transporting employees, equipment, and supplies from one part of the building to another.

A small, specialized kind of elevator called a **dumbwaiter** is used for moving food, normally for short distances between floors. For example, if the main kitchen in a large hotel is one or two floors below the dining rooms and banquet rooms, a dumbwaiter way be installed to transport food and materials between kitchen and the foodservice facilities.

Dumbwaiters are not normally used to transport personnel and, consequently, lack the internal operating controls found in elevators. Staff members usually place food and other items in a dumbwaiter, close the door from the outside, and control it by depressing a button on the wall next to the dumbwaiter shaft.

Escalators are normally used to transport large numbers of people for short distances—one or two floors up or down. They are more commonly used with banquet and meeting facilities, so that those attending meetings, dinners, and other events can get into and out of the facility quickly and easily. If it becomes necessary to move large numbers of people into or out of a facility quickly, all escalators can be made to move in the same direction—up or down. With this arrangement, greater numbers of people can be moved more quickly than would be possible using elevators.

Waste

The **waste system** in a lodging property is designed to facilitate the removal of solid and liquid wastes produced in the property. Solid waste includes paper, glass, fabric, plastic, metal, wood, and food. Liquid waste is primarily waste water being drained into a sewage disposal system.

Solid waste is normally collected throughout a lodging establishment by employees who transport it to one central area. From there, it can be put out for pickup in plastic bags, trash cans, or dumpsters, depending on type, volume, and local regulations. Alternatively, it can be compacted before being put out or incinerated on premises. Many large hotels accumulate huge amounts of solid waste daily. In many areas, local regulations now identify certain solid wastes as recyclables and require that they be separated and made ready for special handling or collection.

In contrast, the disposal of liquid waste is normally quite simple. In areas with public water supply systems, there are also public sewer systems, and disposal is a simple matter of connecting to that system. In other areas, some other means must be found. The most common alternatives are treatment plants and underground drain fields.

Fire Safety

A **fire safety system** is designed to detect, contain, or extinguish fires and to alert both guests and employees to the danger. Some are also designed to summon fire and police personnel to the scene. A fire safety system consists of

1. sensing devices for detecting heat, smoke, flame, or some combination of these;
2. devices for containing or extinguishing fires, such as doors that close automatically to prevent the spread of fire, sprinklers, and portable extinguishers containing water, carbon dioxide, foam, or other chemicals;
3. warning devices for alerting guests and employees, such as fire horns, fire alarms, and flashing lights.

Because of the public nature of lodging establishments, all but the smallest are required by law to have some type of fire safety system. The nature and extent of the systems required clearly vary from one area to another and from one size and type of lodging facility to another.

Energy Control

The **energy control system** in a lodging establishment is designed to manage the use of energy in the building efficiently, minimizing its use and consequent cost. It consists of various devices that turn energy-consuming equipment on and off at optimum times or that prevent excessive use of energy in any system or subsystem. There are four common types of systems.

Time Clock. This is the simplest and least costly of the systems. It uses time clocks to turn on and off the flow of electricity to such devices as exterior lights, lighted signs, and even swimming pool filtration systems, ensuring that they will operate only when needed and for the proper length of time.

Automatic Sensor. Some lodging operators control energy costs by installing automatic sensors that detect the presence or absence of people in a room. These are used primarily to turn lights on and off, ensuring that lights are off when there is no one in a room. They may also be used to turn off such appliances as television sets when guests have left a room.

Electric Demand. These systems are designed to limit the amount of energy of one type that can be used at any one time. This may entail limiting the length of time that a given device can operate continuously or preventing the use of a given device while another is in use. These systems are more commonly used in large buildings where, for example, three major air conditioning systems serve different parts of the building. An electric demand control system may be used to prevent two or more from operating together and to limit the length of time that any one of them can run before being automatically turned off to enable a second to operate.

Computerized System. Computerized systems are the most flexible, efficient, and effective in use today. These are the systems most commonly installed in newly constructed lodging facilities. They can be programmed to control energy use and are capable of all the controls exercised by the three systems described above.

Because proper use of an appropriate energy control system can result in considerable savings in energy costs—some manufacturers claim up to 40 percent—owners of lodging properties are normally interested in selecting systems that will produce minimum energy costs for their facilities.

Communications System

Communications systems in lodging establishments are designed to enable guests, managers, staff members, and others outside the lodging property to communicate with one another. This system may be as simple as a telephone system used by guests, employees, and managers to reach one another to communicate simple messages. This would be the case in the Value Lodge, for example, where an overnight guest may use the telephone only to call the front desk to request information or to request a morning wake-up call so that he or she can get an early start the following morning. However, some communications systems in lodging properties today are far more complex.

A typical modern communications system may link telephones, televisions, computers, and various audiovisual devices. The communications may range from telephone calls between front desk and guest room to interactive televised conferences linking groups in two or more cities via satellite transmission. They may involve business travelers using computers with modems in guest rooms or suites to communicate with their offices via telephone lines. They may even provide a means for guests to view and approve their room bills via the television sets in their rooms. The possibilities for developing increasingly complex telecommunications equipment for installation and use in lodging enterprises are growing with each development in this relatively new field. Therefore, those purchasing communications systems for lodging facilities will be challenged to select systems and equipment that will not soon become obsolete as new systems are developed.

▶ Summary

In this chapter, concept, legal requirements, and product line are introduced as fundamental to the layout and design of lodging facilities. Product line is described as having three components: accommodations, services, and ambiance. Case studies describing three different lodging facilities—Value Lodge, Mountain Inn, and Kensington hotel—are presented as aids to understanding facilities layout and design. The layout and design of three areas central to lodging operations are illustrated and discussed: front office, guest room, and housekeeping area. The layout and design of these three in the Value Lodge and the Kensington hotel are described, compared, and contrasted. Finally, ten engineering systems are identified as the basic elements in lodging properties that make it possible for people to inhabit lodging facilities buildings in reasonable comfort and safety.

 Key Terms

Air Conditioning System	Front Office
Accommodations	Heating system
Ambiance	Housekeeping
Check-in	Information
Check-out	Product Line
Communications System	Reservations
Concept	Service
Dumbwaiter	Transportation System
Electrical System	Ventilation System

Energy Control System   Waste System
Escalator   Water System
Fire Safety System

1. Define the term *product line* as used in lodging operations.

2. List and discuss the three elements in the service product line of a lodging enterprise.

3. What are the activities common to all front office operations that must be taken into account in their layout and design?

4. How would you expect the front office layout and design for a seventy-five room budget motel to differ from that for a five hundred room luxury hotel?

5. Identify by name and size eight types of beds commonly used in lodging properties.

6. Provide the size range in square feet for each of the following: sub-budget motel room; budget motel room; commercial hotel/motel room; luxury motel room; hotel junior suite; hotel standard suite; suite in an all-suite property.

7. Compare and contrast the size and furnishings of a budget motel room with those of a luxury hotel.

8. How would the layout and design of the housekeeping area in a fifty room motel be likely to differ from that in a five hundred room luxury hotel?

9. Why would there be great differences in the size, space allocation, and equipment found in the housekeeping areas cited in number 8?

10. List and discuss ten engineering systems found in lodging facilities.

11. Distinguish between centralized and decentralized air conditioning systems.

12. How often should air be changed in the ballroom of a large hotel? In the kitchen serving the ballroom?

13. List four possible sources of water for lodging operations having no access to a public water supply.

14. What are dumbwaiters? For what purposes are they used in lodging facilities?

15.   What are the principal components of a fire safety system?

16.   Identify four common types of energy control systems.

1.   Visit a lodging facility with at least 150 rooms. From your own perspective, describe the concept around which this operation is established.

2.   For the lodging facility you have identified in number 1 above, describe its product line as completely as you can.

3.   Describe the layout and design of the front office in the lodging operation you discussed in numbers 1 and 2.

Lodging Operations

After reading and studying this chapter, you should be able to:

1 Name the three basic elements common to all lodging operations.

2 Identify six additional services offered by some, but not all, lodging operators.

3 List and state the goals of the four activities associated with front office operation and describe the functions of each.

4 List the advantages of using electronic locks rather than traditional locks with metal keys.

5 Describe three possible variations of the checkout procedure used by hotels, motels, and similar properties.

6 Identify two common problems that have induced some lodging operators to overbook reservations.

7 Describe a minimum of ten tasks that can be assigned to the housekeeping operation.

8 List a minimum of ten tasks required to make a room ready for occupancy.

9 Identify three methods used to assign daily work quotas for room attendants in hotels, motels, and similar properties.

10 Discuss the key differences between security measures used in large center-city hotels and those used in smaller rural and suburban properties.

11 Identify the kinds of activities normally associated with front service.

12 Name three services offered by the telephone system in modern lodging operations.

13 List and describe the three types of foodservice facilities found in lodging establishments.

14 Identify eight personal services offered by some, but not all, lodging properties.

▶ Introduction

In the previous chapter, the basic similarities of lodging establishments were illustrated by means of case studies describing three specific properties: the Value Lodge, the Mountain Inn, and the Kensington hotel. Chapter 8 will serve as the foundation for this chapter, which will identify significant concepts that lie at the heart of lodging operations.

In this chapter, we will point out similarities in lodging establishments that are sometimes obscured by the vast array of differences. We will define and describe a number of important operations—elements and processes—that lodging establishments have in common.

▶ Basic Elements of Lodging Operations

The elements and processes that one encounters in lodging can be divided into two basic groups.

1. Those that are found in all lodging establishments
2. Those that are found in some, but not all

Elements in the first group are common to all lodging facilities; without them, an enterprise would not be considered a lodging establishment. Elements in the second group are used selectively, depending on the goals of a particular lodging establishment.

Group 1 is made up of:

1. Front office

2.   Housekeeping
3.   Security

Group 2 is made up of:

1.   Front service
2.   Telephone service
3.   Food and beverage services
4.   Recreation/entertainment
5.   Parking
6.   Other personal services

Lodging operators choosing to provide some or all of these services have two basic options:

1.   hire employees to provide the service, or
2.   engage an outside contractor to do so for a fee.

For purposes of this text, we will consider that either option results in the addition of an activity to the lodging facility—one devoted to providing the service. In addition, guests using the service will consider that activity part of the lodging facility regardless of whether it is provided by employees of the lodging establishment or those of an outside contractor.

▶ Group 1

As indicated above, the three operations in this group—front office, housekeeping, and security—are common to all lodging establishments. However, although this is true, discussion of housekeeping or security in a small boarding house would be much less enlightening than discussion of those activities in a hotel, motel, or similar commercial lodging enterprise. Therefore, much of the following discussion relates to those kinds of properties—the kinds illustrated in case studies 8.1, 8.2, and 8.3.

▶ Front Office

Front office is a term commonly used to refer to the location where the front desk is situated within a lodging property. To guests, the front

The front office is a guest's principal point of contact with the hotel. Here, at the Breakers, guests who have just checked in are receiving an electronic room key from the desk clerk. Pictured is the workstation used by the clerk to find their reservations, assign their rooms, establish their accounts, and prepare their room keys. (Photo courtesy of the Breakers.)

office represents the lodging property: it is their first point of contact on arrival and last point of contact at departure.

The front office operation consists of four primary activities that are known in the lodging industry by the following terms:

1. Check-in
2. Information
3. Check-out
4. Reservations

Together, these four activities comprise front office operation.

Check-In

Check-in refers to a process by which people become guests in a lodging establishment. Check-in takes place in a reception area, another name for that part of a front office known as the front desk. Here, guests register, are assigned accommodations, and pick up keys for these accommodations. In the Kensington, the check-in process proceeds in the following manner.

An arriving guest goes first to the front desk, normally located in the lobby near the main entrance. A **room clerk**[1], a job title for the

---

[1]There are a number of titles for this job, including desk clerk, assistant manager, desk attendant, guest services attendant, and receptionist. For simplicity, we will only use the terms room clerk and desk clerk in this text.

person on duty at the front desk, greets and welcomes the arriving guest and asks if he or she has a reservation. If so, the room clerk asks the guest to register, a term which refers to filling out a form known as a registration card. A registration card is a printed front office form on which guests record their names, addresses, and other information. The clerk then updates information about the guest in the computer and confirms the number of nights a guest expects to stay. If the guest has no reservation, the room clerk will describe available accommodations and rates, thus attempting to "sell" a room to the individual. If successful, the room clerk will ask the individual to register. Once the guest has registered, the room clerk assigns a suitable accommodation.

In some operations, the guest does not write the necessary information on a registration card but dictates it to a room clerk who inputs this essential information into a computer terminal. After the information has been input, a form with this information is printed from the computer record, and the guest is asked to sign this hard copy.

Today, most hotels, motels, and similar lodging establishments determine at the time of arrival how guests intend to settle their bills. In general, bills are settled by one of three means: credit, cash (or check), or billing to a third party. If a credit card is to be used, the guest is asked to produce the card so that a record can be made of the credit card number. This gives the lodging operator some reasonable means of verifying that the guest has sufficient credit available. If payment is to be with cash or check, the guest is likely to be asked for credit identification. Credit identification is verifiable proof that an individual has sufficient credit to cover his or her hotel bill. Without credit identification, guests are usually asked to pay cash in advance. If the bill is to be settled by a third party, some suitable arrangement is normally made when the reservation is taken. The Mountain Inn, for example, accepts both cash and national credit cards, but virtually all its guests present credit cards at check-in and settle their bills at the time of departure. In contrast, the Value Lodge requires that all guests either pay for their accommodation in cash as they check in or sign credit card vouchers imprinted with their card numbers. Most of the guests pay cash.

In order to be able to assign guests to rooms, room clerks must quickly be able to determine which rooms are occupied, which have been vacated but not cleaned, and which are both vacant and ready. To enable room clerks to do this, lodging establishments use either manual or electronic means to maintain the necessary information. The latter refers to computers, of course, and computers are fast becoming the preferred means in most properties. Computers used for guest check-in are typically part of an overall *property management system*—a term for a computer system designed to perform a variety of tasks formerly accomplished by manual means.

In some properties—the Value Lodge, for example—the information needed by room clerks is maintained manually in a device called a room rack; in many other more complex operations—the Kensington, for example—property management systems are used. Detailed information about specific equipment and techniques for registering guests is normally covered in a rooms management course.

The important point to remember is that the check-in process in all lodging establishments has at least two common goals: to assign guests to accommodations and to insure payment.

After a room number has been assigned and questions of billing have been attended to, guests are given access to their assigned accommodations in one of two possible ways: either they are given keys to their assigned rooms or their keys are given to bellstaff, who accompany guests to their rooms. In the Value Lodge, there is no bellstaff; guests are simply given keys and directed to their rooms. By contrast, room clerks in the Kensington are required to give the keys to bellstaff, who always accompany guests to their rooms. At the Mountain Inn, guests are offered their choice of being accompanied by bellstaff or finding their own way.

Modern technology has changed the nature of the room keys used in many hotels and motels. Although many operations still use the traditional lock with metal key (the kind inserted into a lock, then turned to unlock a door), growing numbers are now using new types of locks that open by means of cards rather than traditional metal keys. Two types of cards are common. The first has information electronically encoded on magnetic strips. To enter a room, the guest inserts the card into an electronic device that reads the code and opens the lock. The second type is a thick card made of plastic or some other material in which round holes have been punched. With either type, the guest insets the card in the lock and that allows the door to be opened.

These new types of "keys" have several important advantages over traditional metal keys, which have always given hotel and motel operators constant problems. When lost or stolen, they are sometimes used by burglars to enter rooms illegally and steal guests' money and valuables. In addition, lost keys must be replaced, an expensive and time-consuming requirement in a large property. Some large hotels have traditionally employed full-time locksmiths to make duplicates of lost metal keys and to change locks in guest room doors when necessary. The newer card "keys" eliminate many of the problems associated with metal keys. Frequently, no room numbers are visible, so that a lost card is useless to the finder. In properties using cards with magnetic strips, the code is changed each time a guest checks out, and this is the same as changing the lock. In properties using cards with punched holes, it is relatively easy to change the code in the door lock and prepare a new "key" if the card is lost.

Information

The goal of the **information** activity in a hotel or motel is to serve the special needs of guests and employees for information about:

1. Guests
2. Goods and services

Guest Information. The front office serves as a center for guest information. In effect, it maintains a data bank with the names and addresses of current guests, their room numbers, the status of their accounts, and considerable additional information. As guests check in, information about them is added to this data bank; as guests leave, the data bank is changed to keep it current. Thus, the front office of a hotel or motel always has up-to-date information about all current guests and about the status of each room—whether occupied or vacant. This information may be maintained in any number of possible forms: data in a computer, typewritten slips of paper, or handwritten sheets of paper are some of the possibilities. The information is used constantly.

Without this information, any number of routine front office matters would be very difficult. For example, in the Kensington, one of these routine matters is assisting guests who have forgotten their room numbers. When such a guest goes to the front desk, the clerk on duty finds the guest's name and room number in the data bank and is thus easily able to give the guest her room number. In the Value Lodge, a small property, the owner has the same need for information but maintains the records in a very different way: the registration cards are simply kept in a file box in alphabetical order.

In front office work, some of the other tasks that require the use of this guest information include the following: placing mail and messages for guests in numbered mailboxes that correspond to their room numbers; directing incoming telephone calls to guests' rooms; assisting visitors in finding the guests they have come to see; verifying the room numbers of guests who have signed guest checks in the restaurant or bar; determining the number of occupied rooms that are expected to be vacated by guests checking out on the current day; counting the number of rooms vacant at any given time during the course of a day; determining the house count, a term meaning the number of guests registered in the property; advising housekeepers that a room has been vacated so that it can be cleaned; and calculating the percentage of guest rooms occupied.

Information about Goods and Services. Many transient guests find themselves in strange surroundings when they have registered in a hotel or motel. Most are strangers to the community and need some orientation and assistance. In many hotels and motels, the front office may have maps, guidebooks, and other sources of information to help guests. Room clerks and other employees may be asked to recommend restaurants, give directions to places of interest, or help guests find sources for any number of goods or services that the community offers. The front office in the Mountain Inn, for example, has maps of the surrounding region that it makes available without charge to guests interested in sightseeing. Similarly, the owners of the Value Lodge provide guests with free copies of a directory listing the locations of all other motels in the chain, from coast to coast.

In hotels, motels, and other lodging establishments that offer services beyond sleeping accommodations, guests normally ask many questions about the available services. They may ask about the hours of operation of restaurants, bars, swimming pools, stables, or other facilities. They may ask about the regulations governing the use of the golf course or the availability of child care services, hairstylists, or travel agents; they may ask details about the kinds of exercise equipment, the types of computers and printers, or the hair dryers available in these facilities. An unlimited number of questions can be asked about the facilities and services of the property itself. Consequently, room clerks and other employees are expected to provide all sorts of information to guests quickly and courteously.

Check-Out

Check-out refers to a process by which guests terminate their status as guests of a lodging establishment. The goal of check-out activity in hotels, motels, and other lodging operations is to accomplish this process.

There are several variations of the check-out process. In the Value Lodge, overnight guests typically pay their bills in advance at check-in, so most simply leave their keys in the rooms and drive away. Because of the size of the property, the owners normally see or hear guests depart and thus know that the vacated room needs to be cleaned and made ready for its next occupant.

In the Mountain Inn, the procedure is different. All guests are expected to stop at the front office to settle their accounts and leave their keys. As indicated above, these accounts are created and maintained in the front office. When guests leave, employees update the front office data bank and make the room number available to housekeepers so that the room will be made ready for the next guests.

In the Kensington, by contrast, guests have access to advanced technology that enables them to "check out" before they leave their rooms. This is accomplished by using the television screen in their rooms to review and settle their bills. While the approaches differ from one establishment to another, the goal is the same in all three: to accomplish the check-out process.

Today, because so many lodging operations require that guests sign credit card vouchers or pay cash at check-in, there are fewer problems

▶ Hotels: The Next Generation ◀

Hotels are studying ways to serve guests better. In the near future, you can expect check-ins to be hassle free and rooms to be a lot smarter.

As you approach the hotel, a chip imbedded in your frequent guest card will not only alert the front desk to your imminent arrival but will also identify you so staff members can call you by name as you enter the property. In some properties, you may not see any members of the staff: to check in, you may simply use a credit card, inserting it in a machine that will assign you a room and provide you with a key. When you reach the room of the future, motion detectors will sense your entry and turn on heat or air-conditioning.

Your night's rest may be like sleeping on air. In fact, the room will have a mattress with inflatable pockets that each guest can adjust to achieve his preferred degree of firmness. It will also have an interactive television monitor that will enable you to call home on a videophone, use an on-line service to shop, plug in your laptop to receive your E-mail messages, and check your bill before you check out.

Adapted from USA Today, *June 6, 1995.*

with unpaid and uncollectible bills than was the case years ago. Because credit cards can be verified as guests check in, hotels, motels, and similar lodging establishments do not have as many *skippers,* an old hotel term used to refer to guests who leave without paying their bills.

Reservations

The term **reservation** refers to an arrangement by which lodging operators hold accommodations for guests who will be arriving at some later time. This may be later in the day on the date the reservation is made or at some date in the future. The reservations operation in a hotel or motel is designed to make such arrangements. There are two major goals of reservations activity.

1. To provide assurance to prospective guests that suitable accommodations will be available to them at a specific price for a specified period.
2. To ensure that the greatest number of rooms possible are occupied each day and that the rates charged for those rooms are the highest possible.

The first major goal is to serve the needs of people seeking assurance that accommodations will be available to them when needed. Individuals intending to travel to a distant location want to be certain that they will have rooms to stay in when they arrive. Reservation operations are intended to meet this need. A potential guest can call or write the reservation office in a hotel, motel, or other lodging establishment to arrange for a room to be held for the necessary number of nights.

The reservations operation in a lodging establishment typically consists of an office with some number of employees, known as reservation clerks or reservationists, who respond to requests for accommodations from potential guests. Requests may be for the coming night, some date in the distant future, or any time in between. These requests usually arrive by telephone, fax, or mail. Each request for a room reservation must be answered promptly with a definite *yes* or *no; maybe* is never an acceptable response to a potential guest. In order to give definite answers, reservationists must have access to information about the number of rooms already reserved for each night, the number of rooms remaining available for those same nights, sold-out dates for which no reservations can be taken, and rates for the rooms available for any given night. Without such information, no reservationist would be able to give a prompt response to someone calling on the telephone to ask about the availability of, say, a room for one person for three nights, beginning next Tuesday. Potential guests need immediate, unequivocal answers to requests of this nature, and reservationists must be able to provide them.

Assuming that an appropriate room is available at an acceptable rate for the nights requested by a caller, the reservationist must record some information quickly. This normally includes name, address, dates for which the room is to be reserved, type of room required, rate, expected time of arrival, and intended method of payment. Some lodging operators may require additional information—telephone number, for example. Many require deposits from guests before they will confirm reservations. Others reserve rooms only for guests who provide national credit card numbers when they make their reservations.

The information taken from guests is recorded either on a paper form or at a computer terminal. If the paper form is used, additional processing is required to add the reservation to others for the same arrival date. If a computer terminal is used, the reservation is automatically added to the reservations database. The Value Lodge, for example, uses inexpensive paper forms for recording reservations and files all the reservations for one date in one folder. By contrast, the Kensington has a computerized system, and all reservations are recorded at terminals and added to the reservations database.

Each day, the reservations that have been taken for that particular day are given to the front desk so those on duty will have the names, addresses, and other information about guests who are expected to check in during the course of the day. In the Value Lodge, the owner has a single folder at the desk that contains all reservations for the current day. In the Kensington, the morning desk clerk uses the computer system at the front desk to print the list of reservations for the day. In some hotels, no list would be printed: desk clerks would use the computer system to look up arriving guests' reservations.

The second major goal of the reservations operation is to ensure that the greatest number of rooms possible are occupied each day and that the rates charged for those rooms are the highest possible.

The ideal goal in a hotel or motel is to have every room occupied each night at the highest possible rate. This is obviously the way to earn maximum revenue. Although it is desirable, however, it is nearly impossible to accomplish. In order to come as close to this ideal as possible, an owner or manager must establish a rate structure that will enable reservationists to sell as many rooms as possible. There must be a range of rates that appeal to the target clientele—that group of individuals and businesses that management wants to attract to the property.

Yield Management. In recent years, many hotels have instituted a reservation system taken from the airline industry called **yield management.** Although each hotel chain has a different variation of it, the goal is the same for all—to obtain maximum occupancy at maximum rates.

The yield management system at the Mountain Inn works as follows: a yield management team consisting of the reservation manager, front office manager, and director of sales meet once each week to review current reservations and establish specific room rates for times in the future. The Mountain Inn has three rates for its double rooms—A, B, and C. Rate A is their highest rate, rate B is their standard rate, and rate C is their lowest rate. During a future holiday period, the team expects demand for accommodations to be very high, and the Mountain Inn is expected to be sold-out for the entire time. The team has decided that only rate A will be quoted to potential guests seeking accommodations for that period. The week immediately after the holiday will be busy, but the Mountain Inn is not expected to be sold-out. After discussion, the team decides to quote rates A and B for that week. The team also decides to review room demand for that week at a future meeting. If reservations for that week are strong, the Mountain Inn will continue to quote only rates A and B. If there are many rooms still available for that week, the team will open up rate C to customers who request a lower rate.

In the fashion described above, the Mountain Inn yield management team reviews all weeks for a six-month period. Demand for accommodations is assessed based on past occupancy and current conditions. During periods of low demand, all rates are available to potential guests. During periods of high demand, only the highest rates are quoted. In that way, only those willing to pay the higher rates are accepted during periods of high demand, and those who are seeking only low rates can be accommodated during slack periods. This method assures the Mountain Inn maximum revenue and maximum occupancy.

One of the more difficult and interesting problems of lodging operations results from customers who make reservations and either cancel at the last minute or fail to check in. Those who fail to check in are called **no-shows.** Last minute cancellations and no-shows may result in vacant rooms and lost revenue. Potential guests, whose requests for

▶ No Room at the Inns ◀

Harris Rosen of Orlando, Florida, is one of the most successful independent hotel operators anywhere. Over the last decade, the occupancy rates in his hotels have averaged 96 percent while those of his competitors have never exceeded 78.8 percent. Much of his success has been attributed to a version of yield management that he has developed for his properties. Each day he sets the rate structure required to fill his vacant rooms for the coming night and establishes the rates his employees must quote as they take reservations over the telephone or sell rooms at the front desks. His approach is quite simple: openly cut prices during the day to lure guests, even if you have to reach rock-bottom rates to fill the last vacant rooms.

Mr. Rosen compares his method to the airlines' practice of yield management—lowering fares at various times on seats that could remain unsold.

Adapted from the New York Times, *November 23, 1995.*

reservations were turned down when it appeared the hotel would be sold-out, have then gone to other properties and may be permanently lost.

Historically, lodging operators have attempted to deal with this problem by **overbooking,** which means taking more reservations than the number of anticipated rooms available. Many transient hotels have used this method with some success. They have accepted 10 to 15 percent more reservations than they had rooms available, knowing from historical data that some customers will cancel and others will not arrive to claim their reservations.

Some difficulties arise when the anticipated number of cancellations fails to materialize, or when more people than anticipated arrive to claim their reservations. On these occasions, some guests must be **walked**—a hotel term meaning to send guests with confirmed reservations to other lodging properties because their reservations cannot be honored.

A few lodging operators have sometimes been guilty of serious overbooking. The vast majority have not. Nevertheless, almost all have found themselves in the unfortunate position of having to walk guests. When this happens, most attempt to find suitable accommodations for the guest at other properties, then pay for the guest's transportation to that property. Some even pay for the first night's accommodation.

In recent years, lodging operators have developed new strategies for dealing with the last minute cancellations and no-shows. They include

1. Confirming reservations with the provision that they will only be held until a specific time—5 P.M., for example. Thus, hotels do not need to overbook to any great extent because they can rent rooms to walk-in guests after that time.

2. Taking only **guaranteed reservations,** meaning that the lodging establishment will hold a room and charge the guest for that room unless the reservation is canceled prior to arrival by a specified date or time. Properties taking guaranteed reservations require a deposit in the form of cash, check, or credit card number when the reservation is made; hotels will not accept guaranteed reservations without one of these. Guests with guaranteed reservations are typically registered and charged for their rooms whether or not they actually arrive.

Resort hotels have long required advance payment for accommodations. The typical resort hotel will require a substantial advance deposit, and some resort hotels require full payment in advance. All have refund policies for customers who must cancel, but they vary greatly. Some will refund only a portion of the advance payment; others will refund the entire amount if the reservation is canceled within two or three weeks prior to scheduled arrival. Some have a sliding scale that provides a percentage refund ranging from 100 percent to 0 percent, depending on when the reservation is canceled: The closer the cancellation is to arrival time, the less of a percentage is refunded. No-shows are seldom a problem with resort hotels that require advance deposits. Thus, many of them do not overbook, and some will overbook only slightly, knowing that a few cancellations will occur.

▶ Housekeeping

The second major element in lodging operations is **housekeeping.** The principal goal of housekeeping is to serve the needs of guests by providing appropriate care for their accommodations and for various other areas in the lodging property. Although this may sound simple, it entails numerous large and small tasks, many of which are very easy for staff members to overlook. However, survey after survey has shown that guests notice and rate overall cleanliness in hotels, motels, and similar properties. These surveys also reveal that positive or negative feelings about housekeeping in a given property play a pivotal role in determining whether or not a guest will return to stay in the property again. In housekeeping operations, even the smallest task can be of very great importance to guests.

Providing appropriate care for guest rooms and other areas includes changing bed and bath linens, making beds, and cleaning rooms for current guests; providing the same services in rooms vacated by guests who have checked out, thus preparing these rooms for new occupants; cleaning hallways and such areas as the lobby, meeting rooms, public bathrooms, and offices used by the management; and insuring the availability of a supply of clean bed and bath linens either by operating an on-site laundry, by using a commercial laundry, or by making suitable arrangements with a linen rental company. In addition, the housekeeping departments in some properties have responsibility for looking after the supply of uniforms for uniformed employees in all departments and the supply of *food linen,* the general term for all linens used in food and beverage departments. Housekeeping may also have responsibility for redecorating and rehabilitating rooms, looking after articles in the property's "lost and found," maintaining floors through-out the property (for example, washing and waxing floors, vacuuming and shampooing carpets), washing windows, raising and lowering flags, moving furniture, repairing torn fabrics, attending to the rooms of employees who live in the property, and cleaning such outside areas as porches or sidewalks that surround the building. The tasks assigned to housekeeping are limited only by the imaginations of those who make the decisions in hotels, motels, and similar lodging properties.

The housekeeping operation can be complicated. Housekeeping is commonly the largest single department in a lodging property, and it is managed by an individual who is usually given such a title as head housekeeper, supervising housekeeper, executive housekeeper, or some variation on one of these. A head housekeeper manages a staff that may include people with such job titles as maid or housekeeper, room attendant, rooms inspector, houseman, laundry manager, linen room manager, assistant housekeeper, floor supervisor, and many other pos-sibilities. Job titles vary considerably from one property to another.

While many of the particular responsibilities of housekeeping may vary from one property to another, one major responsibility is com-mon to all: giving daily attention to guest rooms occupied the previous night, whether or not the guests in those rooms check out on the cur-rent day.

Attending to Guests' Rooms

Each guest room in a property is monitored daily by the housekeeping department to determine whether it is occupied or vacant. In most major hotels and motels, daily comparison is made between housekeeping's determinations and front office records of occupancy so that any differences can be identified and investigated.

When an occupied room becomes vacant because of a guest checkout, the housekeeping office is informed and a maid or room attendant is advised so that the room can be made ready for a new occupant. The room is considered **on change** until it has been made ready again for occupancy. This entails removing all soiled bed and bath linen from the room; replacing it with fresh, clean linen; making the bed(s); cleaning the bathroom; vacuuming the floor; dusting or polishing furniture; cleaning mirrors; emptying wastebaskets; replenishing supplies of tissue, toilet paper, matches, laundry bags, soap, and such amenities as shampoo, hair conditioner, and shower caps; and checking electric lights, televisions, clock radios, heating/cooling units, hair dryers, shoeshine machines, and other devices to be sure they are working properly. It may also require washing ashtrays; replenishing supplies for in-room coffee- and tea-making devices; restocking supplies for in-room bars; reporting items used from an in-room bar to the front office for billing purposes; checking the number of hangers in closets; and many other possibilities. There can be so much to do in every room in some properties that staff members are often given printed checklists to help insure that nothing is forgotten.

For rooms that will continue to be occupied by the current guests, the procedures may be essentially the same, although some properties do not change bed linens every day for guests staying several nights. It should be noted as well that it is probably not possible to do a thorough job of cleaning when guests' belongings are in the room. This is particularly true when clothes and other items are scattered around the room.

If a room has remained vacant since it was last made ready for a new occupant, it is not normally necessary to do more than check it quickly, just to be sure it is still fresh and clean.

In order to have adequate supplies of linens and other materials available as they work, room attendants normally have mobile carts that can be pushed from room to room. Each of these carts typically has a canvas bag for storing the soiled laundry taken from guests' rooms. All soiled laundry collected in the course of one day is normally taken to a single area for processing, which may entail separating it by type and reloading it in other carts that will be collected by a commercial laundry or linen rental company, or preparing it for processing by the in-house laundry.

In the larger hotels and motels of major cities, the work of room attendants may be inspected by supervisors, who verify that rooms have been properly cleaned and meet the standards established for the property. After a vacated room has been made up and inspected, the supervisor may have responsibility for reporting it ready for occupancy by informing the front office directly or by reporting it via the housekeeping office. In a number of the smaller properties, room attendants may have little or no immediate supervision and may report directly to the front office.

The number of room attendants and the manner in which their work is assigned varies greatly from one property to another. In some, they are paid by the hour and are expected to work at a reasonable pace, completing as many rooms as possible. In others, they are given a work quota for the seven-hour day that is stated in terms of the number of rooms or beds that must be done. In still others, they are paid by the room. In most cases, they are assigned a station, a term used to describe the particular section of property or the group of rooms assigned to a room attendant. The station may be a complete floor or a specific number of rooms on one floor, for example. Some hotels, motels, and similar properties use a team approach, assigning more than one attendant per room. The amount of time required to clean a room will depend on the number of attendants assigned to it as well as the size of the room, the number of beds, the extent of cleaning expected each day, and whether or not the room is a check-out. When a room is occupied by the same guests for several days, the amount of time attendants must spend in that room daily is somewhat less than the time they must spend in check-outs.

In those hotels that are considered luxury properties, room attendants normally have more work to do in each room. In some properties they must polish fine antique furniture; in others, they may be required to place arrangements of fresh flowers in rooms daily. In luxury hotels, standards of cleanliness are typically higher than in many other types of properties, so that a greater amount of time is expected to be taken for each room. In many luxury operations, guests may be provided with services not provided in other types of properties. In some, room attendants visit each occupied guest room during the early evening to supply fresh towels, empty wastebaskets, and turn down bedding.

At the Kensington and many other similar properties, these services are routinely performed for each guest. It is necessary, therefore, for the hotel to employ additional room attendants for this purpose. They are supervised by an assistant housekeeper who works an afternoon and evening shift. The Kensington uses housekeeping teams to clean rooms. Two room attendants spend approximately one half hour working together to clean a typical room; that is, one full hour of working time in each room. This is about 50 percent more time than is spent by room attendants at other hotels in the area.

The Mountain Inn and the Value Lodge assign specific rooms to each room attendant. In the Mountain Inn, each is assigned a permanent station consisting of ten rooms on one floor, which are to be completed in one seven-hour shift. In the Value Lodge, room attendants are expected to do fourteen rooms in the seven-hour shift, and those who complete the work satisfactorily in less time are allowed to do additional rooms for extra pay. Thus, room attendants in the Mountain Inn complete each room in an average of forty-two minutes, whereas those in the Value Lodge take about thirty minutes.

Caring for Linen

Caring for linen is one of the major responsibilities of any housekeeping department in any lodging operation. Without adequate supplies of appropriate linen, it is impossible to operate a lodging facility properly.

Linen—bed linen, bath linen, and, in some establishments, food linen—is one of the major problems and largest expenses in a lodging operation. Every bed in every room must be made up and ready for use at all times, whether or not the room is occupied. In addition, the property must have an adequate supply of linen on hand each day to change the linen on each bed, just in case the bed was used the previous night. Finally, there is always some linen in the process of being washed and ironed or folded, whether in the property's own laundry or at that of an outside service. In effect, any lodging operation must have at least three complete sets of linen for each bed and an additional quantity in inventory to replace items that are worn, torn, lost, or stolen. To make up a bed, one would need at least two sheets and one or more pillowcases, depending on the bed and the standards of the property.

In addition to bed linen, housekeeping should have at least three complete sets of bath linen for each guest that the property can accommodate. A set of bath linen would consist of at least one bath towel, one face towel, and one face cloth. Most properties also supply one tub mat for each bathroom. Considerable money is invested in the bed linens and bath linens that lodging establishments need for operation.

Better lodging establishments typically change bed and bath linens for each guest daily. Others—some economy motels and a number of inexpensive resorts—provide guests with changes of bath linens daily and changes of bed linens every two to three days. Still others—boarding houses, typically—are likely to change all linens just once a week. Every responsible lodging establishment would certainly change all linens in any guest accommodation after each check-out.

In general, there are three possible approaches to obtaining clean linen. The lodging operator can

1. own linen and install a laundry on premises to wash, iron, and fold it;
2. own linen and send it out to a commercial laundry to be washed, ironed, and folded;
3. rent clean linen.

Each of these approaches has advantages and disadvantages.

1.   Many hotels and motels maintain their own laundry equipment on premises. Space is set aside for the specialized equipment needed to wash, dry, and iron linens, which may have the name of the property embroidered or woven into the fabric.

Having one's own laundry has several advantages over other approaches. Linen does not leave the premises, so it is easier to control. If linen remains on the premises, it does not get lost as easily as when other methods are used, and personnel do not have to count linen leaving or returning to the building. The lodging operation is not dependent on an outside laundry, which can sometimes be late in returning clean linens and is thus less likely to encounter the kinds of difficulties caused by linen shortages. Finally, maintaining an in-house laundry is often more cost-effective than other approaches. In order for a lodging establishment to justify the expense of the investment in equipment and the ongoing cost of operating a laundry, however, the establishment must be large enough to keep the laundry operating several hours each day. Because of its remote location, the management of the Mountain Inn takes this approach.

2.   There are many lodging operations that prefer to own their own linen but are not large enough to justify the installation of laundry equipment on premises or the cost of using employees to wash and fold linen. In these cases, lodging operations must use the services of a commercial laundry. This choice still permits management to choose linen of the desired quality and inscribe it with the prop-

erty's name, logo, or both. However, those who send their laundry out to a commercial establishment must separate and either count or weigh all sheets, pillowcases, towels, and other items going to and coming from the laundry. Billing is often a problem when the hotel's count or weight does not agree with that of the commercial laundry. In addition, commercial laundries may lose, tear, or otherwise destroy items sent out to be washed, and this can be a source of difficulty and misunderstanding.

The Kensington has judged it less expensive to send its laundry to a commercial laundry located in a nearby suburb than to allocate space and pay the higher wages required to have it laundered on premises.

3.   Many lodging operators choose to rent clean linen rather than own it and have it laundered either on premises or in a commercial laundry. This is the most convenient of the three approaches: there is no investment in either linen or equipment, and management does not have the problems associated with operating a laundry. Many rental companies do not keep accurate records of the amount of linen returned by lodging operators because it is too time consuming to do so. Thus, lodging operators that rent clean linen may not have to account for it. They simply pay for the number of clean pieces they are sent and return the soiled linen. Laundries may not know how much linen they are losing to any one lodging operation, so they build the replacement cost of the lost linen into the rental prices charged to all lodging operators using their services.

Renting is typically the most costly of the three approaches, which is a distinct disadvantage. Another is that the lodging operator must accept the quality of linen supplied by the rental laundry, except in some special situations in which the rental laundry agrees to purchase higher quality linens for a specific lodging operation.

For many smaller operations, renting clean linen is the most desirable of the three approaches. The Value Lodge uses this approach because the owners of the motel are satisfied with the quality of the linen supplied by the rental company. Also, they lack the time to deal with laundry, they choose not to make any investment in linen or laundry equipment, and they do not want to add laundry staff to their payroll.

Redecorating and Rehabilitating Rooms

A very important function of the housekeeping operation is long-term upkeep. This is the process of maintaining the appearance of guest rooms by attending to the many items that make rooms attractive and appealing to guests, including paint, wallpaper, fixtures, carpeting, furniture, lamp shades, curtains, draperies, and other fabrics. All these must be kept in the proper condition. This may mean touching up the paint on one wall, patching damaged wallpaper on another, or replacing a burned patch of carpet, a damaged lamp, a tattered lamp shade, or a broken mirror—the list is endless. If the quality of guest rooms is allowed to deteriorate, they become less appealing to potential guests, and fewer people are willing to stay in them. Over time, lodging operators who ignore this important element of housekeeping find that the establishment has deteriorated below the original standards of the property.

Many hotel and motel operators refurbish guest rooms regularly on a planned rotation system. Each year, a certain number of rooms are taken out of service to be completely refurbished. They are stripped, then redecorated and refurnished. One well-known hotel in New York completely refurbishes several floors each year. Over the course of several years, every room in the property is completely redone.

▶ Security

The third of the front office operations is that devoted to providing security. Security is one of the most important services provided for guests.

Hotels have both moral and legal obligations to protect guests from harm and safeguard their property. The goal of security is to provide the necessary protection to keep guests and their property safe. The extent of this protection varies from establishment to establishment and from location to location. Danger to guests may came from intruders, other guests, or from such hazards as fire or unsafe conditions in the property.

Major metropolitan areas typically have greater crime problems than rural areas, and large hotels in the centers of cities tend to have greater difficulty with burglary and robbery than do small properties in outlying areas. Thus, major hotels in major cities need to take greater security measures than their rural counterparts.

Hotels have always attracted thieves. Transient guests, after all, tend to have many of the items thieves seek: cash, credit cards, jewelry, and other valuables. And although all states have laws stating that lodging operators cannot be held responsible for losses of these valuables unless they are deposited in management's safe, many guests fail

Traditionally, hotel front offices have provided guests with safe-deposit facilities similar to those provided by banks. Instead, some have begun to provide in-room safes similar to that from the Sentry Group, illustrated above. (Photo courtesy of Sentry Group.)

to do so. Many keep cash, jewelry, and other valuables in their rooms, where it is subject to theft either by professional thieves or sometimes even by unscrupulous employees of the establishment (although this is rare).

In some hotels, motels, and similar establishments, prostitution presents problems. Most major cities have prostitutes who find willing customers among hotel and motel guests. It is not uncommon for guests to meet prostitutes in bars and invite them to their hotel rooms. Sometimes guests give their room keys to prostitutes who promise to come to the hotel room. Often they do. Sometimes, however, they merely give or sell the keys to professional thieves.

Major hotels, motels, and similar properties normally provide safe-deposit boxes for guests. In most establishments, these are located in the front office and are exactly the same as those used by banks. Some, however, provide in-room safes. In contrast, smaller and older properties, including small inns and motels, may provide nothing more than a single safe in the front office where valuables can be placed.

Fire and smoke represent continuing threats in most lodging operations. Sometimes guests accidentally start fires in their rooms. During the day, when people are awake, this is a difficult enough problem; at night, when guests are asleep, it is a terrifying threat to life. Newer establishments have smoke detectors and alarms to signal fire stations and to alert employees. But such systems are not universally required, and fire continues to be a danger. The security department of a large hotel in a major city may include personnel who patrol all floors of the building at night with watchmen's time clocks, looking for any signs of smoke or fire as well as for any other potential threats to guests.

Unsafe conditions that exist within the lodging property present a very serious threat to the welfare of guests and employees. Therefore, identifying, reporting, and remedying such conditions is of major importance in any lodging operation. Doing so is not the sole province of security, however; it is or should be one element in the job of every lodging employee. For example, room attendants who note frayed electric cords on hair dryers, lamps, televisions, or other appliances should be trained to report these so that repairs can be made.

Similarly, instances of torn carpets, broken glass, burned-out lights in stairwells, broken chairs or other pieces of furniture, elevators that do not function properly—all such hazards should be reported immediately by the employees who spot them, to prevent unnecessary harm or injury to guests and to other employees.

An important element in providing security for the guests of hotels, motels, and similar properties is that group of individuals known as the security staff. As indicated previously, they may be hotel or motel employees, or they may work for an outside company that provides security services on contract.

Larger properties may have some security personnel in uniform, while others work in plain clothes. Many of those employed as security personnel have backgrounds in law enforcement and are trained to spot people who are likely to present problems—potential thieves, confidence artists, prostitutes, and others. Security personnel are often placed in locations from which they can observe everyone who enters and exits the property. Resort properties, such as the Mountain Inn, often follow this procedure. They may employ a director of security, who supervises several security guards who work in plain clothes. Some may observe entrances and exits, while others mingle with guests in bars, nightclubs, and other recreational facilities.

By contrast, the large transient hotels and motels in major cities may install closed-circuit television cameras to monitor entrances, cor-

Security is one of the most important services provided to protect guests from harm and to safeguard their property. Security personnel in many hotels monitor some areas with cameras to provide maximum coverage with minimal staff. (Photo courtesy of Pinkerton Security & Investigation Services.)

ridors, storage facilities, and other important areas. Properties such as the Kensington commonly have modern closed-circuit television networks that are used to monitor a number of areas in these properties—particularly areas that are deserted at night and those from which food, liquor, and other hotel property may be stolen. In the Kensington and similar properties, employee entrances are typically locked during late evening and night hours, and security guards are posted at these entrances during the day to prevent their use by unauthorized individuals.

Small motels and similar properties cannot normally afford the number and type of security personnel employed in the larger operations just described. In the small property, the owner or manager, who is normally on premises most or all of the time, typically serves as the security staff. On a small scale, he must attend to all the security routines for which major city hotels employ security staff. Typically, this means keeping watch for suspicious or unusual activities. In the Value Lodge, for example, the owner must note carefully who enters and leaves the rooms and watch for strangers attempting unauthorized entry. The owner of such a property will normally walk throughout his property several times during the evening.

▶ Group 2

Most commercial hotels, motels, and similar lodging properties provide more than the basics, in keeping with the wishes of their guests. The majority provide additional services, some of which are listed above in group 2. Because the number of possibilities is so great, we will restrict the following discussion to those listed earlier in the chapter, which are those most often provided by the operators of hotels, motels, and similar properties.

The extent to which these services are provided to guests will vary. Some motels will provide few if any of them and some luxury hotels may provide them all; other hotels, motels, and similar lodging properties will offer a limited number.

One of the most common and important of the services and operations offered in lodging operations is front service.

▶ Front Service

Front service is a term used to identify the operation that provides a variety of useful and desirable personal services for guests. These

The front-service staff consists of uniformed personnel with such job titles as bellperson, concierge, and doorperson (pictured right). (Photo courtesy of The Park Hyatt Hotel, Washington, D.C.)

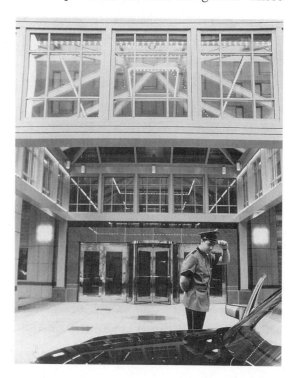

include attended service at the front door for handling luggage, obtaining taxicabs, and opening doors; escorting guests from the front desk to the assigned accommodations, as discussed in the section on check-in; carrying luggage for guests; opening guest room doors for those having difficulty with their keys; delivering newspapers, mail, packages, or telephone messages to guests' rooms; providing information about restaurants, theaters, shopping, and sightseeing (if this is not done at the front desk); making reservations or providing tickets, or attending to both of these, for shows, tours, sporting events, and transportation.

The employees engaged in front service are normally uniformed and have such job titles as bellman or bellperson, doorman or doorperson, baggage porter, concierge, superintendent of service. People in these positions are typically paid low hourly wages and receive gratuities or tips from those for whom they perform services.

▶ Telephone

Telephone service has the obvious goal of providing a means for voice communication for guests and employees. Additionally, a telephone communication system may be used to provide guests with voice mail, wake-up services, and the means for sending and receiving fax messages. In some properties, guest rooms are equipped with the necessary jacks for linking laptop and notebook computer modems to the telephone system—a requirement of growing numbers of guests.

Today, the telephone service in most lodging establishments is automated. Guests in many hotels and motels can dial local and long-distance calls directly. Charges are calculated by computerized call accounting systems and automatically charged to guest accounts. Telephone operators in major metropolitan hotels do not make individual wake-up calls to guests: these are now accomplished by computer. And in many properties, guest rooms are equipped with clock radios so that guests no longer need wake-up calls.

In some properties—the Kensington, for example—the telephone system is operated as a separate department, with round-the-clock operator service available. In others—typically smaller establishments such as the Value Lodge—the telephone operation is actually part of the front office operation. The desk clerk on duty serves as telephone operator in addition to other duties.

▶ Food and Beverage

The food and beverage operation can be critical to the overall success of some lodging operations. For a number of luxury establishments, the quality of the food and beverage products offered in the restaurants and bars are among their major attractions.

For those hotels, motels, and similar lodging operations that offer food and beverage services, the primary goal of the operation is to provide food and beverage products and services that meet the quality standards established by the owners and managers.

Food and beverage operations in lodging establishments offer their services in three distinctly different types of facilities.

1. Restaurants and bars
2. Guests' rooms
3. Banquet rooms

Restaurants and Bars

Many commercial hotels, motels, and similar lodging operations operate food and beverage facilities that are normally open to guests of the property and to the public at large. These facilities include formal and informal restaurants—specialty restaurants, coffee shops, snack bars, and cafeterias among them—as well as bars, cocktail lounges, and nightclubs.

The type and quality of food and beverage products and services available to guests in lodging establishments vary, of course, from one establishment to another. Some properties—motels, most commonly— provide only vending machines with packaged foods. Other motels have vending machines that contain frozen meals, which can be cooked with microwave ovens installed in the lobby or near guests' rooms. By contrast, many luxury hotels take pride in providing the finest food and beverage products and services available. These properties have talented staffs of professionals in their food and beverage departments who are the equals of those in the finest restaurants. In between these two extremes are the majority of hotels, motels, and similar lodging establishments—those that serve guests and customers from the surrounding community foods and beverages that are comparable to those served in most restaurants.

Guests' Rooms

Most first-class and luxury hotels provide **room service,** a type of service that provides guests with food and beverages that may be ordered from and consumed in their rooms.

The most popular meal for room service is breakfast, even though some hotels provide room service twenty-four hours a day. Room service menus typically include items that are similar to or the same as those offered on menus in the public rooms. However, the prices for items offered on room service menus are normally higher than regular menu prices.

Even with higher prices, however, room service is not always a profitable enterprise. One of the primary reasons is that room service is labor intensive and relatively inefficient. It is necessary to have a separate staff of servers for room service, and these individuals may have few orders and little work much of the time. In addition, delivering room service orders can be a very slow and time-consuming busi-

Room service, available in all fine hotels, provides food and beverage service in guests' rooms. Here, a server at the famed Hyatt Regency in St. Louis delivers breakfast to a guest on a mobile cart, often called a room-service table. (Photo courtesy of Hyatt Regency St. Louis at Union Station.)

ness: food that comes from the main kitchen often must be transported great distances to guest rooms. For all of these reasons, labor cost associated with a given room service order is higher than that for the same item served in a public restaurant.

Banquet Rooms

Most establishments with extensive food and beverage facilities make concerted efforts to attract banquet business. The term **banquet** is used to refer to the prearranged service of food and beverages to a group of people in a private room not in use as a public dining room. Banquet business is normally very profitable—often more profitable than restaurant or bar business—because exact numbers of guests are guaranteed in advance, making it comparatively easy to achieve planned food and labor costs.

The availability of food and beverage products and services in some or all of the above can increase the appeal of a given property to potential lodging customers. Some guests return to particular lodging operations time after time because of the excellent food offered in the dining room or because of the superior wine list available. Some may enjoy the great luxury of having breakfast or some other meal served in the comfort and privacy of a guest room or suite. In some instances, those planning one or another type of banquet function will reserve sleeping rooms in the hotel, bringing revenue that would otherwise not have come to the property. Sometimes groups will select a particular hotel and reserve large numbers of rooms for a convention because the hotel has the capacity to provide banquet service for a very large group—five hundred or more people. The presence of a food and beverage operation can be very important in a lodging operation and can make a difference in the amount of revenue the property can generate both from food and beverage sales and from room sales.

▶ Recreation and Entertainment

Recreation and entertainment can be major factors in attracting guests to a lodging operation. In some cases, one or the other of these may be the only reason guests decide to go to a particular property. Recreation and entertainment are broad categories that can include an array of activities and events that guests find appealing.

One category of recreation and entertainment includes a number of well-known and popular athletic and sporting activities: tennis, skiing, horseback riding, golf, and swimming, for example. However, this category also includes such simple activities as Ping-Pong and pool found in some small family resort properties.

Another category includes the nightclubs and other showplaces featuring star-quality entertainers that one finds in many mountain and shore resort properties across the country, in the major hotels and motels of Las Vegas and Atlantic City, and on such closely related facilities as cruise ships.

Still another category is gaming, a highly profitable and very popular attraction in many of the hotels of Las Vegas and Atlantic City as well as on Native American reservations, riverboats, and in some areas outside the United States. Along the same line as gaming are the bingo games, card games, and coin-operated machines of various sorts that are available in many properties because they appeal to guests.

The operators of lodging properties who believe the addition of one or more of these is likely to increase the appeal of the properties, their profitability, or both will probably attempt to include them.

▶ Parking

Facilities for parking are of ever-growing importance to guests and lodging operators, as more and more travelers use automobiles—those they own and those they rent. Many properties are so far removed from any public transportation that guests must have automobiles to get around the local area.

Those properties surrounded by adequate land have relatively little difficulty using it for parking—either outdoor parking near the doors to guests' accommodations or on a simple lot, or indoor parking in a purpose-built structure. By contrast, many newer properties have parking facilities within their structures, permitting guests to drive inside buildings and to park their own cars before proceeding to lobbies to check in.

A number of older hotels in the centers of cities have been forced to arrange alternative parking. Because they had no surrounding land and could not create parking space within their structures, many have had to make arrangements for parking with nearby garages and lots. Some provide pickup and delivery service, so that guests need never go farther than the front door to leave or retrieve their vehicles.

▶ Other Personal Services

There are any number of other possibilities for offering personal services to guests of hotels, motels, and similar lodging operations. The following are the most common.

Banking Services

For the convenience of guests, some lodging operations provide banking services at the front desk. Cashiers normally make change, and in some properties they cash both personal checks and travelers checks. Given the increased number of international travelers, a growing number of lodging operations convert foreign currencies for dollars.

Guest Laundry

A large number of hotels, motels, and other commercial lodging operations provide personal laundry service to guests. In many instances, guests can arrange for soiled shirts, blouses, underwear, and other clothing to be collected from their rooms, laundered, and returned to their rooms. Some even provide same-day service. Another approach is to provide self-service facilities for guests to attend to their own laundry by making washers, dryers, irons, and ironing boards available.

Dry Cleaning

Most properties that provide laundry service also provide dry cleaning services for guests. Guests can arrange to have suits, skirts, trousers, and other garments collected from their rooms, cleaned, pressed, and returned to their rooms. As with laundry, some provide same-day service. Dry cleaning services in hotels are normally referred to as valet services.

HairStyling

Many lodging properties provide facilities for men's and women's hair styling. In a few properties, these are still known by the older terms barber shop and beauty salon, terms that are disappearing from the lodging lexicon. Some facilities offering hairstyling may also offer nail care, cosmetics treatments, and related services.

Office Services

Some hotels, motels, and other lodging properties offer an array of office services, primarily for business travelers. They may provide copy machines, fax machines, computers and printers, modems, typewriters, and tape recorders for dictation. Some have this equipment—as well as such simple items as staplers, staple removers, and paper clips—set up in special rooms for use by guests twenty-four hours a day. A very few will provide personal assistance on request.

Health Facilities

Because many guests are very health conscious and because of the increased emphasis on exercise, a number of lodging operations provide a variety of facilities for exercise. Some have health clubs, saunas, and steam rooms on premises. Others have set up a room or an area with exercise equipment. Some have small swimming pools for exercise. Still others assist joggers in finding appropriate routes at various hours of the day.

Newsstands

In a lodging establishment, the term *newsstand* can refer to a small counter at which a few newspapers and magazines are sold, or to a larger enterprise selling newspapers, magazines, books, candy, cigars, cigarettes, souvenirs, and such personal articles as disposable razors, shaving cream, antiperspirants, toothpaste, and the like.

Language Services

Hotels, motels, and similar lodging establishments that accommodate tourists and business travelers from other nations often employ individuals who are fluent in two or more languages. Such people can be very helpful to visitors who are not fluent in English.

Other Shops

Hotels and other major lodging properties in large cities are very likely to rent space to shopkeepers who provide various goods and services to guests as well as to people from the surrounding area. It is not unusual to find travel agencies, jewelers, luggage shops, and clothing boutiques, among many other possible shops, in the lobby areas of these properties.

The availability of some or all of these commonly increases the appeal of a hotel, motel, or similar lodging establishment to guests. Therefore, the property offering these typically enjoys some competitive advantage over those that do not.

▶ The Interrelatedness of Lodging Operations

It should be apparent that the several operations that are the very essence of a lodging facility—front office, housekeeping, and security, identified as part of group 1—as well as those that enhance the quality of the lodging operations—front service, telephone, food and beverages services, and others, identified as part of group 2—must function effectively, both individually and as a group, for the operation to achieve its goals.

Within the front office operation, reservations must be accurately recorded if the room clerks are to know how many rooms they have available to rent to persons without reservations. Room clerks must properly record information about arriving and departing guests if the housekeeping department is to have accurate data to perform its job. Housekeepers must clean and prepare vacated rooms properly and report the room numbers of made-up rooms to the front desk promptly and accurately so that newly arrived guests can be assigned to suitable accommodations.

In the front services operation, bellpersons checking guests into rooms should note and report the numbers of any rooms that are not up to standard—those with burned-out lightbulbs, damaged furniture, or dripping faucets, for example. This information helps housekeeping identify problems and keep guest rooms in the proper condition.

In the food and beverage operation, room service employees must accurately verify the names and room numbers of guests ordering from their rooms so that the items ordered can be delivered to the correct room quickly. Similarly, employees in restaurants must verify the names and room numbers of guests who charge food and beverages so that the bills of those guests can be properly charged.

Employees attending to guests' laundry and dry cleaning requirements must be particularly careful to obtain and record room numbers correctly so that garments can be returned to the right rooms and charges for the service can be recorded on the right bills.

Because the operations in a lodging establishment are interrelated, all must be functioning properly and in a coordinated way for the lodging operation to achieve its goals. When any given operation is not performing as designed or intended, other operations are affected. For example, if the housekeeping operation in the Kensington fails to clean rooms quickly, the front office operation will be affected: room clerks may be forced to tell guests that there will be a delay in assigning them to rooms, thus disappointing some guests and possibly angering some others. In addition, this may affect the behavior of room clerks toward guests.

If one or another of the lodging operations fails to perform properly, the overall operation will not achieve its goals.

▶ Summary

In this chapter, lodging operations are examined. Front office, housekeeping, and security are identified as the basic operations that are common to all lodging facilities. Front service, telephone, food and beverage, recreation/entertainment, parking, and personal services are identified as six additional activities not common to all lodging operations but used selectively by some to aid in achieving their goals. Examples are drawn from three different types of lodging properties—the Value Lodge, the Mountain Inn, and the Kensington. Finally, the interrelatedness of activities in a lodging enterprise is emphasized and offered as a basis for examining and understanding complex lodging operations.

Key Terms

Banquet	No-Shows
Check-in	On Change
Check-out	Overbooking
Front Office	Reservation
Front Service	Room Clerk
Guaranteed Reservation	Room Service
Housekeeping	Walk
Information	Yield Management

Questions

1. Name the three operations common to all lodging facilities.

2. List and state the goals of the four activities associated with the front office and describe the functions of each.

3. Identify six additional services offered by some, but not all, lodging operators.

4. What are the advantages of electronic locks over traditional locks and metal keys?

5. Describe three variations on check-out procedure used by hotels, motels, and similar facilities.

6. Define the terms *overbooking* and *no-show.* Describe two problems that have caused some lodging operators to overbook.

7. What is the goal of housekeeping?

8. Describe ten tasks that may be assigned to housekeeping.

9. List ten tasks typically involved in making a room ready for occupancy.

10. Why would a guest room in a luxury hotel take more time to make ready for occupancy than one in an economy motel?

11. Why is it necessary to redecorate or rehabilitate guest rooms every few years? List the kinds of tasks likely to be required for the complete rehabilitation of a guest room in a luxury hotel.

12. Describe several security measures that would typically be taken in a large center-city hotel. Contrast those with security measures typically taken in a small motel in a rural community.

13. List ten guest services normally associated with front service.

14. Identify three services provided to guests by a modern telephone system.

15. List and describe three different types of facilities in which food and beverage services are available in lodging operations.

16. Of the services offered in the three types of food and beverage facilities identified in number 15, which is the most profitable? Why?

17. Is it more important for lodging properties in remote rural areas to have parking facilities for their guests than for those located in city centers? Why?

18. List eight personal services identified in the chapter that are offered by some but not all lodging properties.

1. Visit a lodging property in your community. Identify the services offered to guests. Are there any services offered in the property that are *not* discussed in this chapter?

2. You are the desk clerk of a local motel. The reservation department has overbooked for the current day. Unfortunately, the anticipated number of cancellations did not materialize, and a guest with a confirmed reservation is now at your front desk. This particular guest has given the telephone number of your motel to a large number of potential buyers of his products, and many of these people will be calling to make appointments with him. You do not have a vacant room, so it is necessary for you to walk the guest. In your own words, explain how you would do this. Describe what you would do, what you would say, how you would say it, and how you would deal with the guest if she were very angry.

3. You are the evening desk clerk at a motel located in a remote area in the western part of the United States. At 9:00 P.M., you have no vacant rooms left except for one you are holding for a Mr. Nern, an individual with a guaranteed reservation who has not yet arrived. Your records show that the anticipated arrival time for the guaranteed reservation was 6:00 P.M. A woman without any reservation is at your front desk asking if any rooms are available. You check with other lodging establishments in the area, but find they have no vacant rooms either. She is desperate, because the next area with lodging facilities is over one hundred miles away. She is too tired to attempt that long drive at this hour. What would you do?

Part Five

Hospitality Management Perspectives

T e n

Hospitality Operations Management

After reading and studying this chapter, you should be able to:

1 Define the term *operations management.*

2 List and define the functions of management.

3 List the six steps in the organizing process.

4 Discuss the significance of an organization chart.

5 List and discuss the four steps in the control process.

6 Define *marketing* as used in hospitality operations.

7 List and describe the four elements of marketing.

8 Define the term *human resources management* and describe the activities it includes.

9 Identify three important steps taken by management to enhance employee safety in the workplace.

10 Define the term *accounting* and identify the two major financial statements derived from accounting records.

11 Define the following terms:

   a Asset

   b Current assets

    c   Fixed assets
    d   Liability
    e   Current liability
    f   Long-term liability
    g   Owner's equity
    h   Income statement
    i   Revenue
    j   Expense
    k   Profit
    l   Loss

12 Identify the formula for calculating each of the following:
    a   Food cost-to-sales ratio
    b   Beverage cost-to-sales ratio
    c   Labor cost-to-sales ratio
    d   Percentage of occupancy

13 Identify each of the following:
    a   Inventory turnover
    b   Return on sales
    c   Average sale per customer
    d   Average rate per occupied room

14 Define the term *budget.*

15 Describe the importance of cost control to the management of a hospitality operation.

16 Identify benefits that computers can provide for hospitality operations.

▶ Introduction

Previous chapters have identified various types of hospitality establishments, discussed hospitality facilities, and described basic elements common to hospitality operations. This chapter will be an introduction to operations management in the hospitality enterprise.

Operations management is a term that requires some explanation. In the hospitality industry and in this text, the term **operations management** is defined as the day-to-day activities that managers engage in to achieve the goals of the operations they manage.

Those with any experience in professional hospitality operations are likely to be familiar with some or all of the areas that these activities encompass, and they are known to hospitality managers by such traditional business terms as *marketing, accounting,* and *human resources management.* These and others similar to them are areas in which managers must be able to apply certain specific skills.

▶ The Functions of Management

In formal texts devoted to the subject, management at all levels is often said to have four specific functions.

1. Planning
2. Organizing
3. Directing
4. Controlling

▶ Planning

Planning is the primary task of managers at all levels. At the highest level—many refer to it as top management—planning is the process of defining goals and objectives for an organization and determining the appropriate means for achieving them. In its broadest sense, planning is an attempt to define the organization's future: to determine today what the state of organization should be in the future—one year or five years from now. In the hospitality industry, top management must make plans today for the future. These are likely to center on such considerations as the service products that will be offered in the future, the rate of expansion for the organization, the rate of sales increases necessary to sustain that growth, and the means for financing the expansion.

To illustrate planning in one hospitality organization, we will cite several examples from Marecki Foods, the business and industry hospitality organization described in chapter 5. In the Marecki organization, top management is developing plans to enlarge the business. These plans include increasing the number of clients by 10 percent per year and expanding the company from its present regional base to one that is more national in scope. This is an example of the type of high-level and long-range planning that top managers do.

At the next highest level—middle management—planning tends to be more pragmatic and more short range. In the Marecki organization, the middle managers are the district managers. Their plans are linked to the day-to-day realities of the units they oversee. At Marecki Foods, the district manager of the area that includes the Mountain Bank and six other units is one of several middle-level managers. She works with unit managers to plan annual budgets to submit to the main office once a year. She also makes plans for unit renovations as needed and for such major purchases as kitchen equipment and computer systems.

At the lowest management level—the supervisory level—planning tends to be for the very near term. Supervisory managers must make plans for today, tomorrow, and next week. Their plans deal with such problems as having adequate staff and sufficient food available in the kitchen to prepare and serve the next meal and meals for the balance of the week. They commonly make plans, for example, for having enough servers and linens on hand in the dining room to prepare for heavy demand for the next three days. In the Mountain Bank unit, the manager plans menus as well as the food purchases necessary to prepare those menus, and he plans staffing levels for the operation, including the daily work schedules for employees.

▶ Organizing

Organizing follows planning as the next logical step in the management process. It is the second function of management. After a manager has developed plans designed to achieve some objective, those plans must be carried out. That is the purpose of the additional steps in the management process—organizing, directing, and controlling.

Organizing means coordinating the use of resources, human and otherwise, to achieve established objectives. To organize work in a hospitality operation, a manager determines how human and other resources will be combined and activated to achieve established objectives.

Organizing is accomplished by means of the following series of steps:

1. Determine what work must be done to execute plans and achieve objectives.
2. Arrange that work into logical patterns or structures.
3. Assign the work to specific jobs.
4. Allocate the resources required to accomplish the work.
5. Coordinate the work activity.
6. Evaluate the results of the organizing process.

Assume that in the Steak Shack, the restaurant described in chapter 5, the chef has completed plans to feed the expected number of customers for the following week. The first step in the organizing process is to determine what must be done to carry out the plans. Clearly, food must be ordered and a staff schedule must be set up. The second step is to group the work into logical patterns. To do this, the chef must decide which menu items should be prepared by each of the stations in the kitchen. The third step is to assign the preparation of the various menu items to specific cooks. Next, each cook will be told the number of portions of each item to prepare and will be given recipes to use. Additionally, the chef will make provision for the ingredients to be on hand when needed. Next, he will coordinate the work activity, synchronizing the efforts of all personnel so that the established goals will be achieved; that is, that the various menu items will be ready on time. He will specify the times at which roasts and potatoes are placed in ovens and soup and sauces cookery begins so that all these items will be properly done at the time needed. As the work proceeds, he will continually evaluate the results of the organizing process to determine whether or not changes or alterations are required.

Once the organizing process is completed, each of the six steps does not necessarily have to be repeated each day. When work is satisfactorily organized, it simply becomes a daily routine. Although these daily routines should be reevaluated on a regular basis, they are unlikely to be changed unless new, more effective or efficient ways are found.

Hospitality Organization

The work in any hospitality enterprise can be organized in any of several ways. One way is to create departments in which the focus is on employees whose work is logically grouped. For example, all of the employees working in the dining room of the Steak Shack can be grouped into one department known as the dining room service department. This department is headed by a dining room manager and includes all servers and bussers. Similarly, all employees working in the front office of the Kensington hotel can be grouped into a front office department headed by a front office manager.

Organization Charts

An organization chart is simply a diagram of the formal structure of the business organization. In a small organization like the Steak Shack, an organization chart shows the departments in the organization and the relationship of the departments to one another. In figure

10.1, the organization chart of the Steak Shack, the lines connecting the various departments show the reporting structure. The reporting structure in an organization indicates to employees which workers report to particular supervisors. From figure 10.1, it is clear that the dining room manager and the chef both report to the general manager of the restaurant. It is also clear that cooks and dishwashers report to the chef, while servers and bussers report to the dining room manager. The owner/manager of the Steak Shack considered other possible organizational structures before settling on the one illustrated, but rejected them as unsuitable for this specific operation.

It is especially important in an organization to ensure that no employee has more than one immediate supervisor—a practice identified as unity of command. If an employee reports to more than one manager, there is a strong possibility—even a probability—that the employee will be given opposing or contradictory instructions by these managers. This will result in conflict and confusion. If, for example, the chef identified in figure 10.1 were to begin giving instructions to servers to serve plates of food from the right, the servers could become confused and frustrated because the dining room manager had instructed them to serve from the left. Some would be angry at being criticized by the two managers for failing to follow directions. If the chef wanted an item served in a particular way, the correct procedure would be to discuss it with the dining room manager, who could, in

Figure 10-1

Organization chart: Steak Shack

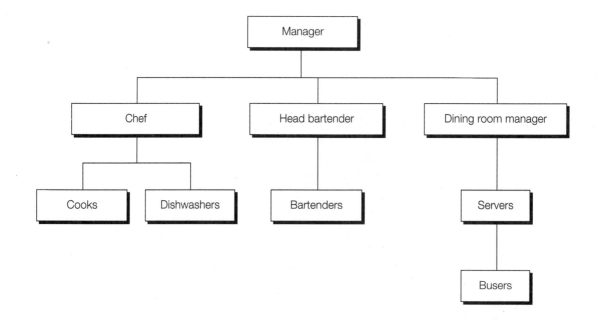

turn, instruct the servers. Similarly, if the manager wanted to change a standard recipe, she would be wrong to go directly to the cook preparing that item. Proper procedure would be for the manager to discuss it with the chef, who would in turn instruct the cooks. When one employee has two or more bosses giving him contradictory orders, confusion and conflict are sure to result.

▶ Directing

The third management function is directing. **Directing** is the process of achieving organizational goals by leading, motivating, and supervising subordinates. Directing is important at all levels of management, but it is particularly important at the supervisory level. Hospitality operations tend to be more labor intensive than other businesses. This means that a larger proportion of hospitality employees report to managers at the supervisory level.

In the Mountain Inn, the front office manager is the supervisory manager with responsibility for leading, motivating, and supervising the front office staff. One of her activities aimed at fulfilling this responsibility is to hold regular meetings with staff to deal with some or all of a range of important topics, including procedures for handling credit cards, dealing with complaining guests, selecting and assigning rooms for arriving guests, and plans for room renovations over the next six months. In addition, because the front office manager is normally at the front desk during periods of heavy arrivals, she is in an excellent position to observe employees and to make note of problems that should be addressed during the meetings. This is just a small sam-

Front office managers and other supervisors commonly hold meetings of the front office team to deal with such important topics as procedures for handling credit cards and selecting and assigning rooms for arriving guests, among many others. (Photo courtesy of Red Lion Hotels and Inns.)

ple of the dozens of activities required of the front office manager of the Mountain Inn.

The vast majority of hospitality employees report to chefs, front office managers, dining room managers, and other supervisory managers. In hospitality operations, the employees who report to supervisory managers are those whose job titles are best known to the public, including servers, desk clerks, cooks, reservationists, dishwashers, housekeepers, and bartenders. Employees reporting to supervisory managers account for as much as 90 percent of all hospitality employees.

▶ Controlling

The fourth function of management is controlling. **Control** is a process used by managers to regulate and sometimes restrain the actions of people in order to achieve desired goals. Controlling consists of decisions and actions taken by managers to assure that desired goals are achieved.

Assuming that plans are made to achieve goals and objectives, the enterprise is organized, and managers direct the efforts of employees, it is unlikely that goals and objectives will be achieved unless managers exert control over those efforts to assure that goals will be reached. In part, they do this by preventing incidents and problems.

The Control Process

The control process consists of four steps.
1. Establish standards and standard procedures for operation.
2. Train employees to follow established standards and standard procedures.
3. Monitor employee performance and compare actual performance with established standards.
4. Take appropriate action to correct deviations in performance.

One example will serve to illustrate.

In the Steak Shack, one of the three soups listed on the menu is an onion soup served with a small toasted slice of rye bread covered with mozzarella cheese. The item is placed briefly in a broiler just before service to melt the cheese. In recent years, the restaurant has earned a reputation for having the best onion soup in the area, and the owner/manager wants to keep that reputation. To do so, he must be sure that all portions of onion soup are identical to one another day after day. The best way to achieve this is to establish a standard procedure for preparing the item. This is done by writing a standard recipe, a recipe that kitchen personnel are required to use each time the item is prepared. The recipe is printed on a card and is accompanied by a color photograph of one portion prepared as it is to appear to each customer. Staff members must be trained to follow the recipe. If they do so correctly and see that every portion looks like that in the photograph, there is some reasonable assurance that all portions will be identical and the reputation will be maintained. The chef must monitor employee performance, comparing actual portions of onion soup with the standard portion defined by the standard recipe and photograph. If there are portions that do not measure up, steps must be taken to correct performance. The nature and type of corrective actions will depend on what went wrong.

▶ Operations Management

As indicated earlier in this chapter, *operations management* is defined as the day-to-day activities that managers engage in to achieve the goals of the operations they manage. These activities cover a number of key areas, including marketing, human resources, accounting, budgeting, cost control, and computers. In this chapter, we will suggest how all these key areas are linked to an operations manager's job in the hospitality industry. Successful performance as an operations manager in hospitality requires considerable knowledge of these key areas. In the course of demonstrating this, the chapter will provide a sense of the broad range of daily activities that face the typical manager in the hospitality business.

▶ Key Area 1: Marketing

The very best manager cannot make an enterprise meet its financial goals if too few customers patronize it. Restaurants must serve a given number of customers per week and hotels must insure that a given number of rooms are occupied if these hospitality operations are to be financially healthy. Our discussion of marketing will focus on the activities associated with obtaining the number of customers or guests required for a foodservice or lodging operation to achieve the necessary degree of financial health.

▶ Definition of Marketing

The American Marketing Association defines marketing very broadly. It states that marketing is "the process of planning and executing the conception, pricing, promotion, and distribution of ideas, goods, and services to create exchanges that will satisfy individual and organizational objectives."[1]

While this definition is entirely suitable for organizations that manufacture and sell goods that customers tend to use in their homes and businesses, it needs to be adjusted slightly to apply to service products that customers tend to consume in hospitality establishments. Our adjusted definition for hospitality operations is as follows: **marketing** is the process of planning service products, finding the right place to locate, and pricing and promoting products to attract sufficient numbers of customers/guests and to create exchanges that will satisfy both their needs and the goals of the hospitality enterprise.

▶ Elements of Marketing

The above definition has four key elements.

1. Product
2. Place
3. Price
4. Promotion

Product

One basic decision to be made in hospitality marketing is the nature of the service products to be offered. To some extent, that is defined by the characteristics of the type of establishment one intends to operate. Some of the many possible foodservice types are discussed in chapter 4, including fast-food restaurants, family restaurants, specialty restaurants, fine-dining restaurants, cocktail lounges, and taverns. A number of the possible lodging types are identified in chapter 7.

Each characteristic type of foodservice or lodging enterprise is associated with some general type of service product line. Based on

---

[1]"AMA Board Approves New Marketing Definition," *Marketing News* (March 1, 1985): p. 1.

that knowledge, customers seeking a particular type of service product are likely to look for the type of establishment they expect will offer it.

Among the foodservice examples cited, the Steak Shack character-izes itself as a neighborhood family restaurant, and has a product line consisting of eight entrees that are among those most favored by resi-dents of the area. By contrast, Frog's Pub, which caters to an entirely different group of people, has chosen to emphasize imported beers—36 varieties—and to treat its hospitality product line as secondary. Among the lodging examples, the Kensington is a luxury hotel offering the full range of services and amenities normally associated with that type of property, while the Value Lodge is clearly a budget operation offering clean, comfortable sleeping accommodations but few addi-tional services.

Place

The second element in hospitality marketing is **place.** In the hospital-ity world, *place* is a synonym for *location.* The location of a hospitality operation can be an essential element in its marketing effort.

Physical location is critical to the success of many hospitality oper-ations. A family restaurant like the Steak Shack must generally be located within a reasonable driving distance of the population it intends to serve. By contrast, any fast-food restaurant must be in the immediate vicinity of its customers to attract great numbers of them. In the lodging industry, it is well-known that location is probably the single most important consideration. If the Value Lodge were not situ-ated within sight of an exit from a major interstate highway, it proba-bly would not attract enough customers to survive.

For marketing managers, physical location is a fact of life that can-not normally be changed: hotels, motels, restaurants, and bars do not normally change locations. One of the major challenges of marketing is to develop a product line that is suitable for the existing location.

Price

The third element in hospitality marketing is **price;** that is, the prices charged for hospitality service products—menu prices in a restaurant, room rates in a lodging operation. In general, customers and guests tend to be more easily attracted to operations with lower prices and rates than to similar establishments that charge more. Price is only one consideration, however, in the consumer's decision to purchase a ser-vice product from one operation rather than from another. The three other elements of marketing—product, location, and promotion—may also play important roles in the decision-making process.

Establishing the price structure for any hospitality operation is a difficult process. Unfortunately, there is no simple formula that will enable one to determine the right price structure. Many judgments must be made, most of which are subjective.

Menu pricing is one of the most difficult challenges facing hospitality operators. If menu prices are too high, customers may go elsewhere. If they are too low, the establishment may not be profitable. At the Mountain Bank, where operating costs are subsidized, menu prices are kept low to encourage bank employees to use the facility and to remain on premises throughout the working day. The Steak Shack has earned an excellent reputation for superior food, and menu prices can be somewhat higher than would be possible without that reputation.

The same basic problem of pricing faces operations managers in the lodging industry. If room rates are higher than those in similar operations nearby, customers may patronize those competing establishments. If, for example, the room rates in the Value Lodge were $10 per night higher than those in a comparable new motel just across the highway, the Goodsons would lose considerable business.

To establish menu prices for food and beverages or rates for hotel rooms, operations managers take the following factors into account.

1. Product costs: ingredient costs in a restaurant, or such costs as bed and bath linen in a hotel or motel
2. Labor costs, including benefits and payroll taxes
3. Overhead costs
4. Prices at competing establishments
5. The effect of prices on the numbers of customers or guests likely to patronize the establishment

It should be obvious that hospitality operations cannot operate profitably if the prices or rates charged are less than the product costs. Also, operating costs are not limited to product costs: there are labor costs and such overhead costs as real estate taxes, telephone bills, insurance bills, utility bills, cleaning supplies, and others. All of these costs must be taken into account before setting menu prices and room rates, because there must be adequate revenue from product sales to cover all costs of operation.

Labor costs reflect both the levels of skill and the amounts of employee time required to prepare service products for sale. These must be factored into the menu prices and room rates. For example, fine-dining establishments employ talented and highly paid chefs and cooks because they have the high level skills required to prepare the menu items. In contrast, most fast-food restaurants can operate successfully with relatively unskilled employees who earn far lower wages. The menu prices at both of these types of establishments reflect the levels of difficulty and amounts of employee time required to prepare menu items. These differences help to account for the higher menu prices charged in fine-dining establishments than those charged in fast-food restaurants.

The same considerations are important in lodging operations. In luxury hotels like the Kensington, labor costs are much higher than those in budget motels like the Value Lodge. The higher room rates charged by luxury hotels reflect greater numbers of employees and the higher levels of skills they bring to their jobs.

For the majority of hospitality operations, neither menu prices nor room rates should be established until one has considered prices in competing operations. Those who ignore the prices of their competitors risk having potential customers and guests go elsewhere.

Hospitality operators who seek to attract a large number of customers or guests usually establish low prices. For example, one of the major reasons for the success of fast-food hamburger chains has been this ability to attract many customers by pricing their products low. They are able to make a satisfactory level of profit by instituting strict controls over costs. For many foodservice operations, low pricing is a key element in marketing. This has also been the case in a number of the successful budget motel chains.

Promotion

The fourth element in hospitality marketing is **promotion.** For hospitality operators, promotion is the process of informing, influencing, and persuading customers to purchase their service products. There are five types of promotional activities.

1. Personal selling
2. Advertising
3. Sales promotion
4. Merchandising
5. Public relations

Personal Selling. Personal selling requires personal contact between buyer and seller. It typically takes place in a face-to-face encounter.

Personal selling enables a salesperson to communicate directly with a buyer—to ask and answer questions and to use personal powers of persuasion to sell the service product. In restaurants, servers come in direct contact with customers. Each server is in an excellent position to engage in personal selling—to make suggestions and respond positively to questions, with the aim of increasing sales. In addition, servers can be trained to promote the sale of those items with the highest profit margin—the items that it is in the best interests of the establishment to sell in greater quantities. In lodging operations, desk clerks come in direct contact with guests. The desk clerk is also in an excellent position to engage in personal selling—to suggest accommodations that may be larger, more luxuriously appointed or better located, and at higher rates than the more basic accommodations. Personal selling can be a major sales tool in hospitality operations.

Advertising. Advertising is paid, nonpersonal communication directed to potential buyers. A vast number of hospitality organizations promote their service products by advertising. Advertising is costly, however, and most organizations have limited amounts of money to use for purchasing advertising.

One of the important goals in advertising is to reach specific potential customers and to avoid reaching those who cannot or will not purchase the advertised service product. The familiar term *market* refers to a group of people who are willing and able to purchase a product. The owner/manager of the Steak Shack has identified as his market those families living within easy driving distance and having upper-middle-class incomes. The Goodsons, owners/managers of the Value Lodge, have identified transient travelers on Interstate 80 as their market.

Once a hospitality operator has decided to advertise his establishment, he must then decide where to advertise. There are a number of possibilities from which to choose, including broadcast/cable television, radio, newspapers, magazines, outdoor ads, direct mail, and even the yellow pages—a directory of business telephone numbers readily available to everyone. There are both advantages and disadvantages associated with the use of each of these for hospitality advertising.

Sales Promotion. A **sales promotion** is an inducement offered by a seller to persuade a buyer to make an immediate purchase. Sales promotions are intended to persuade consumers to take action immediately rather than to wait. In hospitality operations, sales promotions

Advertising is paid, non-personal communication directed to potential buyers. The selection of hotel advertisements reproduced above offers weekend packages with meals and other features included.

are intended to attract customers to an establishment immediately, or at least to make reservations immediately for dining or lodging.

Hospitality operators frequently offer sales promotions to increase business. Some restaurants offer entrees at reduced prices on specific nights. For example, the manager of the Steak Shack has developed a sales promotion for his slowest night, Monday, offering a 50 percent discount on all fried shrimp dinners. One aim is to attract business during slow periods. By contrast, Frog's Pub offers a 50 percent discount on the special imported beer of the week on Monday and Tuesday afternoons between the hours of 4:30 P.M. and 6:00 P.M. This would be illegal in some places, but not in the area where Frog's Pub is

Yellow Page Ads
Call Attention to Your Restaurant

oday's diners have a nearly unlimited choice of places to eat. Every day, many of these diners go to the yellow pages of the telephone directory to help choose a restaurant. They use the yellow pages because of the availability of such information as type of food, location, value, healthy food choices, and quick service.

According to Statistical Research, Inc., adult American consumers referred to the yellow pages restaurant headings an estimated 1.3 billion times in one recent year. This makes the restaurant's heading the second most referenced heading in the yellow pages—a statistic that has been constant for approximately ten years.

Almost nine out of ten yellow pages users answering a recent survey indicated that they did respond to restaurant ads in the yellow pages, and that about 75 percent of these made purchases. About 37 percent were new customers to the restaurants they patronized. When they call, customers are reportedly seeking information about

- ▶ The menu
- ▶ Times and days the restaurant is open
- ▶ Exact location
- ▶ Possible delivery service
- ▶ Reservations policy
- ▶ Dress code
- ▶ Other services available—catering facilities, private rooms, and so on

Adapted from an article in Restaurants USA, *August, 1995.*

located. In the lodging industry, sales promotions are also very common. In the Kensington, a center-city property where weekend business is light, there is a discounted weekend package for two that includes a room for two nights, breakfast from room service, dinner in the dining room, and theater tickets.

Merchandising. **Merchandising** is a term used to describe those actions taken to increase sales to those customers who are already in the establishment. Merchandising differs from sales promotion. Sales promotions are aimed at attracting new customers to the establishment; merchandising activities are designed to increase sales to existing customers—diners seated at tables in the dining room, or guests who are passengers in hotel elevators, for example.

Merchandising tools used by hospitality operators include posters, carefully written menus, literature placed in guest rooms, table tent cards in a dining room, and displays of breads, desserts, fruits, and wines. Some restaurants use dessert carts; others may use tent cards to merchandise specific desserts. In the Steak Shack, tent cards on tables promote the sales of desserts, especially fruit pies. In the Kensington, signs in the elevator promote reservations in the gourmet dining room, while literature in the rooms promotes the hairstylist.

Public Relations. **Public relations** is a term used to refer to those activities and efforts designed to do any of the following: (1) improve or enhance the image or reputation of an organization; (2) promote the organization's name; or (3) improve an organization's relations with its employees, customers, suppliers, stockholders, or any other individuals or groups thought to be important to the organization.

Public relations activities and efforts can take many forms. Supporting local charities or sponsoring worthwhile activities is one form.

▶ Marketing on the Internet ◀

According to the vice president for marketing for Hampton Inns, "Instead of opening the newspaper or turning on the TV or making a phone call to buy a product, people will be turning on the computer." In fact, many are already hailing the information superhighway, the Internet, as the wave of the future. Best Western, Choice Hotels, Hampton Inns, Holiday Inn, and Hyatt already have property directories on line, making it possible for potential guests to determine whether or not a particular chain of hotels or motels has a property in a given city or town. Others are soon to follow. Some are already beginning to take the next step: allowing guests to book reservations over the Internet. Several chains, including Best Western, are testing direct booking of reservations, and many others will be doing the same in the near future.

Adapted from an article in Lodging, *July, 1995.*

The owner of Frog's Pub sponsors a little league team by purchasing uniforms, and the management of the Kensington hosts a fund-raising dinner once each year with the proceeds going to purchase equipment for the local hospital.

All of the four elements of marketing discussed above—product, place, price, and promotion—are important components in the marketing efforts of hospitality organizations of every size and type. Decisions about marketing are major concerns in operations management, so managers of hospitality establishments must understand the components of marketing and be prepared to use them effectively.

▸ Key Area 2: Human Resources

The hospitality industry is labor intensive, meaning that many people are needed to do the work required in the hundreds of thousands of hospitality operations in the United States. Of all the resources available to hospitality managers, none are of greater value than human resources.

This industry is known to have a high rate of *employee turnover*, a term used to refer to the number of new employees required to replace employees who have left. It is not unusual for a hospitality operation to have an employee turnover rate of 100 percent during the course of a year.

Because of the ongoing need to retain present employees as well as to hire and train new employees, hospitality managers commonly spend considerable amounts of time with various activities that are commonly grouped under the heading of human resources.

▸ Human Resources Management Defined

Dr. Mary L. Tanke, in her book *Human Resources Management*, defines **human resources management** as "the implementation of the strategies, plans, and programs required to attract, motivate, develop, reward, and retain the best people to meet the organizational goals and operational objectives of the hospitality enterprise."[2]

From this definition, it is quite clear that human resources is a broad field that includes a number of specialized areas, including plan-

---

[2]Mary L. Tanke, *Human Resources Management* (Albany: Delmar Publishers, 1990), p. 5.

ning staff requirements, recruiting suitable applicants, selecting new employees, orienting them to the organization, providing them with the proper training, conducting performance appraisals, developing suitable compensation and benefits packages, attending to their various health and safety considerations, and making every reasonable effort to retain the services of personnel in whom a great deal of time and effort has been invested. And in organizations with employees covered by contracts negotiated by labor unions, labor relations constitutes another yet another specialized challenge.

The activities cited above are the major responsibilities of a human resources manager. In one sense, all managers are human resources managers, because working with people and supervising their activities is a human resources activity and is a major part of any supervisor's job. In large organizations with extensive human resources departments, such as the Kensington, supervisory managers are relieved of the need to attend to all the details of recruiting, selecting, and training employees for their departments. However, in a number of smaller organizations, such as the Steak Shack and the Value Lodge, human resources activities are somewhat limited because managers have limited time to devote to them. We will discuss the human resources activities to which managers in these circumstances would be most likely to devote their limited time.

▶ Recruiting Applicants

Recruiting is a process used by managers to find suitable applicants to fill vacant jobs. It may begin when there are actual vacancies to be filled because employees have left. Alternatively, it may begin in anticipation of vacancies that are likely to occur in the near future. This is a wise approach in an industry with high rates of employee turnover. Hospitality managers have found that applicants for particular jobs can be found by means of recommendations made by current employees, unsolicited resumes received in the mail, walk-ins, classified advertisements in newspapers, public and private employment agencies, vendors, unions, colleges and universities, trade journals, and competitors.

The decision whether or not to use any one of these sources will depend on the nature of the jobs to be filled. Many hospitality operations with labor contracts are required to seek new employees for jobs covered by the union contract through the union hiring hall. Applicants for jobs other than those covered by a union contract may be obtained through classified advertisements in the help wanted sections of newspapers. In contrast, entry-level management trainees can often be recruited at colleges and universities. Candidates for supervisory positions and for such skilled positions as chef and front office manager often come from employment agencies.

▶ Job Descriptions

Before attempting to recruit anyone for any position, a manager must have a clear idea of the specific duties and tasks that someone in that position will be required to carry out. This is to say that there should be a job description for every job in any hospitality enterprise. As the term implies, **job descriptions** are detailed written statements that describe jobs. In many instances, job descriptions list very specific duties and directions for performing jobs. The job description for any specific job should answer three important questions.

1. What is to be done?
2. When is it done?
3. Where is it done?

A job description typically has three parts.

1. A *heading* that states the job title and the department in which the job is located. In some organizations, the heading may include such information as the number of positions with that particular job title, the specific hours, days, or shifts worked by those with the job title, and the supervisor to whom those with that job title report.

2. A *summary* of the duties of the job, typically written in paragraph form. The summary enables the reader quickly to gain a basic understanding of the nature and purpose of the job. By reading the summaries of all the jobs in a particular department, one could obtain a great deal of information about the department in a very short period. This might be of great benefit to a new manager, for example.

3. A *list of the specific duties* assigned to the job. These should be as detailed as possible, to the point that well-written job descriptions can be used as step-by-step instructions for doing the work required of those holding the jobs. As we will see, having job descriptions can be of great value to those charged with appraising employee performance.

A job description is particularly important for prospective employees. By having detailed descriptions of the duties required, job applicants and newly hired workers know specifically what is to be done by someone holding a particular job.

Job descriptions are also very important for employers. They enable employers to hold employees accountable for doing the work assigned to a job. Employees who have read job descriptions but fail to perform the assigned work cannot successfully use the age-old excuse, "Nobody ever told me I had to do this."

Job descriptions offer the added benefit of forcing managers to assign specific work to each job holder. If all the normal duties of a department are identified with specific job descriptions, the department will be better organized and will operate more smoothly.

Figure 10.2 is an example of the kind of job description that one might find in a foodservice enterprise. Note the degree of detail provided.

Figure 10.2

Steak Shack Job Description

JOB TITLE:	Server
SUPERVISOR:	Dining Room Manager
WORKING HOURS:	Schedule varies: hours and days vary each week.
JOB SUMMARY:	Server reports in uniform at scheduled time, sets up stations, and follows standard service procedures.

DUTIES:

1. Following the appearance standards identified below, server reports in uniform to supervisor at scheduled time. Appearance standards are as follows:

   a. *Uniform.* Servers provide own uniforms: black pants or skirt; white dress shirt with long sleeves and buttoned cuffs; black bow tie; polished black shoes with flat heels (no high heels). Server will be given a weekly allowance to care for uniform, which must be clean at the start of each shift.

   b. *Personal grooming.* Servers must be showered or bathed just before reporting to work; underarm deodorant required; clean fingernails; hair clean and neat; no excessive jewelry.

   Males:
   a. Clean shaven preferred. Mustache permitted if neat and trimmed.
   b. No facial or ear jewelry.
   c. Hair cannot extend beyond shirt collar.

   Females:
   a. No excessive jewelry, makeup, or perfume.
   b. Long hair must be in hair net.
   c. No long false nails.

2. Server sets up tables in station assigned by dining room manager.

3. After opening, server attends to guests seated in assigned station by pouring water, taking food and drink orders, placing orders in kitchen and bar, picking up and serving food and drink, presenting check(s) to guest(s), and clearing/resetting tables. Service standards are as follows: serve food from guest's left, beverages from right; remove china, glassware, and flatware from right.

▶ Selecting Applicants for Employment

One purpose of the recruiting effort is to develop a sizable pool of applicants from which the best person for a job can be selected. The value of job descriptions for this purpose should be evident. In their efforts to obtain sufficient information about applicants to ensure the selection of the best one, human resources personnel use a number of common "tools." These include application forms, résumés, selection tests, interviews, and background checks. The following constitutes a standard selection process used by many organizations.

1. Preliminary interview
2. Application form
3. Selection test
4. Interview
5. Reference check and background investigation
6. Selection
7. Physical examination

Some or all of these are normally included in the selection process followed by managers in hospitality firms. However, each hospitality firm tends to develop its own preferred routine for selecting the best candidate.

▶ Orientation of New Employees

All new employees should be given a suitable **orientation** to the organization prior to their first day of work. New employees normally have some concern and uncertainty about beginning a job, and it is important to get them started with as little uneasiness as possible. In addition, some basic information should be given to every new employee. In most well-managed hospitality organizations, basic orientation includes

1. Organization policies, procedures, and rules. Among the concerns to be addressed are wages, work hours, overtime, sick leave, time cards, insurance, and keys, among others. In the hospitality industry, answers must be provided for such common questions as, "What meals do employees get?" "How do I get a clean uniform?" "Where do I change into uniform?" "How does the health insurance plan work?"

2. The mission and objectives of the organization. It is important that every employee in the organization work toward the same goals

and that the goals be understood by every employee from the very first day on the job.

3.   A tour of the work area to point out offices and facilities with which all employees should be familiar. The tour should include opportunities for the introduction of such personnel as the chef or the front office manager—any managers with whom workers should be acquainted.

Some organizations rely on a mentor system to provide each new employee with a more complete orientation. A new employee will be paired with an experienced employee who will "show him the ropes." For example, a cook who has been with the Steak Shack for ten years may be made the mentor for a new cook. The experienced cook could give the new cook an orientation tour of the property and kitchen, pointing out such details as the locker room, storeroom, specific pieces of equipment, requisitions, recipes, uniforms, and refrigerators. The experienced cook might also explain the chef's policies for reporting to work, cleaning equipment, laundering uniforms, and other matters. In the Kensington, a new desk clerk might be paired with an employee of some years of experience who would give the new employee a tour of the property, pointing out particular elements with which any desk clerk should be familiar.

▶ Training Employees

Training is generally required of all new employees—even those who come to an organization with considerable experience. Every hospitality operation has its own way of doing things—its own methods for performing tasks and accomplishing work. It is important, therefore, that people who already know how to perform a job be shown the specific methods and procedures used by the organization for which they have just started to work. For those who are inexperienced, more formal training is likely to be needed.

Training can be done on an individual basis, or it can be done in groups. Individual training is undoubtedly the most effective, but it is very expensive: the trainer must devote time to training only one person at a time.

Training can be done on the job or off the job. On-the-job training is commonly used with experienced workers who need only be shown the methods used by the hospitality operation. For example, the new cook in the Steak Shack may be put to work immediately under the guidance of an experienced cook who will show the new cook such details as how requisitions for supplies are filled out, how orders are placed for menu items, and how the establishment garnishes particular menu items.

For inexperienced employees, on-the-job training can be used effectively when their work can be easily monitored and corrected before it has negative impact on customers or when new employees can work side by side with experienced workers. For example, a new desk clerk in the Mountain Inn can be trained effectively if assisted by an experienced clerk. The experienced clerk can show the new employee the normal routine for checking in new guests and checking out departing guests.

▸ Employee Safety

Another important human resources concern in hospitality operations is employee safety. Accidents are costly to both employees and employers—costly in terms of lost wages, medical bills, and higher insurance premiums, among the many possibilities. Therefore, when feasible, responsible employers prefer to develop educational campaigns and training programs aimed at improving safety in the workplace and reducing the number of accidents. Efforts to do this normally come under the heading of human resources.

One agency of the federal government, the Occupational Safety and Health Administration (OSHA), sets safety and health standards for workers in the United States. The basic standard is that an employee's workplace should be free from recognized hazards—those that are likely to cause physical harm to the employee. Most states have also adopted legislation aimed at protecting workers from physical hazards.

The potential for physical harm in the hospitality industry is at least as great as that in many other industries. Such areas as kitchens, bars, stairwells, guest rooms and baths, boiler rooms, elevator shafts, and many others present great potential for physical harm. Management must take three important steps to enhance employee safety in the workplace.

1. Know the applicable federal, state, and local safety regulations, and take all necessary and appropriate actions to comply.
2. Develop policies, procedures, methods, guidelines, and work rules aimed at maintaining a safe work environment for all employees.

3. Conduct appropriate safety training for all categories of employees, giving special emphasis to those who work with potentially dangerous materials and equipment.

Human resources issues are major concerns in operations management, so managers of hospitality establishments must have considerable knowledge and understanding of this broad subject and be prepared to make critical decisions in this all-important area.

▶ Key Area 3: Accounting

Accounting has been broadly defined as the process of identifying, measuring, and communicating economic information to permit informed judgments and decisions by users of the information. In practical terms, it is the process of analyzing, recording, classifying, reporting, and interpreting financial information that reflects the financial condition of an organization. Accounting principles are the rules generally accepted by the accounting profession for analyzing, recording, classifying, reporting, and interpreting this financial information.

A hospitality manager should have sufficient knowledge of accounting principles to be able to look at information provided by an accountant, understand it, and make judgments about the financial condition of the organization. This is one reason that educational programs in hospitality management commonly include at least one course in financial accounting.

▶ Financial Accounting

Financial accounting is a branch of accounting concerned with analyzing, recording, classifying, and summarizing the day-to-day transactions that occur in an organization. Analyzing means preparing data to be recorded. Recording means entering data into the formal records of the organization. Classifying is arranging the data into useful categories, so that data will be reported in a way that can be understood. Reporting is summarizing the information into statements for managers, owners, and others.

Some people think of financial accounting as bookkeeping, and indeed bookkeeping is one part of financial accounting. Bookkeeping is record keeping; it is clerical in nature and a fundamental element in accounting.

▶ The Accounting Cycle

Accounting cycle is a term that refers to a sequence of procedures used to record and summarize transactions for an accounting period, to organize the summary data into financial reports, called statements, and to prepare for the next sequential accounting period. The normal accounting period is one year. Accounting data, however, are typically summarized monthly and used to prepare monthly statements.

The two most important financial statements prepared by accountants are balance sheets and income statements.

▶ Balance Sheet

A balance sheet is a financial statement that lists the assets, liabilities, and the value of ownership claims to the assets of a business on a specific date. Figure 10.3 shows a balance sheet for the Steak Shack; figure 10.4 shows a balance sheet for the Value Lodge.

Assets

On the left-hand side of the balance sheet are the assets of an organization. An **asset** is anything of value. Any asset belonging to an organization belongs on the organization's balance sheet. Examples of assets are cash, food, beverages, furniture, and automobiles.

Assets are classified as current assets or fixed assets.

Current Assets. **Current assets** are those that are not expected to last beyond one year. They are normally used up in the course of doing business. Current assets are listed on the balance sheet in order of liquidity. The term *liquidity* refers to the ease with which an asset can be converted into cash. Obviously, cash is the most liquid of all assets, so it is listed first. In figures 10.3 and 10.4, accounts receivable (money owed to a business) are listed second and are followed by such other current assets as food in the Steak Shack and cleaning supplies in the Value Lodge.

Fixed Assets. **Fixed assets** are those that will last beyond one year. In figure 10.3, the fixed assets of the Steak Shack are identified as furniture, equipment, and an automobile. In figure 10.4, the fixed assets of the Value Lodge are listed as land, building, furniture, equipment, and an automobile. Note that the values of some of the fixed assets have

Figure 10-3 Steak Shack Balance Sheet, December 31, 19XX

Assets			Liabilities and Owners' Equity		
Current Assets			**Current Liabilities**		
Cash	$9,322		Accounts payable	$4,250	
Accounts receivable	3,893		Wages payable	2,312	
Food	16,891		Sales taxes payable	1,567	
Liquor	9,633		Rent payable	2,000	
Supplies	4,540		**TOTAL CURRENT LIABILITIES**		$10,129
Office supplies	561				
TOTAL CURRENT ASSETS		$44,840	**Long-Term Liabilities**		
			Note payable		2,355
Fixed Assets			**TOTAL LIABILITIES**		$12,484
Furniture and equipment	$243,600				
Less accumulated depreciation	23,678	$219,922			
Automobile	18,700		**Owner's Equity**		
Less accumulated depreciation	6,400	12,300	Capital at January 1, 19XX	$111,100	
TOTAL FIXED ASSETS		$232,222	Net income for 19XX	153,478	
			TOTAL CAPITAL		$264,578
TOTAL ASSETS		$277,062	**TOTAL LIABILITIES AND CAPITAL**		$277,062

Figure 10-4 Value Lodge Balance Sheet, December 31, 19XX

Assets				Liabilities and Owners' Equity			
Current Assets				**Current Liabilities**			
Cash		$3,560		Accounts payable	$2,300		
Accounts receivable		2,575		Wages payable	350		
Cleaning supplies		620		Sales taxes payable	375		
Office supplies		75		TOTAL CURRENT LIABILITIES		$3,025	
TOTAL CURRENT ASSETS			$6,830				
				Long-Term Liabilities			
Fixed Assets				Mortgage payable		$993,000	
Land	$65,000			TOTAL LIABILITIES		996,025	
Building	$1,500,000						
Less accumulated				**Owner's Equity**			
depreciation	100,000	1,400,000		Roger and Jane Goodson			
Furniture and equipment	50,000			Capital at January 1, 19XX		$314,467	
Less accumulated				Net income for 19XX		$115,233	
depreciation	14,285	35,715		TOTAL CAPITAL		$429,700	
Automobile	12,500						
Less accumulated							
depreciation	5,000	7,500					
TOTAL FIXED ASSETS			$1,508,215				
TOTAL ASSETS			$1,515,045	TOTAL LIABILITIES AND CAPITAL		$1,515,045	

been reduced by amounts shown on the balance sheets as accumulated depreciation.

Accumulated depreciation is a bookkeeping figure that indicates a theoretical lessening in value of assets from the time they were purchased. It should be noted that accumulated depreciation is only a bookkeeping figure and that the real value of fixed assets—their market value—may be either higher or lower than shown on the balance sheet. For example, the furniture and equipment shown on the balance sheet of the Steak Shack as having a value of $243,600 less $23,678 in accumulated depreciation may really be worth more or less than that if it were sold. Assets are listed at cost because it is impossible to know their true market value unless and until they are actually sold.

Liabilities

Liabilities are financial obligations to others. Stated another way, liabilities indicate what the business organization owes. Liabilities are generally incurred as a normal consequence of doing business. They are classified as current liabilities and long-term liabilities.

Current Liabilities. **Current liabilities** are those financial obligations that are due to be paid within the next accounting period. On the illustrated balance sheets, there are several current liabilities, including accounts payable, wages payable, sales tax payable, and rent payable. Accounts payable refers to amounts owed to suppliers for goods and services. Wages payable refers to wages earned by employees but not yet paid to them. Sales tax payable refers to sales taxes collected from customers but not yet remitted to the government agency that collects the tax. Rent payable refers to amounts owed to a landlord for use of the premises but not yet paid to that landlord.

Long-Term Liabilities. **Long-term liabilities** are financial obligations due beyond the accounting period. The Steak Shack has a note payable, and the Value Lodge has a mortgage payable. The amounts remaining on these are shown on the illustrated balance sheets as long-term liabilities.

Owner's Equity. *Owner's equity* is the term used to describe an owner's claims to the value of assets listed on a balance sheet. The term *capital* is sometimes used as a synonym. In the Steak Shack, capital (the owner's claim to the assets) at the beginning of the year was $111,100. The restaurant made a profit of $153,478 last year, and that amount is added to the start-of-year capital to arrive at the total figure of $264,578 at the end of the year. In the Value Lodge, capital at the beginning of the year was $14,467. The motel had net income of $115,233 for the year, making the end-of-year capital figure $429,700.

▶ The Income Statement

The second important financial statement is the income statement. An **income statement** shows sales (or revenues) and expenses of an organization for a given time period. That period is normally one year, but

Figure 10-5

Steak Shack
Income Statement

<table>
<tr><td colspan="2" align="center">**The Steak Shack**
Income Statement
Year Ended December 31, 19XX</td></tr>
<tr><td>**Sales**</td><td></td></tr>
<tr><td>Food</td><td>$853,066</td></tr>
<tr><td>Beverage</td><td>223,355</td></tr>
<tr><td> **TOTAL SALES**</td><td>**$1,076,421**</td></tr>
<tr><td>**Cost of Sales**</td><td></td></tr>
<tr><td>Food</td><td>$349,757</td></tr>
<tr><td>Beverages</td><td>51,372</td></tr>
<tr><td> **TOTAL COST OF SALES**</td><td>**401,129**</td></tr>
<tr><td>Gross Profit</td><td>$675,292</td></tr>
<tr><td>Other Income</td><td>4,356</td></tr>
<tr><td> **TOTAL INCOME**</td><td>**$679,648**</td></tr>
<tr><td>**Controllable Expenses**</td><td></td></tr>
<tr><td>Salaries and Wages</td><td>$333,548</td></tr>
<tr><td>Employee Benefits</td><td>78,692</td></tr>
<tr><td>Direct Operating Expenses</td><td>45,187</td></tr>
<tr><td>Energy & Utility Services</td><td>48,341</td></tr>
<tr><td>Administrative & General</td><td>16,528</td></tr>
<tr><td>Repairs & Maintenance</td><td>8,976</td></tr>
<tr><td> **TOTAL CONTROLLABLE EXPENSES**</td><td>**$531,272**</td></tr>
<tr><td>Income Before Occupancy Costs,
  Interest, Depreciation,
  and Income Taxes</td><td>$148,376</td></tr>
<tr><td>Occupancy Costs</td><td>80,025</td></tr>
<tr><td>Income Before Interest,
  Depreciation, and Income Taxes</td><td>$68,351</td></tr>
<tr><td>Interest</td><td>1,258</td></tr>
<tr><td>Depreciation</td><td>13,615</td></tr>
<tr><td>Restaurant Profit</td><td>$53,478</td></tr>
</table>

income statements can be prepared for any period of time. The income statements of the Steak Shack and the Value Lodge are shown in figures 10.5 and 10.6.

Sales and **revenue** are the terms used for the income an organization receives as a result of doing business. Expenses are the costs of doing business. Note the differences between the income statements of the Value Lodge and the Steak Shack. The income statement of the Steak Shack uses the term *sales* rather than *revenue*. This is simply a difference in terminology and is not significant. The income statement for the Steak Shack indicates two sources of revenue: food sales and beverage sales. The income statement also has a section labeled cost of

Figure 10-6

Value Lodge
Income Statement

	The Value Lodge Income Statement Year Ended December 31, 19XX	
Revenue		
Room sales		$584,040
Miscellaneous		3,682
TOTAL REVENUE		**$587,722**
Operating Expenses		
Wages	$51,162	
Employee benefits	7,665	
Laundry	57,838	
Cleaning supplies	25,632	
Uniforms	1,820	
Office supplies	5,591	
Repairs & maintenance	15,267	
Energy costs	26,722	
Telephone	11,115	
Automobile expense	4,451	
Commissions	3,334	
Reservation network fees	4,245	
Franchise fees	23,368	
Credit card fees	6,379	
TOTAL OPERATING EXPENSES		**$244,589**
Income Before Fixed Charges		$343,133
Fixed Charges		
Property taxes	$34,600	
Insurance	26,500	
Interest expense	99,300	
Depreciation	67,500	
TOTAL FIXED CHARGES		**$227,900**
Net Income Before Income Taxes		$115,233

sales, in which the food and beverage costs are subtracted from total sales to determine gross operating profit. This is customary in hospitality operations whenever there are expenses that can be attributed directly to a specific revenue source.

The Value Lodge also has two sources of revenue. The major source is identified as room sales—income received from renting accommodations to guests. The secondary source is identified as miscellaneous income—that received from selling postcards, maps, and food in the vending machines.

Expenses on income statements are commonly grouped into two categories: operating (or controllable) expenses and fixed expenses, sometimes identified as fixed charges. Operating, or controllable, expenses are those that managers can control or change. They are direct expenses, which tend to increase and decrease as business volume increases and decreases. These expenses include wages, laundry, cleaning supplies, and office supplies. Fixed charges, by contrast, are those that managers cannot change in the near term. Fixed charges include rent, mortgage payments, and property taxes—expenses that must be met even if the business has no sales revenue. In the Steak Shack, fixed charges include occupancy costs, interest, and depreciation; in the Value Lodge, they include property taxes, insurance, interest expense, and depreciation.

The income statements of the Steak Shack and the Value Lodge are comparatively simple and provide useful information about financial operations to the owners. The total dollar amount in each category listed on an income statement can be compared with the amount anticipated or budgeted for that category. For example, if the amount shown for wages is higher than anticipated or budgeted, the owners can attempt to determine a reason and take precautions to hold wages to a lower figure in the next operating period.

If revenues exceed expenses for the period covered by an income statement, the result is termed *profit*. If expenses exceed revenues for the period, the result is termed *loss*.

The value of accounting information is not limited to the specific figures listed on income statements and balance sheets. Additional useful information can be obtained by anyone willing to spend a few moments performing some comparatively simple calculations, several of which are described below. There are literally dozens of ratios, averages, and other figures that managers can calculate from financial reports and then use to analyze business performance. The following are just a few, selected to suggest the broad range of possibilities.

▶ Ratios

Ratios compare one number to another for purposes of making judgments. Most students are familiar with the concept, if not the term. For example, if there are ten questions on a test, a student who answers eight correctly can be said to have performed well. Her ratio of correct answers to total questions is eight to ten, written numerically as

$$\frac{8}{10} = 0.8 \text{ or } 80\%$$

Thus we determine that the student's grade—an evaluation of performance—is 80 percent.

Ratios are used very commonly in hospitality operations to evaluate financial performance. The following are a few of the ratios that managers calculate and use. Note that all answers are rounded.

▶ Cost-to-Sales Ratios: Cost Percents

Food and Beverage Cost-to-Sales Ratios

The ratios of food cost to food sales and beverage cost to beverage sales are considered very important by hospitality managers. The ratio of food cost to food sales is also known as the **food cost percentage;** the ratio of beverage cost to beverage sales is known as the **beverage cost percentage.** Managers believe these two ratios, or cost percentages, indicate how well these important costs are being kept under control. Cost-to-sales ratios are calculated as follows:

$$\frac{\text{cost}}{\text{sales}} = \text{cost - to - sales ratio, or cost percentage}$$

For the Steak Shack, food and beverage cost-to-sales ratios are calculated as follows:

$$\frac{\text{food cost}}{\text{food sales}} = \text{food cost - to - sales ratio}$$

$$\frac{\$349,757}{\$853,066} = 0.4099, \text{ or } 41.0\%$$

$$\frac{\text{beverage cost}}{\text{beverage sales}} = \text{beverage cost - to - sales ratio}$$

$$\frac{\$51,372}{\$223,355} = 0.23, \text{ or } 23.0\%$$

The food cost percentage is 0.4099 or 41 percent. This figure can be compared with planned cost percentage and with industry averages for other restaurants of that characteristic type. The beverage cost percentage is 0.23 or 23 percent. As in the case of the food cost percentage, a manager would compare it with the planned cost percentage and might compare it with an industry average. In this instance, both the food cost percentage and the beverage cost percentage compare favorably with industry averages.

Labor Cost-to-Sales Ratio

From figure 10.5, the dollar figure appearing on the line marked salaries and wages is $333,548. That on the line marked employee benefits is $78,692. The sum of these, $412,240, is the cost of labor for the period. Using this figure, one can calculate a labor cost-to-sales ratio by dividing the cost of labor by total sales, $1,076,421.

$$\frac{\$412,240}{\$1,076,421} = 0.38297 = 38.3\%$$

This figure, 38.3 percent, is the **labor cost percentage.** As with food cost percentage, a manager would compare labor cost percentage with that planned and with industry averages. In this case, the labor cost percentage compares favorably with industry averages for these types of establishments.

Some additional ratios that can be calculated very simply using readily available figures include the following.

Other Operating Ratios

Operating ratios measure overall performance in specific areas. Four ratios commonly used in hospitality are percentage of occupancy, seat turnover, inventory turnover, and profitability.

Percentage of Occupancy. Percentage of occupancy is used in lodging operations to express the ratio of occupied rooms to total rooms available for sale. It is calculated as follows:

$$\frac{\text{occupied rooms}}{\text{total rooms available for sale}} = \text{percentage of occupancy}$$

To illustrate, we will use the Value Lodge, which has fifty rooms. On a given night, forty of those rooms are occupied, so the percentage of occupancy for that night is 80 percent, calculated as follows:

$$\frac{40 \text{ occupied rooms}}{50 \text{ rooms available for sale}} = 0.8 = 80\%$$

Lodging operations normally determine the percentage of occupancy each night. Managers then make comparisons with their percentages of occupancy the same night the previous week and the same night the previous year. By doing so, they are able to make some general assessment about the state of business for that one night compared with other nights. In some major cities, night managers in the major hotels normally exchange information about percentages of occupancy so that managers of the properties can compare their percentages of occupancy to those of their competitors.

Seat Turnover. **Seat turnover** relates the number of diners served in a given time period to the number of seats available in the dining room. Viewed another way, it indicates the average number of customers served per seat in the time period. Often called *turns* in the hospitality industry, it is calculated as follows:

$$\frac{\text{number of diners served}}{\text{number of seats available for diners}} = \text{seat turnover}$$

In the Steak Shack, with one hundred tables seating 250 persons, the number of customers served on a given Friday night was 575. Seat turnover for that night is calculated as follows:

$$\frac{575 \text{ diners served}}{250 \text{ seats available for diners}} = 2.3 \text{ turns}$$

Foodservice managers often keep records of the number of turns so that comparisons can be made between days and dates.

Inventory Turnover. **Inventory turnover** ratio measures the rate at which inventories are used up and replaced during an operating period. The ratio is calculated as follows:

$$\frac{\text{cost of goods sold}}{\text{average inventory}} = \text{inventory turnover ratio}$$

For the Steak Shack, there are two inventory turnover ratios to calculate: one for food, the other for beverage. Food inventory turnover rate is calculated as follows:

$$\frac{\text{cost of food sold}}{\text{average inventory}} = \text{inventory turnover rate}$$

The inventory figures from the balance sheet of the Steak Shack are shown as $16,891 for food and $9,633 for beverages. We will assume that these represent the average inventories of the restaurant. Costs are shown on the income statement as $349,757 for food and $51,372 for beverage. Given this information, the inventory turnover rates would be calculated as follows:

$$\frac{\$349,757}{\$16,891} = 20.71 \text{ food inventory turnover rate}$$

$$\frac{\$51,372}{\$9,633} = 5.33 \text{ beverage inventory turnover rate}$$

The food inventory rate is 20.71 times per year or just under two times per month. This ratio would be considered about right for many restaurants. Because food is perishable, it should be used up and replaced about every other week.

The beverage inventory turnover rate is 5.33 per year or about every other month. Except for beer, alcoholic beverages are not considered perishable. Therefore, it is not uncommon for foodservice establishments to have large liquor inventories. This is particularly true for those that stock fine wines.

Profitability Ratios. Profitability ratios are said to measure the efficiency of organizations. They are very important to both investors and managers because they are an indication of the quality of management. One important ratio is return on sales.

Return on sales, or net profit margin, shows the portion of each sales dollar that an organization earns as a profit. It varies considerably from one type of business to another. Return on sales is calculated as follows:

$$\frac{\text{profit}}{\text{sales}} = \text{return on sales}$$

For the Steak Shack, it is calculated as follows:

$$\frac{\$53,478}{\$1,076,421} = \text{return on sales}$$

$$= 0.04968 \text{ or } 5.0\%$$

For the Value Lodge, it is calculated as follows:

$$\frac{\$115,233}{\$587,722} = 0.196067 \text{ or } 19.6\%$$

The ratio for the current year can be compared with those for prior years and with industry averages. For the Steak Shack, the ratio is probably somewhat lower than the owner would like; for the Value Lodge, many would consider it to be reasonable for that type of property.

▶ Averages

In addition to ratios, owners and managers of foodservice and lodging operations commonly use various averages to evaluate business operations. An **arithmetic average,** the kind most commonly used, is determined by adding a series of figures to obtain a total, then dividing that total by the number of figures it includes. Suppose, for example, one wanted to determine the average grade earned by a student whose scores on four quizzes were 68, 82, 88, and 90. To determine the arithmetic average, one would add the scores on all quizzes and divide by the number of scores.

$$68 + 82 + 88 + 90 = 328 \text{ total of all scores}$$

$$\frac{328 \text{ total of all scores}}{4 \text{ scores}} = 82 \text{ average score}$$

Two of the most common arithmetic averages in hospitality operations are average sale per customer in restaurants and average rate per occupied room in hotels.

Average Sale per Customer

Average sale per customer is calculated by dividing total dollar sales for a given time period by the number of customers served in that period.

$$\frac{\text{total dollar sales}}{\text{number of customers}} = \text{average sale per customer}$$

In the Steak Shack, for example, total sales on a given day were $3,150.40. The number of customers served on the day was 220. Therefore, the average sale per customer on that day was $14.32, calculated as follows:

$$\frac{\$3,150.40 \text{ total sales}}{220 \text{ customers}} = \$14.32 \text{ average sale per customer}$$

Average Rate per Occupied Room

Average rate per occupied room is calculated by dividing the room revenue for a given period by the number of rooms occupied in that period.

$$\frac{\text{total room revenue}}{\text{number of rooms occupied}} = \text{average rate per occupied room}$$

In the Value Lodge, total room revenue for a given night was $1,640, and 40 rooms were occupied. Average rate per occupied room was $41.00, calculated as follows:

$$\frac{\$1,640 \text{ room revenue}}{40 \text{ occupied rooms}} = \$41.00 \text{ average rate per occupied room}$$

A variety of useful averages can easily be calculated, and many hospitality managers do so regularly. Some of the possibilities include average sale per waiter, average rate per guest, average food sale, and average beverage sale, among others.

Accounting is generally described as "the language of business," and hospitality managers should have more than a passing knowledge of the subject. Accounting questions are major concerns in operations management, and managers of hospitality establishments must be prepared to make full use of accounting information in making critical decisions about operations management.

▶ Key Area 4: Budgeting

Budgeting is a necessary element in business operations. A **budget** is a financial plan developed for a period in the future. Therefore, a budget can be viewed as a manager's attempt to project future financial performance. Successful businesses need to look ahead and make specific plans to reach revenue targets while keeping expenses within certain predetermined bounds. Without financial planning, management is leaving the future health of a business to chance.

There are various types of budgets, including operating budgets, capital budgets, sales budgets, advertising budgets, and cash flow budgets. For a hospitality manager, the most important of these is likely to be the operating budget.

▶ Operating Budget

An **operating budget** is a financial plan for generating a given amount of revenue at a given level of expenditure in a coming period. Operating budgets are usually based on income statements from the most recent operating periods. Normally, one assumes that past performance is the best indicator of future performance and that the enterprise will continue to operate more or less as it has been operating. If one could assume no change of any kind, then a recent income statement could be adopted as a future budget. However, there are always changes being planned and trends becoming evident. Changes include rewriting a menu, increasing the number of servers in a dining room, and raising menu prices or room rates to offset increasing costs. Trends include increases or decreases in sales revenue due to the opening or closing of other hotels or restaurants in the area, or, in the case of restaurants, to increases or decreases in the number of people living in the surrounding area. The manager of the Steak Shack, for example, has noted that the number of customers has been increasing at approximately 5 percent per year, a figure that matches the increase in population in the neighborhood the restaurant serves.

One element in budgeting is to identify tomorrow's changes and trends today because they will obviously affect tomorrow's revenues and expenses. The more difficult element is to quantify the changes and trends—to identify the net effect in dollars that these changes and trends will have on various categories of revenue and expense. In the budgeting process, managers attempt to project the effects all changes will have on each.

Figure 10.7 illustrates a budget for the Value Lodge for the coming year. Before preparing it, Roger and Janet Goodson analyzed revenues and expenses for the year just ending, then identified changes anticipated in the coming year—such items as the normal affect of inflation on expenses, planned increases in hourly wages for employees, an increase in reservation network fees, and a decrease in local real estate taxes reported in the local newspaper.

The Goodsons plan to increase wages to the staff by 10 percent, which will increase the expenses for both wages and employee benefits (which is normally a percentage of wages). They anticipate that most other operating expenses will increase by approximately 4 percent, except for reservation network fees, which are expected to rise by 10 percent. The remaining three operating expenses—commissions, fees to franchisor, and credit card fees—are expected to remain the same

Figure 10-7

Value Lodge
Budget

The Value Lodge Budget Year Beginning January 1, 19XX		
Revenue		
Room sales		$613,242
Miscellaneous		3,682
Total Revenue		**$616,924**
Operating Expenses		
Wages	$56,278	
Employee benefits	8,432	
Laundry	60,151	
Cleaning supplies	26,657	
Uniforms	1,893	
Office supplies	5,815	
Repairs & maintenance	15,878	
Energy costs	27,791	
Telephone	11,560	
Automobile expense	4,629	
Reservation network fees	4,670	
Commissions	3,508	
Fees to franchisor	24,536	
Credit card fees	6,700	
Total Operating Expenses		**$258,498**
Income before Fixed Charges		**$358,426**
Fixed Charges		
Property taxes	$33,562	
Insurance	36,500	
Interest expense	99,300	
Depreciation	67,500	
Total Fixed Charges		**$236,862**
Net Income Before Income Taxes		**$121,564**

percentage of revenue. Fixed charges are expected to remain the same, except for property taxes, which will decrease by 3 percent, and insurance costs, which will increase by $10,000. Next, having considered the general overall increase in expenses, the Goodsons have decided to increase room rates by 5 percent. Finally, they have quantified these changes and prepared the budget shown in figure 10.7.

Once an operating budget has been prepared, managers and others who need to purchase supplies and hire personnel have a guideline for doing so. The guideline is the budget. For example, once the budget has been prepared for the Value Lodge, the Goodsons have a budgeted figure for employees' wages for the year—a figure to be used as the guide for spending in that category for the period. From that budgeted figure, the Goodsons will be able to determine the number of housekeepers and other employees they can have on the payroll.

Without budgets, managers have limited means of assessing whether or not operations are progressing satisfactorily and whether or not financial objectives are likely to be reached. Budgets are very important to operations managers, so those intending to follow careers in hospitality management must have some reasonable level of knowledge of this important subject and be prepared to develop and work within budgets throughout their careers.

▸ Key Area 5: Cost Control

Cost control activities are very important to managers in hospitality operations. Cost control is the process of regulating costs and guarding against excessive costs.

Managers need to know the costs of the hospitality service products they sell to customers and guests. For example, a hotel manager needs to know the total cost of preparing a vacated hotel room for the next guest. There are many elements to that total cost, including the wages of the housekeeper who will clean the room and the costs of the bed linen, bath linen, soap, and various other supplies that go into it. Restaurant managers need to know the costs of the ingredients in the menu items they prepare so that suitable prices can be established and printed in menus. Some need to know the labor cost of preparing standard quantities of particular menu items.

Determining these costs, as well as many others, is part of the cost accounting activity that take place daily in hospitality operations. It is important that these costs be known before sales prices are established for hospitality service products. The costs associated with cleaning and maintaining a hotel room clearly should be known before one sets room rates. And the costs of food and beverage items on menus should be established before setting menu prices. One example will suffice.

One of the items on the lunch menu at the Steak Shack is a charcoal-broiled hamburger served on a sliced, sesame seed bun. The standard portion size for a hamburger is 6 ounces. Hamburgers are made from ground chuck, which is purchased at $2.40 per pound. Hamburger buns are purchased fresh daily at $1.50 per dozen.

The cost of the 6 ounce hamburger is $.90, determined by dividing 16 ounces into the $2.40 cost per pound to find the $.15 cost per ounce, then multiplying by 6 ounces in each portion.

$$\frac{\$2.40 \text{ cost per pound}}{16 \text{ ounces in each pound}} = \$.15 \text{ cost per ounce}$$

$$\$.15 \text{ cost per ounce} \times 6 \text{ ounces per portion} = \$.90 \text{ cost per portion}$$

The cost of the bun is \$.125, determined by dividing the cost of the dozen, \$1.50, by the number of buns in the dozen, 12.

$$\frac{\$1.50 \text{ cost per dozen}}{12 \text{ buns per dozen}} = \$.125 \text{ per bun}$$

Thus the basic food cost per portion for the hamburger and bun is:

hamburger	\$.90
bun	0.125
total	\$1.025

To this, one would add the costs of any other items accompanying the hamburger—ketchup, mustard, pickles, and so on—to determine the total cost of the item. If the other items are assumed to cost \$.225, the total cost of the item would be \$1.25.

It should be obvious that any foodservice operator should know the basic cost of every item on a menu before setting menu sales prices. If the hamburger above is listed on the menu at \$1.50, the cost of the food alone will use up all but \$.25 of the sale price. However, if the item can be priced at \$2.50, the sales price will be twice the food cost.

In the first case, food cost percent would be 83.3 percent, calculated as

$$\frac{\text{food cost } \$1.25}{\text{sales price } \$1.50} = 0.833 = 83.3\%$$

In the second, food cost percent would be 50 percent, calculated as

$$\frac{\text{food cost } \$1.25}{\text{sales price } \$2.50} = 0.5 = 50.0\%$$

Once the portion cost for an item has been determined, the manager has a responsibility to control the cost of all portions of that item prepared in the kitchen. In general, this means that the manager must establish procedures aimed at regulating portion costs and guarding against excessive costs. Those procedures should ensure that

1. purchases of specified ingredients of specified quality are made in appropriate quantities and at proper prices in a timely manner;

2. foods purchased are received, stored, and issued under secure conditions and in a manner that will preserve their quality until they are needed for production; and

3. food production is accomplished with minimal waste and results in appropriate numbers of portions of correct quality and quantity, prepared according to specific recipes.

For example, the manager of the facility in the Mountain Bank must limit the spending for food purchases to the amount specified in the budget. This requirement has led her to take a number of steps aimed at controlling the cost of hamburgers. These include

1. specifying that the only beef to be used for hamburgers will be ground chuck, U.S. Choice, with fat content not to exceed 20 percent;

2. estimating the amount of ground chuck needed each week and ordering only enough for one week at a time;

3. seeing that beef is moved to refrigerated storage immediately after it is received and that it is stored securely and under proper conditions until needed; and

4. installing a machine to make hamburger patties that features a dial to control the number of ounces per hamburger.

Many operations managers devote considerable amounts of time to setting up and overseeing extensive procedures for keeping costs under control. Cost control is of critical concern to operations managers in this industry, so anyone intending to pursue a career as a hospitality manager must have considerable understanding of the subject and be prepared to establish and maintain control over costs at every stage of that career.

▶ Key Area 6: Computers

In the hospitality industry today, **computers** are of critical importance to operations managers. Operations managers are using and relying on computer systems principally because they provide the kinds of information and types of control measures that owners and managers require to help insure efficient operation. In fact, it is becoming difficult to find a hospitality operation of consequence that lacks some type of computer system.

Figure 10-8

Layout of the Steak Shack, showing the elements of the restaurant's computer system, with terminals and workstations at several key locations: manager's office, dining room, bar, and kitchen.

At this point, it will be useful to describe the computer system used in the Steak Shack. It is typical of many found in foodservice operations today. Figure 10.8 is the floor plan of the restaurant showing the following system components linked together on a network:

1.   In manager's office, a large capacity microcomputer used as a file server, which is the hub of any computer network
2.   Terminals with keypads and printers at two servers' stations
3.   One microcomputer with monitor and printer at the manager's desk
4.   Remote printers at service stations at the front bar and at the cooks' station

Operations proceed along the following lines. Servers arriving for work change into uniforms, then proceed to their side stands in the dining room. On each of the two side stands is a small terminal with keypad and printer that dining room personnel use to log in. In other words, they record their arrival or work much as they would with a traditional time clock. Other personnel log in at the terminal in the manager's office.

Guests enter by the front door and leave their coats in the coatroom. They are seated by the dining room manager, who leaves menus at the table. Servers greet the guests and take their orders for drinks; the orders are written on ordinary white pads rather than on guest checks. Each server proceeds to a terminal and opens an account in computer memory. This account is equivalent to a guest check. The process requires that the server enter his personal code, the table number, the number of guests, and a special code used for creating a new account. With the account opened, the server uses a numerical code to enter the customers' orders for drinks. This information, together with the time of the order, is stored in computer memory. The computer has been programmed with correct prices for each drink.

The system is programmed to send the recorded drink orders to the service station at the front bar. There, the bartender gets the drink orders on a remote printer. The hard copy provided by the remote printer is an order for the bartender to prepare the drinks. This hard copy includes the server number, table number, and order time.

The bartender removes the hard copy of the order from the printer and places it on the tray with the prepared drinks, thus eliminating questions about which drinks are for which server and what time the orders were entered. At the appropriate time, the server follows similar procedures for placing food orders. With different codes used for foods and drinks, the computer is programmed to send food orders to the remote printers at the cooks' station. All menu items ordered are stored in memory, but the only items appearing on the remote printer at any specific preparation station are those appropriate to that station. Thus food order are not sent to the service bar, and orders for coffee, handled by the servers themselves, do not appear on any remote printers.

After a diner has finished his or her meal, the server obtains a guest check by going to the terminal and printer at the side stand and requesting one. With this system, the guest check is a hard copy of the data stored in the computer, accessed by table and server number. This hard copy is removed from the printer and given to the diner. In the Steak Shack, each server acts as a cashier for his own checks, and settlement for each check is recorded at the terminal as the server receives cash or a credit card.

At the end of a shift, the server reports to the manager's office to turn in the cash, checks, and credit card vouchers for his or her sales. The manager uses his terminal to print out summary data showing charge and cash sales for that particular server. He collects the appropriate amount of cash and all charge vouchers from the server. The totals collected from each must obviously equal the amounts recorded on the print out. Finally, each server logs out, using the manager's terminal, before changing out of uniform and leaving the premises.

At the end of the day, the manager obtains a detailed breakdown of the day's business on a computer printout. The system provides considerable information, including total dollar sales categorized into cash sales and charge sales, with the charge sales divided by type of credit card; total dollar sales separated into food sales and beverage sales, with the food sales broken down into dollar sales by menu category and by individual menu item; average dollar sale per customer, per server, per seat, per table, and per hour; seat turnover; number of orders of each hospitality item sold; total dollar sales per hour; sales in any category for the period to date; total payroll cost for the day, for any part of the day, or for the period to date; and a vast amount of hospitality cost data.

Using this system, the manager of the Steak Shack can monitor operations as the day progresses. Such data as gross sales volume, number of customers served, number of checks outstanding, number of portions of particular items sold, and any number of other possibilities may be of special interest at given times throughout the day.

Because computer systems are of such importance in operations management, hospitality managers should have reasonable knowledge of computer operations. Any hospitality manager should be prepared to take full advantage of the capacity of the systems available in today's hospitality environment.

From the foregoing, it should be apparent that marketing, human resources management, accounting, budgeting, cost control, and computers all play important roles in hospitality operations management. Those planning careers in hospitality management should develop their knowledge of the topics discussed in this chapter and learn as much as possible about additional subjects and complex topics that can best be covered in the more advanced courses commonly offered in hospitality management programs.

▶ Summary

In this chapter, *operations management* is defined as the day-to-day activities that managers engage in to achieve the goals of the operations they manage. The four functions of management—planning, organizing, directing, and controlling—are identified as primary skills required by operating managers. Marketing, human resources, accounting, budgeting, cost control, and computers are described as key areas in operations management. Examples from the Steak Shack, the Mountain Bank staff dining room, and the Value Lodge facility illustrate these six key areas of operations management and provide a sense of the day-to-day work that consumes much of the time of a hospitality manager.

 Key Terms

Accounting	Labor Cost Percentage
Accounting Cycle	Liabilities
Advertising	Long-Term Liability
Arithmetic Average	Marketing
Asset	Merchandising
Average Rate per Occupied Room	Operating Budget
Average Sale per Customer	Operations Management
Beverage Cost Percentage	Organizing
Budget	Personal Selling
Computer	Place
Controlling	Planning
Cost Control	Price
Current Asset	Product
Current Liability	Promotion

Directing   Public Relations
Expense   Ratio
Financial Accounting   Recruiting
Fixed Asset   Return on Sales
Food Cost Percentage   Revenue
Human Resources Management   Sales
Income Statement   Sales Promotion
Inventory Turnover   Seat Turnover
Job Description   Training

Questions

1. Define the term *operations management.*

2. Define the term *planning* as used in management.

3. What does the term *organizing* mean?

4. List the six steps in the organizing process.

5. What does the term *reporting structure* refer to?

6. What are some possible consequences of failure to follow the practice known as unity of command?

7. What is an organization chart?

8. What does the term *directing* mean?

9. What does the term *control* mean?

10. List and discuss the four steps in the control process.

11. Define *marketing* as used in hospitality operations.

12. List and describe the four elements of marketing.

13. List five factors taken into consideration in establishing menu prices.

14. List and describe five types of promotional activities.

15. Define the term *human resources management.*

16. What does the term *recruiting* mean in hospitality?

17. What is a job description?

18. List and discuss the three parts of a job description.

19. Identify ten possible sources from which human resources personnel can recruit applicants for employment.

20. List and discuss the seven basic steps that constitute a standard procedure for selecting the best candidate for employment.

21. Identify three principal elements that should be included in a basic orientation for new employees.

22. Identify three important steps taken by management to enhance employee safety in the workplace.

23. How is accounting defined in the chapter?

24. Identify the two major financial statements derived from accounting records and list the principal parts of each.

25. Define the following terms:
    a. asset
    b. current asset
    c. fixed asset
    d. liability
    e. current liability
    f. long-term liability
    g. owner's equity
    h. income statement
    i. revenue
    j. expense
    k. profit
    l. loss

26. Identify the formula for calculating each of the following:
    a. food cost-to-sales ratio
    b. beverage cost-to-sales ratio
    c. labor cost-to-sales ratio
    d. percentage of occupancy

27. Given the following information, determine seat turnover for the Steak Shack for March 15: number of diners—900; number of seats available for diners—250.

28. Identify each of the following:
    a. inventory turnover
    b. return on sales
    c. average sale per customer
    d. average rate per occupied room

29. What is a budget?

30. Discuss the importance of cost control to the management of a hospitality operation.

31. Determine the portion cost for each of the following:
    a. 5 ounce portion of tomato juice if tomato juice is purchased in 46 ounce cans costing $1.38 each.
    b. 1 order of toast consisting of two slices of bread from a loaf of 24 slices costing $1.44, plus one ounce of butter purchased at $1.60 per pound.
    c. 1 order consisting of 2 eggs and 3 strips of bacon if eggs cost $.96 per dozen and bacon costs $3.36 per pound, and each pound consists of 16 strips.

32. Identify the benefits that computers provide for hospitality operations managers.

1. You are the assistant manager of a fine-dining restaurant located in a midsize city. The chef has developed two new entrees that are unique and exciting. You have been asked by the manager to suggest ways of promoting these new entrees. Make a list of those you would suggest, explaining each in as much detail as possible.

2. You have just been hired as the front office manager for a two hundred room motel. During your first day on the job, you notice that the procedure for selling rooms is performed differently by each desk clerk. Some clerks explain which types of rooms are available and the rates for each, and then ask which type of room the guest would prefer. Others offer only the highest rates and suggest lower rated room only if the prospective guest refuses the highest rated room. Still others offer only the lowest rates in an attempt to sell as many rooms as possible. How do you deal with this problem?

3. Write a job description for the most recent full-time or part-time job you have held.

4. Go to a nearby restaurant or hotel. Interview a supervisor to learn in detail about the work he does, then write a job description for the job.

Part Six

Travel and Tourism Perspectives

E l e v e n

Dimensions of Travel and Tourism

After reading and studying this chapter, you should be able to:

1 Identify at least ten travel motivators.

2 List and discuss eight social and economic changes that have led to increased travel.

3 Explain the role of local, state, and federal governments in travel and tourism.

4 List the four criteria used to establish the status of an individual as a traveler or a tourist.

5 Define the terms *traveler* and *tourist*.

6 Identify the three segments of the travel industry.

7 Discuss the size and scope of international travel.

8 Identify the nations that are the world's leading travel destinations.

9 Identify the nations whose citizens spend the most on international travel.

10 Discuss the conditions and documents that make international travel possible.

11 Identify the nations that send the most visitors to the United States.

12 Describe the importance of domestic travel to the U.S. economy.

13 Define and describe the economic, cultural, social, and environmental impacts of tourism.

14 Identify several nations, states, areas, and localities that rely on tourism for jobs and income.

▶ Introduction

Earlier chapters have pointed out the close relationships that four areas significant to the hospitality industry have had to one another: economic progress, the development of roads and transportation, the scope of hospitality facilities, and the extent of travel. We have indicated that those nations with the most advanced economies have had the most highly developed transportation networks and the greatest numbers of travelers. We have shown that hospitality enterprises develop as a direct consequence of the development of transportation and that as transportation modes change, so too do the locations of hospitality operations. We have discussed the foodservice and lodging industries in detail and described characteristic types of operations in each.

In this chapter and the two that follow, we will turn our attention from the specifics of food, beverage, and lodging operations to the larger industry of which hospitality operations are a part: travel and tourism. In the first of these, we will discuss the importance of travel and tourism to various nations and states, and then take a close look at the economic, social, cultural, and environmental impact of travel and tourism on them. In the second chapter, we will describe travel services. In the third chapter, we will describe recreation and entertainment facilities to which people travel for a major nonbusiness purpose: pleasure.

▶ Travel Motivators

People travel for many reasons. The list below includes just a few of the many possibilities.

Convention attendance
Visiting family or friends
Business

Health problems
Climate
Rest and relaxation
Theme parks
Exhibits
Concerts
Sports events
Sightseeing
Education
Visiting the birthplace of parents or grandparents
Weddings
Funerals
"Getting away"

Some of these would have been unknown before the twentieth century. In the 1600s and 1700s, for example, very few people would have had the time or the money just to travel because they wanted to go to a warmer climate, and no one would have traveled to ski or to visit a theme park: ski slopes and theme parks were not developed until the twentieth century.

▶ Americans Need Vacations ◀

A recent survey by Hilton Hotels appears to prove that American workers need vacations: of those surveyed, 20 percent reported calling in sick at least once last year just to get a day of relaxation! And nearly 80 percent preferred the idea of a two-week vacation to an opportunity to work two additional weeks for additional pay.

In another survey, Americans reported that their top choices among domestic vacation destinations include Florida, California, Colorado, Arizona, and Hawaii. For foreign destinations, top choices include Canada, the Bahamas, England, France, and Australia.

The results of various surveys are making it quite clear that in the 90s, Americans consider free time among their most valuable commodities.

Adapted from an article in the Boston Sunday Globe, *July 23, 1995.*

In recent years, a number of important social and economic changes have led to increased travel. These include the following.

▶ Early Retirement

The retirement age for a large part of the population is earlier than it used to be. The social security system in the United States grants retirement benefits as early as age sixty-two, and many retirement programs are linked to years of service rather than age. In some retirement programs, particularly government programs, it is possible to retire at age fifty-five with substantial benefits after working twenty-five or thirty years. Early retirement leads to greater numbers of travelers as the retirees set out to see the world.

▶ Longer Life Span

The average American or Canadian can now expect to live well into their seventies, and many will live considerably longer. This is in contrast to conditions a few generations ago, when the average life span was considerably less. A growing population of people over sixty provides a larger base of travelers—many of whom can afford extended periods of travel.

▶ Shorter Workweek

In the first third of the twentieth century, the six-day week was standard for most workers. Today, the five-day week is standard, and a four-day week is not uncommon. The resulting longer weekends, combined with faster and easier transportation, enable many workers to take weekend trips. This may include driving to visit friends and relatives, attending weddings and receptions, and traveling to various places and events that people did not have time to attend only a few years ago.

▶ More Leisure Time

Workers have greater amounts of leisure time today than ever before. American, Canadian, and west European workers have more vacation time than any groups of workers in history. Most receive a minimum of two to four weeks of vacation each year, and many work for organizations that offer additional vacation time for those with greater numbers of years of service. Some of the leisure time available to Americans is in the form of holidays, many of which are now scheduled to fall on Mondays and Fridays. These create three- and four-day weekends that make it possible for people to get away. One example is the addition of Martin Luther King Day, celebrated on a Monday in mid January. This has created a long weekend that has had a major impact on travel destinations. In the northeastern United States, for example, it has turned a relatively quiet weekend into a record weekend for the ski areas.

▶ Greater Disposable Income

Many families have more disposable income available than ever before. Higher wages and two-earner households account for much of this increase. This makes it possible for consumers to spend more for goods and services, and travel appears to be one of the services that consumers want most.

▶ Greater Mobility

Improved roads and better transportation make travel easier and more comfortable each year. The U.S. interstate highway system is now virtually complete, making travel faster between points distant from one another. Most people in the United States are near a major airport or one that provides service to a major airport.

▶ Smaller Families

The average size of American families has decreased significantly, making it easier and cheaper for the average family to travel: with fewer family members, travel costs less.

▶ Change in Consumer Spending Patterns

The growth in public and private retirement programs has prompted a "live now" attitude and a feeling that the future will take care of itself.

Improved roads and better transportation make travel easier and more comfortable each year. (Photo courtesy of San Francisco Convention and Visitors Bureau.)

Many people are not as concerned as their parents were with saving for retirement, and they are more willing to spend their growing incomes on travel. Significantly, travel has become a major element in the lifestyle of many people.

▶ Government Role in Travel and Tourism

In many countries, the national government plays an important role in travel and tourism. Some national governments own and operate airlines as well as national rail systems. Some also own and operate hotels, motels, and other tourist facilities. In addition, most national governments establish tourism goals, gather statistical data, regulate tourist facilities, and advertise internationally to promote tourism.

In the United States, the national government has taken a much more limited role. Until recently, the official government agency promoting travel and tourism was the United States Travel and Tourism Administration. However, funding for the agency was eliminated. In its place, Congress established a thirty-six-person National Tourism Board, with its members appointed by the president. Congress did not provide the board with funding, so there are serious questions about what it can accomplish.

Statistical data concerning travel in the United States is gathered by the Bureau of the Census and by several other agencies. However, most people interested in obtaining travel-related data about the United States tend to rely on information from private agencies. The principal private organization providing data in this area is the U.S. Travel Data Center, based in Washington, D.C.

In the United States, the responsibility for promoting and regulating travel and tourism in each state falls to state governments. All state governments have offices charged with that responsibility, but their names and the departments to which they report vary from one state to another. In some, there is an independent state travel department; in others, the office responsible for travel and tourism is part of a larger department—commerce or transportation, for example.

At the local level, most U.S. cities and regional areas have chambers of commerce that promote tourism in those communities where tourism is important. City governments frequently have convention and visitor's bureaus that promote travel to the city. They receive inquiries that they refer to hotels and motels for follow-up. They provide such services to meeting planners as orientations to the city and introductions to convention hall managers, hotel convention managers, and other suppliers of hospitality services. These bureaus frequently act as housing coordinators for groups that come to the city, referring delegates to hotel properties. In some instances, convention and visitor's bureaus are funded by a tax added to hotel bills in the city. This is not the only approach to funding these bureaus, however. In other cases, their operating costs are met by some combination of funds contributed by tourism-related businesses and matching funds from state or local government.

▶ Definitions of Traveler and Tourist

Most people would agree that a traveler is someone who goes from one place to another beyond his normal commuting distance, and a tourist is a person who travels for pleasure. However, when one examines those definitions critically, it becomes apparent that categorizing a specific person as a traveler or a tourist is not as easy as it first appears.

There are four criteria that have been used to establish the status of an individual as a traveler or tourist.

1. Distance
2. Residence
3. Purpose
4. Length of stay

Various governments, states, and organizations concerned with travel and tourism have tended to develop their own definitions of travelers and tourists based on these four criteria. These definitions are important because they are used to count and categorize travelers. Unfortunately, governments, states, and organizations still disagree on both the definitions of traveler and tourist and on the importance of each of the four criteria in those definitions.

The question of who should be considered a traveler is particularly thorny. Should someone who is going to work on a special assignment twenty miles beyond his normal commuting distance be considered a traveler? What about someone who is going shopping in a city fifteen miles from home? And what about someone who visits a friend in a nearby town and returns home the same day? Is she a traveler? Should a person who goes from New Haven, Connecticut, to New York City to see a baseball game and returns home the same day be considered a traveler? If he or she should stay overnight in New York, does that change his or her status?

To be counted as a traveler by the U.S. Bureau of the Census, a person must travel to a place at least one hundred miles away from home and return. The U.S. Travel Data Center uses a broader definition: a traveler is "any resident of the United States regardless of nationality who travels to a place 100 miles or more away from home within the United States or who stays away from home one or more nights in paid accommodations and who returns home within twelve months, except for commuting to and from work or attending school."[1] Of the fifty state governments within the United States, a majority have now adopted this U.S. Travel Data Center definition, although some are using a distance of 50 rather than one hundred miles.

Because travel and tourism are important to the economic health of so many nations of the world, even the United Nations has become

---

[1]*The Economic Review of Travel in America* (Washington, D.C.: U.S. Travel Data Center, 1995), p. 3.

involved in establishing definitions. In 1993, the United Nations Statistical Commission adopted "Recommendations on Tourism Statistics," proposed by the World Tourism Organization. Included in the document are definitions aimed at establishing some uniform approaches to collecting data.

Tourism comprises the activities of persons traveling to and staying in places outside their usual environment for not more than one consecutive year for leisure, business, or other purposes.[2] All travelers engaged in tourism are described as visitors, and visitors are separated into two groups—domestic visitors and international visitors.

In everyday usage, the terms *traveler* and *tourist* tend to be used interchangeably; the two terms are quickly becoming synonyms for one another. In this chapter, our definition of the word **travelers** will be the same as that of the U.S. Travel Data Center, explained above, and the words **traveler** and **tourist** will be used interchangeably.

▶ Make-Up of the Travel Industry

The travel industry is made up of firms and people who serve the needs of travelers. Professor Chuck Gee, a well-known authority in the field, divides the **travel industry** into three segments.[3]

1. Direct providers of travel services
2. Support services
3. Tourism development

▶ Direct Providers of Travel Services

Direct providers of travel services are those firms and people who are in direct contact with travelers and who provide the services necessary for their travel. They include

Airlines
Bus companies

---

[2]There are some exceptions, including migrants, students traveling to and from school, crews, and temporary workers.

[3]Chuck Y. Gee et al., *The Travel Industry,* 2d ed. (New York: Van Nostrand Reinhold, 1989), pp. 7–9.

Camps
Car rental companies
Credit card companies
Cruise lines
Entertainment and recreation centers
Hotels/motels
National and state parks
Railroads
Rental companies specializing in campers and recreational vehicles
Restaurants
Shops selling goods and services to travelers/tourists
Travel agents

This is not a complete list of the all the direct providers of travel services. However, it does offer a good cross section of firms whose primary business activity is to provide a travel service. It is important to emphasize that this segment of the travel industry is not restricted to transportation, lodging, and foodservice. It includes any firm that provides a travel service directly to the traveler: travel agents who make travel arrangements; shops that sell souvenirs to travelers; tour guides; entertainers who provide music and cultural activities for tourists; businesses that supply rental bicycles, rowboats, or sailboats for tourists; and many, many others.

▶ Support Services

Support services is a segment of the travel industry that includes the firms and individuals who provide services and supplies to the direct providers. These firms and individuals depend on the travel market for all of their business or for a large part of it. They provide the necessary goods and services that make it possible for direct providers to perform travel services.

A list of these support service firms includes purveyors of food and beverages to hotels and restaurants; laundries that supply the linen for lodging properties; firms and individuals who supply travel mementos to gift shops; employment agencies that specialize in providing hospitality workers; management firms that run hospitality operations; foodservice firms that provide food for airline passengers; and many, many others.

▶ Tourism Development

Tourism development is a term used to identify the individuals and organizations that have impact, direct or indirect, on direct providers, support services, and individual travelers. This category includes those with an interest in travel and tourism but who would not be classified as direct providers, support services, or travelers. Examples of individuals and organizations in tourism development include

1.   Organizations associated with direct providers. These include the American Society of Travel Agents, the American Hotel & Motel Association, the National Restaurant Association, the International Air Transport Association, and the Cruise Lines International Association. Each of these organizations represents its respective hospitality or travel industry and consists of member firms from those or allied industries. They provide a voice for their industries to the U.S. Congress and to the public, they provide information about their industries to their members, and in some cases, they make policy decisions relating to the sales of their services, the business or professional practices of their members, or both. For example, the International Air

In the United States, the responsibility for promoting and regulating travel and tourism falls to each state and is usually overseen by the department of commerce, transportation, or tourism. This includes advertising (as shown right) in print, television, and radio to contribute to the development of tourism within the state. (Photo courtesy of Virginia Department of Economic Development-Tourism Group.)

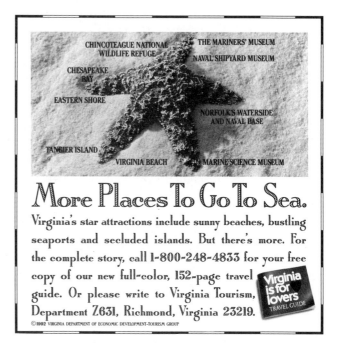

CHINCOTEAGUE NATIONAL WILDLIFE REFUGE   THE MARINERS' MUSEUM

NAVAL SHIPYARD MUSEUM

CHESAPEAKE BAY

EASTERN SHORE

NORFOLK'S WATERSIDE AND NAVAL BASE

TANGIER ISLAND

VIRGINIA BEACH   MARINE SCIENCE MUSEUM

More Places To Go To Sea.

Virginia's star attractions include sunny beaches, bustling seaports and secluded islands. But there's more. For the complete story, call 1-800-248-4833 for your free copy of our new full-color, 152-page travel guide. Or please write to Virginia Tourism, Department Z631, Richmond, Virginia 23219.

Virginia is for lovers
TRAVEL GUIDE

©1992 VIRGINIA DEPARTMENT OF ECONOMIC DEVELOPMENT-TOURISM GROUP

Transportation Association establishes international airfares for member airlines.

2.   Government agencies, including the National Tourism Board, as well as various state and local travel offices. These government organizations promote travel and tourism to their countries, states, and localities and are important components of the travel industry.

3.   Private agencies that promote travel and tourism and gather statistical data. One example is the World Tourism Organization (WTO)—a private organization located in Madrid, Spain. The WTO promotes international tourism, gathers statistical data on world tourism, and is an official consultant to the United Nations. Another important private organization is the World Travel and Tourism Council (WTTC), located in Brussels, Belgium. The WTTC is the newest of the international organizations and has recently published a study of world tourism.

4.   Schools, colleges, and universities—public, private, and proprietary—that prepare individuals for careers in hospitality and tourism. Numerous public and private institutions train cooks, chefs, desk clerks, and travel agents, among many others. In addition, more than eight hundred two- and four-year colleges offer majors in foodservice, lodging, or tourism. Among the first colleges to develop such programs were Cornell University, Michigan State University, and Pennsylvania State University. One of the first to develop a culinary program was the Culinary Institute of America in Hyde Park, New York, which offers a program that has won national and international acclaim. The oldest of the four-year colleges offering a comprehensive program in travel industry management is the University of Hawaii.

The travel industry is made up of a broad range of private and government firms and agencies. It is a collection of organizations serving the needs of travelers. Many firms in the travel industry have little in common except their dependence on travelers for their primary business.

▶ The Size and Scope of the Travel Industry

Travel is the world's largest industry. In 1994, the WTTC estimated that world spending on domestic and international tourism reached $3.4 trillion. This represents about 11 percent of the total amount of money spent at the retail level on goods and services. Worldwide, travel and tourism employs more than 204 million people.

Table 11.1 **Growth of World Tourism**

International Tourist	
Year	**Arrivals**
1950	25,282,000
1960	69,320,000
1970	165,787,000
1980	284,282,000
1990	455,673,000
1994	528,461,000[1]

1   Preliminary estimates.

Source: *World Tourism Organization.*

Table 11.2 **Annual Increase in World Tourism**

Period	Average Annual Increase in International Arrivals
1950–1960	10.6%
1960–1970	9.1%
1970–1980	5.5%
1980–1993	4.6%
1950–1993	7.3%

Source: *World Tourism Organization.*

▶ The Scope of International Travel

International travel is travel between countries. There has been continued growth in the number of people traveling internationally, as shown in tables 11.1 and 11.2.[4] The data in tables 11.1 and 11.2 includes international arrivals only. The many millions of travelers who travel within their own native countries are not included.

Some will note that these two tables appear to offer conflicting information. Table 11.1 shows a sizable increase in the number of arrivals over the years, while table 11.2 indicates a decline in the percentage of increase in international tourism for each of the periods shown. For example, between 1950 and 1960, the increase in interna-

---

[4]The data in this chapter is the latest available as this revision is prepared. The presentation of data is always delayed by at least two years because of the time required to collect, tabulate, analyze, and publish it.

tional tourist arrivals was 44,038,000 (69,320,000 minus 25,282,000), and the percentage increase per year for that period was 10.6 percent. Yet between 1970 and 1980, the increase in international tourist arrivals was 118,495,000 (284,282,000 minus 165,787,000), but there was only a 5.5 percent annual increase for that period. The reason for this is that the base numbers used to calculate the annual percentage increases were larger in the latter period, and this results in a smaller percentage increase. For example, an increase of 500 in the number of visitors to an area from 1,000 to 1,500 would be a 50 percent increase. Yet that same increase of 500 in the number of visitors the next year from 1,500 to 2,000 is only a 33 percent increase.

For the purposes of this chapter, it is important to note that there has been a significant and steady increase in international travel. One of the primary reasons is the decreased cost of transportation relative to income, making transportation more affordable for great numbers of people. Others include greater periods of vacation time and greater numbers of holidays in many countries.

▶ World's Leading Tourist Destinations

The world's leading tourist destinations are shown in table 11.3. A destination, as used in this table, is a country that receives visitors, regardless of whether they come by plane, ship, train, or automobile.

Table 11.3 **World's Leading Tourist Destinations, 1993**

Rank	Country	Number of Arrivals
1	France	60,100,000
2	U.S.A.	45,793,000
3	Spain	40,085,000
4	Italy	26,379,000
5	Hungary	22,804,000
6	United Kingdom	19,154,000
7	Austria	18,257,000
8	Poland	17,000,000
9	Mexico	16,440,000
10	Canada	15,105,000

Source: *World Tourism Organization.*

France receives more international arrivals than any other country. One of the reasons for this is France's central location in western Europe. Residents of the countries of western Europe frequently travel from one country to another, and France is both an excellent destination and a country that travelers must pass through when traveling to other countries by automobile. France's central location means that many visitors counted in the statistics include people who are passing through France on their way to Germany, Italy, or other destinations.

Second on the list is the United States. Discussion of travel to the United States is found later in this chapter.

The third leading travel destination is Spain. Its sunny, warm climate and its relatively low prices make it a very popular travel destination, particularly for those residents of colder climates. It is thus perhaps the leading vacation country for European travelers. The Spanish government has made a consistent effort to keep the monetary rate of exchange very favorable for visitors in order to attract as many tourists as possible.

Italy, the fourth leading tourist destination, is important historically, particularly because the Vatican is located there, and there is much else to see in Rome, as well as in the rest of the country. Many tours of Europe start or end in Rome.

In nations that are high on the list of tourist destinations, there are many jobs created to provide food, lodging, and other travel services for tourists. The jobs created by tourism are important to the economies of these nations, as will be discussed in greater detail later in this chapter.

▶ World's Leading Spenders on International Tourism

Table 11.4 shows the amount spent on international trips by residents of countries ranked as the top ten in spending for international travel.

The United States leads the list of international spenders. Discussion of U.S. spending abroad is found later in the chapter. Germany is second on the list. The Germans have always been frequent travelers. A primary reason for this is the economic prosperity of Germany and the high standard of living in that country. In addition, German workers typically have considerable time for travel. On average, they receive ten holidays and six weeks of paid vacation.

Third on the list is Japan. Japan has become a leading economic power by exporting automobiles, televisions, cameras, computers,

Table 11.4   **World's Leading International Travel Spender Nations, 1993**

Rank	Country	Amount Spent[1]
1	U.S.A.	$41,260,000,000
2	Germany	37,514,000,000
3	Japan	26,860,000,000
4	United Kingdom	17,431,000,000
5	Italy	13,053,000,000
6	France	12,805,000,000
7	Canada	10,629,000,000
8	Netherlands	8,974,000,000
·9	Austria	8,180,000,000
10	Taiwan	7,585,000,000

1   Excludes international transportation.

Source: *World Tourism Organization.*

radios, and many other products. Japan has become a significant member of the world community, and its citizens are leading international travelers. The average Japanese worker now receives more vacation time than the average American, and the Japanese government actively encourages its citizens to travel abroad.

It should be noted that the list of leading tourist spenders is made up of the most developed nations. None of the so-called *underdeveloped nations* are included. This has been the pattern historically.

Current trends suggest that travel will continue to increase. Recent political changes in eastern European nations have resulted in many who were formerly prohibited from traveling by their governments now becoming part of the world's growing number of travelers. In addition, these former Eastern-bloc countries are becoming attractive destinations for growing numbers of international travelers.

The world is fast developing a global economy. As nations become more and more dependent on one another, travel will increase.

▶ Conditions and Documents Required for International Travel

Before international travel can take place, nations must recognize each other through formal, diplomatic channels; certain specific agreements and arrangements must have been made, and the travelers themselves must have proper documentation.

Diplomatic Recognition

The first requirement for international tourist travel is diplomatic recognition between countries. This recognition can take two forms.

1. **De jure recognition.** The government of one country recognizes that the party in power in another country is that country's legitimate government.

2. **De facto recognition.** The government of one country does not acknowledge the legitimacy of the party governing another country but acknowledges, at least, that the party does govern.

When discussions between two nations result in diplomatic recognition, government officials from each take up residence in the other and additional negotiations begin to establish the procedures and routines for travel. Without diplomatic recognition, there is no suitable way to negotiate procedures for travel between nations, and travel between them is normally prohibited.

The procedures for travel are negotiated by diplomatic officials known as consuls or ambassadors. They serve as the official links between nations. Diplomats work out detailed procedures for travel between nations and for assistance and protection to travelers. Diplomats also negotiate agreements that facilitate travel, such as landing rights for aircraft.

International travelers must have appropriate documentation. The basic document needed for visits to most nations is the **passport.** Passports are issued by the government of a nation to its citizens. A passport provides specific data about the individual to whom it is issued, including name, date of birth, residence, occupation, and citizenship. It also has a photograph of the passport holder.

In addition to the passport, many nations require a **visa.** A visa is either an endorsement on the passport or a separate document showing that the passport holder has received permission from the government of the country he intends to visit to enter that country. Visas are usually obtained by applying to a consulate of the country to be visited well in advance of the intended dates of travel.

Passports and visas are stamped by immigration authorities as visitors enter a country. These official stamps show the date and port or border of entry and indicate the permissible length of stay for the passport holder. Permission to stay in a country is normally granted for only a limited period of time.

United States citizens need only a passport to visit most western European countries; one does not need to obtain a visa. Passports are not required for U.S. citizens to visit Canada, Mexico, or most Caribbean nations. Valid identification and proof of citizenship are required, however. For some countries, a driver's license is sufficient; for others, further proof is needed—a birth certificate, for example. A visa is required to visit most eastern European, Middle Eastern, Asian, and African countries. In many South American countries, visas are required for some travelers and not for others. There, visas are normally required for business travelers and for those staying three months or more.

Additional travel requirements exist for many parts of the world. Typical of these are vaccination certificates proving immunity to certain infectious diseases that travelers are likely to encounter in the country being visited. Cholera vaccinations are commonly required in many African nations, including Angola, Chad, Ghana, and Liberia. Cholera vaccinations are also required in many parts of the Middle East, the Pacific region, and South America. Yellow fever vaccinations are required in Bolivia, Brazil, Colombia, Ecuador, and Peru, and malaria vaccinations are required in several nations during those times of the year when the risk of contracting the disease is great.

Proof of financial ability—a return ticket or a stated amount of cash—and other documentation are also frequently required. For example, to enter Ecuador, a tourist must have a ticket to leave and proof of sufficient funds. A passport is required, and a visa is necessary for a stay of three months or more. An American traveling to El Salvador must have both passport and visa along with a photograph and a notarized letter from the traveler's employer. Presumably, these strict travel requirements result from past difficulties.

Governments frequently prohibit citizens from visiting nations at war, those where the safety of visitors may be at risk, or those that have not been officially recognized. For many years, U.S. citizens were prohibited from visiting China because that nation did not have diplomatic relations with the United States.

Some countries restrict the amount of money their citizens can take from the country. Citizens of Indonesia, Israel, and Malaysia have been restricted in this way, for example. Some countries, including India and Burma, have prohibited tourists from taking any local currencies out of the country.

Governments sometimes prohibit some citizens of other nations from entering. Most do not allow criminals, suspected terrorists, and similar undesirables to enter, for example.

Most nations restrict the types and quantities of goods that visitors can bring with them. For example, pork products, alcohol, and pornographic materials are prohibited by Saudi Arabia. Many nations limit the amounts of alcohol, tobacco, and perfume that can be brought in.

Some countries require that departing travelers obtain exit permits. When travelers return home from abroad, governments commonly require that they show passports and any other travel documents to a government official at entry. Most also restrict both the type and value of goods that citizens can bring home. United States citizens must declare all articles purchased abroad and currently in their possession, as well as the price paid for each. However, individuals are permitted to declare orally goods up to a total value of $400, the maximum that can be imported duty-free. There are some exceptions in which greater amounts from some specific places are permitted. If the value of goods exceeds the permissible limit, travelers are charged an import tax known as a duty. Travelers are not permitted to bring goods intended for resale into the United States without the proper permits.

Officials also verify that travelers entering a country are not bringing prohibited goods. In the United States, prohibited goods include illegal drugs, explosives, firearms, and certain plants, animals, and related items.

▶ Travel to and from the United States

United States citizens have always been leading world travelers. Americans spend more on international travel than any other nationality ($41.3 billion annually), as illustrated in table 11.4. Perhaps the most significant reasons for this are

1. The United States has a large, prosperous group of middle-class citizens who can afford to travel internationally.

2. Many Americans have roots in other countries. This leads many to visit the homeland of their ancestors.

3. Travel is an integral part of the American heritage. Compared to citizens of other nations, Americans tend to move more frequently from one town or city to another. Because many Americans have relatives in other parts of the country, they tend to travel distances to see them.

4. International travel is easier for Americans than for the citizens of many other countries. The United States government has relatively few travel restrictions, making it possible for most Americans to travel freely outside the country. The amount of money Americans can

take along when traveling outside the country is not restricted. Neither is the amount of time they can spend outside the country or their frequency of travel.

5. English is the most widely spoken of the international languages, making it possible for Americans to travel without having to know other languages. In many countries, English is nearly a universal second language, required in schools and used by many. Employees in hotels, restaurants, airline offices, and other travel services throughout the world speak English.

The United States is also the leading country for tourism receipts ($56.5 billion), as illustrated in table 11.5.

The United States is a vast country with innumerable sights and attractions for foreign visitors. The many features they enjoy include such imposing cities as New York and Chicago, with their tall buildings and cultural diversity; the impressive scenery in the national parks; excellent facilities for such sports activities as golf and skiing; and places of special interest such as Disney World, historic Williamsburg, and Sea World.

It is interesting to note which countries send the most visitors to the United States (see tables 11.6 and 11.7). The greatest number of foreign visitors to the United States come from Canada and Mexico. The proximity of these two countries to the United States is the obvious reason for the large number of Canadian and Mexican visitors. For most, it is both easy and inexpensive to drive across the American border when compared with the distance and cost associated with overseas travel.

Table 11.5 **World's Top International Tourism Earners, 1993**

Rank	Country	Amount Spent[1]
1	United States	$56,501,000,000
2	France	23,410,000,000
3	Italy	20,521,000,000
4	Spain	19,425,000,000
5	Austria	13,566,000,000
6	United Kingdom	13,451,000,000
7	Germany	10,509,000,000
8	Hong Kong	7,562,000,000
9	Switzerland	7,001,000,000
10	Canada	5,897,000,000

1 Excluding international transportation.

Source: *World Tourism Organization.*

Table 11.6 **Foreign Visitor Arrivals in the United States, 1993**

Origin	Number
Canada	17,306,883
Mexico	9,824,000
Overseas	18,661,819
Western Europe	8,297,055
Eastern Europe	233,405
Asia	5,165,147
Middle East	418,703
Africa	168,969
Oceania	609,435
South America	2,026,391
Central America	544,602
Caribbean	1,098,110
All Countries	45,793,000

Source: *"United States Travel and Tourism Administration,"* in Somerset R. Waters, Travel Industry World Yearbook: The Big Picture, 1994–1995 *(New York: Child & Waters, 1995), p. 70.*

Table 11.7 **Overseas-Visitor Arrivals in the United States, 1993**

Country	Number
Japan	3,542,546
United Kingdom	2,999,301
Germany	1,826,757
France	844,644
Italy	555,758
Brazil	555,102
China	504,407[1]
Australia	448,507
Venezuela	444,355

1 Mostly from Taiwan.
Source: *"United States Travel and Tourism Administration,"* in Somerset R. Waters, Travel Industry World Yearbook: The Big Picture, 1994–1995 *(New York: Child & Waters, 1995), p. 70.*

The pattern of travel to the United States from overseas has changed in recent years. Table 11.7 shows where the most overseas visitors to the United States originate.

In recent years, the Japanese have traveled to the United States in very large numbers and now lead the list of overseas visitors. This is indicative of both the role of Japan in the world economy and the importance of the United States as an importer of Japanese goods. Americans have very strong economic ties to Japan. The Japanese have invested heavily in the United States, and Americans purchase more goods and services from Japan than from any other single country. The Japanese people come to the United States for many reasons, not the least of which is to play golf, a sport they have embraced with a passion. Golf is a very expensive sport in Japan and is therefore available to only a relatively few people there.

The United Kingdom is second in the number of visitors. Britain has always accounted for many travelers to the United States. A major reason for this appears to be a common heritage and language. America also received large numbers of immigrants from the United Kingdom in past centuries, so many Americans can trace their family roots there.

▶ Travel within the United States

The scope of travel/tourism in the United States is truly impressive. According to the *Travel Industry World Yearbook*, total spending for tourism services in the United States was estimated at $726 Billion for 1993.[5] This represents over 11 percent of the gross domestic product of the United States.

Table 11.8 reveals some interesting information about travel patterns in the United States. Several observations can be drawn from this data. Nearly all travelers in the United States use family automobiles, trucks, recreational vehicles (RVs), or airplanes to reach their destinations. Seventy-five percent of all travel over one hundred miles is by automobile, and 21 percent is by airplane. Ninety-six percent of all trips taken use these two modes of transportation. Trains and buses are rarely used for long-distance travel. It appears that their primary use is for commuting to and from work.

The major reason that people travel long distances within the United States is to visit friends and relatives—37 percent of all trips. Most of the trips over one hundred miles—93 percent—involve at least one overnight stay, and a large number of overnight stays are at the homes of friends and relatives.

Thus, the statistics confirm the importance of the family automobile to the traveling public. This is in contrast to many other nations, particularly the less developed nations, in which comparatively few people own automobiles, roads are poor, and train, bus, and bicycle are still the primary means of transportation.

---

[5]Somerset R. Waters, *Travel Industry World Yearbook: The Big Picture, 1994–1995* (New York: Child & Waters, 1995), page 15.

Table 11.8 **U.S. Trip Profile—1993 Adult Travelers**

Mode of Transportation	% Of Trips
Auto/truck/RV	75
Airplane	21
Bus	2
Train	1
Other	1
Trip Duration	
0 Nights	7
1 Night	11
2 or 3 Nights	43
4 to 9 Nights	30
10 Nights or more	7
Type of Lodging	
Friends' and relatives' homes	37
Hotel or motel	49
Rented cabin or condo	3
Owned cabin or condo	4
Camper, trailer, RV	4
Other	4
No overnight stay	7

Source: Somerset R. Waters, *Travel Industry World Yearbook: The Big Picture, 1994–1995* (New York: Child & Waters, 1995), p. 20.

▶ The Impact of Tourism

Tourism affects every nation and many localities within those nations. For some, tourism has a major impact on the economy, the culture, the society, and the environment. The effects can be both positive and negative and are greater in some countries and areas than others. Let us examine these in more detail.

▶ The Economic Impact of Tourism

The **economic impact** of tourism is a term used to refer to the increased level of economic activity in an area that results from tourism. It is generally measured in additional jobs and income to an area.

Travelers and tourists purchase goods and services. They spend money for transportation, lodging, food, drink, and entertainment. They

▶ Lots of Help for Those Traveling by Car ◀

Those traveling by car can now find lots of help in various computer programs from Rand McNally, the American Automobile Association, and DeLorme Mapping, among others. These programs are designed to help travelers do their own routing, and the programs are complete with ideas for attractions along the way as well as lodging facilities and restaurants.

One program, Precision Mapping 2.0, comes with a CD–ROM that allows users to find any of 17 million streets and road segments in the United States. Users can create their own maps, plan their own itineraries, and determine distances between various points they intend to visit.

Other programs under development will enable users to map their vacations, select lodgings along the route, and book reservations over the Internet. Soon, those with laptops, portable printers, and cellular telephones will be able to change their plans en route by canceling existing reservations, booking new reservations, and printing updated maps showing their revised routes.

Adapted from an article in the Boston Sunday Globe, *June 4, 1995.*

also purchase other goods and services in the areas they visit. The money they spend comes from outside the area and is brought to the area by tourists in the form of cash, traveler's checks, and credit cards. It is "new" money; that is, money not generated from internal economic activity but brought to the area by tourists. It is money that would not get into the local economy without travel and tourism.

The direct or immediate effect of this additional spending is likely to be an increase in the number of jobs in the area and an increase in the income of many local citizens. For example, in an area being developed for tourism, new hotels, motels, and other lodging establishments must be built to accommodate travelers. This creates construction jobs. Once the facilities are built, staff must be hired to operate them. Wages are paid to employees, and these wages are spent in the area to purchase housing, food, clothing, and many other goods and services. Retail establishments selling these items receive income that they would not have had if the hotels, motels, and other lodging facilities had not been built. In addition, the lodging properties must purchase various supplies, including food, beverages, linens, and a host of other items. If these goods are bought locally, the food purveyors and suppliers of other goods gain income they would not have had otherwise.

Besides these immediate effects, there are also very important "ripple" effects. The additional income going to local businesses as a result of tourism enables the owners of these enterprises to hire more employees to handle the extra business. The new employees also spend their wages in the locality, so more jobs are created and more income is generated as a secondary effect of the original new spending. And the cycle does not stop there. There may be third, fourth, and additional rounds of new jobs created as these new employees spend their money locally. Where there was only one restaurant in the area, for example, there may now be several, catering to the tourists, the growing and more prosperous local population, or both.

The total economic impact on an area is the sum of this increased economic activity. It may be greater than the original amount spent or it may be less, depending on how much of the original new money is spent locally and how much of it is spent outside the area. For example, suppose that a new hotel hires workers who commute from a dis-

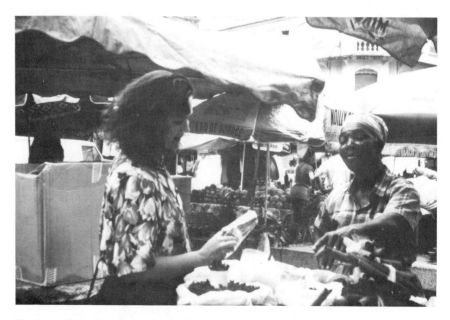

Tourism affects the economic development of any region to which tourists travel, generally increasing the region's jobs and income. For example, tourism to Guadelupe spawned shopping areas and recreational activities. (Photo courtesy of Joe Petrouck.)

tance away, and that the hotel also purchases its goods and services from firms outside the local area. Under these circumstances, the economic impact on the immediate area would be limited, because very little of the new money would be spent there. This was the case in Atlantic City, New Jersey. The legalization of casino gaming led to the construction of many new hotels, but the economic impact in the immediate area was minimal. There were three principal reasons for this.

1. Gamblers tended not to leave the casino hotels and consequently spent very little in other Atlantic City businesses.
2. Comparatively few casino hotel employees established residence in Atlantic City, so they tended to shop for goods and services outside the city.
3. A major portion of the goods and services purchased by the casino hotels were from vendors located outside the city.

The economic impact of tourism varies considerably from one part of the country to another and from one location to another. The economic impact of travel and tourism is high in some areas and low in others. For example, tourism is the most important industry in the state of Florida. In one recent year, $51.6 billion was spent by tourists in that state. This spending directly and indirectly created about 1.1 million jobs, which accounted for 18 percent of the state's civilian labor force. The economic impact of tourism is high in Florida because most of the wages paid to workers are spent in the state, and a large proportion of the goods and services purchased by the travel industry come from Florida businesses. By contrast, in Bermuda, the economic impact of tourism is relatively low even though tourism is also the most important industry, accounting for about 60 percent of the jobs. The impact is lower than in Florida because Bermuda grows relatively little food and manufactures very few products for the travel industry. Although employees do spend their wages in the local community, hotels, shops, and other businesses must purchase food and other goods from suppliers outside Bermuda. In both Florida and Bermuda, tourism is the most important economic activity. The economic benefits from tourism are greater in Florida because the direct and indirect economic impacts are greater.

Another important economic benefit is the increased government income from taxes. Every state in the United States imposes taxes on tourists. Most have sales taxes on rooms and meals. These are frequently higher than the sales taxes imposed on other goods and services. For example, the state of New Hampshire has an 8 percent tax on rooms and meals, yet it has no sales tax on other goods and services sold in the state. New York City imposes special sales taxes on hotel rooms. A traveler staying in a New York hotel may be charged as much as 15 percent in state and city taxes for hotel accommodations.

Finally, the foreign exchange earned as a result of tourism is a major economic benefit to many nations. A nation needs foreign exchange to pay for goods and services imported from abroad, and tourism is one of the principal means of earning it.

▶ The Cultural Impact of Tourism

Tourism can have a significant impact on the culture of a nation—the customary beliefs, social forms, and daily life of a racial, religious, or social group. Culture manifests itself in art, dance, religion, food, drink, and other aspects of a society. Tourism may help preserve native culture, but at the same time it will speed the process of cultural change.

Tourism helps preserve a culture when large numbers of people travel to observe that culture. Music and dance, religious rites and other ceremonial activities are performed for tourists and thus become profitable. The repetition of these performances and the income they provide offers an incentive to preserve the culture. It is said that traditional ceremonies still performed on several Caribbean and South Sea islands would have disappeared if tourists had not been drawn to the islands to see them.

One reason travelers go to other countries is to sample the local food and drink. Irish stew, German sauerbraten, Italian cannelloni, and Japanese sukiyaki and sashimi are dishes served in the traditional way for tourists. Many are convinced that these dishes somehow have different and more authentic flavors in their homelands.

Travelers also go to other countries to see the remains of past civilizations. The Roman Colosseum and the excavated ruins of Pompeii, for example, attract large numbers of visitors, and the money spent by tourists helps to preserve them.

Over the long term, tourism may bring about changes in the culture of a region or a country. Two important areas that may be affected are food and clothing.

Food

Tourists bring their social and cultural attitudes and values with them when they visit other countries. They may be eager to sample the food

Tourism impacts culture in two ways. For example, it may help to preserve art or dance in performance or cuisine in preparation, but it may also influence changes in a culture through contract with travelers and the devaluation of once sacred rituals through commerce. Shown above are the Lion Dancers at the Merlion Festival, held on the last day of the Merlion Week. (Photo courtesy of Singapore Tourist Promotion Board, all copyrights reserved.)

of the countries they visit, but they commonly look for foods as well, seeking those similar to foods served at home. Hotels and restaurants willingly accommodate them. The local residents discover these "foreign" foods and begin to try them, and some of these foods eventually become part of the local culture. For example, imported frozen foods and American whiskey are now popular throughout the Caribbean. This was not the case before Americans began to visit in large numbers.

Fast-food hamburger chains are now spreading throughout the world. McDonald's is now all over the world, and Burger King has expanded into China. There are American-style restaurants in Japan. Eventually, the American foods served in these restaurants will be included in the diets of those countries, and their cultures will have been altered. It is said that the many Puerto Rican dishes have all but disappeared from the diets of those living on that island. The Puerto

Rican diet now clearly resembles that of the American mainland. San Juan has many fast-food restaurants offering typical American mainland cuisine.

Clothing

Tourism also can change the manner in which local populations dress. Tourists wear clothing that is popular at home. Local shops begin to sell clothing that will appeal to tourists, and it is noticed by the local residents, some of whom begin to adopt it. As it becomes more popular with local residents, more traditional clothing may become less common. It may be replaced gradually by the new styles from abroad. A classic example of this has taken place in Russia, where Levis and other jeans have become very popular and command high prices.

▶ The Social Impact of Tourism

Tourism can also have dramatic—and often negative—effects on the social climate in a country. It can affect the way the host society feels about citizens of other countries, and it can affect the behavior of citizens of the host country. These changes manifest themselves in many ways, including

1. Resentment
2. Family problems
3. Social problems
4. Crime and violence

Resentment

Tourists going to poor, less-developed countries sometimes create feelings of resentment and jealousy among the local population. They do this by being demanding—sometimes demeaning—and by seeming to spend excessive amounts of money.

Local workers see tourists check into first-class and luxury hotels. The rates paid by these tourists are usually high by local standards. The room rate charged for one night in some of these properties may be the equivalent of several weeks' wages for a local worker. Some tourists can be very demanding, requiring instant service or a special service that may not be readily available in the area. Other tourists can be demeaning, talking to the hotel staff as if they were inferior. The considerable amount of money spent by the tourists can create jealousy. Tourists sometimes appear to spend money as if it meant very little. Native workers with lower standards of living become jealous of the more affluent tourists and develop a dislike for them.

If the behavior of tourists is grossly inappropriate, local workers are likely to become resentful and react by being impolite. These feelings are transferred to the local population, as workers go home and discuss events with family and friends. Americans have poor reputations in some countries because some American tourists have behaved inappropriately and insultingly. Thus, local residents have assumed that all Americans are like the unpleasant ones they have seen at the hotels.

This problem is not restricted to other nations: it can be seen within the United States. For example, tourists from large cities, such as New York, who go to rural areas in New England may appear to local residents to "throw money around." Given the cost of living in major cities, they are accustomed to spending more for goods and services, but they appear to be spending more than the local population feels these goods and services are worth. The prices of goods and services generally rise in response to this. In reality, prices in the rural areas may be considerably cheaper than in large cities, such that tourists do not feel they are paying too much. Nevertheless, the native population resents them for driving up prices, crowding the highways, polluting the area, and generally "acting superior"; and although local residents typically are willing to take their money, they resent the presence of the outsiders.

Family Problems

Tourism can affect the family relationships of local residents when one or more members of the family work in the tourist industry. Several years ago, a study of Hawaiian families showed that the divorce rate of workers involved in tourism was rapidly rising. The study concluded that women who dressed in native Hawaiian costumes to greet and entertain tourists sometimes faced jealousy from their husbands, who accused the women of carrying on with the tourists. In addition, many of the women began to earn higher wages than their husbands, which led to further problems.

Social Problems

Tourism obviously creates the need for work in hotels, restaurants, and other businesses catering to the traveler. Many of these workers are drawn from the local population, but some may come from other areas and settle among the local population. Communities that have always been of a single culture find that people of different backgrounds, beliefs, values, and lifestyles are now living in their neighborhoods. The new residents act differently, go to different churches, may speak a different language, and even eat different foods. Past social patterns are upset and cultural collision occurs. If the new residents are accepted by the community, the dissimilar cultures can exist peaceably together. If not, there may be conflict.

Crime and Violence

When areas grow in population as a result of tourism, negative changes can take place. A once peaceful, rural community may become a busy town or a small city. Tourists, who tend to carry larger amounts of money than they would when not traveling, become targets for amateur and professional thieves. Houses and stores are broken into; a larger police force is required; and local residents who had never found it necessary to lock their homes and cars find an urgent need to do so.

▶ The Environmental Impact of Tourism

The impact of tourism on the environment can be positive or negative, depending on the specific area and one's personal views. On the one hand, everyone would agree that some tourist areas such as Atlantic City, Miami Beach, or Waikiki do not now have the natural beauty that existed prior to development. On the other hand, many would argue that resort areas such as Bermuda, Nassau, or Maui are nicer, cleaner, and more charming than they were prior to their development for tourism.

Some people feel that more people in an area and such changes as new roads, hotels, and restaurants are harmful to the environment. To them, all tourism is harmful to the environment. The general arguments for both the positive and negative points of view are as follows.

The Positive

Development of all kinds has a tendency to destroy natural as well as historical and cultural elements in an area. One cannot develop an area without building new roads, creating hotels and other structures, and installing power lines for electric power. In the process, some historical or cultural symbols may be destroyed. Many countries and areas lack the incentive or the economic means to undertake large-scale projects for the conservation of beautiful scenery, rare and interesting natural environments, or historically important sites. The local population may have little use for "unspoilt nature" and will develop these areas in ways that will bring in the most money— whether it be for factories, mining, or some other kind of business.

Tourism changes all that. It encourages the restoration of ancient monuments and archaeological treasures. It provides a reason for the preservation of historical buildings and the creation of museums. The Roman Colosseum would not be preserved if there were no tourists to see it; the same can be said for the Acropolis in Greece—probably the best known "ruins" in the world. Natural scenery and historical sites as well as traditional towns become economic assets. In fact, some attractions may be more beautiful than the natural land—golf courses and parks, for example.

Tourism provides not only the incentive but the economic means to preserve the environment. It discourages the development of heavy industry and other unsound uses of the land.

The Negative

The benefits of tourism are overshadowed by its side effects. The development of tourism often brings large numbers of people, accustomed to relatively high standards of amenities, to a previously secluded natural or cultural environment. Tourism necessitates the development of roads, airports, foodservice, lodging facilities, and shops.

In the process, many tourist sights are inevitably transformed. At best, their natural attractiveness will be lost as they become regulated tourist attractions with parking lots, food outlets, and bathrooms. At worst, major and often irreversible environmental damage will be caused by a rush to build tourist facilities on the most attractive sites. In many instances, the natural environment is lost forever.

Crowds of tourists litter the area and damage the fragile environment. Local water, sewage, and other facilities become overburdened, causing pollution and unclean air. In the long run, tourism, like any other industry, contributes to environmental destruction.

Most people find that both points of view are somewhat off the mark. Perhaps the most compelling argument falls somewhere between these two extremes. If there is to be development—if an area is to have economic progress—tourism is one of the very best alternatives. If properly controlled and regulated, tourism can be the least damaging of any form of economic development and can actually improve the environment of an area. The key to preserving the environment and allowing for economic progress is in controlling the rate of growth, attending to the necessary support (water, sewage, roads), and developing a plan that will preserve the best environmental assets of the area. This usually requires government involvement in tourism planning.

The Importance of Tourism (to Nations, States, Areas, and Communities)

Tourism is more important to some nations, states, areas, and communities than to others. In many nonindustrialized nations, for example, tourism is the single most important source of income and economic activity. This is true of Spain and most of the Caribbean islands, where tourism produces about 43 percent of the income for the region. Leading the list of income generators in the Caribbean are the Bahamas, Puerto Rico, Dominican Republic, the U.S. Virgin Islands, and Jamaica. Taken together, these five account for over one half of the tourist-generated dollars in the region.

The economic importance of tourism is not limited to nonindustrialized nations. Some industrialized countries also rely heavily on tourism to provide foreign exchange. France is now the world's leading travel destination and receives about 10 percent of all international tourists. The United States is a close second. Countries such as Canada, Italy, and the United Kingdom also rely heavily on tourism.

Within the United States, tourism is very important to some states and less so to others. Those states in which tourism is particularly important—where large numbers of tourists visit the state or where more than 20 percent of the jobs in the state can be traced directly or indirectly to tourism—are frequently labeled destination states. Heading the list of destination states is California. More tourist dollars go to California than to any other state. Other destination states include Florida, New York, Texas, New Jersey, Hawaii, New Hampshire, Vermont, Nevada, Colorado, Arizona, Maine, and South Carolina, among others. In some of the destination states, tourism is the leading industry, accounting for more jobs than any other industry in the state. This is true in Hawaii, Florida, Vermont, Maine, and Nevada.

For many states, tourism is not the leading or even the second leading industry but is still a major factor in the economy, accounting for 10 to 20 percent of total employment. This is true in Virginia, West Virginia, Georgia, Tennessee, Louisiana, Michigan, Missouri, Illinois, Wisconsin, Minnesota, North Dakota, Montana, Utah, Idaho, Oregon, Washington, Alaska, Massachusetts, Connecticut, and others.

In some areas and many local communities, tourism is the only significant industry. In these places, most jobs and income can be traced directly or indirectly to tourist dollars. This is true for such destinations as Cape Cod, Bar Harbor, the White Mountains of New Hampshire, the Catskills, the Poconos, Atlantic City, Myrtle Beach, Orlando (Disney World), White Sulphur Springs, Sea Island, Great Smokey Mountains National Park, New Orleans, Hot Springs, the Black Hills, Yellowstone, Scottsdale, Sante Fe, Las Vegas, Sun Valley, Yosemite, and Vail.

It would be impossible to list all of the areas in the United States where tourism is the only significant industry. Hundreds of smaller areas, such as Boothbay Harbor, Maine, or Long Beach Island, New Jersey, are not well known outside their regions but rely heavily on tourism for employment and income.

To many, tourism is the industry of the future. As more people have greater amounts of leisure time, the number of people traveling will increase. As transportation becomes cheaper, faster, and more comfortable, travelers will venture farther and farther from home. As disposable income increases, travel will become even more a part of our lifestyle. As the population lives longer and the quality of medical care enables more people to be healthy and mobile for greater numbers of years, more older people will travel. These and other changes in society, mentioned at the beginning of this chapter, insure that travel and tourism will continue to be a leading growth industry.

▶ Summary

In this chapter, the dimensions of travel and tourism are explored. The motivators for travel and changes in society that have caused people to travel more frequently are listed. The government role in travel and tourism is examined, and major government and private travel organizations are identified. The terms *traveler* and *tourist* are discussed, and definitions are provided for each. The composition of the travel industry—direct providers, support services, and tourism development—is explained. The size and scope of international and domestic travel are examined. Conditions and documents necessary for travel are described, as are the economic, cultural, social, and environmental impacts of tourism. Finally, the importance of tourism to nations, states, areas, and communities is discussed.

De Facto Recognition

De Jure Recognition

Direct Providers of Travel Services

Passport

Support Services

Tourism Development

Tourist

Traveler

Travel Industry

Visa

1. List at least ten motivators for travel.

2. Describe eight social and economic changes that have led to more frequent travel.

3. How does the role of the U.S. government in travel and tourism compare to that of other nations?

4. What organization publishes most U.S. travel data?

5. List the four criteria used to determine a person's status as a traveler.

6. How does the U.S. Bureau of the Census define *traveler*?

7. How does the definition of a traveler from the U.S. Bureau of the Census differ from that of the United States Travel Data Center?

8. Define *tourism*.

9. List ten examples of direct providers of tourist services.

10. What kinds of firms would be classified as support services to the travel industry?

11. Give one example of each of the four types of organizations or agencies classified as tourism development.

12. How much money is spent on world domestic and international travel and tourism?

13. List the countries that are the top three international tourist destinations.

14. The citizens of which five countries are classified as the top five spenders on international tourism.

15. Distinguish between de jure and de facto diplomatic recognition.

16. What basic document is required for Americans to visit most European countries? Canada? the Caribbean islands?

17. What is a visa?

18. List the five nations that earn the largest amounts from international tourist spending.

19. From which two countries do the largest number of foreign tourists come to the United States? What accounts for these large numbers?

20. From which countries do the largest number of overseas visitors to the United States come?

21. How much is spent on domestic travel in the United States?

22. Which mode of transportation accounts for the greatest share of domestic travel?

23. What is the primary reason for domestic travel?

24. What does the phrase "economic impact of tourism" mean?

25. Identify three major benefits that national governments derive from tourism.

26. In what primary way does tourism preserve the culture of a nation?

27. In what ways can tourism affect human relations in a society?

28. The chapter describes the points of view of those favoring and those opposing tourism. Summarize each in one short paragraph. Do you accept either? Why?

29. List five destination states for tourists.

30. List ten areas or localities where tourism is the only significant industry.

1. You are discussing a possible career in the travel industry with a friend. He states that he does not believe the industry will grow significantly in the coming years, and thus would not be a wise choice for a career. What is your response?

2. You are planning a trip to Mexico. What information do you need to obtain about entering the country?

3. Select a nearby area that caters to tourists and assess the environmental impact of tourism on the area. Has it been positive, negative, or mixed? Respond in an essay of suitable length, including as much factual information as possible to defend your position.

Twelve

Travel Services

After reading and studying this chapter, you should be able to:

1 Define the term *travel intermediary.*

2 Define the term *package* as used in the travel business.

3 List the advantages and disadvantages of purchasing travel packages over making travel arrangements independently.

4 Describe the contents of each of the following types of packages: (a) all-inclusive; (b) fly/cruise; (c) fly/cruise/hotel; (d) fly/drive; (e) motor coach; (f) accommodations; (g) accommodations and meals; (h) family vacation; (i) events; (j) special-interest; (k) affinity group; (l) incentive; (m) convention and meeting.

5 Explain the advantages and disadvantages of making travel arrangements directly with a supplier of travel services.

6 Describe the typical packages provided by (a) airlines; (b) bus companies; (c) cruise lines; (d) hotel companies; (e) railroads.

7 Identify the percentage of travel agency business going to each of the following: airlines, cruise lines, hotels, car rentals.

8 Identify the number of travel agencies in the United States and the dollar sales of the average agency.

9 Explain the importance of travel agents to the suppliers of travel services.

10 List the prerequisites for a travel agency to sell travel tickets.

11 Define the terms *travel wholesaler* and *tour operator.*

12 Define the term *specialty channeler.*

13 Identify and explain the role of each of the following specialty channelers in selling travel: (a) hotel representatives; (b) state and local tourists offices; (c) corporate travel offices; (d) incentive travel firms; (e) convention and meeting planners.

▶ Introduction

In the previous chapter, the dimensions of travel and tourism were explored. The travel industry was shown to consist of direct providers of travel, support services, and tourism development. Data were supplied to show that international and domestic travel has increased steadily over the years, such that the travel industry is now the world's largest industry, accounting for more than one in every ten dollars spent at the retail level.

Mass travel—extensive long-distance travel by the middle class as well as by the wealthy—really began shortly after World War II. Prior to that time, the middle class generally had neither the time nor the money for long-distance travel, except for job-related purposes, immigration, or some urgent purpose. For many Americans, serving with the armed forces during a war provided the single opportunity for travel that they would have in their entire lives.

Long-distance travel for pleasure was highly unusual for most Americans. After World War II, however, more people had greater amounts of free time to travel. They had automobiles that could be used for travel, and they were earning higher wages that gave them the disposable income for travel. Airlines evolved into a major means of public transportation, making it possible for virtually everyone to travel long distances at relatively low prices. The age of large-scale selling of travel to the public began after World War II.

In this chapter, we will provide a broad description of the travel business. We will identify the two basic options for those intending to travel and then examine the roles of travel agencies, travel wholesalers, travel specialists, and other related organizations in developing travel packages and making arrangements for travelers.

Once an individual has made the decision to travel, there are two possible options for making the necessary arrangements: she may either seek the help of an individual or firm in the business of making travel arrangements, or she may take the do-it-yourself approach.

If the traveler elects the do-it-yourself approach, he must make direct contact with the supplier or suppliers of the services required and attend to all the necessary arrangements. The traveler must obtain detailed information about fares, schedules, and dates directly from suppliers.

The difficulties associated with making these arrangements have led many travelers to take the other approach; that is, having all arrangements made by a travel professional known as an intermediary. The term **travel intermediary** refers to a person or firm that makes travel arrangements for individuals or groups. When the arrangements are made by an intermediary, the traveler need only call or visit the intermediary, discuss the various options, then leave the detailed arrangements to this professional.

One of the more familiar travel intermediaries is the travel agent. A **travel agent** is one who is in the business of making travel arrangements for others. When travelers use the services of a travel agent, travel arrangements can be tailored to their particular needs and desires. Specialized itineraries can be prepared for them. The travel agent inquires into their needs and makes specific reservations for airlines, hotels, transfers, rental cars, or other requirements. If specialized travel arrangements are not required, the travel agent may recommend a common alternative: a travel package. **Travel package** is a term used to describe two or more travel services bundled together and sold at one price.

Travel packages are among the most important elements in the travel business. Travel agents typically find that sales of travel packages represent approximately 18 percent of annual bookings. Approximately 32 percent of Americans traveling to foreign overseas destinations book packages. Because of the important role they play in the travel business, it is useful to examine various types of packages and the firms that develop them.

▶ Travel Packages

There are many different kinds of travel packages. Some are group packages, arranged so that a given number of travelers are together for the duration of a trip. Others are individual packages that enable a traveler to travel independently without regard to others who select the same package. In some instances, the independent package requires that the individual travel at specified times; thus, the air transportation may be arranged along with others taking the tour. In other instances, the independent tour does not require a specific departure or return date. Travelers choose those dates for themselves and travel entirely independently of others taking the same package.

Packages can be very different from one another. Some packages are vacation packages to specific locations—a hotel on a Caribbean island, for example. Others are packages with travel to several locations—London, Paris, Rome, and Berlin, for example. Packages may last for only a few days or for a week or longer, and they vary in price according to the quality of the package and the length of time involved.

Some packages provide deluxe accommodations; others include accommodations in properties of lower quality. Some packages are geared to specific activities—golf, for example.

Some packages include all the necessities: travel, accommodations, meals, tips, transfers, sports, and entertainment. Others include only a few: accommodations and a rental car, for example. The firm that assembles the package makes judgments about the combination of services it believes are most appealing and can best be sold to potential customers.

The following are characteristic types of packages sold to travelers.

▶ All-Inclusive Packages

As the name implies, **all-inclusive packages** provide most or all of the necessary elements of travel. They generally include transportation, accommodations, meals, transfers (ground transportation between an airport and a hotel or similar lodging property), entertainment, sightseeing, sports, taxes, and gratuities. However, they do vary considerably. Some offer all meals; others offer a specified number of meals. Some include admission to special events; others do not. Other specifics in the travel package may also vary.

▶ Fly/Cruise Packages

Fly/cruise packages include air transportation to and from a point of departure, transfers, and a cruise. Fly/cruise packages are almost always all-inclusive, meaning that the package price includes the cost of airfare, accommodations, all meals, and entertainment. Gratuities and sightseeing are typically extra.

A page from a brochure featuring all-inclusive vacation packages, detailing accommodations, foodservice, activities, and other points of interest. A myriad of travel packages are available, offering travelers savings through volume sales and the convenience of having most of the important arrangements made. (Photo courtesy of Club Med Sales, Inc., all rights reserved.)

Located on the southeast Atlantic coast of St. Lucia on 95 acres, five minutes from Hewanorra International Airport. The pastel pink, marble-trimmed central atrium leads to a large swimming pool, open-air cocktail lounge, boutique, theater and modern nightclub. Tiny Maria Island dots the horizon. For ages 2 and over.

Accommodations

Air-conditioned, double occupancy rooms in four-story beach and garden-front lodgings with a private balcony overlooking the ocean. Each has oversized twin beds and a private bathroom with shower. Connecting rooms (request upon arrival) and single rooms (extra charge; request when reserving) are subject to availability.

Restaurants

At the main dining room in the village center, enjoy lavish buffets at breakfast, lunch and dinner. For quiet, intimate dinners served at your table for two or more, visit the open-air Club House for French cuisine, and the new Cadi's Pub for classic American favorites.

Sports and Activities*

- Scuba diving: beginners to experts; near the Pitons (departure is a five-minute bus ride from the village); intensive program
- Horseback riding: English and Western; intensive English horseback riding program for all levels of skill
- Windsurfing: experienced boardsailors only; advanced training program
- Tennis: 8 composition courts (all night-lit); clubhouse with showers
- Circus workshops
- Fitness center
- Aerobics/Calisthenics
- Water exercises
- Practice golf

- Archery
- Volleyball/Basketball
- Soccer
- Softball
- Ping-pong
- Bocce ball
- All-day snorkeling picnics and boat rides
- Nightly entertainment and dancing

Beyond the village*

Castries, Soufriere (hot sulfur springs), island helicopter tour, the Grenadine Islands, Martinique, snorkeling excursion, sunset cruise.

Especially for kids

Scuba experience in the pool from age 4-12. Carriage, pony and horseback rides, according to age and ability, with intensive program from age 8*. Go-cart racetrack, complete with traffic lights, road signs and individually-timed races. Kids-only circus instruction and equipment, complete with flying trapeze, trampoline and more, from age 4. Snorkeling, tennis and practice golf for age 6. Basketball, softball and volleyball on smaller courts.

Open-air Petit Club (2-3 years) with air-conditioned nap room, Mini Clubs (4-7 years), and Kids Club (8-11 years), open from 9:00 am – 9:00 pm. Wading pool.

Highlights

- *Dramatic Windward island setting*
- *Plenty for every member of the family*
- *Unique children's program with scuba diving, horseback riding, go carting, circus school and more, plus Kids Free!*

Kids Free — Youngsters 2-5 years are invited to St. Lucia absolutely free of charge! Please refer to page 1 for dates and details.

*Extra charge for horseback riding, scuba certifications, and excursions. Refer to the "General Sports Information" section in the back of the main brochure for more information about our sports programs.

ST. LUCIA VILLAGE FACTS

Address:
Club Med-St. Lucia
P.O. Box 246
Vieux Fort
St. Lucia
West Indies

Telephone:
(809) 45-46-546

Telex:
341 6324

Fax:
(809) 45-46-017
Incoming calls/telexes/faxes reach our switchboard; messages are posted.

Transfers:
Airport: Hewanorra (UVF) approx. 3 miles from village; 10 minutes by transfer; approx. $5 one way taxi fare plus $2 per extra person
Alternate airport: Vigi (SLU), approx. 28 miles from village, 1 hour; approx. $45 one-way taxi fare

Time difference:
EDT all year

Currency:
Eastern Caribbean dollar

National language:
English and Creole

Languages spoken in the village:
English and French

Form of payment in the village:
Traveler's Checks
American Express
Visa
MasterCard
Cash

Laundry:
Washers, dryers, irons and ironing boards available

Voltage:
220 volts; adapters and converters are necessary

Car rental:
At village and at airport

Medical assistance at the village:
Infirmary/2 Nurses

Medical assistance outside the village:
Doctor
Hospital 10 minutes from village

Climate:
Tropical*

	High	Low
November	85	71
December	83	70
January	82	69
February	83	69
March	84	69
April	87	71

*average daily highs and lows

▶ Fly/Cruise/Hotel Packages

Fly/cruise/hotel packages normally include air transportation, a cruise, and a specified number of nights at a hotel. These packages are typically offered by cruise-line companies (such as Cunard), which own resort hotels in the general vicinity of the ship's point of departure.

▶ Fly/Drive Packages

Fly/drive packages typically include airfare and rental car only. They are intended for travelers who prefer to make their own travel plans. Fly/drive packages are usually prepared by airlines in partnership with rental car companies.

▶ Motor Coach Packages

Motor coach packages are special purpose bus tours for those interested in shopping, sightseeing, or attending a particular sports event, for example. They are planned by motor coach operators and other tour companies. If a particular tour is to take more than one day, it will normally include accommodations, meals, and entertainment.

▶ Accommodations Packages

Accommodations packages usually include only lodging. They are really just discounts on room rates. Some are only available for particular seasons or on specified dates. Others are limited to particular numbers of nights. Many international airlines offer very attractive accommodations packages for use in major cities abroad. Accommodations packages sometimes include such additional features as continental breakfasts, transit passes, or theater tickets.

▶ Accommodations and Meals Packages

Accommodations and meals packages include hotel accommodations and meals. They vary considerably. Some include three meals per day; others include certain specified meals: full English breakfast daily, or dinner the second night, for example. Some include free access to sports facilities, such as golf courses and tennis courts. Others offer discounts on sporting activities. Some also offer sightseeing and other entertainment.

▶ Family Vacation Packages

Family vacation packages always include accommodations at specific destinations and attractions that appeal particularly to families:

Disney World, Sea World, or Busch Gardens, for example. They normally include other appealing features, as well: some type of child care for part of the vacation, for example, so that adults can have time for themselves. These packages are typically designed to provide value to families.

▶ Events Packages

Events packages are special packages that focus on particular events or performances: football games, festivals, theater, art exhibits, and so on. The possibilities are endless. These packages usually include transportation and admissions to the event or performance, and they may include such other features as accommodations, meals, and rental cars.

▶ Special-Interest Packages

Special-interest packages are designed for groups of people who share a particular interest, such as a sport or a particular hobby. The common interests around which these packages are developed include golf or tennis, photography, wine, fall foliage, and many others.

▶ Affinity Group Packages

Affinity groups are groups of people who share a common bond. They may be students in the same college, alumni of one university, members of a social club, a religious organization, or a fraternity or a sorority. They may all be in the same profession: doctors, dentists, or lawyers, for example. **Affinity group packages** enable the group to share a common experience. It can be a tour, a vacation at a particular resort, a cruise, or any other activity that appeals to the group.

▶ Incentive Packages

An **incentive package** is a vacation package sponsored by a corporation and offered to employees as a reward for superior performance—high-volume sales of a product or service, or some other achievement beyond the norm. Some companies offer all-inclusive vacations to

Hawaii, for example. Any type of package can be used as an incentive package as long as it provides incentive for employees to improve performance.

▶ Convention and Meeting Packages

Convention and meeting packages are typically offered by hotels and sponsoring organizations. They frequently include accommodations, meals, sightseeing, and other activities.

Packages have several advantages over individual travel arrangements. They are typically less expensive, because the person or firm preparing the package purchases the travel arrangements in quantity and is able to pass on savings to the traveler. For example, an intermediary putting together a vacation package to London, England, for forty-five people might be able to obtain rooms and meals at a particular hotel for 70 percent of the normal price. The hotel manager may be glad to sell these rooms at that price, because he is assured of selling a large number of rooms, and the cost of providing food for these guests might be less than for regular customers. In addition, the hotel does not have to pay a travel agency commission because the commission is paid to the travel agent by the intermediary.

It is also possible to purchase airline seats at a discount. Some of the savings that result from making these arrangements at discounts are passed on to the purchaser of the package, and sufficient profit is left for the intermediary making the arrangements. The total price of the package is considerably less than it would be for an individual to make the same arrangements on his own.

Another advantage of a package is that the traveler knows precisely what the trip will cost. All essentials of the trip are normally included in the price, and any extra charges are stated in the promotional materials.

Finally, if the travel is complicated, the tourist traveling on a package has to make only a very few decisions. Once the tour package has been selected, there are normally relatively few choices to be made. Many people prefer to travel without having to make important decisions about where to stay and what sights to see. Good packages assure the traveler that the important events and sights will be seen.

▶ Package Developers

Many suppliers of travel services develop travel packages. A list of these suppliers and the packages they develop includes the following.

▶ The Best Off-Season Packages ◀

Off season—when the crowds are gone—can be the best time to travel: package prices are the lowest and travel can be the easiest. The following are examples of fall packages that offer excellent values.

The Sabena Eurostar package, from Sabena Airlines, includes round trip airfare to Brussels, a one-way coach ticket on the Eurostar, a train traveling from Brussels to London through the channel tunnel, and a return flight to Brussels. The price is as low as $499 per person. This package is available beginning November.

If you want to travel to Florida and beat the winter crush, the Sanibel Harbour Resort and Spa, in Fort Meyers, will provide two people with a room and breakfast for $99 a night, Sunday through Thursday until December 15.

Orient Flexi-Pax Tours offers the Beijing Super Saver package. It includes round-trip airfare on United Airlines, a room for five nights, and daily buffet breakfast. Prices are only $1,199 per person from San Francisco. Departures are scheduled through October.

CEI Tours International has developed a Mystical Ireland Package that begins with one night in Dublin. The next day, travelers head north for overnight visits to the coastal resorts of Bangor and Ballycastle and the lakeside town of Enniskillen. The package includes round-trip transportation from New York or Boston and covers seven nights' accommodations, daily Irish breakfast, most dinners, and sightseeing. Prices start at $1,418. It is available in the fall, until October 20.

These are just a few of the many values in travel packages available to those who can travel in the fall, after the summer rush.

Adapted from articles in Travel Holiday, *September and October, 1995.*

▶ Airlines

Airlines create a large number of packages, the most popular of which are fly/drive packages and accommodation packages.

Fly/drive packages are designed for travelers who wish to be on their own. Airlines create these packages to provide incentives for travelers to go to destinations served by the airlines. They frequently offer these packages on dates or days of the week when they are not normally fully booked.

Accommodations packages are also very popular with airlines. These are typically individual travel packages rather than group packages. Airlines work closely with hotels to provide accommodations at rates that may be below the normal room rates offered by the hotels. Hotel companies are willing to do this because when they establish links with the airlines, they obtain bookings they might not otherwise get.

Many accommodations packages offered by airlines do not include airfare, and some do not include meals or other normal expenses. For example, American Airlines offers accommodations packages to more than twenty Caribbean islands and has established package rates with several hotels on each of these islands. The basic package rate is very appealing but includes only the hotel room. Transfers to the hotel, taxes, airfare, food, drinks, entertainment, and activities are all extra. Many of the same hotels participating in the American Airlines package plan, however, do allow customers to opt for an all-inclusive rate that includes drinks and some activities.

Other packages offered by airlines are more extensive and may include airfare as well as other costs. For example, Northwest Airlines offers packages to Bangkok, Hong Kong, and Singapore that include airfare, hotels, land transportation, sightseeing, and entertainment.

The buyer of an airline package must look very closely at the specific contents of the package to determine if it includes the elements he or she is looking for.

▶ Bus Companies

Bus packages are increasingly popular, particularly with senior citizens. These packages are offered by bus companies that own or lease buses and by many other firms that contract with bus companies for required bus service.

Bus tours vary considerably in quality, length, price, and amenities. Some are as short as a few hours, while others may take days. One of the most popular tours is the gaming tour, a bus tour that takes potential gamblers to a casino and returns them to the point of departure. The casino hotels of Atlantic City, New Jersey, play host to many of these tours from the surrounding region—New York, Connecticut, Pennsylvania, Delaware, Washington, D.C., and other nearby areas.

Bus tours—which vary in quality, length, price, and amenities—are gaining in popularity. Each has a tour guide, who provides interesting and informative commentary about sights along the way, as this Tauck Tours guide is doing in the photograph right. (Photo courtesy of Tauck Tours.)

These tours frequently include bus fare, entertainment, and a number of quarters or gaming chips of sufficient value to make the cost of the tour very reasonable.

Extended bus tours are, by nature, all-inclusive tours because the people on the tour must be housed and fed. These bus tours, like other all-inclusive tours, vary in quality and in the amenities offered. At the economy level, bus tours will stay at budget lodging properties. Meals will offer few if any menu choices and travelers may be charged extra for admissions to events. At the luxury level, those on the tour will be accommodated at luxury hotels, will have a number of choices from the hotel menu, and will not pay for admissions to events.

One of the more interesting professions is that of a bus tour manager or tour guide. She meets the travelers at the point of embarkation and stays with them throughout the tour. Duties of the tour manager include confirming that all reservations for hotels, restaurants, and events are in order, assigning seats and establishing a seat rotation plan on the bus, keeping the tourists informed of sights along the way, keeping order on the tour, making sure baggage gets to hotel rooms and back on the bus, attending to illness and other emergencies, and attending to the myriad details of a bus tour and the countless needs of travelers. Tour managers typically are not paid high salaries, but they do receive tips at the end of the tour. In some cases, they also receive commissions from gift shops and other retail establishments when buses stop at these places. Thus, many tour managers are able to earn comfortable incomes and live interesting lives.

Domestic bus tour companies generally price their package tours without airfare. International bus tour companies, however, have package prices that include airfare. For example, Cosmos, a European-based bus tour company, has various packages to Europe. Their twenty-seven day escorted budget tour of Europe can include airfare and offers transfers, tourist-class hotels, private baths, twenty-five continental breakfasts, twelve dinners, and visits to various sights. These and other bus tours are sold directly to the public as well as through travel agents.

▶ Cruise Lines

Major cruise lines prepare all-inclusive packages that include airfare, transfers to the ship, and the cost of the cruise. Included in the cruise are accommodations, meals, and entertainment. Passengers are required to

Carnival Cruise Line's 2,040-passenger SuperLiner Ecstasy passes the tip of Miami Beach as it heads from the Port of Miami to Caribbean ports of call. The 855-foot-long, $275 million floating resort features a seven-deck-high atrium, twelve thousand-square-foot health spa, dazzling casino, state-of-the-art lounge, and an array of imaginatively themed public rooms reflecting a "visionary metropolis" motif. (Photo courtesy of Carnival Cruise Line.)

pay only for drinks, gratuities, and excursions from the ship. Most cruise lines are noted for the quality and quantity of their food. A typical day will include breakfast, lunch, mid-afternoon tea or snacks, dinner, and midnight buffet.

The cruise lines use a variety of airlines to transport passengers from their homes to the ship. Interestingly, the typical cruise price is usually the same from any city in the United States. This means that cruise passengers coming long distances pay the same as those coming from near the port of embarkation. Usually, cruise lines will deduct the airline portion of the package for those passengers who choose not to take advantage of the "free" air transportation.

Some cruise lines have packages that include one or more nights in a hotel before or after the cruise. These combinations are particularly attractive to those who wish to see the sights while they are in the vicinity of the port. Some offer packages that include a one-week cruise and a second week at a resort hotel owned by the cruise line.

Travel agents account for 95 percent of all cruise sales, virtually all of which are packages. The packages cruise lines create are obviously the most important element in their sales effort.

▶ Railroads

As mentioned in earlier chapters, rail travel was once the most important form of pubic transportation. In Europe and other parts of the world, it is still important, but in the United States, rail travel is used primarily for commuter service. Amtrak does issue a Discover America pass, but it is not what one would call a package because it does not contain features other than the train ride. In Europe, a Eurailpass enables travelers to see Europe relatively inexpensively. In several South American countries, trains are a relatively popular transportation mode for excursions, although the trains are not particularly modern or comfortable. Trains may be part of packages prepared by others, but railroad companies have not been leading developers of packages.

▶ Lodging Companies

Many of the companies operating hotels, motels, and other lodging properties create travel packages that are sold directly to customers as well as through travel agents. For example, Club Med, one of the largest chains of resort hotels, has developed all-inclusive packages for their resorts around the world. These packages include transportation, transfers, taxes, gratuities, meals, entertainment, and accommodations. Recreation is also included in the package price, although the resorts charge extra for certain sports, such as golf, horseback riding, and deep-sea fishing. In contrast to cruise packages, the price of Club Med packages is not the same from all cities. Those who travel the farthest are charged more than those who come from nearby points. Interestingly, Club Med is now also in the cruise business and offers a cruise package aboard its Club Med 1, a motor-sailing vessel, advertised as the largest and most beautiful sailing ship in the world. The vessel has 191 outside staterooms.

Other accommodations packages offered by hotels vary significantly. Many hotels offer packages that include accommodations, all meals, and recreation. Some offer only accommodations and breakfast, plus specified entertainment. There are several all-inclusive resorts that offer packages with accommodations, meals, recreation, sports, gratuities, taxes, and even unlimited drinks at the bar. It is almost impossible to spend money at these resorts.

▶ Tour Wholesalers and Tour Operators

Tour wholesalers and tour operators are important developers of travel packages. As the name implies, a **tour wholesaler** prepares tours and other travel packages and distributes them through retail outlets. The wholesaler organizes the tour, prepares promotional material, and distributes it to travel agencies and other retail firms. Wholesalers may also conduct the tour. **Tour operators** traditionally have been individuals and firms that carry out ground arrangements—for bus tours or guides, for example.

One example of a tour wholesaler that prepares and operates tour packages throughout the world is Collette Travel Service, based in Pawtucket, Rhode Island. This company offers group tours and independent tours to Australia, Europe, Alaska, Africa, Asia, Hawaii, Canada, and the continental United States. The packages range from fly/drive vacations to escorted tours that include land and sea transportation, accommodations, a number of meals, and many of the tour sights. Airfare to the starting destination is additional and is arranged with TWA and other airlines. Collette relies heavily on travel agents to sell their tours.

Of course, when the wholesaler makes travel arrangements, there is a risk that all of the available space will not be sold. If tours are not sufficiently popular, the wholesaler may lose money or may have to cancel the tour.

Any individual or firm can act as a wholesaler. There are virtually no government regulations or requirements for becoming a tour wholesaler. There are more than two thousand independent tour wholesalers and operators in the United States, although the largest forty account for the major share of the business. One of the major problems of dealing with tour wholesalers and operators is that some of the smaller ones are not well managed. Some have gone into bankruptcy, causing serious loss to customers, travel agents, and suppliers of travel services. In recent years, several large tour wholesalers have abruptly gone out of business, and the travel industry is addressing this problem. The U.S. Tour Operators Association, which represents many of the largest international tour operators, has established a bonding program that assures payment in the event of the failure of a travel wholesaler or tour operator.

In many instances, the tour wholesaler and tour operator are two separate firms. The wholesaler makes the travel arrangements for hotel accommodations, meals, and visits to sites along the way. He also prepares the promotional material and distributes it to travel agencies. The tour operator actually conducts the tour, providing the bus to meet travelers at their departing or arriving point and conducting the tour for the travel wholesaler.

There is an increasing degree of overlap in the functions of tour wholesalers and tour operators. Some tour wholesalers arrange all of the details for tours and also act as tour operators. Some tour operators act as tour wholesalers, preparing tour packages and promotional materials and distributing them to retail travel outlets. Thus, travel wholesaler and tour operator sometimes appear to be one and the same. In fact, travel wholesalers are often referred to as tour operators.

Frequently, travel agencies act as travel wholesalers. They do this by developing their own package tours and offering these both to their own customers and to those of other travel agencies. They make arrangements for airline travel, hotels, ground transportation, and all other features of the tour. One of the largest of these firms is American Express, which acts as both tour operator and travel agent.

▶ Travel Agents

The most important retail sellers of travel are travel agents. Interestingly, they are a relatively recent addition to the travel industry. The first travel agent was Thomas Cook, a British publisher and lecturer on the evils and sins of alcohol. In 1841, he conceived of the idea of chartering railroad trains to bring his temperance supporters to meetings, and on July 5 of that year, he transported 570 passengers round-trip on a train from Leicester to Loughborough, England. The distance was twelve miles each way, and the reported cost to each passenger was one shilling.

The trip was very successful, and Cook's services were soon sought by others interested in group travel. By 1845, he was organizing relatively complex travel for individuals and groups over several railroad lines. In 1851, he organized tours to the exhibition in London, and in 1855, he organized similar tours to the Paris exhibition. Shortly thereafter, he opened an office in London.

Thomas Cook was the first man to organize and conduct an around-the-world tour, a feat he accomplished in 1872. His travel agency business continued to grow, becoming one of the world's

An office in a typical travel agency. The most important retail sales channel for travel sales in the United States, travel agents provide the majority of sales for the airline, international hotel, cruise-line, and packaged tour segments of the industry. With access to a wealth of information, travel agents can provide their clients with travel arrangements that best suit their needs and expectations. (Photo courtesy of American Society of Travel Agents.)

largest travel organizations. In 1994, parts of that organization were acquired by American Express, but the name Thomas Cook is still among the best known in the travel industry.

Travel agents are professionals with expertise in arranging travel for clients. Good travel agents, like good doctors, lawyers, or accountants, are highly trained individuals. They have extensive knowledge of travel destinations, accommodations, transportation, and all other aspects of travel. They are able to find the most direct or the least expensive travel route to any destination. They can determine which hotel in a given city is most convenient to a particular site. They can advise travelers about the best time of year to travel to specific destinations. They can advise customers about the proper type of clothing to pack for a specific destination at a particular time of year. They can tell clients whether or not a visa is required to visit a particular country. They can even advise clients on the best routes from the airports to their hotels.

Like other professionals, some travel agents have specialties. Some are particularly knowledgeable about travel in specific parts of the world—Africa, China, or Russia, for example. Others have extensive knowledge of particular types of vacations—cruises or bus tours, perhaps. All travel agents have access to information about the elements of travel, and all should be able to make appropriate travel arrangements for their clients.

Good travel agents have one very important trait in common—the ability to match customers with travel that is suitable. For example, assume that a customer goes to a travel agency looking for a vacation on a cruise ship. Each cruise line and cruise ship is different. Some cruise ships are more formal than others and require formal dress at meals. Some have music and entertainment that appeals to younger people, and others are more suitable for older adults. Some cruise ships sail at night and dock during the daytime at different ports. A good travel agent will be able to determine which cruise best suits the needs, desires, and budget of each individual. To be able to do so requires an understanding of the customer—the kinds of activities, entertainment, and food he or she prefers, as well as the most suitable shipboard environment, type of accommodation, size of ship, and price. Only by understanding both the customer and the cruise lines can the travel agent properly match the customer and the cruise. If the travel agent does a poor job of this, the customer will not be satisfied and will find the travel agent at fault.

Travel agents have immediate access to a wealth of travel information that would take customers long hours to find if they were attempt-

▶Choosing the Options in Caribbean Accommodations ◀
That Are Right for You

When visiting the Caribbean, travelers have several options in accommodations. Choosing the right one may be the key to a successful vacation. Travel agents can best advise vacationers which accommodations are best for them.

All Inclusive Resorts First made popular by Club Med in the 1950s, all-inclusives now offer an even wider range of activities and amenities. At the new breed of "super inclusive" resorts, the daily rate usually includes an air-conditioned room, meals, drinks, airport transfers, and activities like tennis lessons, windsurfing, and snorkeling. Base prices are higher than standard resort prices, but they are excellent values for fun-loving guests prepared to take advantage of everything these resorts have to offer. Jamaica boasts the most all-inclusive resorts. They range from those that cater to couples only to those that accept singles only to those catering to families.

Family-Run Inns These intimate resorts provide the experience of an extended family in the Caribbean. Most do not offer room service but do offer a friendly house-party atmosphere imbued with the personality of the host. Sociability is important, as regulars arrive ready to mingle.

Classic Resorts Most of these properties provide the elegant island style of the 1960s but with updated amenities, and many cater to groups. Guests are not required to participate in activities unless they want to, and unlike all-inclusive resorts, they pay only for food and drink they purchase.

Villa Rentals For some, a Caribbean villa means peace, privacy, and independence—all with an ocean view. A two-bedroom house can provide ample room for two couples or a family and allow the occupants freedom to make their own schedules. Many villas come with privileges at tennis and golf facilities, and frequently, a complex will include the amenities of a full resort.

The travel agent is best able to match the needs of travelers with the type of accommodation suited for them, and there is no cost to the traveler. Travel agents receive their commissions from direct providers of travel services.

ing to make their own arrangements. For example, an individual intending to fly from Boston to San Francisco would have to spend considerable time on the telephone calling the airlines that fly out of Boston to determine if they fly to San Francisco. He would have to ask about flight schedules and fares from each of those airlines. If he were to require a hotel room in San Francisco, he might have to call someone in California who had access to the yellow pages for San Francisco to determine the names, addresses, and telephone numbers of local hotels. He would then have to call, fax, or write the hotels to inquire about reservations.

All of this information is readily available to travel agents through computers and publications on hand in their offices. Within moments, travel agents can determine which airlines fly to San Francisco, the schedules for all flights, and the availability and cost of seats on each flight. They can also advise the customer about which hotels are located in the city, their rates, and their locations, and they can easily determine the availability of rooms. All travel arrangements including air, hotel, rental car, and travel insurance can be made by travel agents in a very short period of time.

The travel agent performs all of these services at no cost to the client. This is because the income to a travel agent comes in the form of sales commissions paid by airlines, hotels, and other suppliers of travel services. This sales commission is normally a stipulated percentage of the price of the particular travel service arranged.

Frequently, travel agents can obtain travel and hotel reservations at lower prices than can a customer attempting to make individual travel arrangements. The agent's familiarity with rates and sales practices of airlines, hotels, rental cars, and other services makes it possible for her to find the lowest rates. Under most circumstances, travelers are wise to use the services of travel agents for travel that requires public transportation, accommodations, rental cars, or other travel services. Good travel agents have the expertise to advise clients on the best travel arrangements and can usually make these arrangements at equal or lower cost than arrangements made independently.

Travel agents gain their expertise in a variety of ways. Most have studied at post-secondary institutions—some at colleges and universities offering degree programs in travel and tourism, others at schools that offer shorter professional training programs for travel agents. They complete courses in travel agency management, geography, computer operation, ticketing, customer relations, and other professional subjects. However, coursework alone is normally not enough. Experience is a major element in the development of an expert travel agent.

Travel knowledge and expertise is gained on the job and by means of **familiarization trips,** commonly known as FAM trips. These are trips to resorts, cities, sights, and the like that are sponsored by airlines and by other travel suppliers at the destination. The cost of these trips is usually absorbed by the airlines and the sponsoring organizations. The organizations that sponsor FAM trips do so with the obvious objective of creating referrals and bookings from the travel agencies.

▶ The Number of Travel Agencies and Their Size

Although travel agencies have been in existence since the mid 1800s, when Thomas Cook started the first one, the number was comparatively small until after World War II, when the era of mass travel began. Since then, the increase in the number of travel agencies has kept pace with the growth of travel. Table 12.1 shows the growth in the number of travel agencies in the United States.

The total sales of all U.S. travel agencies in 1993 was estimated at $93.5 billion, and a majority of agencies booked less than $2 million in sales.[1]

Airlines provide the largest share of income to travel agencies, as shown in table 12.2. In 1993 the total sales in a "typical" agency from airline tickets, hotel accommodations, and car rentals, for example was $2.88 million. The average sales commission received from all sources was just over 9 percent of sales, which would mean that actual income to pay salaries, meet other expenses, and provide profit was

Table 12.1 **Number of U.S. Travel Agencies**

Year	Number of Travel Agencies[1]
1985	27,193
1987	30,169
1990	37,807
1993	42,709

1   Including satellite ticket printer locations.

Source: *"Airlines Reporting Corporation," in Somerset R. Waters*, Travel Industry World Yearbook: The Big Picture, 1994–1995 *(New York: Child & Waters, 1995), p. 147.*

---

[1] Somerset R. Waters, *Travel Industry World Yearbook: The Big Picture, 1994–1995* (New York: Child & Waters, 1995), pp. 146–49.

Table 12.2 **U.S. Travel Agency Sales, 1993**

	$ Billions	Percent of Total Sales
Airlines	$55.9	60%
Cruise lines	14.0	15
Hotels	10.3	11
Car rental	6.6	7
Other sales	6.5	7
Totals	$93.4	100%

Source: *"Louis Harris Survey for Travel Weekly," in Somerset R. Waters, Travel Industry World Yearbook: The Big Picture, 1994–1995 (New York: Child & Waters, 1995), p. 149.*

about $260,000. This "typical" agency employed six full-time travel agents and two part-time agents, 84 percent of whom were women.

▶ Supplier Dependence on U.S. Travel Agents

Much of the travel industry is dependent on travel agencies for survival. Airlines, international hotels, cruise lines, and many firms that prepare tours rely heavily on travel agencies. Table 12.3 shows the importance of travel agents to the major segments of the travel industry.

The airlines rely on travel agents for 80 percent of domestic business and 85 percent of international business. Cruise lines are almost

Table 12.3 **Supplier Dependence on U.S. Travel Agents**

Supplier	Estimated % of Volume Booked by Travel Agents
Airlines	80 domestic
	85 international
Hotels	25 domestic
	85 international
Cruise lines	95
Rail	37
Bus	Less than 10
Rental cars	50
Packaged tours	90

Source: *Somerset R. Waters,* Travel Industry World Yearbook: The Big Picture, *1994–1995 (New York: Child & Waters, 1995), p. 131.*

totally dependent on travel agencies, and some international hotels are very heavily agency dependent.

For the supplier of travel services, there are several critical reasons to promote the use of travel agencies. One of the most important is that travel agents act as one's sales representatives in all parts of the country. Table 12.1 shows that there are over forty-two thousand travel agencies in the United States. If the average travel agency has six employees, there are more than two hundred and fifty thousand sales-people working to sell travel. This is a powerful incentive to promote their use, particularly when one considers that agencies are paid only when the agents are successful in selling travel.

The use of travel agents is particularly important for suppliers of travel services that cannot afford to have sales representatives in all parts of their marketing areas. For example, a two hundred room resort hotel in the Caribbean obviously could not afford to maintain offices in all the major cities in the eastern United States.

Travel agencies are equally important for the larger suppliers of travel services. Travel agencies enable them, in effect, to expand the number of offices selling their services without increasing their over-head costs. For example, major airlines might be forced to consider having a sales office in every city of in the United States if there were no travel agents to represent them.

▶ Prerequisites for a Travel Agency to Sell Travel Tickets

One cannot open up a travel agency and sell airline, cruise line, or other travel tickets as easily as one can open other types of retail establishments. This is because the travel agency receives its income from the suppliers of transportation services, and most of these suppliers will not pay commissions to organizations that they have not approved or that have not been approved by a travel association.

Approval to sell tickets for transportation services is only given to a travel agency when it receives an appointment to one or more of the various conferences that represent travel services. The term *conference* does not mean a meeting, as one might think; it is a regulatory body that sets standards for travel agencies. The following are the most important conference approvals needed by travel agencies:

ARC   Airline Reporting Corporation
CLIA   Cruise Lines International Association
IATA   International Air Transport Association

Each conference has specific requirements that travel agencies must meet in order to gain approval and the right to sell the services offered by conference members. Conference requirements are very strict, because travel agents issue tickets and collect funds that must be turned over to the companies whose services they sell. Requirements for conference approval typically include the following:

1. The travel agency must have a manager with at least two years' experience and at least one employee with one year's experience as a travel agent.
2. The agency must have a net worth of about $100,000 or a bond—a type of insurance policy—covering the normal amount of business expected for a period of time.
3. The agency must be clearly identifiable to the public and be open for business a given number of hours (typically at least thirty five) per week.
4. The agency must pay an application fee and annual fees to the conference, plus additional charges for blank ticket forms and for computer and other costs.

Each conference has its own requirements, but those listed above are representative. After receiving conference approval, travel agents can issue tickets and are entitled to commissions on the sale of tickets.

▶ Computer Use in Travel Agencies

Just a few years ago, travel agents used telephone, telex, and the mails to make all travel arrangements. A travel agent booking an airline seat looked up the airline schedule in a publication known as the *Official Airline Guide* and then called the airline to find out about seat availability.

Today, virtually all full-service travel agents make these travel arrangements using one of the computer programs that airlines have developed. American Airlines, with its Sabre system, has a greater number of network users for its program than any other system. United Airlines has the Apollo system, and TWA has a system called PARS. These programs make it possible for travel agents to determine which airlines fly between any two points and to obtain the schedule of flights between those two points for any given day. They enable the travel agent to determine seat availability for each flight and the prices for various classes of tickets. If a customer wants to reserve a seat, the travel agent can make the reservation by computer. The computer prints the ticket in the travel agent's office, and it is issued to the customer. The entire transaction may take as little as five minutes.

New computer programs now available enable travel agents to obtain information about many hotels, motels, and resort properties. Agents can even obtain layouts and floor plans of properties as well as information about special features they offer. Telephone calls and the mail still have their place, of course, but fax machines and computers have largely replaced older methods of communication at travel agencies.

▶ Other Travel Specialists

In addition to the various direct providers, travel wholesalers, tour operators, and travel agents discussed above, there are a number of other specialists that assist travelers by making arrangements for some or all of their needs.

▶ Specialty Channelers

Specialty channelers are individuals or firms that represent either buyers or sellers of travel services. They make travel arrangements for the parties they represent and do so either directly with the travel supplier or through a travel agent. Because specialty channelers deal directly with travel customers, they can have great impact on where they go and how they get there. There are two types of specialty channelers.

The first type of specialty channelers that represent sellers of travel services include (1) hotel representatives and (2) state and local tourism offices.

Hotel Representatives

A *hotel representative,* usually called a *hotel rep,* is an individual or firm that represents hotels—usually a number of them in many different locations—and sells the services of those hotels directly to individuals, businesses, and groups. Hotel representatives are not employees of the hotels; they usually have contractual agreements with the hotels they represent, and they develop and book both individual and group business for those hotels.

Hotel representatives may be individuals, travel agencies, or other firms, and they are normally located in specific large metropolitan areas, such as New York, Chicago, and Los Angeles.

Hotel representatives seeking group business have detailed knowledge of the businesses and groups in their area that require hotel facilities for meetings and conventions. Many maintain close contact with travel agencies and thus provide a link between the hotels they represent and local travel agencies.

Hotel representatives are able to meet the needs of the businesses and groups they contact because they represent a great number of hotels in many areas. Thus, they have a number of varying service products to meet the specific needs of the businesses and groups they contact. Some hotels have a number of hotel representatives, such as one in each of several parts of the country. Their compensation comes in the form of retainers—fees paid to professionals for services rendered—and commissions for the business they book in the hotels.

State and Local Tourism Offices

All states have tourist offices that promote hotels, motels, and other travel services in their states. They advertise travel opportunities and attempt to connect potential customers with appropriate properties and organizations. They often have information offices located on highways that direct customers to appropriate travel destinations, properties, and businesses.

All states have tourist offices that promote hotels, motels, and other travel services in their states. They often have information offices to direct customers to appropriate travel destinations, properties, and businesses. (Photo courtesy of the Virginia Division of Tourism.)

Chambers of commerce perform similar functions for local areas. They advertise the local area and refer inquiries to specific properties and businesses. Most chambers of commerce have offices that provide information and assistance to travelers and refer them to local hotels, motels, and other properties.

Most cities with populations over 1 million have convention and visitors' bureaus. These bureaus typically focus their attention on attracting groups, businesses, conventions, tours, and the like to their cities. They frequently assist in convention arrangements and often act as housing coordinators for convention groups.

The second type of specialty channelers that represent buyers of travel services include (1) corporate travel offices, (2) incentive travel firms, and (3) convention and meeting planners.

Corporate Travel Offices

An example of a specialty channeler who represents the buyer of travel services is a corporate travel officer who makes travel arrangements for corporate personnel. Corporate travel officers may make the arrangements directly with suppliers of travel services or they may book through travel agencies. Corporate managers, sales personnel, and employees in various jobs with other titles account for a considerable amount of travel, and many corporations have established travel departments to make the necessary arrangements. These travel departments are generally not official travel agencies because they are not members of the various travel conferences and cannot receive commissions on their travel arrangements. Frequently, however, they make the same arrangements as travel agencies—booking transportation, accommodations, and other required travel services directly with the suppliers of those services. Some make travel arrangements through travel agencies in just the same way as other travel agency customers.

There are a number of reasons to explain why firms establish corporate travel offices. Sometimes they are set up to be a convenience for employees, providing a central office where travel arrangements can be made. Frequently they are established as a means for corporations to control travel costs. Travel departments have information indicating which personnel are permitted to travel at company expense, which may be permitted to travel first class, how much each is allowed for accommodations and meals, and various other related questions. It should be obvious that corporate travel departments have great influence over the airlines and hotels used by company employees.

Incentive Travel Firms

As part of programs aimed at encouraging personnel to work toward achieving company goals, many organizations provide rewards for employees who exceed specific targets. These are called *incentive programs* because employees are offered some incentive to perform above and beyond some norm. Sometimes the rewards offered are in the form of company-paid travel. Firms that specialize in developing—and sometimes administering—such programs are called *incentive travel firms*. They specialize in assembling incentive packages—transportation, accommodations, meals, and entertainment, for example.

Incentive travel firms are of two broad types: those that charge fees for their services and those that receive their fees in the form of commissions from the travel suppliers.

Those that charge fees are called *full-service incentive companies*. They are employed by corporations to establish incentive programs, prepare promotional material, supervise the operation of the programs, and make the travel arrangements. They make these travel arrangements either directly with the suppliers of travel services or through travel agencies.

The second type of incentive travel company does not charge fees but receives commissions directly from the travel suppliers. Travel agencies sometimes have incentive travel departments that specialize in making these travel arrangements. These departments typically do not establish the incentive programs or supervise their operation as a full-service company would. Instead, they limit their activity to providing advice to interested companies on establishing incentive programs and making the travel arrangements. Incentive travel firms of both types obviously have great influence over the travel arrangements of the incentive packages they book.

Convention and Meeting Planners

Convention and meeting planners are employees of or consultants to corporations, government agencies, or other large organizations. Their profession is planning and running conventions and meetings.

Convention and meeting planners organize meetings and conventions ranging from small board meetings to conventions attended by thousands of people. They typically attend to all of the planning details including budget, travel, accommodations, meeting programs, and billing. They supervise the meetings or conventions and ensure their success. Conventions and meetings account for more than $50 billion per year; thus, these individuals and firms have influence over large expenditures for travel. They make travel arrangements directly with travel suppliers or they work through travel agencies.

Given this broad description of the travel business, it should be apparent that the selling of travel is a major and growing industry in the world today. The roles of travel agents, travel wholesalers, tour operators, and other travel specialists are of greater importance than ever before both to the industry and to the economies of the communities and nations that are coming to rely heavily on the tourism dollar as a source of income.

▶ Summary

In this chapter, the individuals and businesses that sell travel services are examined. The term *travel package* is defined, and characteristic types of packages are identified and explained in detail. The advantages and disadvantages of travel packages are described. The terms *tour wholesaler, tour operator,* and *specialty channeler* are defined and their roles in travel are described.

The role of travel agents and their importance and significance are examined. The size and scope of the travel agency industry, supplier dependence on travel agents, requirements for a travel agency to sell transportation, and the importance of computers in modern travel agency operation are discussed in detail. Finally, the role of such specific specialty channelers as hotel representatives, state and local tourist offices, corporate travel offices, incentive travel firms, and convention and meeting planners are described.

Key Terms

Accommodations and Meals Package	Fly/Drive Package
Accommodations Package	Hotel Representative
Affinity Group Package	Incentive Package
All-Inclusive Package	Incentive Travel Firm
Convention and Meeting Package	Motor Coach Package
Convention and Meeting Planner	Special-Interest Package
Corporate Travel Office	Specialty Channeler
Events Package	Tour Operator
Familiarization Trip	Tour Wholesaler
Family Vacation Package	Travel Agent
Fly/Cruise/Hotel Package	Travel Intermediary
Fly/Cruise Package	Travel Package

1. Define the term *travel intermediary.*

2. When did the era of mass travel begin?

3. What is a travel package?

4. List three advantages of purchasing a travel package over making arrangements directly with the providers of the travel services included in the package.

5. Describe each of the following characteristic types of packages, identifying the features normally included.
   a. all-inclusive
   b. fly/cruise
   c. fly/cruise/hotel
   d. fly/drive
   e. motor coach
   f. accommodations
   g. accommodations and meals
   h. family vacation
   i. events
   j. special-interest
   k. affinity group
   l. incentive
   m. convention and meeting

6. What are the advantages to the traveler of making arrangements directly with the supplier of travel services rather than making arrangements indirectly through a travel agent? What are the advantages to the direct supplier?

7. List and describe the typical packages provided by
   a. airlines
   b. bus companies
   c. cruise lines
   d. hotels and motels

8. Who is generally considered to have been the world's first travel agent? For what purpose did he organize his first group tour?

9. When was the first round-the-world tour? Who arranged and conducted it?

10. List six reasons why it is advisable to use a travel agent to make travel arrangements.

11. What is the approximate number of travel agencies in the United States?

12. What is the total annual dollar sales of the "typical" travel agency?

13. Sales of tickets for which two modes of transportation provide the most income to travel agents?

14. What percentage of sales of international airlines are booked through travel agents? international hotels? cruise lines?

15. Why are conference appointments necessary for travel agencies? What are the typical requirements for a travel agent to obtain a conference appointment?

16. Name two computerized airline reservations systems used by travel agents.

17. Define the terms *tour wholesaler* and *tour operator* and distinguish between the two.

18. Define the term *specialty channeler.*

19. Define and explain the role of each of the following in the travel industry.
    a. hotel representatives
    b. state and local tourist offices
    c. corporate travel offices
    d. incentive travel firms
    e. convention and meeting planners

1. You are preparing family vacation packages for Disney World. Of the travel packages described in this chapter, which would you prepare to appeal to families coming from a distance away?

2. You have a friend interested in a job as a bus tour guide for a tour company in the United States. He tells you that he sees the job as relatively easy, because his primary job is to entertain the customers on the bus, and there is very little else he must do. Is he correct? If not, what other types of duties is he likely to have if he takes the job?

3. You are interested in going to Mexico for your vacation. What advantages do you see in making your travel arrangements through a travel agent rather than making them directly with the airline, hotel, and car rental firms?

Thirteen

Recreation, Entertainment, and Other Tourism Attractions

After reading and studying this chapter, you should be able to:

1 Distinguish between recreation and entertainment.

2 Identify the types of national parks operated by the United States National Park Service.

3 Distinguish between primitive, transient, and vacation camping.

4 List five different resort areas and identify the recreational activities for which they are noted.

5 Define the term *theme park* and list several well-known theme parks, identifying the theme commonly associated with each.

6 Define the term *entertainment area* and list several nationally known entertainment areas, citing the types of entertainment for which each is best known.

7 Distinguish between economy, standard, and luxury motor coach tours.

8 List ten kinds of performances, musical and nonmusical, that bring tourists to an area.

9 Identify several national and international fairs and festivals that take place each year.

10 List several annual parades and ceremonies that have positive economic impact on various tourist businesses.

11 Discuss the importance of legal gambling to the economies of some regions of the United States.

12 List ten forms of gambling that are legal in at least one state.

13 Identify five types of special events that have positive economic impact on the areas where they are held.

14 Specify the four principal features of cruises that tend to make them appealing to vacationers.

15 Describe how shopping serves as a tourist attraction for some areas.

▶ Introduction

Some of the major reasons for travel have been identified in earlier chapters: business, vacations, conventions, conferences, exhibits, concerts, theatrical performances, sports events, sightseeing, education, visiting the birthplace of parents or grandparents, and attending weddings or funerals are among the many thousands of possibilities. This chapter will focus on some of the major attractions that draw tourists to an area—recreation, entertainment, and other significant attractions that induce travel.

In recent years, a number of important social and economic changes have made it possible for greater numbers of people to travel. These include early retirement, longer life span, shorter workweek, more leisure time, increased disposable income, greater mobility, smaller families, and changes in spending patterns. In fact, as the figures in table 13.1 indicate, a total of 38 percent of U.S. travelers in 1993 were away from home for purposes of entertainment or outdoor recreation, and another 7 percent indicated that their trips were for combined business and pleasure. It is quite clear that recreation, entertainment, and other similar activities account for a major share of travel.

Given the definition of a **traveler**—"any resident of the United States regardless of nationality who travels to a place 100 miles or more away from home within the United States or who stays away from home one or more nights in paid accommodations and who

Table 13.1 **U.S. Trip Profile—1993 Adult Travelers**

Primary Purpose of Trip

Visit friends, relatives	32%
Outdoor recreation	9%
Entertainment	29%
Business	17%
Conventions	2%
Combined business/pleasure	7%
Other	3%

Somerset R. Waters, Travel Industry World Yearbook: The Big Picture, *1994–1995 (New York: Child & Waters, 1995), p. 20.*

returns home within twelve months, except for commuting to and from work or attending school"[1]—it is clear that many travelers are contributing to the economic health of the areas to which they travel and the businesses they patronize while traveling.

A list of the activities that generate tourism—recreation, entertainment, and others—would be nearly endless. Think of the possibilities.

Visiting theme parks
Going to resort areas
Gaming
Attending performances—theater, concerts, dance,
Witnessing events—religious events, parades, patriotic ceremonies
Engaging in hobbies—photography, collecting
Going on cruises
Watching sporting events—football, baseball, various kinds of races (horse, dog, automobile, bicycles), the Olympic games
Visiting national, state, and local parks
Engaging in outdoor activities—golf, tennis, skiing, hiking, climbing, fishing, hunting, boating, swimming, surfing, snorkeling, water-skiing, beaching, sunning, taking various kinds of walks (bird-watching, nature walks)
Attending festivals
Camping, RVs
Taking tours to see landmarks, sights, museums, fall foliage
Shopping at major malls or discount shopping centers

---

[1]*The Economic Review of Travel in America* (Washington, D.C.: U.S. Travel Data Center 1995), p. 3.

While there are no universally accepted definitions for the terms **recreation** and **entertainment,** it will be useful to attempt some differentiation at this point in the chapter.

Recreation is an interesting term meaning to create anew, to restore, or to refresh. The idea of activity is commonly linked to recreation; people often refer to recreational activities. Thus, recreation has to do with activities aimed at restoring or refreshing one's mind, body, or both, presumably after some sort of work. The annual vacations that working men and women look forward to each year are probably of a recreational nature for many, used to restore their minds and bodies in ways they find interesting.

By contrast, **entertainment** is a term commonly used to refer to something diverting or engaging, presumably something that will hold one's attention and occupy one's mind for some period. It does not normally suggest physical activity of the type that one associates with recreation. There may be some limited physical activity associated with reaching the entertainment, but once at the entertainment site, the individual is commonly said to be watching, seeing, viewing, or hearing—all verbs that tend to suggest something more passive than the real physical activity associated with such recreational activities as tennis or swimming, for example.

Because of the extent to which recreation and entertainment in the United States impact the travel and tourism industry (including the hospitality industry), a number of the better-known examples are examined below. We have chosen to make three lists—one for locations or activities associated with recreation, a second for those associated with entertainment, and a third for "others," by which we mean some that could be described as either recreation or entertainment, both recreation and entertainment, or neither recreation nor entertainment. One possible example of this is a family trip to one of the largest shopping centers in the world, the West Edmonton Mall in Alberta, Canada.

▶ Recreation

There are a number of sites that people visit for the purpose of recreational activity. Among the most significant are the following.

▶ National and State Parks

National and state parks have become very popular destinations for American travelers. The national park system, operated by the

National Park Service, part of the U.S. Department of the Interior, includes recreation parks, recreation areas, battlefields, historic sights, monuments, and memorials, and it brings to mind such well-known parks as Yellowstone, Glacier, Sequoia, and Grand Teton. The majority of the parks are entirely traditional, but some of the newer parks might best be described as innovative. One national park is actually underwater! The John Pennekamp Coral Reef Park, in Florida, offers an underwater lodge for tourists. Jules' Undersea Lodge, reached only by diving and passing through an airlock, is a bit small, with just two suites available for travelers. In 1993, the National Park Service reported two hundred, seventy-three million visits to the 367 sites in the national park system.

For 1991, the U.S. Forest Service, which operates 156 national forests and twenty grasslands in forty-two states and Puerto Rico, reported 279 million recreation visitor's days. Accumulated data for 1991 from the various state systems indicates a total of seven hundred, thirty-four million visits to the 5,256 state parks in that same year.

It is quite clear that people are visiting these parks in great numbers for various recreational and educational purposes: to experience the natural landscape; to see plants and animals in their natural environment; to view the Grand Canyon, Old Faithful, and other major sights; to learn about significant battles in the various wars fought in

National and state parks have become very popular destinations for American travelers. Grand Canyon National Park is one of the most popular. (Photo of Mather Point, Grand Canyon, Arizona, courtesy of the Arizona Office of Tourism.)

North America and other significant events from history. They are also taking advantage of the various recreational activities available in the parks, such as skiing, hiking, boating, fishing, swimming, skating, and so on.

Many of these parks have excellent facilities—hotels, motels, lodges, and campgrounds, as well as foodservice facilities of many kinds. The foodservice and lodging facilities are all licensed by the National Park Service. Some of the lodging facilities are quite modern, while others are somewhat rustic. For example, in Everglades National Park, the nation's only tropical national park, tourists are able to stay at the Flamingo Lodge, a relatively modern property, privately operated, with 102 rooms and twenty-four bungalows. Guests can take advantage of such activities as watching flocks of waterbirds, seeing alligators and crocodiles, and taking guided tours of the park, then return to the relative comfort of a modern inn. One hotel in Yosemite National Park offers an interesting contrast. Built in 1879, the Wawona Hotel was once a stagecoach inn. It is a two-story property with 105 rooms that is a national historic landmark. It is not modern: only half the rooms have private baths, and none have telephones or television.

People have found that the park systems provide excellent opportunities for recreational activities of all kinds. Many parks have developed various businesses outside their borders to meet the needs of the growing numbers of tourists. Hotels, motels, inns, lodges, and foodservice operations of all kinds abound near the parks, offering travelers sleeping accommodations and meals at a wide variety of rates and menu prices.

It is interesting that the number of visitors to some of the parks has grown to the extent that many are now concerned about the potential threats to the environment posed by too many visitors to the parks. In fact, in some of these parks, there are no new tourist facilities being developed in spite of growing demand in order to prevent further damage to the environment. Some existing tourist facilities in some of these parks are even being shut down to reduce the risk.

▶ Campgrounds

The national and state park systems offer excellent opportunities for camping. Camping has become an increasingly popular activity—particularly for families—partly because it is comparatively inexpensive. Camping is by no means restricted to national and state parks: there are many private campgrounds from coast to coast.

In general, there are three kinds of camping.

1. **Primitive camping** is normally associated with public lands—forests and large national parks. The areas set aside are normally unimproved and appeal only to dedicated backpackers who are willing to make the best of it for a very few nights. Those choosing to hike along the Appalachian Trail that runs from Maine to Georgia have no camping choice other than primitive.

2. **Transient camping** is for those who intend to remain for no more than a very few nights. The areas set aside for transient camping are somewhat improved, with electricity, bathing facilities, and toilets available. The campsites are more or less organized, and many are privately run. This type of camping is more likely to appeal to individuals who are put off by the rigors of primitive camping.

3. **Vacation camping** is for those who plan to spend a greater number of nights at a single site—from four or five nights to a period of several weeks or more. Vacation camps are improved, with electricity and bathroom facilities. Some even provide cabins that can be rented by the day or the week. Improved camps commonly have stores selling basic supplies and recreational facilities for such activities as baseball, volleyball, swimming, boating, and waterskiing, among others.

Camping has also led to the growth of tourism-related business in some areas. Many of those on camping trips patronize foodservice and lodging facilities of one type or another before, during, or after the camping activity. Some will stay overnight in a motel before setting out early in the morning on a trip into the wilderness; others will do so on their return. Many are especially eager to find foodservice facilities after several days of cooking over a campfire.

One interesting element in the growing popularity of camping has been the accompanying increase in the popularity of recreational vehicles, commonly known as RVs.

Recreational vehicles—wheeled vehicles with temporary living quarters—include motor homes, travel trailers, park trailers, truck campers, folding camping trailers, and van campers. They are a significant part of the American scene. About 8.5 million people in the United States own some form of recreational vehicle, and about twenty-five million people regularly use them on an average of about twenty-three days per year. About one out of ten families owns at least one RV.

When RVs first became popular in the early and mid 1970s, a large number of them were sold. However, gasoline prices increased signifi-

Recreation vehicles (RVs) are a significant part of the American scene. More than 8.5 million people own them, and over 25 million use them regularly. (Photo courtesy of Winnebago Industries, Inc.)

cantly in the late 1970s and early 1980s, when there was a recession, and interest rates on automobile loans were very high. This led to a dramatic drop in the number sold. In recent years, sales of RVs have not only recovered considerably but have begun to climb to new heights. Recreational vehicle sales and rentals have made this a $14.5 billion industry in the United States today.

Recreational vehicles range in price from just a few thousand dollars to over $100,000. There are many different types. These include fold-down trailers, very large trailers pulled behind automobiles and trucks, campers that fit into the back of pickup trucks, and self-motorized vacation vans of many sizes that are actually homes on wheels.

▶ Resort Areas

Resort areas are geographic areas that have become well known regionally, nationally, and, in some cases, internationally as centers for some recreational activity.

Like national and state parks, resort areas offer opportunities for recreational activities of various kinds. Some resort areas are noted for specific activities. Scottsdale in Arizona, Palm Springs in California, and both Hilton Head Island and Myrtle Beach in South Carolina have all earned strong reputations as golf resorts. Many communities on the Atlantic and Gulf coasts of Florida—Miami Beach, Daytona Beach, Panama Beach, for example—are known as beach resorts. Aspen and Vail in Colorado, Taos in New Mexico, the White Mountains in New

Hampshire, and Killington in Vermont are all known as ski resorts. Parts of Maine and Minnesota are well-known fishing areas, while Newport, Rhode Island and San Diego, California are noted for sailing.

In some cases, the reputations these areas enjoy have been very carefully developed and nurtured. In any event, their reputations have led to considerable tourist travel to these areas over the years, and this has generated considerable income for individuals and businesses.

▶ Entertainment

People enjoy entertaining experiences. Those experiences take various forms, and seeking some form of entertainment has long been one of the primary reasons for travel.

▶ Theme Parks

Of all the recent developments in tourism, perhaps the best known and most interesting may be the creation of that modern entertainment center known as the **theme park.** One of the first of these was Hershey Park, founded in the early years of this century by Milton S. Hershey, the founder of the Hershey Corporation, internationally known for chocolate products.

Water is the obvious unifying theme at Water Country USA. The "Malibu Pipeline," pictured right, features double water flumes completely enclosed, sending riders "flying blind" through several twists, turns, and drops before plummeting into a waterfall and splash pool. (Photo courtesy of Busch Entertainment Corporation, copyright 1995, Water Country, USA.)

The term *theme park* refers to a tract of land on which a developer has created a series of exhibits, rides, and other elements that tend to be designed around some unifying idea: Knott's Berry Farm, in California, uses the old West as a theme; Busch Gardens, in Florida, uses wild animals; Disney World uses the cartoon characters created by Walt Disney. While theme parks have some such unifying theme, they commonly have other elements that are not related to the theme in any way. These may include exciting or entertaining rides, interesting and educational exhibits, or both. Knott's Berry Farm, for example, has 135 attractions, including roller-coasters. In addition to over three thousand wild animals, Busch Gardens has trained animal shows, reconstructed African villages, and various rides—roller-coasters, monorails, boats, miniature trains, and others. It also offers Broadway-style shows and a tour of an Anheuser-Busch brewery.

The term has come to be used rather loosely to refer to any number of operations that were once known as amusement parks. These lacked any kind of unifying theme and were usually little more than collections of assorted rides, with or without such accompanying elements as minor shows and exhibits. Many of these provided wonderful opportunities for a day's entertainment and brought substantial numbers of tourists to the various areas where they were located. Some of today's theme parks are really old style amusement parks with a new name.

Examples of some better-known theme parks include the following.

Opryland

Adjoining the legendary Opryland Hotel, near Nashville, Tennessee, the Opryland theme park features a major outdoor theater offering varied musical performances—country, jazz, rock, folk, and blues—in addition to a vast collection of rides of all types.

Sea World

In Orlando, Florida, near Disney World, Sea World offers indoor and outdoor exhibits of sea life, including sharks, sea turtles, and many others as well as shows featuring dolphins, sea lions, and whales.

Six Flags Great Adventure

Located in central New Jersey, this one thousand, seven hundred acre theme park offers over one hundred attractions, including carousels, giant roller-coasters, and other exciting rides as well as vaudeville shows and a drive-through safari zoo.

Universal Studios

These popular parks in Los Angeles, California, and Orlando, Florida, offer thrill rides based on well-known motion pictures, such as *King Kong, Jaws, ET,* and *Back to the Future.* Other attractions include a theater offering screen tests to audience volunteers and a walk-through backlot featuring set locations for a New England village, a San Francisco street, and New York City's upper East Side.

Tivoli Gardens

Located in the center of Copenhagen, Denmark, this special park, considered by many to be the oldest in the world, features miniatures of such famous sites as the Eiffel Tower in Paris and Mount Rushmore National Monument in South Dakota. Tivoli is also a world-class amusement park with rides, games, and theaters for shows, plays, pantomimes, and concerts.

Among the very best known and most popular theme parks today are four created by the Disney organization—Disneyland, in Anaheim, California; Walt Disney World, near Orlando, Florida; Disneyland Paris, near Paris, France; and Tokyo Disneyland, near Tokyo, Japan.

Disneyland

Disneyland is the original Disney theme park, opened in 1955, by the late Walt Disney. Although smaller than the more recent Disney World in Florida, it is considered the archetype of modern theme parks and has been visited by over three hundred million people since it opened. Among the sixty attractions featured are Fantasyland, Pirates of the Caribbean, Frontierland, Adventureland, Sleeping Beauty's Castle, and Carnival of New Orleans. Several of these names were later used in Disney World. One of the more recent additions is Star Tours, an outer space Disneyland.

Disney World

Disney World is the largest and most famous theme park, or amusement park, in the world. It covers over twenty-seven thousand acres—

an area twice the size of the island of Manhattan. It really is three separate amusement parks—Magic Kingdom, EPCOT, and Disney-MGM Studios—linked by road and monorail.

Magic Kingdom is organized into six miniature villages: Adventureland, with a boat tour through the jungle; Fantasyland, which features the Walt Disney characters; Frontierland, with a traditional far West theme; Liberty Square, which features presidents of the United States; Main Street, U.S.A., a turn-of-the-century small town; and Tomorrowland, with a space adventure theme.

EPCOT, an acronym for Experimental Prototype Community Of Tomorrow, is based on a twenty-first century theme. It features "Window on the World"—recreations of famed elements of many nations—as well as theme pavilions sponsored by world-class industrial corporations, the world's largest aquarium, and a huge eighteen story sphere which is universally recognized as the symbol of EPCOT.

Disney-MGM Studios, based on motion-picture themes, offers such varied features as film making, backstage studio tours, and ride-through attractions that transport visitors through such classic films as *The Wizard of Oz, Raiders of the Lost Ark, Alien,* and *Singing in the Rain.*

In addition to these parks, Disney World includes a seven thousand, five hundred acre forest reserve, two artificial lakes, three golf courses, camping facilities, every imaginable sport—tennis, sailing,

The eighteen-story sphere in Orlando, Florida, which is universally recognized as the symbol of EPCOT. (Photo courtesy of The Photo Works.)

swimming, waterskiing, fishing, and horseback riding—plus a dozen hotels and innumerable foodservice operations.

Disneyland Paris and Tokyo Disneyland offer interesting comparisons to those in California and Florida. Disneyland Paris has had to address some difficulties new to the Disney organization: low attendance and employee unrest. These have given Disney new challenges to meet, but history suggests that innovative solutions will be found. By contrast, Tokyo Disneyland has been entirely successful, with over sixteen million visitors spending an average of $85 each in 1993. It has known neither low attendance nor labor strife and continues to set new records each year.

Theme parks have become a major force in tourism worldwide in recent years. In the United States, theme parks attracted one hundred and forty million visitors in 1993, accounting for $11.3 billion in revenues. Walt Disney World alone attracts over thirty million visitors to central Florida each year and is the major tourism attraction in the

▶ New Theme Park Thrills Range from Rides to Barney ◀

The latest trend in the theme park world is to develop thrills aimed at people of every age. Some—like "A Day in the Park With Barney" at Universal Studios in Orlando, Florida—are intended for younger children. This attraction features Barney in an enclosed, environmentally controlled park-like setting with brilliantly colored flowers and trees, indoor clouds, and special effects designed to appeal to children.

To attract teenagers and younger adults, Six Flags parks has constructed thrilling new Viper rides that vary in thrills from vertical loops to speeds greater than fifty-five miles per hour to sudden ten story drops and even upside down loops!

To reach a broader audience, Sea World of California, in San Diego, has developed a tropical adventure land called Shamu's Happy Harbor, which has more than twenty interactive play and water attractions.

Because theme parks are anxious to attract return customers for new thrills, the trend toward new and innovative attractions is sure to continue.

Adapted from an article in the Boston Sunday Globe, *July 23, 1995.*

area. The success of so many existing theme parks has led developers to plan many more for coming years.

▶ Entertainment Areas

In a very real way, Orlando, Florida—with the Disney enterprises, Sea World, and various other features—has become an **entertainment area.** In fact, it is clearly the entertainment capital of Florida. Keeping in mind that Orlando is within two hours' drive of such additional tourism attractions as Cape Kennedy, Daytona Beach, and Cypress Gardens, it does not require too much imagination to think of Orlando as the entertainment capital of the Southeastern United States.

Another community that has achieved status as a well-known entertainment area is Branson, Missouri. A small but growing community in the Ozark Mountains of southwestern Missouri, Branson has become a focal point for musical entertainment. It is home to a number of nationally-known entertainers, many of whom have built and operate their own musical theaters. There are over twenty-five theaters in Branson that offer over forty live country music and variety shows daily to growing numbers of tourists. These tourists require the usual in lodging and foodservice, and there are now over ten thousand hotel rooms in Branson, along with growing numbers of the kinds of restaurants that cater to tourists. There are no signs that growth in the area is about to slow down.

In addition to Orlando and Branson, other places in America that can be regarded as entertainment areas include New York City, known for Broadway; Nashville, Tennessee, known the world over as the center for country music; and New Orleans, which has earned a strong reputation for performing arts, jazz, and sports. The Superdome in New Orleans is the largest enclosed stadium in the world.

Another city that many would list with entertainment areas is Las Vegas, Nevada. Las Vegas draws millions of tourists each year who go there to enjoy its many features. Some attend performances in the great showrooms featured in the famed Las Vegas hotels. The Hilton Las Vegas features the Moulin Rouge Revue, while Bally's Casino Resort, Caesar's Palace, and the Dunes Hotel all have huge showrooms that feature nationally-known performers. Others go for the golf: Las Vegas has some of America's finest golf courses. It is also well-known for its foodservice facilities—over seven hundred of them—that offer some of the finest food imaginable at some incredibly low prices. The area has over eighty-five thousand hotel rooms, over five thousand of which are in the world's largest hotel, the MGM Grand Hotel. In addition, gambling has been legal in Las Vegas since 1931, so it has had many years to develop its reputation in that field. While some classify gambling as entertainment, that view is not universal. Thus, gambling will be discussed later in the chapter under "Other Tourism Attractions."

▶ Tour Destinations

Every nation of the world has its own special collection of unique sights for tourists to see. In the United States, tourists from abroad often go to Washington, D.C., to see many of the important government buildings that they have seen on television and in film over the years, such as the White House, the Capitol, and various others. Or they may go on a bus tour through northern California that includes a national park and several other sights. In France, tourists from abroad visiting Paris would be likely to see the collection of magnificent sights for which the city is famous—the Eiffel Tower, the Louvre museum, Notre Dame cathedral, the palace at Versailles, the Champs-Elysees, and many others. In England, tourists visiting London would be likely to see Buckingham Palace, Parliament and Big Ben, St. Paul's cathedral, Westminster Abbey, the Tower of London, and the British Museum. Similarly, in the minds of tourists, Egypt is always linked to the Sphinx and the great Pyramids, India to the Taj Mahal, China to the Great Wall, Japan to Mount Fuji; and Rio de Janeiro to Copacabana Beach. These all tend to be focal points for tourists and thus important locations for the development of businesses that cater to the tourists.

For many vacationers, tours are the preferred way, and to great numbers, motor coach tours (bus tours) are an entertaining and relaxing way to spend some time—any period from an hour or two to ten days or more. Some take very short trips—an interesting, educational, or enjoyable trip from a city center to some site twenty or more miles outside the city. Others take an overnight excursion that includes hotel accommodations—from home to a sports event in a city one hundred or more miles away. Still others go on longer motor coach tours—a ten-day trip with meals and lodging to see the leaves change color in the mountains of New England.

Tourists from abroad—both Americans visiting other lands and foreigners visiting America—commonly enjoy their first views of the sights from aboard bus tours. Sometimes these tours are just a few hours long and introduce tourists to well-known sights in the center of a city—a tour of central London, New York City, or Chicago, for example. After this short introduction, tourists have time to decide for themselves which sights they will visit again to spend more time. Sometimes these tours are a full day, designed to take tourists on excursions from a city center to some important destination outside. Examples include bus tours from central London, England, to Windsor Castle and from San Diego, California, to Death Valley National Monument. Sometime these bus tours are several days long and can best be regarded as a package tour.

Because tour and vacation packages are grouped together, it is difficult to estimate the actual number of tours. The number is significant, however. There are more than two thousand tour operators in the United States today, and the largest share of the business is handled by the top forty. Motor coach tours are popular with citizens of all nations. Many Americans take motor coach tours that last for periods of one week or more. So do large numbers of foreign visitors, many of whom take motor coach tours that are conducted in languages other than English.

Essentially, there are three classes of motor coach tours: economy, standard, and luxury. The differences can be found in the level of quality evident in the various elements of the tours as well as in the amenities included in the price.

Economy bus tours include a seat on the bus—it may not be the most modern bus—and the basics required. If accommodations are included, they are likely to be in a budget motel. If there are meals, the fare is likely to be plain: extensive menu choices are unlikely, and so is gourmet cuisine. If the tour includes admissions to events, the tickets are not likely to be the best in the house.

Standard bus tours, by contrast, are likely to use more modern and comfortable buses. They are likely to have toilets on board. If lodging is included in the price, it is likely to be provided at a property somewhat above the level of a budget motel. Meals are likely to be tastier, with more menu choices available. Tickets to events are likely to be for better seats.

Luxury bus tours are quite different. Many offer the best of everything, and the prices are set accordingly. The motor coach will be as comfortable as any available anywhere. Lodging will be in luxury hotels and similar superior properties, and meals will be excellent. If there are tickets included, they will be for the best available seats. On luxury tours, everything is usually included in the tour price, so those on the tour have no need to pay for extras, except for personal needs.

People who go on luxury tours are often convinced that there is no more pleasurable way to travel.

While a great number of tours are planned or scheduled and offered on a recurring basis throughout the year, others are nonrecurring, having been arranged to meet a particular demand at a particular time, such as bus tours aimed at fans of a particular baseball team who want to see their team play in another city. The possibilities for these are endless, including, for example, motor coach tours to see Mardi Gras in New Orleans, the Rose Bowl Parade, or a college football game played away from home. All these are positive generators of tourism income for the cities or areas visited.

Another interesting variation on touring that tends to generate tourism income for an area is the automobile tour. Automobile tours are often individual family tours for the purpose of seeing sights, monuments, or anything else of interest to the particular family. Similar in many ways are the tours that high school groups take to Washington, D.C., and other places of historic interest or educational value. All these tend to be individually arranged by the schools or families intending to take the tours, so data on their number and duration tends to be limited. However, all these individualized tours also tend to be economic generators for the cities and regions visited, as the tourists spend their money on accommodations, meals, admissions, and gifts for family members and friends back home.

▶ Performances

There are literally millions of people who travel regularly or occasionally to the thousands of performances that take place in countries all over the world each week. There are performances of every conceivable type. Some are musical—concerts by groups ranging from rock groups performing in theaters, stadiums, and other large venues to symphony orchestras playing in well-known concert halls, such as Lincoln Center and Carnegie Hall in New York City, or Royal Albert Hall in London. Others are performances by individuals ranging from rock stars, folk singers, popular singers, and opera stars to instrumentalists and classical artists.

These kinds of musical performances are not the only type that serve as tourism attractions. People also travel to see plays, musicals, and operas in major cities and in many more rural resort areas. Other performances that bring tourists to an area include magicians, dancers of all kinds—folk, ballet, and tap, for example—acrobats, jugglers, and circuses, including the famed Ringling Brothers Barnum & Bailey Circus. Some people will even travel great distances for lectures delivered by all sorts of people—retired military leaders, politicians, self-help artists, and various characters who have gained some high level of notoriety, assorted felons and con artists among them.

▶ Fairs and Festivals

Fairs and **festivals** constitute another class of entertaining activities that tend to increase tourism in all parts of the world. There are literally thousands of fairs held each year—especially in the summer months. In the United States, there are state fairs, county fairs, village fairs, Grange fairs, and church fairs. There are equivalents of many of these in countries around the world, and every few years there is even a world's fair in one nation or another.

Every year, there are dozens of state fairs. The Alaska state fair features some interesting activities, including wood splitting, ax throwing, bow sawing, potato digging, and water hauling. The Indiana state fair, by contrast, features farm animal competitions, including a workhorse show. The New Mexico state fair features a rodeo, with thousands of dollars in prize money awarded to winners, while the Big E, the regional fair for the six states of New England, features important local food products, including apples, clams, maple syrup and cranberries.

If there are thousands of fairs, there are even more festivals. There are festivals dedicated to film, dance, music, art, religious figures, ethnic pride, heritage, the old West, days gone by, assorted flowers and fruits, crafts, balloons, beer, wine, boats, seasons, and various fish and sea creatures, among others. There are so many festivals annually in New England alone that one list of them consumes six pages, single-spaced.[2]

Festivals range from those that are truly major, such as those that are internationally renowned and respected, to many that are minor and some that are a bit unusual, with every possibility in between. For example, there are major international film festivals annually in Sidney, Australia; Tokyo, Japan; Montreal, Toronto, and Vancouver, Canada;

---

[2]Kathy Kincade and Carl Landau, *Festivals of New England* (San Francisco: Landau Communications, 1989), pp. 1–6.

Venice, Italy; Edinburgh, Scotland; London, England; and San Sebastian, Spain. There are certainly other, less-known film festivals in other smaller cities as well. There are also such festivals as the annual oyster festival in Milford, Connecticut, and Log Days, in Skowhegan, Maine (a week-long salute to the logging industry and its influence on that part of the state).

Some of the more important examples of festivals held in the United States include

▶ The music festival at Tanglewood, in the Berkshires, featuring the Boston Symphony Orchestra, the Boston Pops Orchestra, and various guest orchestras, artists, and conductors from around the world.

▶ National Cherry Festival in Traverse City, Michigan, a week-long festival featuring cherries from the orchards of northwest Michigan served in every conceivable way, accompanied by parades, jazz and band competitions, sports events, and non-stop live musical entertainment.

▶ Dodge City Days, held annually in Dodge City, Kansas, the nineteenth-century shipping point for cattle on the old Santa Fe Trail, to celebrate the area's heritage from the old West.

▶ New York Film Festival, considered one of the finest, with showings in Alice Tully Hall, at Lincoln Center, of over thirty films selected by a prestigious jury.

▶ Mardi Gras, held in New Orleans, Louisiana, on Shrove Tuesday, the day before Ash Wednesday. It includes several parades—the Rex parade, the Zulu parade, and the Indian parade among them—with elaborate floats, magnificent costumes, and great revelry.

▶ Parades and Ceremonies

Major **parades** and various important **ceremonies** are also important factors in the tourism equation. Both can play significant roles in bringing tourism dollars to a community, supporting employment, and generating income for those in tourism-related businesses.

Some of the better-known parades held in the United States are the Thanksgiving Day parade in New York, sponsored by Macy's; several St. Patrick's Day parades held in Boston, New York, and other cities having large populations of citizens with Irish ancestry; the Columbus Day parade in New York; the Tournament of Roses, often called the

Rose Bowl parade, held in Pasadena, California, on New Year's Day; the Mummers' parade, held in Philadelphia, also on New Year's Day; the Inauguration Day parade held every four years in Washington, D. C. on the day the president in sworn into office; Memorial Day, Independence Day, and Veteran's Day parades held in major cities on those holidays; and the so-called Easter parade in New York, which is not a parade at all—just a mass of people milling about on Fifth Avenue on Easter Sunday. Each of these brings tourists from varying distances to the parade area. Once there, they will see the parade and seek the goods and services that tourism-related businesses provide.

There are important ceremonies held in areas across the country that also serve to attract tourism to those areas. Sometimes these ceremonies are held in conjunction with parades, especially in the case of patriotic national days such as Memorial Day and Independence Day. Sometime they are have no relationship to parades. Religious ceremonies, for example, have always been positive forces for tourism. A visit by the Pope and a Billy Graham Crusade for Christ both offer excellent examples from the religious community. Commencement ceremonies offer an example from the academic world. These and many others help to enhance the role of tourism in a local economy.

▶ Sports Events

Sports events of all kinds are also great tourism builders. Such team sports as baseball and football, in particular, as well as basketball and hockey account for considerable travel by tourists. Individual sports, such as tennis and golf, and individual sports events such as the New York Marathon, the Boston Marathon, and others held across the country each year also attract tourists. Professional, collegiate and other amateur sports increase tourism in varying degrees for various sports. A substantial number of college and university football teams help the economies of their local communities by winning games and thus increasing the level of tourism activity in those communities.

The Olympic Games provide another example of sports events that increase tourism. Both Summer Olympics and Winter Olympics increase the level of tourism in the areas where the games are held, and there is always keen competition among cities wishing to host the games. Selection as the site for upcoming Olympic Games also leads to other economic activity in a region. It normally helps the construction industry in the region because new facilities, including stadiums, must be constructed to accommodate the athletes and the games.

▶ Other Tourism Attractions

In addition to recreation and entertainment, there are a number of other tourism attractions that do not lend themselves readily to being classified as one or the other. Any list of these would certainly include gambling, special events, cruising, and shopping.

▶ Gambling

Gambling in one form or another is legal in forty-eight of the fifty states—all but Hawaii and Utah. At present, thirty-five states operate state lotteries and other games of chance using such names as Lotto, Pick-3, Pick-4, Instant Winner, and so on. Taken together, these accounted for $30 billion in revenues in 1992. One can add to that such other legal gambling as pari-mutuel betting on horse races, dog races, and jai alai; betting on professional sports; card games, such as blackjack and poker; bingo, including both charity and Native American; as well as roulette, wheels of fortune, various dice games, and slot machines. The total amount bet legally in the United States in one recent year was estimated at over $300 billion. This is an enormous amount of money—considerably greater than the sum of the gross domestic products of several industrialized nations.

Some states operate lotteries while others permit racetracks for thoroughbred racing, harness racing, or dog racing. While some of these legal gambling activities have given rise to some limited increases in tourism in a few areas, none have had the same degree of impact on tourism as casino gambling.

Gaming—another term for casino gambling—is probably the fastest growing and most powerful force today in tourism within the United States. In the years since state and local governments and various Native American tribes realized the potential for easing all sorts of financial problems with income from legal gambling, casinos have begun to appear all across the country. In fact, it has been reported that more Americans visited casinos than ball parks in 1993[3].

Until quite recently, casino gambling was restricted to one state—Nevada—and one city—Atlantic City, New Jersey. Now, however, casino gambling is well established in a number of states, includ-

[3]Somerset R. Waters, *Travel Industry World Yearbook: The Big Picture, 1994–1995* (New York: Child & Waters, 1995), p. 18.

ing Colorado, Connecticut, Iowa, Louisiana, Mississippi, and South Dakota. In many instances, the casinos are on Native American lands and operated by Native American tribes.

The casino in Foxwoods, Connecticut is an interesting example of this relatively new development: casinos run by Native American tribes. By 1995, over 150 Native American tribes were either operating some form of gambling or had plans to begin doing so in the near future.

In addition to land-based locations, casino gambling is also found on the water. In some instances, it is conducted on riverboats and is known, obviously, as riverboat gambling, which is nothing more than casino gambling conducted on a boat. Riverboat gambling is available in Iowa, Missouri, Louisiana, Illinois, and Indiana. In Mississippi, casino gambling is conducted on barges that are permanently moored and do not have engines or other means of locomotion.

In spite of the growth in the numbers of sites where casino gambling is available, the best-known centers of casino gambling activity continue to be in the state of Nevada—especially Las Vegas, Laughlin, and Reno—and Atlantic City, New Jersey.

Las Vegas and Reno have both become well known for casinos and casino hotels—mammoth hotels of three thousand, four thousand, and five thousand rooms. The MGM Grand Hotel, Caesar's Palace, Bally's Casino Resort, and the Hilton Las Vegas, all with huge casinos, feature superior rooms at reasonable rates, excellent food and beverages at modest prices, and lavish stage shows with nationally known entertainers. But the newer properties in Las Vegas are much more than fine hotels with huge casinos. Increasingly, Las Vegas hotel operators are positioning their properties to appeal to the broadest possible markets, striving to attract tourists of every kind. They have long since abandoned the idea of appealing to gamblers alone, partly because it is a comparatively small segment of the tourism market and partly because of increasing competition for the gambling dollar from other jurisdictions.

Casino gambling will continue to be available in Las Vegas, but the city will be able to offer so many additional attractions for tourists that it will be difficult for other areas with casino gambling alone to compete. Attractions aimed at drawing tourists to Las Vegas include a fifteen thousand, two hundred seat arena for sporting events and concerts at the MGM Grand as well as an Emerald City theme park taken from the fictitious city in the *Wizard of Oz;* a replica of King Tut's tomb in the Luxor, a new two thousand, five hundred room hotel and casino; Treasure Island, a two thousand, nine hundred room hotel and theme park modeled on the famed novel of that name, where a British frigate

Las Vegas hotel operators are positioning their properties to appeal to the broadest possible markets and to attract tourists of every kind. Many are fascinated with the Luxor Burial Chamber in the Tut Museum at The Luxor, Las Vegas. (Photo courtesy of The Luxor, Las Vegas.)

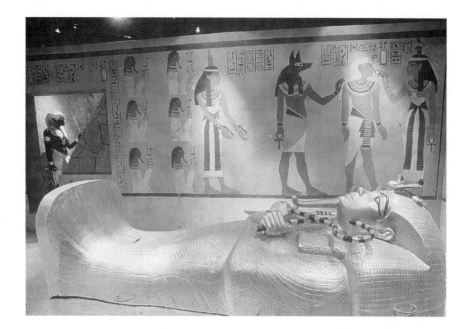

does battle with a pirate ships six times a day in the hotel "lagoon." These and such additional attractions as the Excalibur Hotel and Casino, with its $290 million Camelot theme park, offer formidable competition for cities, towns, and regions attempting to build tourism and attract tourist dollars.

▶ Special Events

There are hundreds of **special events** held every day of the year that serve as tourism attractions in various areas. Some are nationally and internationally known, attracting great numbers of people; others are far smaller. Each, however, plays an important role as a tourism attraction in the area where it is held.

Many of these special events are quite large—too large to be accommodated in the facilities available in a single hotel or other similar facility, and thus they become area-wide events. They attract large numbers of visitors to a city, and they are often planned and managed with the cooperation of a local convention and visitor's bureau. Hundreds of these take place in cities that have the basics required to support major public events: a major airport, good local transportation, a sufficient number of hotels, and a facility large enough to accommodate the event.

A number of cities in the United States and countries around the world have built facilities to house major events. Facilities of this type are known by a variety of names, including convention center, exhibition center, expo center, and civic center. The very fact that cities have spent many millions of dollars to build these facilities to attract these events is testimony to the importance of such events to the local economy. Examples of facilities constructed for this purpose include McCormick Place in Chicago, Jacob K. Javits Convention Center in New York City, the Pennsylvania Convention Center in Philadelphia, and the Astroarena and Expo Center in Houston. There are facilities of this nature in hundreds of American cities, including Ft. Lauderdale, Florida; San Francisco, California; Las Vegas, Nevada; and Baltimore, Maryland. In addition, growing numbers of cities in other nations have also built convention centers for the same general purposes, including Adelaide, Canberra, Melbourne, and Sydney, Australia; Toronto, Calgary, Edmonton, Montreal, Ottawa, and Vancouver, Canada; London and Birmingham, England; Frankfurt, Germany; and Acapulco, Cancun, and Mexico City, Mexico.

Convention facilities are commonly used for several types of special events of particular interest, including expositions, trade shows, exhibitions, conventions, and rallies and marches.

Expositions

An **exposition** is a large show that is open to the public. They are often known simply as shows. Examples of expositions held in various cities include automobile shows, boat shows, garden shows, and computer shows. Producers or manufacturers of the goods or services that serve as focal points for such expositions typically rent exhibit space in the facility in order to place their wares on view for the public. An automobile show would provide manufacturers of American and foreign automobiles with an opportunity to display current automobiles and prototypes of future automobiles to the consuming public. Many people are ready to pay reasonable admission fees to attend such expositions, so they can be profitable ventures for their sponsors and for those operating hospitality and other businesses that serve people attending and working at the show.

Trade Shows

Trade shows restrict admission to those who are part of a particular industry or trade. They are sometimes called expositions. Trade shows are not open to the public. Producers or manufacturers of the goods or services that serve as focal points for a trade show rent exhibit space in the convention facility to advertise or demonstrate their products to people likely to be interested in buying. The exhibitors at these shows feature goods or services of interest to those in a specific field and provide opportunities for people in the field to see and compare goods and services available from various competing vendors.

There are two excellent examples of hospitality industry trade shows: the National Restaurant Show held each May in Chicago's McCormick Place, sponsored by the National Restaurant Association, and the International Hotel/Motel & Restaurant Show, held each November in New York's Jacob K. Javits Convention Center and jointly sponsored by the American Hotel & Motel Association, the New York State Hospitality & Tourism Association, and the Hotel Association of New York City. These shows feature exhibits of interest to people in hospitality as well as lectures, seminars, and other educational presentations that focus on solving current industry problems. Admission to both of these is restricted to individuals who are directly involved in the hospitality industry, either working in hospitality or in some directly related field.

Exhibitions

An **exhibition** is a show, but usually a smaller show than an exposition. Exhibitions can be aimed at entertaining, enlightening, or instructing the public, offering specific goods or services for sale, or providing opportunities for competition and judging. These, too, are simply called *shows* in many cases. Some of these are held in convention centers, but many are held in other popular venues that may be known by such names as armories, museums, and halls. Some are even held out-of-doors.

There are many kinds of exhibitions that attract people to central locations—arts, crafts, antiques, and pets, to name a few. One held out-of-doors in New York City each year is the Washington Square Art Show, during which Washington Square Park and the surrounding streets are lined with artworks offered for sale by their creators. A very different kind of exhibition held in New York City, at Madison Square Garden, is the annual cat show, where cat fanciers are able to see various breeds of these popular pets and to learn which have been judged best in each of the classes of competition held.

Cities all across America and in every industrialized nation have any number of exhibitions of varying types and sizes throughout the

▶ Exhibitions Are Big Business ◀

Exhibition attendance in the United States and Canada is growing by leaps and bounds. From thirty-nine million in 1990, attendance figures have jumped nearly 300 percent in the last five years to an estimated one hundred and thirteen million in 1995, the most recent year for which data is available. There were over four thousand exhibitions in 1995, generating direct economic impact of over $22 billion. Attendees spent an average of $221 per person and occupied hotel rooms for the equivalent of one hundred million nights. In addition, attendees who used airlines to reach exhibitions spent an average of about $500 for their airline fares. Airline ticket sales amounted to more than $20 billion.

Because of the strong positive impact these events have on the economic life of communities, there is extraordinary competition to build suitable facilities and to lure new exhibitions to cities.

Adapted from an article in World's-Eye View on Hospitality Trends, *summer, 1995.*

year. All of them attract visitors from near and far and result in positive contributions to the economic health of the host cities.

Conventions

A **convention** is an assembly of people who are members of an organization, delegates representing members, or simply individuals with a common interest or concern. Conventions are special events, typically held annually, and are normally international, national, or regional in scope.

Each year there are many conventions held in the United States and in many other nations around the world. A great number of these are small enough to be held in a single convention or resort hotel. Others, however, attract too many people to be accommodated in one hotel, and thus they assume larger roles in the communities that play host to them. Three of the larger conventions held in the United States are those of the American Bar Association, the American Medical Association, and the Veterans of Foreign Wars. One annual convention that is much smaller but of great significance to hospitality educators is that of International CHRIE, the International Council on Hotel, Restaurant, and Institutional Education.

Conventions are held in all kinds of key locations across the United States each year. Some are held in major cities and may be large enough to require a convention center for some of the meetings. Examples of this type include the national conventions held every four years by the Republican and Democratic Parties to nominate candidates for president and vice-president. By contrast, one recent convention of CHRIE was held at a single Stouffer property, the Esmeralda Resort, in Indian Wells, near Palm Springs, California.

Many national organizations vary the locations of their conventions each year to be sure that the site is relatively near each member's home at least once every few years. Some organizations select a West Coast site one year, a Midwest site the next, and an East Coast site the third. This approach attempts to equalize the travel costs of members and offers some tourism-related inducements to convention attendance.

Conventions can have significant impact on the economic life of the communities selected as their sites, and there is keen competition for convention business among major American cities. These special events can be important contributors to the economic health of the cities that serve as their hosts as well as to hospitality businesses in the area.

Rallies and Marches

Every year, there are newspaper and television news accounts of **rallies** and **marches** held in key cities across America by groups of people interested in influencing public opinion. Those sharing some particular view of a public question gather to make their views known by marching, by carrying signs, and by listening to and applauding some speaker who can verbalize their point of view effectively. These marches and rallies clearly have impact on public opinion and public policy, though not necessarily the impact their supporters hope to have. However, these special events in public life can have significant impact on the economic life of the communities where they take place. Those attending the rallies and marches commonly seek the same goods and services as other visitors—foodservice, lodging, and so on.

Special events of all kinds are important contributors to the economic health of the hospitality industry.

▶ Cruises

Cruising is an important attraction that can be classified as recreation, entertainment, or both. Worldwide, about $6.5 billion is spent annually on vacation cruises, with 81 percent of it spent in North America. This represents about 3.6 million passengers. The types of people who take cruise vacations are changing. Years ago, vacationing aboard cruise ships—cruising, as it is known—was selected by older, more affluent individuals who had the time and the money for it. Cruising required both. In more recent years, cruise-ship passengers have tended to be younger, and the lengths of the cruises they select have become shorter. The average cruise-ship passenger is now less than fifty, with an income level more likely to be middle class, and the duration of the average vacation cruise is likely to be three or four days. Interestingly, only about 5 percent of Americans have ever been on vacation cruises. Cruise-ship vacations and getaways are becoming increasingly popular, however, with a growth rate of about 10 percent each year.

Cruises are often sold as packages with airfare, transfers, and the actual cruise all included in one price. The only additional costs for passengers on cruise packages are those for shore excursions and gratuities.

New cruise ships are being built to accommodate the expanding market. There are nearly two hundred cruise ships worldwide, with more being added each year. Most ships carry between eleven hundred and sixteen hundred passengers, but there are some notable exceptions: some of the newer ships carry more than two thousand passengers. Examples include the Royal Caribbean *Sovereign of the Seas*, which carries 2,280 passengers, and its sister ship *Majesty of the Seas*, which carries 2,354. Carnival Cruise Line's *Fantasy* carries 2,025 passengers. There are also a number of smaller ships that carry very limited numbers of passengers. For example, Cunard's *Sea Goddess I* and *Sea Goddess II* each carry fifty-eight couples. Exploration Cruise Line's *Colonial Explorer* carries only 102 passengers, and Ocean Cruise Line's *Ocean Islander* carries 250.

The appealing features of cruises have not changed over the years. They continue to be

1. Food
2. Activities and entertainment
3. Weather
4. Elegance and comfort

Cruise ships normally offer quantities of excellent food. Passengers on vacation cruises are typically offered breakfast, mid-morning bouillon, lunch, afternoon tea, dinner, and a midnight buffet supper. Passengers can eat as much as they like, and the high quality of the food is a major attraction.

Cruise ships have an entertainment staff that provides activities all day long. A typical day might start with exercises, or swimming in one of several pools. During the day, ongoing activities include cards, bingo, dance lessons, sports, and movies. If the ship is docked or anchored, there are shore excursions ranging from shopping to visiting rum factories to going underwater snorkeling. In the evening, there is live entertainment and dancing as well as more movies.

One of the main attractions for many passengers is the weather. Most voyages take place in the warm climates of the Mediterranean, the Caribbean, or along the Mexican coast. When the weather is cold in much of the United States and northern Europe, the temperatures in the Mediterranean and the Caribbean are very appealing. Vacation cruises in colder climates—Alaska, for example—are restricted to the warmer summer months. Many ships cruise the northern waters in the summer and the warmer waters nearer the equator during the winter.

Modern ships provide a level of elegance and comfort that can be found only in luxury resort hotels and private villas. Facilities on board the larger ships include theaters, night clubs, gambling casinos, swimming pools, saunas, exercise rooms, beauty and barber shops, gift shops, and various sporting activities. Public rooms are tastefully decorated, lounge and deck chairs are plentiful, and staterooms are comfortable. Stabilizers prevent most ships from rolling in high seas, even when the weather is stormy. Thus seasickness, which used to be a problem for some passengers, has been virtually eliminated.

The level of service on many ships is as high as that in luxury hotels. Cabin stewards are available twenty-four hours a day and provide turndown service in the evening. Food and beverage service is commonly available day and night, and all sorts of recreational activities are available at any given time. Pursers are there to store valuables, cash checks, and convert currencies. Because of the high level of service, a cruise on one of these luxury liners can be an elegant and refreshing experience.

▶ Shopping Centers

Shopping has long been a favored American pastime. Years ago, shopping was an activity that one engaged in by going "downtown" to a major shopping street—every village had one, and cities had more than one. The street was lined with an array of stores offering shoppers the goods they needed and wanted, and people walked along looking in the shop windows at the goods on display. Now, with automobiles, the preferred mode of transportation for most Americans, retailers have moved to make shopping easier than ever before in history. New travel-related alternatives to traditional shopping have been developed. The most significant of these are malls and discount outlets.

Malls

Major shopping malls are enclosed structures designed to accommodate numbers of stores and common walkways under one roof, making shopping possible in virtually any weather. Some shopping malls are very large, multilevel affairs, enclosing hundreds of retail shops, several department stores, and such other varied enterprises as banks, restaurants, food markets, and movie theaters. Some have facilities for child care and arcades with computer games as well as carousels and other rides for children. They normally have extensive parking facilities to accommodate the hundreds or thousands of automobiles and vehicles that shoppers use to reach the malls.

While these malls have been developed with retail sales as the primary focus, many are attracted to them for the entertainment value. On hot summer days, people flock to malls for the air conditioning; on any day, numbers of people are there just to "people watch" and to look at and ask questions about merchandise they may never be able to buy. Some of the largest malls—the Mall of America in Bloomington, Minnesota, and the West Edmonton Mall in Alberta, Canada, for example—are actually tourist destinations, drawing hundreds of bus tours each year, some from thousands of miles away. In a very real way, these malls are entertainment centers for a sizable segment of the population.

Discount Outlet Centers

Rather than develop malls of the type described above, some communities have taken advantage of the American penchant for shopping by permitting the development of discount outlet centers—collections of retail stores specializing in the sale of name brand merchandise at discount prices. In effect, entire areas have become entertainment centers. Reading, in Pennsylvania, and Secaucus, in New Jersey, have well-known discount outlet centers that attract thousands of shoppers daily. Many of these are travelers who have come some considerable distance just to take advantage of the shopping. Some arrive in their own automobiles while others come in tour buses. All bring tourism dollars to the area, spending money in hotels, motels, restaurants, and other tourism-related businesses, as well as in the discount shops.

▶ Summary

In this chapter, we identify recreation, entertainment, and other features that attract tourists to an area. We provide general definitions to distinguish between the terms *recreation* and *entertainment*. We list and discuss a number of sites for recreational activities, including national and state parks, campgrounds, and resort areas. We identify and discuss significant forms of entertainment that can be found at theme parks, entertainment areas, tour destinations of various types and lengths, performances, fairs and festivals, parades, ceremonies, and sports events. Finally, we cite a number of other important tourism attractions that are not usually classified as either recreation or entertainment, including gambling, special events, cruises and shopping.

 Key Terms

Ceremony	Primitive Camping
Convention	Rally
Cruising	Recreation
Economy Bus Tour	Recreational Vehicle
Entertainment	Resort Area
Entertainment Area	Shopping
Exhibition	Special Event
Exposition	Sports Event
Fair	Standard Bus Tour
Festival	Theme Park
Gaming	Trade Show
Luxury Bus Tour	Transient Camping
March	Traveler
National and State Park	Vacation Camping
Parade	

 Questions

1. Distinguish between recreation and entertainment.

2. Identify four types of national parks operated by the United States National Park Service.

3. Distinguish between primitive, transient, and vacation camping.

4. What is an RV? Why do you suppose so many Americans own them?

5. List five different recreational activities and identify at least one resort area that is noted for each.

6. What is a theme park? List five well-known theme parks and identify the theme commonly associated with each.

7. What is an entertainment area? List four nationally known entertainment areas and cite the types of entertainment for which each is best known.

8. Motor coach tours are great favorites with tourists. If you were asked to developed the itinerary for a half-day tour of your local area, which sites would you include?

9. Distinguish between economy, standard, and luxury motor coach tours.

10. List ten kinds of musical and nonmusical performances that bring tourists to an area.

11. Identify the five best known fairs and festivals that take place each year in your state.

12. Are there any annual parades and ceremonies in your area that have positive economic impact on various tourist businesses? Identify them, then identify several steps that could be taken by local groups to increase the economic impact.

13. In how many states of the United States is gambling legal in some form?

14. List ten forms of gambling that are legal in at least one state.

15. Identify five types of special events that have positive economic impact on the areas where they are held.

16. What are the four principal features of cruises that tend to make them appealing to vacationers?

17. Over the last fifty years, the age and economic status of cruise passengers have changed. How?

18. In what way does shopping serve as a tourist attraction for an area? In addition to the shopping, what other features are there to attract tourists?

1. You have been hired by a group of hotel and motel owners in your area to prepare a list of interesting local attractions that could be included in tour packages being developed to promote business for their lodging establishments. Identify at least ten you would recommend along with your principal reasons for selecting each. What kinds of package tours could be developed that would include these attractions? What kinds of visitors do you think would be interested in these packages?

2. You have been contacted by a group of hospitality educators looking for a site for a regional convention they intend to hold in your part of the state in early August of next year. The site must have the following:

    a. guest rooms to accommodate up to four hundred people
    b. room rates no higher than $100 double occupancy
    c. a minimum of ten meeting rooms accommodating up to forty people, four meeting rooms accommodating up to one hundred, and one meeting room accommodating up to four hundred, all within ten minutes of one another
    d. at least four popular-priced restaurants within ten minutes of the meeting rooms
    e. a catering facility offering several banquet menus under $35 per person for groups up to four hundred
    f. nearby recreation and entertainment facilities for attendees and their families

    Determine the best site in your area for this convention, then identify the foodservice, lodging, and other facilities meeting the specifications provided above.

Part Seven

Future
Perspectives

F o u r t e e n

Hospitality and Tourism Tomorrow

An Issues Overview

After reading and studying this chapter, you should be able to:

1 Identify six social and economic changes that suggest a bright future for the hospitality and tourism industry.

2 Describe the growth in demand for the service products of the foodservice and lodging industries.

3 Identify and discuss specific issues that tomorrow's hospitality and tourism managers are likely to face in each of the following areas: (a) marketing, (b) legal climate, (c) human resources, (d) operations, and (e) consumer affairs.

▶ Introduction

In preceding chapters, a number of significant topics have been introduced, including the history of hospitality and tourism and the dimensions of its principal segments. Understanding these topics gives one an excellent foundation for planning a career in the industry. These chapters will also serve as background for later coursework or for the experiential learning that is so critical for anyone pursuing a professional career in hospitality.

▶ The Bright Future of Hospitality and Tourism

In recent years, a number of important social and economic changes have occurred that suggest a bright future for the industry. These have been addressed briefly in several previous chapters, but it will be useful to review them here.

▶ Social and Economic Changes

Early Retirement

Today, many workers are retiring at earlier ages than was the case in previous generations. There are several factors that contribute to making this possible.

1. The social security system provides benefits to those as young as sixty-two years of age.
2. Many employee retirement programs are tied to years of service rather than to age.

In some retirement programs, particularly government programs, it is possible to retire and receive full benefits after just twenty-five or thirty years of service, making it possible for many to retire by age fifty-five.

With greater numbers of people retiring early, more people now have the leisure time and the income to see and experience the world, which translates into increased sales for tourist businesses in general, including hotels, motels, restaurants, and other hospitality businesses.

Longer Life Span

The average citizen of one of the industrialized nations can now expect to live well into his seventies, and many will live longer. This is in contrast to earlier generations, when the average life span was considerably less. The increasing population of older, retired citizens provides a larger base of potential customers for the tourism industries, including hospitality operations.

Shorter Work week

Sixty years ago, the six-day workweek was standard for most working people. Today, the five-day workweek is standard, and the four-day workweek is not uncommon—leaving several days for other activities. The resulting increase in leisure time, combined with faster, more comfortable, and more accessible transportation makes it possible for many to take weekend vacations, drive to visit friends and relatives, attend weddings and receptions, and generally travel to a degree they could not have attempted just a few short years ago. Hospitality and tourism benefit immeasurably from this increase in travel.

More Holidays

Americans now celebrate greater numbers of holidays than was the case in the past, and these holidays are often observed on Mondays and Fridays. This creates three- and four-day weekends that provide people with still more opportunities for patronizing hotels, motels, restaurants, and other hospitality businesses. One comparatively recent addition to the list of holidays is Martin Luther King's birthday. It is celebrated on a Monday in mid January. This has created a long weekend that has had major impact. In the Northeast, for example, it has turned a relatively quiet weekend into a record weekend for the ski areas.

Greater Disposable Income

The average family is likely to have more money to spend than ever before. Higher wages and growth in the number of two-earner households account for much of this. A large portion of the additional disposable income is being spent on consumer goods and services, and businesses that are tourism-dependent appear to be receiving an important share of it.

Greater Mobility

Better highways and improved transportation make travel easier each year. The interstate highway system has dramatically reduced the time required for automobile travel between any two points in the United States. In addition, most Americans live close enough to a major airport to select air travel more readily than would have been the case forty years ago. These increases in travel have had a strong positive impact on hospitality and tourism sales.

▶ Growing Demand

Today, the foodservice industry ranks as one of the largest in the nation. A recent publication by the National Restaurant Association (NRA), the industry's principal trade association, states that "eating and drinking places are first among all retailers in the number of establishments and the number of employees." Today, there are over seven hundred and thirty-nine thousand eating and drinking establishments, employing over nine million people. The number of managerial and administrative positions in the industry is approaching five hundred thousand. In fact, one out of every four retail outlets in the nation is an eating or drinking establishment.

On a typical day, foodservice establishments provide approximately 30 percent of American adults with lunch and nearly 25 percent with dinner. Of those patronizing these establishments, over 50 percent are males. On this typical day, over 55 percent of adult males eat out, compared with under 50 percent of adult females. Well over 70 percent of the adult population of the United States eats at a restaurant once a month.

The growth of food and beverage sales has been continuous. In 1970, figures gathered by the National Restaurant Association placed foodservice sales at $42.8 billion. By 1975, sales volume had grown to $70.3 billion. By 1980, it had increased by over 150 percent, to nearly $120 billion, and the 1980 figure had nearly doubled by 1990. By 1995, it was approaching $300 billion. If the rate of growth continues at the current rate of approximately 4 percent per year, sales will reach $350 billion by the year 2000. Although not adjusted for inflation, these figures still point out the extraordinary growth in foodservice. Today, food and beverage sales account for nearly 5 percent of the GDP, the gross domestic product (generally defined as the value of all goods and services sold), in the United States. By any measure, this is indeed a major industry.

The demand for foodservice has grown at a very rapid pace. Today, eating in a restaurant is a frequent experience, one parents commonly share with their children. Many have Kid's Meals at Wendy's, then continue to patronize Wendy's and restaurants in general in their adult years. Many adults eat out several times each week—more than ever before in our history. The NRA reports that 43 percent of the money Americans spend on food is spent in foodservice establishments. Americans are consuming ever greater numbers of meals away from home each year, and nationwide food sales continue to increase dramatically. It has been predicted by experts that Americans will soon be eating half of all meals away from home!

The commercial lodging industry is also growing. The American Hotel & Motel Association reports that the commercial lodging industry in the United States now includes approximately forty-five thousand properties, ranging in size from small inns with fewer than ten rooms to giant hotels with over five thousand rooms. In total, the commercial lodging industry in the United States generates nearly $60 billion in sales each year, representing about 1 percent of the gross domestic product. The industry employs approximately 1.6 million people, full time and part time. It is a major industry, and with the increases in leisure time and disposable income, it is continuing to increase in size and in economic importance.

The tourism industry is growing as well. Internationally, the World Travel and Tourism Council reports that world spending on domestic and international tourism is over $3.4 trillion annually. By the year 2000, the figure will exceed $4 trillion. The industry presently employs well over two hundred million people, and that number will certainly grow.

The future of the hospitality and tourism industry is bright in spite of the temporary setbacks that any industry must endure. In one region or another, changes will always occur that have negative implications for various segments of the industry. However, these are unlikely to last. In most areas, hospitality and tourism will continue to be important to the economic vitality of the region.

Issues in Hospitality and Tourism

Although the future of these industries is bright, it is not without problems. Those pursuing careers in hospitality and tourism will find it necessary to be familiar with a number of topics and issues that will have significant impact on the industry in the years ahead.

Students in degree programs commonly confront many of these in their major courses. Some of these have been problems for many years but no generally accepted solutions for them have yet been found. Others are issues that the industry has been dealing with for years but which must now be addressed differently because of changing conditions. Still others are emerging issues, occasioned by social, economic, or technological change. Many of these topics are addressed below—not exhaustively, but to the extent that the significance of each and the areas in which the impact is likely to be felt most are described.

The topics addressed in this chapter can be distributed under the following headings:

1. Marketing
2. Legal
3. Human resources
4. Operations
5. Consumer affairs

The issues identified and discussed in this chapter are certainly not the only matters of concern to hospitality and tourism managers. They are, however, some of the major topics that men and women planning managerial careers in this field should know about. Many are discussed in daily newspapers, in general periodicals, in trade publications, and at industry conferences. Sometimes they are the subjects of programs on broadcast television or on cable networks. They are often central topics for discussion at meetings of hospitality-related organizations. Numerous owners and managers are genuinely concerned about them. Many have to do with the social responsibility of those who own and operate foodservice, lodging, and other tourism-oriented enterprises—social responsibility toward customers, employees, the community, and the environment. Those planning managerial careers are likely to discover that they, too, will become increasingly aware of these and other similarly important issues as their careers progress.

Those considering these topics and the categories under which they are discussed in this chapter may disagree with the inclusion of a given issue under a particular category. Some, for example, might consider it more suitable to cover questions relating to diet/nutrition/health with operations issues rather than with consumer issues. The difference would have more to do with the degree of emphasis given one or another of the elements.

We would certainly not disagree with anyone seeking to categorize any of these issues differently. We are less concerned about classification than about the significance of the issues. We are particularly interested in promoting the idea that responsible hospitality and tourism managers should know about and be engaged in constructive consideration of the issues that face the industry. In our view, all of the issues discussed here will be of considerable significance to managers in the years ahead.

▶ Marketing

Changing Demographics

The population of America is aging. The median is now thirty-three years and is projected to go higher in the coming years. The so-called baby boomers born in the years following World War II are now reaching age fifty. An older population has preferences that differ significantly from those of a younger population, and hospitality providers will find it necessary to adjust their service products to the changing preferences of the market. Thus, changing demographics is an issue of dramatic importance to the industry.

Another changing demographic characteristic is the increase in the number of single-parent households. Single-parent households traditionally have had lower levels of discretionary income and thus have not been as able to support hospitality and tourism businesses. To reach this market, providers will have to continue developing new service products that appeal to this demographic segment at affordable prices.

A third demographic change is the continuing growth in the number of people traveling for personal rather than for business purposes. As indicated in chapter 11, approximately 74 percent of domestic travelers are traveling primarily for some purpose other than business. This group has accounted for growing percentages of the travel market in the past forty-five years, and the growth is sure to continue.

The fourth demographic change is the growth in the number of international travelers in general and in the number of international travelers to the United States in particular. International travelers account for an ever-growing share of hospitality and tourism revenues in the United States. The number of international visitors to the United States is likely to reach sixty million by the year 2000.

In the coming years, hospitality and tourism marketing executives will find it important to take these demographic changes into account as they develop marketing plans for the service products the industry offers.

Changing Vacation Patterns

The length of vacations taken by Americans is changing. The traditional once-a-year vacation of two weeks or more is declining in popularity. For growing numbers of people, vacations are becoming shorter and more frequent. Today, more people are likely to plan minivacations. Some, for example, will add two of their annual vacation days to a three-day holiday weekend to make a five-day minivacation. By doing so, they manage to get away for several days while using only two actual vacation days.

Vacation destinations are changing as well. Travel to and from nations that once were part of the so-called communist bloc has made it possible to plan vacations in countries that were usually considered off limits in the past. The Czech Republic, Hungary, Russia, Romania, and Bulgaria are becoming more popular sites for American and European vacationers. And with industrialization and improvements in transportation, other nations are becoming more popular as well. The People's Republic of China is just one of the nations that were not common destinations a few years ago. Today, China is one of many nations seriously engaged in efforts at tourism development.

Market Segmentation

In the years since 1980, a key term in hospitality marketing has been **market segmentation.** Until the late 1970s, lodging establishments attempted to appeal to broad, general markets; their aim was to appeal to as broad a group of potential guests as possible. In more recent years, the success of the limited-service properties has led to the development of other properties designed to appeal to carefully selected market segments at various points on the guest spectrum. Some of the types of lodging properties to emerge include all-suite properties, residence properties, sub-budget properties, and a variety of budget properties differentiated by their varying services and amenities.

Examples of market segmentation have also been evident in foodservice, particularly in the past ten years. A number of the restaurants that traditionally have offered extensive something-for-everyone menus have begun to see reductions in business as customers have chosen to patronize restaurants offering specialized service products. As new market segments are identified, properties designed to appeal to those segments are likely to be developed.

Frequent Guest Programs

With the proliferation of properties and the growing competition among them, some lodging operators have begun to develop programs to gain repeat business. Modeled on the frequent-flyer programs used so successfully by many airline companies, these plans typically give credits to regular guests. They can be redeemed in the form of reduced rates, upgrades, free accommodations, free meals, or any of a variety

▶ Single Diners Can Add Up to Big Business ◀

The singles population is growing, and singles are eager to spend money on food away from home. Singles spend 44 percent of their overall food budget on food away from home, while households of five or more spend only 29 percent. And there are more singles in the nation today than ever before in history. Foodservice operators who cater to single customers are finding that single diners can add up to big business.

Operators have found various ways to attract singles. Some have advertised that they cater to singles and have seen considerable increase in sales as a result. Some of these establishments have offered free glasses of wine or free desserts to singles. Another approach has been to designate one table as a "communal table" to be shared by single diners who prefer to share a table rather than dine alone. Other names for this communal table include "networking table," "table of friends," and "joiners' table." For those who prefer to dine alone, some restaurants keep a selection of books, newspapers, or magazines available.

In the highly competitive foodservice industry, successful operators are always trying to attract new market segments to keep sales volume high and growing, and singles are proving to be a profitable new segment for many.

Adapted from an article in Restaurants USA, *March, 1995.*

of amenities. In some cases, they can be translated into frequent-flyer miles and used for air travel. As competition becomes even keener, the number of these kinds of programs is likely to grow. Many believe that these programs will gain in the lodging business the same degree of favor they have achieved among airline customers.

Food and beverage managers have long known that it pays to reward regular customers. Many restaurant and bar owners have given their regulars complementary appetizers, desserts, glasses of wine, and other rewards for their regular and continuing patronage. However, they have not followed the formalized approaches adopted by the airline and lodging companies, which require elaborate record-keeping. In most instances, it has been a matter of independent restaurant and bar owners making spur-of-the-moment decisions when seeing frequent customers in their establishments. In some cases, departing customers have been given discount coupons that could be redeemed on their next visit. This approach has been more common with chain operations, some of which have taken an additional step by setting up promotions to offer discounts to all customers purchasing specific menu items during a limited period—severals days in midweek, or the third week of a given month, for example. One aim of food and beverage operators adopting these approaches is to build repeat business. This aim is identical to that of the lodging operator with a frequent-guest program or the airline company with a frequent-flyer program.

Maturation in Segments of the Fast-Food Industry

Segments of the fast-food market are no longer expanding as quickly as was possible in the past. The demand for hamburgers is not growing as fast as it once did, and operators are finding it necessary to develop new products to maintain desired sales levels. Today, for example, establishments that once offered few products other than hamburgers are now test marketing or offering such products as pizza, salads, and various poultry or other meat products. As public tastes continue to change, foodservice operators will need to keep pace—to develop new specialty products to retain an adequate share of the market.

Consolidation in the Commercial Lodging Industry

Some experts are now suggesting that the number of large, nationwide lodging companies will decrease in the years to come. They are fore-

As public tastes continue to change, Kentucky Fried Chicken and other fast-food operators are developing new specialty products to keep their share of the market. (Photo courtesy of Kentucky Fried Chicken.)

casting that a relatively small number of firms will dominate the lodging industry by acquiring smaller chains of regional or national properties. This will enable successful firms to obtain the funds required to expand their operations internationally.

This trend toward consolidation will have significant impact on all commercial lodging operations. Both independent operations and smaller chains will have increasing difficulty competing with heavily advertised national and international brands.

▶ Legal

Liquor Liability

In recent years, public concern has been growing over the alarming number of alcohol-related automobile accidents. Today, substance abuse is a factor in over half of all automobile accidents, and a vast number of these have been attributed to alcohol abuse. This has led to increasing public pressure on state legislatures to act. Although the specifics vary from one state to another, it is generally true that legislators have responded by lowering the levels of blood alcohol at which an individual is considered intoxicated and by increasing penalties on offenders. In addition, many states have imposed new regulations on the serving of alcoholic beverages. In at least one state, new regula-

In response to the growing awareness of the negative effects of alcohol abuse, new state regulations increase liability for establishments that serve alcoholic beverages to intoxicated individuals. In reaction, some restaurant and bar owners either no longer serve alcohol or promote nonalcoholic beverages (shown right). (Photo courtesy of Ocean Spray Cranberries, Inc.)

tions have made the discounting of drink prices illegal, thus bringing an end to the so-called happy hour. In many states, establishments and their owners can be held financially accountable if they serve alcoholic beverages to an intoxicated individual who causes damage or injury after leaving the establishment. In some places, this has caused such huge increases in the cost of liability insurance that some bar and tavern owners have chosen to go out of business. It has caused some restaurant owners to stop serving alcoholic beverages.

Some restaurant and bar owners have changed market strategy: they are now featuring and promoting nonalcoholic drinks. Others have encouraged groups of their patrons to select a designated driver and have provided various incentives for them to do so.

As societal attitudes toward alcoholic beverages continue to change, it will be necessary for foodservice and lodging operators to adjust.

Impact of the Americans with Disabilities Act of 1990

This landmark legislation prohibits discrimination against anyone with a disability. A disabled person is defined as one who has a physical or mental impairment that substantially limits one or more major life activities. While the act has had significant impact on many facets of American life, its impact has been especially significant in hospitality and tourism. In this industry, the **Americans with Disabilities Act** applies to both employees and guests. In lodging, it applies to establishments of more than five rooms; in foodservice, to all restaurants, bars, and similar establishments serving food or drink. In tourism generally, it has had significant impact on every type of business.

The act prohibits discrimination in hiring on the basis of disabilities. It dictates that builders of new facilities must design and construct them to accommodate the disabled; by contrast, owners of existing facilities must make reasonable efforts to accommodate the disabled. In general, it holds that the disabled are entitled to full and equal enjoyment of goods, services, facilities, privileges, advantages, and accommodations.

Although the language of the act is subject to varying interpretations, these will, no doubt, eventually be resolved in the courts. In the meantime, both the National Restaurant Association and the American Hotel & Motel Association have developed publications to guide their members in their efforts to comply with the law. Hospitality and tourism managers are likely to be addressing questions arising from this act for many years to come.

Ethics in Hospitality

Ethics is an academic discipline that deals with the study of codes of moral conduct. *Business ethics* is a term that refers to the application of a particular moral code to relationships, activities, and decision-making in business and industry. It is the code that enables an individual in business to distinguish right from wrong—to distinguish between ethical and unethical behavior.

Ethics has been an issue in hospitality and tourism for thousands of years—since the tavern keepers of earliest recorded history first diluted the drinks of unsuspecting customers. Although this and similar practices are illegal today, it is possible to question the business ethics of some hospitality operators. The following are a few examples: a manager of a new restaurant may hire twenty servers, intending to keep only the twelve most able after the second week of operation; a room clerk may accept bribes to register guests without reservations, even when the property is overbooked; an owner may fail to report all sales on her income tax returns; a server may attempt to cheat on his income taxes by failing to report all tips; an owner may misrepresent his hotel, using idealized artists' renderings rather than photographs in his advertising; an employee in a purchasing department may accept gifts from vendors in return for purchasing inferior products; an owner may cheat on her taxes by charging personal expenses to the business. Business ethics will forever be high on anyone's list of important hospitality issues.

▶ Human Resources

Diversity

More than most other industries, the hospitality and tourism industry has long been known for its diverse workforce. Our workforce has been diverse in the extreme, including men and women of every age, race, ethnic, and religious group. In fact, throughout our history, immigrant groups to the United States have always been able to find employment in foodservice, lodging, and other tourism-related fields.

But while the workforce was diverse, management was inclined to treat all members of all groups identically, without taking into account the characteristic cultural differences of the many groups represented in our workforce. Unfortunately, this tended to create a workforce that consisted of individuals from all sorts of groups who did not really get on well together and thus did not particularly work well together. In general, there was little team spirit among the diverse employees in any given hotel or restaurant.

An example will help to explain. Suppose that people growing up in one culture are taught to be quiet and reserved, not to speak unless someone else speaks first, and never to differ with anyone in authority. When one individual with that cultural background is hired to work in a given restaurant, some on the staff are likely to assume, on the basis of his "different" behavior, that their new coworker is unfriendly and unwilling to fit into the group. The new employee, by contrast, may decide that many on the staff are rude and offensive. The truth may be that both the new employee and the others on the staff simply do not understand one another; neither has had any experience dealing with people from cultural backgrounds other than their own, and thus neither can accept the other as coworkers.

One of the great challenges to managers today is finding ways to manage **diversity** in the workforce. This requires education. Ideally, everyone in the workforce will learn to respect, understand, appreciate, and value the array of individual differences to be found among their coworkers. To that end, there is a growing trend toward diversity training for hospitality and tourism employees. As a result, many managers are finding that this training brings immediate and tangible benefits to the workplace, including competitive advantages in the changing economic environment.

Sexual Harassment

The Federal Equal Employment Opportunity Commission defines **sexual harassment** as "unwelcomed sexual advances, requests for sexual favors, and other verbal or physical conduct of a sexual nature that takes place under any of the following conditions:

1. submission is made a condition of the person's employment;
2. submission to or rejection of such conduct is used as a basis for employment decisions affecting the person; or
3. it unreasonably interferes with the person's work performance or creates an intimidating, hostile, or offensive work environment.[1]

---

[1]Excerpted from the *Federal Register*, vol. 45, no. 219, 29 CFR, chapter XIV, section 1604.11, "Sexual Harassment," promulgated November 10, 1980.

Most cases of sexual harassment involve complaints by females about male coworkers or superiors, although the number of complaints by males has been growing. In the last ten years, as greater numbers of employees have become willing to speak out, the number of these cases has grown.

Because employers are liable for the actions of their employees at work, it is particularly important for employers to take several important steps.

1. Institute a strict policy banning all forms of sexual harassment in the workplace.
2. Develop appropriate training programs for managers and employees so that all will understand and become sensitive to the nature of sexual harassment.
3. Establish procedures for handling all complaints promptly, fairly, and in a sensitive manner.

Employers who have taken these steps have found that the number of sexual harassment complaints has decreased substantially and that the training has had significant and positive impact on the behavior of employees at work.

Employee Turnover

As was pointed out in chapter 10, **employee turnover** continues to be one of the major issues facing hospitality managers. With turnover rates averaging approximately 100 percent per year across the industry, managers are continually faced with the problem of losing experienced employees and hiring replacements with less experience. Faced with inexperienced replacements, many managers believe they have only two choices: to incur the high training costs associated with transforming new employees into valuable workers, or to suffer the equally high costs associated with operating with untrained workers. Too few are willing to acknowledge that they have a third option: to take suitable steps directed toward retaining employees and reducing turnover.

Many hospitality managers understand the prerequisites to reduced turnover. These include adequate wages and benefits, reasonable working conditions, reasonable work schedules, and reasonable treatment of employees by enlightened managers. Comparatively fewer managers are willing to put these into practice.

A number of employers and managers still attempt to treat workers as if they were cogs in some gigantic wheel—metal parts, rather than people. They hire at the lowest possible wages, provide no training, then belittle and berate workers for failing to do work correctly. They assign workers to schedules without any regard to personal preferences, change their schedules without notice, and demand at the last minute that workers report for work on their days off if the need should arise. Then they complain about the ungrateful workers who quit their jobs at the first opportunity to accept seemingly equal jobs with other employers.

Employers who are willing to improve their treatment of employees by giving the employees a sense of importance in the orgnaization find that the result is a significant positive impact on employee turnover.

Employee Assistance Plans

Employee Assistance Plans (EAPs) are included in this discussion of hospitality and tourism issues because they illustrate one of the attempts made by enlightened owners and managers to pay responsible attention to the real, human problems faced by their employees. The problems of those employed in hospitality are essentially the same as the problems of those in the general population. These include substance abuse, psychological problems, family issues, financial issues, legal problems, health issues, and educational issues.

The hospitality and tourism industry traditionally has been among the larger employers of men and women with limited education, including many of the foreign-born with limited knowledge of English. Because of this, managers in the industry have an opportunity—some would say an obligation—to be of unique assistance to workers who might otherwise not have access to help with their problems.

Managers who establish EAPs to benefit employees are likely to develop a more loyal workforce—one that is more willing to strive toward the operational goals of the enterprise. At the same time, managers with the foresight to help employees are likely to see reductions in employee turnover.

▶ Operations

Total Quality Management (TQM)

Total Quality Management—tailoring service to the needs of guests and customers—has become a very important topic in management circles today. One point made several times in earlier chapters is that service products cannot be mass-produced in advance—they are produced only when ordered by a customer. To an important extent, each service product is tailored to suit the guest or customer who has ordered it.

In many operations, managers have developed extensive rules and procedures that all employees are directed to follow when dealing with customers. These can extend to the most minute details—rules forbidding free refills on coffee; strict limits on the number of hand towels per guest; directives prohibiting substitutions on special dinner menus; inflexible rules about checkout time. These—and the many others one sees daily in hospitality and tourism—lead to critical moments of truth that may affect a customer's overall impression of a particular foodservice, lodging, or other tourism enterprise. The negative moment of truth resulting from a refusal to give a customer an extra half cup of coffee may be enough to offset all the positive moments of truth that precede and follow it. For some customers, it may be enough to make them decide never to return.

Many owners and managers have come to realize the futility of attempting to set strict rules to govern every detail of a customer/employee service encounter. Instead, they are now revising their approach, developing policies that are service oriented, and training their employees to provide as many positive moments of truth as possible. They are giving their employees some reasonable degree of latitude to tailor service products to the specific needs and preferences of guests. In effect, they are empowering their employees to make enlightened, educated decisions that will improve service quality for guests without having a negative impact on operations.

Internationalization

Internationalization is a term that can be thought of in at least two hospitality contexts. One of these is the tendency of national hospitality firms to expand operations beyond national borders—to "go global." Another is the special efforts that hospitality firms are making to cater to the needs of international visitors. It is in this latter context that internationalization has become an important issue in hospitality operations today.

The United States has always been a favorite destination for any international travelers who could afford to come. While hotel operators were always glad to book international business, comparatively few went out of their way to provide for some of the special needs of foreign visitors: currency exchange; staff members fluent in languages other than English; special menus; brochures, maps, and similar materials in other languages; climate controls in individual guest rooms; and many others.

Today, the growth in international travel is bringing growing numbers of foreign visitors to the United States. Foreign visitors account for growing percentages of room revenue in many hotels—particularly in major cities on the East and West Coasts—and growing numbers of hotel operators are taking steps to provide the kinds of services that tend to make foreigners feel welcome. Some are requiring that new guest service employees be fluent in at least one language other than English. Many are adopting additional practices such as having international menus in restaurants, posting signs with international symbols, providing foreign newspapers in lobbies, including a currency exchange at the front desk, and any number of others.

Automation

Automation means using electronic and mechanical equipment and machinery to complete some or all of the tasks associated with a given enterprise. Three principal reasons are commonly cited for automating an enterprise.

1. To increase the speed of work
2. To reduce the cost of work
3. To standardize results

Historically, hospitality and tourism managers have always been ready to automate. A few of the historical examples of automation in the industry include peeling potatoes, washing dishes, washing tablecloths and napkins, preserving frozen foods, vacuuming carpets, recording reservations, and maintaining guest accounts.

Today, we are at the point where some foodservice and lodging establishments have automated to the extent that guests and customers need no longer have direct contact with any human staff. Food and beverages can be obtained from vending machines. There are lodging operations where one "swipes" a credit card through an electronic device, enabling one to check in without speaking to a room clerk at the desk. Using touch-sensitive screens on the television sets in their rooms, guests will soon be able to place orders for food and beverages from room service; obtain information about stores, restaurants, theaters and other entertainment facilities in the area; make reservations for dinner at nearby restaurants; and even purchase clothing and other goods of various kinds from stores, requesting immediate delivery. Guests can already use these touch-sensitive screens for reviewing their hotel bills and checking out.

It is interesting that foodservice and lodging operations at the high end of the price spectrum have tended to maintain the appearance of service, even when automated devices have been installed. For example, some hotels with automatic elevators have continued to employ personnel to run the elevators. Guests are still treated to a high level of service but with more modern and efficient equipment than the older manual elevators.

Some are beginning to question whether the industry is pushing automation too far—whether those that automate too extensively are offering any degree of hospitality. Have they automated themselves out of the hospitality industry, so to speak? It is a question that owners and managers of hospitality enterprises, as well as their guests and customers, will continue to ask in the years ahead. And it is sure to be of growing importance, as well. The technological capacity to automate grows daily, and the industry will have to determine the extent to which it should embrace the technology.

▶ Consumer Affairs

Smoking/No-Smoking Areas

As more and more customers and guests of foodservice and lodging enterprises demand smoke-free areas for dining and smoke-free sleeping accommodations, the industry continues to make all reasonable efforts to meet these demands. This will be particularly true in those states and localities in which legislation mandates that appropriate facilities be made available.

To date, this trend has had the greatest impact on the food and beverage sector of the industry. Restaurants and related enterprises have found it desirable, even if not required by law, to apportion sections of their dining facilities to accommodate the wishes of nonsmokers. Some have also found it necessary to install or improve ventilation equipment.

Most mainstream lodging operations have set aside accommodations for nonsmokers—rooms that are free of the lingering effects of tobacco smoke. In some properties, smoking is prohibited in public

To Light Up or Not to Light Up:
The Smoking Debate Continues to Smoulder

Growing numbers of Americans are taking a stand against smoking and are having a significant impact on restaurant operations in many parts of the country. In several states—California, Utah, Vermont, and Maryland—and in New York City and a number of other municipalities, regulations have gone into effect that restrict or prohibit smoking in restaurants. In fact, more than 165 antismoking ordinances have gone into effect in the United States since the mid 1980s.

The effects of these regulations appear to be mixed. In California, a state with a comprehensive restaurant smoking ban, an informal survey by the California Restaurant Association found that 64 percent of respondents reported that business had increased or stayed the same since the ban was imposed; 36 percent reported that business had decreased. On the other hand, a survey of twelve hundred adult smokers by the National Restaurant Association found that a ban on smoking in the workplace would mean $18.2 billion in lost sales for the nation's restaurants, primarily due to lost sales from smokers lingering less over their meals and thus consuming fewer appetizers, desserts, and drinks.

As growing numbers of people press for a smoke-free environment, growing numbers of restaurateurs are complaining that government-imposed smoking regulations are interfering with their right to operate their businesses as they see fit, and the debate is likely to continue.

Adapted from an article in Restaurants USA, *June/July 1995.*

areas—lobbies, corridors, elevators, and other areas—often as a matter of law.

The prohibition of smoking in hospitality operations is an issue that will be of growing significance to owners and managers in the years ahead.

Sanitation and Public Health

No subject is of greater importance in foodservice than sanitation. Everyone agrees that all responsible steps must be taken to prevent illnesses that can be traced to the manner in which food is handled, or to the food itself.

Insuring proper food handling has always been an issue in the industry. Managers must constantly check to see that food is purchased from responsible vendors. It must be kept at suitable temperatures to prevent bacterial growth or under proper conditions to prevent infestation by insects and rodents. Equipment surfaces must be cleaned effectively to ensure that food is not contaminated during preparation. Washing is an ongoing necessity in foodservice—the washing of employees' hands, the washing of some fresh foods to remove chemical residues, and the thorough washing of all china, glassware, flatware, pots, and pans that are used in the preparation and service of foods and beverages.

State and local governments apply strict sanitary standards to food and beverage operations. Some conduct regular inspections and impose sanctions on those found violating the applicable code. The

Although not often emphasized, sanitation is one of the most important operations issues in the hospitality industry. Ensuring proper food handling, supervising vendors, and washing foods, utensils, and equipment are all essential in meeting legal sanitary standards. (Photo courtesy of Cryovac.)

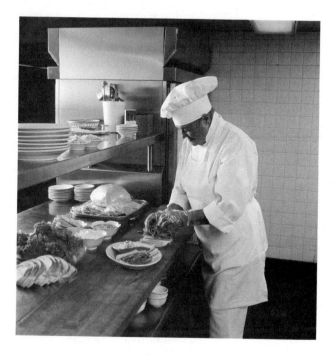

sanctions range from imposing fines to publishing lists of violators in newspapers to closing flagrant violators.

In an effort to ensure their compliance with local sanitary codes, many food and beverage operators hire consultants to conduct regular inspections and to assist in the immediate correction of any violations. As consumers become increasingly aware of the potential for harm from improperly handled food, preventing possible violations of local codes will be an issue of growing importance to food and beverage service operators.

The Environment

In recent years, society at large has become much more concerned with the natural environment than has ever been the case in the past. The public and the business community have become much more aware of a number of key environmental issues, and the hospitality and tourism industry has taken a leadership role in efforts to protect the natural environment. For this industry, the key environmental concerns are recycling, energy conservation, and water conservation.

1.   Recycling. In recent years, there has been a gradual closing of the landfills traditionally used for disposing of solid wastes and a growing awareness of the harmful effects of either burning solid waste or dumping it in the sea. This has led to major waste-disposal problems in some areas.

In some major metropolitan areas, the cost of removing solid wastes is becoming higher than government and citizens are willing and able to pay. In many of these areas, separating recyclable plastic, glass, metal, and certain paper items from other solid waste is now required by law. Separating these recyclables from other solid wastes greatly reduces the quantities requiring disposal.

The trend toward recycling is likely to grow. Many in the hospitality industry who have not previously been affected by this issue will soon see some change. They, too, will find the adoption of a recycling program both necessary and desirable.

2.   Energy conservation. Energy in the form of electricity, gas, and oil is a major element in hospitality. Hospitality operations depend directly or indirectly on energy sources for heating, cooling, lighting, cooking, and operating all kinds of equipment, including elevators. Conservation of energy has become an important national goal and is now an important goal of many hospitality operations. Owners and

managers have instituted many measures to conserve energy. These include

a. Monitoring temperature controls. Managers know that temperature controls for heating and cooling need to be monitored so that energy is not wasted. Some establishments have computer systems that automatically monitor and set temperatures to desired levels. Others set thermostats at the desired level, then lock the controls and provide keys to specific individuals.

   A major concern in the lodging segement of the hospitality industry is climate control in guest rooms—heating and cooling. Policies must be established to prevent unneeded heating and cooling of guest rooms when guests are out or when the rooms are vacant. Members of the housekeeping staff are frequently trained to turn thermostats to desired temperatures after they finish their work in the rooms. Guests are asked to adjust thermostats in their rooms in order to avoid overheating rooms in cold weather and overcooling them in hot weather, particularly when they are away from their rooms. Many hotels offer extra blankets to guests in an effort to encourage them to keep room temperatures lower during nighttime hours.

b. Switching off unnecessary lights. Keeping lights on when not necessary is a waste of energy. Guests are reminded to turn off lights when not in their rooms, and staff are trained to turn off unnecessary lights, particularly in ballrooms and other public space when unoccupied. Some properties have installed sensing devices that automatically turn off lights when there is no motion in a room.

c. Preventative maintenance to increase equipment efficiency. Equipment that is properly maintained typically uses less energy. Additionally, equipment that is properly maintained lasts longer and has fewer repair problems.

d. Sequential start up of HVAC equipment. Electric companies must be able to produce or purchase sufficient electrical power to service peak demand. Because of this, billing for electricity is typically based on peak usage during a given twenty-four hour period. Properties that start HVAC equipment in a staggered fashion do not generate as much usage at one time as they would by starting the equipment all at once. This approach leads to lower electric bills than would otherwise be the case.

e.   Operating washing machines only when filled. Hospitality operations can reduce costs considerably by running washing machines in dish rooms and launderies only when there are full loads. This can produce significant energy savings when followed consistently.

f.   Replacing old equipment with new energy-efficient equipment. Equipment purchased many years ago is usually not energy efficient. No one expected it to be. With today's soaring energy costs, replacing that old equipment may actually save money. Replacing old equipment with new may be a large capital investment, but it frequently pays for itself in energy conservation. For example, kitchen ovens that are old usually have poor insulation and require excessive amounts of energy to maintain desired temperatures. New ovens typically use much less energy and can yield considerable dollar savings in energy costs.

In the hospitality industry, energy costs are an important component of total operating costs. Many owners and managers have found that reducing these costs can contribute substantially to profit.

3.   Water conservation. Like energy conservation, water conservation has become an important element in hospitality. As much as any other industry, hospitality operations require dependable sources of clean water for a vast number of purposes—cooking, drinking, cleaning, washing, and so on. Having a continuing source of water is an urgent necessity in hospitality, and owners and managers have come to understand the importance of conserving water. Conservation of water is now an important goal of many hospitality operations.

The following are typical of the measures taken in hospitality operations to conserve water.

a.   Reducing water consumption in bathrooms with devices that restrict the amount of water used in showers and toilets.

b.   Serving no water to guests in restaurants unless they request it, and then serving the water in smaller glasses.

c.   Sweeping outdoor areas—primarily sidewalks and other walkways—with brooms rather than flushing them clean with running water.

d.   Purchasing water-efficient equipment, such as dishwashers and laundry washers designed to consume less water.

e.   Reusing treated waste water for irrigation, public toilets, and cooling towers.

    f.   Offering conservation-minded guests the option of having their towels and bed linen changed every second day instead of every day.

Truth in Menu

For most foodservice operators, preparing truthful and accurate menus is a normal practice that is never to be violated. A small minority, however, produce menus that are not always entirely accurate indicators of the foods served in their establishments. Some have merely abused such terms as *fresh* and *cooked to order*. Others have been more flagrant, serving U.S. Choice beef when their menus state U.S. Prime. Still others have served portions with fewer ounces than the number listed in the menu. Some have not used the actual ingredients suggested by their menus and have substituted one product for another: turkey for chicken, margarine for butter, generic products for name brands, and domestic products for imported.

In some areas, enough abuses have occurred to produce a groundswell of public opinion in favor of requiring foodservice operators to be entirely truthful. Where such consumer protection legislation exists, those who violate the regulations risk fines and loss of their licenses.

It is important that those in the industry conduct their operations ethically—in such a manner that consumers can have complete faith in the truth of their menus, the wholesomeness of their foods, and the honesty of their business practices.

Diet/Nutrition/Health

With the public becoming increasingly concerned about healthy diets, such as diets containing less fat and fewer calories, many foodservice operators are adjusting or amending their menus to accommodate these changing public tastes. Some are devoting sections of their menus to foods for the diet conscious; others are designating certain of their menu items as appropriate for those interested in foods low in sodium and cholesterol. Growing numbers of restaurants are seeking to attract health-conscious diners. Some have eliminated "unhealthy" foods from their menus.

The trend to healthier dining is certain to continue, and successful foodservice operators will want to give greater attention to the nutritional content of foods in the years ahead.

Fire and Safety

Fire and safety have always been issues of concern in hospitality. In earlier centuries, taverns, inns, and hotels, usually constructed of wood, were regularly demolished by fire. Many burned to the ground, and large numbers of people were killed or maimed.

During the twentieth century, various changes have made hotels, motels, and other hospitality operations much safer. Improvements in design and construction have made a great difference. So have improvements in the fire control systems installed in buildings—electronic smoke detectors, automatic systems to summon fire departments, better sprinkler systems, and so on. Because of these changes, hotels, motels, and other lodging operations have never been safer.

A number of dangers associated with fire remain to be addressed, however. In the event of fire, the guests in some properties today may face danger from the toxic smoke resulting from the burning of furniture, fixtures, and fibers produced from man-made materials. In a fire, many of the artificial fibers used in wall coverings, carpets, draperies, and upholstery produce toxic fumes that can be more dangerous than the flames and smoke.

Another problem relates to construction. In recent years, to reduce heating and cooling costs, new buildings have been particularly well insulated. In some, the windows are not designed to be opened, and temperature and air are controlled by very complex central systems. In the event of fire in such buildings, some danger exists that smoke may be quickly dispersed throughout the building. As a consequence, a shift to individual room ventilation can be seen in properties being built today.

Managers of hospitality and tourism operations universally agree that there is no consideration more important than the protection of their guests and customers from the threat of fire.

▶ Summary

In this chapter, several social and economic changes likely to affect the future of the hospitality industry are described, including earlier retirements, longer life spans, shorter workweeks, more vacation time, greater disposable incomes, and increased mobility. Growing demand for the hospitality service products of both the foodservice and lodging industries is discussed. Many of the key topics and issues that will have significant impact on the industry in the years ahead are identified and categorized in five areas: marketing, legal, human resources, operations, and consumer affairs. Topics and issues in marketing include changing demographics, changing vacation patterns, market segmentation, frequent-guest programs, maturation in segments of the fast-food industry, and consolidation in the commercial lodging industry. Legal topics and issues include liquor liability, impact of the Americans with Disabilities Act of 1990, and ethics in hospitality. Those in human resources include diversity, sexual harassment, employee turnover, and employee assistance programs. In operations, total quality management, internationalization, and automation are discussed. Finally, topics and issues in consumer affairs include smoking/ no-smoking areas, sanitation and public health, environmental issues, truth in menu, diet/nutrition/health, and fire and safety.

Americans with Disabilities Act of 1990	Internationalization
Automation	Market Segmentation
Diversity	Sexual Harrassment
Employee Assistance Plan (EAP)	Total Quality Management
Employee Turnover	

1. List and discuss six social and economic changes that suggest a bright future for the hospitality and tourism industry.

2. Identify the demographic changes that hospitality and tourism marketing executives will find it important to take into account as they develop marketing plans for the industry.

3. Why do hospitality businesses develop frequent-guest or frequent-customer programs? How do frequent-guest programs for lodging operations differ from frequent-customer programs for foodservice operations?

4. What has been the major cause of the large increases in the cost of liability insurance to bar and tavern owners in recent years?

5. What was the primary purpose underlying passage by Congress of the Americans with Disabilities Act of 1990?

6. Identify one positive outcome that diversity training should produce for a foodservice or lodging establishment.

7. How does the Federal Equal Employment Opportunity Commission define the term *sexual harassment*?

8. What steps can hospitality and tourism managers take to reduce employee turnover?

9. Identify the three principal purposes of automation. Discuss the impact of automation on service.

10. List seven key activities that foodservice employees engage in to insure safe and sanitary conditions for food handling.

11. List and discuss four key environmental issues that have had significant impact on the foodservice and lodging segments of the hospitality industry.

1. You are the front office manager in an airport motel of 150 rooms. The company you work for has just given you a promotion: you have been named front office manager of a three hundred room luxury hotel located in the city center. During your first week at the new job, you quietly evaluate members of staff and notice that one desk clerk is far more able than the others. He appears to be a member of a religious minority: he always wears a small neat cap to keep his head covered. It is also quite clear that others on the staff try to exclude him from their conversations and activities whenever possible, and this seems to be having a negative effect on communications and on team cooperation. You overhear one staff member telling another that this desk clerk is "weird" because he always wears a hat. What should you do?

2. You have just taken a job as manager of a white-tablecloth restaurant. One of the featured items is chicken tetrazzini made with fresh chicken breast, cream, and butter. The ingredients are identified on the menu. Early in the dinner hour on Friday night, the chef informs you that he is running out of chicken tetrazzini and there are no more fresh chicken breasts available. He can only make more chicken tetrazzini if he uses a frozen chicken roll from the freezer. What would you direct the chef to do? What would you direct servers to tell customers in the dining room?

3. You are in charge of the marketing department of a large hotel located in a small midwestern city that is home to two large universities—one public and one private. A large percentage of your rooms business comes from the universities. The private university has booked fifty single rooms for a group coming from Saudi Arabia for a conference. You are advised that most of these people speak no English and have never before been outside their native country. The university's conference coordinator informs you that this is a VIP group and that she will gladly pay for special services to make these people comfortable. What special services would you suggest?

4. You are food and beverage manager in a hotel with a restaurant and bar that stays open quite late—until 1:00 A.M. It is now 11:00 P.M., the dinner service is over, and you are in the foodservice area supervising the nightly clean up. You are called to the bar, where you learn that one of the regular customers, a man who lives over twenty miles away, appears to have had too much to drink. The bar is crowded, and this customer is demanding another drink. The bartender does not want to serve him, and the customer is becoming loud and disruptive. What should you do?

Glossary

Accommodations and Meals Package

Accommodations and meals packages include hotel accommodations and meals. They vary considerably. Some include three meals per day; others include certain specified meals: full English breakfast daily or dinner the second night, for example. Some include free access to sports facilities such as golf courses and tennis courts; others offer discounts on sporting activities. Some also offer sightseeing and other entertainment.

Accommodations Package

Accommodations packages normally include lodging alone. They are really just discounts on room rates. Some are only available for particular seasons or on specified dates. Others are limited to particular numbers of nights.

Accounting

Accounting has been broadly defined as "the process of identifying, measuring, and communicating economic information to permit informed judgments and decisions by users of the information." In practical terms, it is the process of analyzing, recording, classifying, reporting, and interpreting financial information that reflects the financial condition of an organization.

Accounting Cycle

Accounting cycle is a term that refers to a sequence of procedures used to record and summarize transactions for an accounting period; to organize the summary data into financial reports, called statements; and to prepare for the next sequential accounting period.

Accounting Principles

Accounting principles are the rules generally accepted by the accounting profession for analyzing, recording, classifying, reporting, and interpreting financial information.

Accumulated Depreciation

Accumulated depreciation is a bookkeeping figure that indicates a theoretical lessening in the value of an asset from the time it was purchased.

Advertising

Advertising is paid, nonpersonal communication directed to potential buyers.

Affinity Group Package

Affinity groups packages are packages designed for groups of people who share some common bond. Examples of affinity groups include students in the same college, alumni of one university, members of a social club, a religious organization, or a fraternity or a sorority, or members of a given profession, such as doctors, dentists, or lawyers.

Airline Catering

Airline catering is the business of providing food for service by an airline crew during a flight.

A la carte

A term used to indicate that each item is individually priced in the menu. See Table d'hôte.

All-Inclusive Package

As the name implies, all-inclusive packages provide most or all of the necessary elements of travel, including transportation, accommodations, meals, transfers (ground transportation between an airport and a hotel or similar lodging property), entertainment, sightseeing, sports, taxes, and gratuities.

All-Inclusive Resort

An all-inclusive resort is one that commonly includes sleeping accommodations, all meals, entertainment, and activities in the quoted rate. Many also include round-trip airfare, liquor, and gratuities. The best known all-inclusive resort is Club Med.

All-Suite Hotel

All-suite hotels do not offer the traditional bedroom and bath accommodations provided by most hotels; they offer only suites that include facilities for limited cooking. Most all-suite hotels do not have traditional restaurants or bars, and most have no public meeting rooms. Many, however, provide some form of limited foodservice, beverage service, or both: free breakfast buffets in the lobby, food vending machines in designated areas, and in-room bars are some of the possibilities.

Ambiance

In the hospitality industry, ambiance is a term used to refer to the aesthetic impact of an establishment on its customers. Ambiance has any number of elements—furnishings, lighting, sound, decoration, theme, table setting, employees' appearances and attitudes, and so on—all aspects of the establishment's environment.

American Plan (AP)

Room rates quoted under the American Plan include three meals daily: breakfast, lunch, and dinner.

American Service

American service is characterized by food portioned and plated in the kitchen, then carried to diners by servers.

Americans with Disabilities Act of 1990

The Americans with Disabilities Act of 1990 is a key act of Congress that prohibits discrimination against the disabled (defined as people with any physical or mental impairment that substantially limits one or more major life activities).

Asset

An asset is defined as anything of value. The term is used to identify those items listed on a balance sheet as having value to an organization. Stated another way, assets are what a business organization owns.

Automation

Automation is a term referring to the use of electronic and mechanical equipment and machinery to take the place of humans in doing physical or mental work of one sort or another.

Average Rate per Occupied Room

Average rate per occupied room is calculated by dividing the room revenue for a given period by the number of rooms occupied in that period.

Average Sale per Customer

Average sale per customer is calculated by dividing total dollar sales for a given time period by the number of customers served in that period.

Back Bar

Back bar is a storage and display facility located behind a bartender. It is commonly used to display some or all of the wines and liquors available at the bar, and it may also be used as a storage area for clean glassware. The compartments underneath are used for storage of bar supplies, which may include beers, wines, liquors, mixers, paper supplies, or any other item used at the bar. If these compartments are refrigerated, they may be used to store bottled beers and such food supplies used in beverage production as milk, cream, lemons, limes, and various fruit juices.

Balance Sheet

A balance sheet is a financial statement listing the assets, liabilities, and value of ownership claims to the assets of a business entity as of a specific date.

Banquet

Banquet is the term used for the prearranged service of food and beverages to a group of people. Banquets are normally held in private rooms but are sometimes held in reserved areas of larger public dining rooms.

Bed and Breakfast Establishments

Bed and breakfast establishments are small owner-operated lodging businesses that include sleeping accommodations and breakfast in the quoted rate. They normally occupy the owner's home. While they vary in quality, a growing number are operated at very high standards, rivaling that of fine hotels.

Bermuda Plan

See Breakfast Plan.

Beverage Cost Percent

Beverage cost percentage is the ratio of beverage cost to beverage sales expressed as a percentage.

Beverages

As used in the foodservice and lodging industries, beverages are those alcoholic and nonalcoholic drinks typically prepared by bartenders.

Beverage Service

The provision of alcoholic and other related beverages for consumption on premises is referred to as beverage service. The term beverage includes all alcoholic beverages and any nonalcoholic beverages typically prepared by bartenders.

Beverage Service Establishment

A beverage service establishment is one that provides beverage service for its customers. In many cases, the beverage service establishment provides its customers with food as well: food sales may even constitute the major source of sales revenue.

Boarding House

A boarding house is a residential facility that provides lodging and meals for guests who normally consider the facility their home, whether temporarily or permanently. The services provided are typically restricted to limited housekeeping and meals, which tends to distinguish them from residential hotels. They are inexpensive, compared with residential and other hotels.

Breakfast Plan (BP)

The Breakfast Plan, sometimes called the Bermuda Plan, includes a full breakfast with the quoted room rate.

Buffet Service

Buffet service is a self-service arrangement characterized by diners serving themselves from a selection of foods attractively displayed on a long table or counter. Typically, each diner carries a plate, determines selections, places desired quantities of selected foods on the plate, then takes the plate to a table to consume the food. A set price is usually charged for each person, regardless of particular foods or quantities selected.

Budget

A budget is a financial plan developed for a period in the future. Therefore, a budget can be viewed as a manager's attempt to project future financial performance.

Business and Industry Foodservice

Business and industry foodservice is a term used to identify organizations that provide food for employees of particular firms in their offices or factories during business hours.

Cafe

A type of food service establishment with roots in eighteenth century France. *Café* is the French word for coffee, and it is probable that cafes were the French equivalents of English coffee houses.

Cafeteria Service

Cafeteria service is a self-service arrangement characterized by diners selecting foods from a complete array of all foods available. Diners typically have trays and proceed to the area where the kinds of foods they want are displayed. Items are priced separately. After the customer finishes making selections, her selections are totaled by a cashier. The customer pays the cashier and takes the tray to a table.

Casino Hotel

Casino hotel is a term used to refer to transient hotels with gaming casinos. These hotels have allocated major amounts of space to casino gaming, which includes games of chance—blackjack, roulette, and poker, for example—and slot machines.

Catering

Catering is preparing and serving food to groups of people gathered for a specific purpose, such as attending a meeting or celebrating a wedding. Some caterers prepare and serve food only in their own halls; others prepare food in their own kitchens but serve only on premises provided by their clients. Some will both prepare and serve on premises provided by the client.

Chain Restaurant

Chain restaurants are those linked by some common identifiable characteristic, such as their products, their ownership, or their physical appearance. Wendy's, Pizza Hut, and Kentucky Fried Chicken are all examples of chain restaurants.

Chambers of Commerce

Chambers of commerce organize businesses in a specific geographical area in order to promote the area and to foster business development and growth in the area. In areas that are economically dependent on travel and tourism, chambers of commerce have offices that provide information and assistance to travelers and refer travelers to local hotels, motels, and other properties.

Check–In

Check-in is the process by which people become guests in a lodging establishment. Check-in takes place in a reception area, another name for that part of a front office known as the front desk. Here, guests register, are assigned accommodations, and pick up keys for their accommodations.

Check–Out

Check-out is the process by which guests terminate their status as guests of a lodging establishment. During check-out, guests surrender the keys, verify the accuracy of their bills, and settle their accounts.

Club Foodservice

Club foodservice operations are those that provide foodservice in clubs and other similar membership establishments.

Coaching Inns

Coaching inns were lodging establishments located along stagecoach routes. At the coaching inns, tired horses were exchanged for fresh horses and stagecoach passengers were fed and given opportunities to rest, frequently overnight.

Coffee House

Coffee houses were foodservice establishments found in England beginning in the sixteenth century. They provided fresh-brewed coffee and light snacks.

Coffee Shop

Traditionally, a coffee shop is an American foodservice establishment with a limited menu designed to attract customers seeking coffee and some light accompaniment—a doughnut, a sandwich, or a slice of pie. Today, most have extensive menus more nearly resembling those of diners.

Commercial Hotel

Commercial hotel is a term used to refer to a specialized property that caters to business travelers, such as executives and sales personnel in need of transient lodgings. The term dates from the early twentieth century, when a number of newly constructed hotels—Statler's Buffalo property among them—were designed to accommodate single business travelers, providing the types of rooms and services that would appeal to those anticipated guests.

Commercial Lodging Industry

The commercial lodging industry is that business-oriented segment of the lodging industry that provides transient accommodations to travelers. It consists of such profit-oriented lodging properties as hotels, motels, and inns.

Condominium

Condominium is a term that identifies a furnished housing unit with kitchen area, living room area, sleeping area, and bath. Condominiums are distinguished from other types of lodging establishments by their ownership characteristics: each condominium unit in a complex is independently owned, but the management of the complex provides maintenance for the outside and the common inside areas of the facility for a monthly fee. In addition, the grounds and other facilities are usually owned jointly by all of the condominium owners.

Conference Center

A conference center is a facility designed especially to accommodate meetings and conference business. Conference centers are typically located in suburban and rural areas and are designed to provide a setting that is comparatively free of distractions. Thus, conference centers tend to be conducive to concentration and learning and are selected by groups that require such settings for productive work.

Contintental Breakfast Plan (CBP)

The Continental Breakfast Plan is a rate plan that includes a light breakfast with the room rate. The composition of the light breakfast varies from one establishment to another. In some, it is limited to juice, Danish pastry—also known as sweet rolls in some parts of the country—and a choice of coffee or tea. In others, it can include an array of juices, fruits, pastries, croissants, rolls, bagels, doughnuts, and a choice of regular or decaffeinated coffee and tea.

Controllable Expenses

Controllable expenses are those that managers can control or change in the near term.

Controlling

Controlling is one of the functions of management. It is a process used by managers to regulate and sometimes restrain the actions of people in order to achieve desired goals. The process consists of managerial decisions and actions aimed at achieving desired goals.

Control Process

The control process consists of four steps.

1. Establish standards and standard procedures for operation.
2. Train employees to follow established standards and standard procedures.

3.   Monitor employee performance and compare actual performance with established standards.

4.   Take appropriate action to correct deviations in performance.

Convention

A convention is an assembly of people who are members of an organization, delegates representing members, or simply individuals with a common interest or concern. Conventions are special events, typically held annually, and are normally international, national, or regional in scope.

Convention Hotel

A convention hotel is one that focuses on conventions as the primary source of business.

Convention and Meeting Package

A convention and meeting package, typically offered by hotels and sponsoring organizations, commonly includes accommodations, meals, sightseeing, and other activities.

Convention and Meeting Planners

Convention and meeting planners are employees of or consultants to corporations, government agencies, and other large organizations. Their profession is planning and running conventions and meetings.

Convention and Visitor's Bureau

A convention and visitor's bureau is a government-sponsored agency established to attract groups, business meetings, conventions, tours, and other forms of tourism to the cities or regions they represent. They frequently assist in convention arrangements and often act as housing coordinators for convention groups.

Corporate Travel Office

A corporate travel office makes travel arrangements for corporate personnel traveling on business.

Cost Control

Cost control is the process used to regulate costs and guard against excessive costs.

Counter Service

Counter service is a type of service characterized by the service of food on a level surface known as a counter, on which servers place customers' selections. The customers may be either seated at the counter or standing, and they may consume the food at the counter or at some other location within the establishment.

Current Asset

Cash or other assets that a business can reasonably expect to realize in cash, to sell, or to use up, normally within a year.

Current Liabilities

Current liabilities are those financial obligations that are due to be paid within the next accounting period.

Cycle of Service

Cycle of service is the complete chain of events experienced by a customer from his first contact with an organization to the point when the customer considers the service complete. It is the sum total of the customer's moments of truth.

De Facto Recognition

De facto recognition is a form of recognition acknowledging the existence of a government without supporting the means by which it came to power.

De Jure Recognition

De jure recognition is a form of recognition acknowledging both the existence of a government and the means by which it came to power.

Desk Clerk

See Room Clerk.

Diner

A diner is a foodservice establishment offering full service that is normally moderately priced and typically open very long hours—sometimes twenty-four hours a day. Diners serve breakfast, lunch, and dinner from a single, multipage menu. In most diners, the customer can order any meal at any hour—breakfast at 11 P.M., for example.

Direct Providers of Travel Services

Direct providers of travel services are those businesses in direct contact with travelers that provide the services necessary for their travel. Examples include hotels, restaurants, airlines, travel agents, and rental car companies.

Directing

Directing is one of the functions of management. It is the process of achieving organizational goals by leading, motivating, and supervising subordinates.

Discount Outlet Centers

Discount outlet centers are collections of retail stores specializing in the sale of name-brand merchandise at discount prices.

Diversity

Diversity is a term used in this text to refer to the fact that both the hospitality workforce and its customer base includes people with differences in ethnicity, gender, religion, sexual orientation, national origin, and cultural background.

Dormitory

A dormitory is a lodging facility affiliated with some educational or other institution. Dormitories provide sleeping accommodations for those in residence in the institution. It is this institutional affiliation that differentiates a dormitory from a lodging house.

Drive-ins

Drive-ins are restaurants within large parking lots. They feature food served to customers seated in their parked automobiles. Orders are taken from customers, conveyed to the kitchen, and served when ready. The food is served on special trays that hook onto the frame of the open automobile window, and customers can eat without leaving their cars. In some drive-ins, servers are equipped with roller skates to speed service.

Drive-Through

A drive-through is an operation at which a customer can drive a vehicle to a window to obtain and pay for food without ever leaving the vehicle. Having received the food, the customer drives away to consume the food elsewhere.

Economy Bus Tour

An economy tour is an inexpensive tour. Accommodations are likely to be in a budget motel. Meals are likely to be simple: extensive menu choices and gourmet cuisine are unlikely. If the tour includes admissions to events, the seats are not likely to be the best.

Employee Assistance Plan (EAP)

The Employee Assistance Plan refers to the collective activities undertaken by an employer to assist employees in dealing with such problems as substance abuse and a range of issues relating to such areas as physical health, mental health, personal and family finance, the law, and education, among many possibilities.

Employee Empowerment

In the service industry, employees are said to be empowered when they have the power to make decisions about how best to meet the particular needs of a guest or customer in a particular instance.

Employee Turnover

Employee turnover is the ratio of new employees replacing departed employees to the total number of employees.

English Service

English service is characterized by a main entree—a roast of beef or lamb, or a turkey, for example—placed in front of the host at the head of the table, who then carves and plates it. A server places the plates in front of diners.

Entertainment

Entertainment is a term commonly used to refer to diverting or engaging sights and sounds, presumably those that will hold one's attention and occupy one's mind for some period. Entertainment does not normally suggest physical activity of the type that one associates with recreation.

Entertainment Area

An entertainment area is a geographical area that has become well known as a center or focal point for some type of entertainment.

Ethnic Restaurant

An ethnic restaurant is one that specializes in foods associated with a particular culture. Among the most common of these are Chinese, Mexican, Greek, Japanese, German, Italian, Spanish, and Indian.

European Plan (EP)

Room rates quoted under the European Plan include no meals. The European Plan has become the standard in most American transient hotels.

Events Package

An events package focuses on particular events or performances: football games, festivals, theater, art exhibits, and so on. Events packages usually include transportation and admission to the event or performance—and may include such other features as accommodations, meals, and rental cars.

Exhibition

An exhibition is an event aimed at entertaining, enlightening, or instructing the public; at offering specific goods or services for sale; or at providing opportunities for competition and judging. They may or may not be open to the public. Exhibitions are usually smaller that expositions and are often simply called "shows."

Expense

An expense is a cost associated with doing business.

Exposition

An exposition is similar to an exhibition, but it is larger and open to the public.

Extended-Stay Hotel

An extended-stay hotel is a property that caters to those who intend to stay longer than typical transient guests and those who seek accommodations other than the traditional hotel accommodation of bedroom and bath. The typical extended-stay hotel provides a home-like environment and attempts to minimize the resemblance to other commercial lodging facilities. Accommodations in extended-stay hotels tend to resemble those in a fine garden apartment complex—a suite consisting of kitchen, living room, bedroom, and bath as well as recreational facilities for swimming and other forms of exercise. Suites in extended-stay hotels commonly feature exterior entrances, with parking by the door.

Family Restaurant

A family restaurant is one that caters to family groups—parents with children and other contemporary family groupings. In order to appeal to families, operators must make a number of important decisions with respect to menu, food quality, menu prices, service, and ambiance.

Family Vacation Package

A family vacation package includes accommodations at specific destinations and attractions that appeal particularly to families: Disney World, Sea World, or Busch Gardens, for example. They normally include other appealing features, such as some type of child care for part of the vacation, for example, so that adults can have time for themselves.

Fast-Food Establishment

A fast-food establishment is one in which there is little or no waiting for food. Many in the industry identify these establishments as fast-service or quick-service restaurants, in recognition of the fact that the service is fast, not the food.

Financial Accounting

Financial accounting is a branch of accounting concerned with analyzing, recording, classifying, and summarizing the day-to-day transactions that occur in an organization.

Fine-Dining Establishment

In a fine-dining establishment, the emphasis is on high-quality foods, expertly prepared and professionally served. Fine-dining establishments tend to use few convenience foods, and most foods are prepared from fresh ingredients. Such restaurants are typically among the most formal and are often among the most expensive.

Fixed Asset

A fixed asset is one that will last beyond one year.

Fly/Cruise/Hotel Package

A fly/cruise/hotel package normally includes air transportation, a cruise, and a specified number of nights at a hotel. These packages are typically offered by cruise-line companies, such as Cunard, that own resort hotels in the general vicinity of a ship's point of departure.

Fly/Cruise Package

A fly/cruise package includes air transportation to and from a point of departure, transfers, and a cruise. Fly/cruise packages are almost always all-inclusive, meaning that the package price includes the cost of airfare, accommodations, all meals, and entertainment. Gratuities and sightseeing are typically extra.

Fly/Drive Package

A fly/drive package typically includes airfare and rental car only. They are intended for travelers who prefer to make their own travel plans. Fly/drive packages are usually prepared by airlines in partnership with rental car companies.

Food Cost Percentage

Food cost percentage is the ratio of food cost to food sales expressed as a percentage.

Foodservice

Foodservice is the act of providing foods fully prepared for immediate consumption on premises or off.

Food Quality

Food quality is a term used to refer to the degree of excellence in food products.

Fortified Wine

A fortified wine is a still wine to which brandy has been added to enhance the flavor and to increase the alcoholic content. Sherry is among the best-known fortified wines.

Franchise

A franchise is a contract between two parties—a franchisor and franchisee—that grants the franchisee the right to use the franchisor's name, sell its products, and participate in its programs and services under set, specific conditions.

French Service

French service is characterized by service from a gueridon, a specially equipped cart or trolley on which food is transported from kitchen to dining room.

Frequent-Flyer Program

A frequent-flyer program is an incentive program that awards mileage for travel on a given airline and provides various rewards for accumulated mileage. The awards may include upgrades to first-class seats, free flights, free car rentals, and free hotel rooms.

Front Bar

A front bar is a fixed counter for beverage service, directly accessible to customers and open for business on a regularly scheduled basis. Front bars are permanently fixed in particular locations within establishments.

Front Office

Front office is a term commonly used to refer to the location where the front desk is situated within a lodging property. To guests, the front office represents the lodging property: it is their first point of contact on arrival and last point of contact at departure.

Front Service

Front service is a term used to identify the people who provide a variety of useful and desirable personal services for guests. These include attended service at the front door for handling luggage, obtaining taxicabs, and opening doors; escorting guests from the front desk to the assigned accommodations; carrying luggage for guests; opening guest room doors for those having difficulty with their keys; delivering newspapers, mail, packages, or telephone messages to guests' rooms; providing information about restaurants, theaters, shopping, and sightseeing (if this is not done at the front desk); making reservations or providing tickets, or attending to both of these, for shows, tours, sporting events, and transportation.

Gaming

Gaming is another term for casino gambling.

"Golden Age of Hotels"

The decade of the 1920s—popularly known as the Roaring Twenties—was a particularly important period of hotel development. It has been characterized as the "golden age of hotels" because of the large number of hotels constructed, their size, and the very high occupancy rates they were able to maintain.

Guaranteed Reservation

A guaranteed reservation is a room reservation that a lodging establishment guarantees to hold provided the guest guarantees payment for one night.

Guest House

See Tourist Home/Guest House.

Guest Ranch

A guest ranch is a resort property that emphasizes horseback riding and related activities. Guest ranches are typically properties of fewer than one hundred rooms that provide housekeeping services, food, and other seasonal recreational facilities—swimming, tennis, and hunting, for example.

Health Spa

Health spa is a general term given to lodging establishments that focus on providing some form of beneficial, health-related services. They tend to specialize—some in weight reduction, others in cosmetic therapy, others in drug or alcohol rehabilitation, among many other specialties.

Hospital

A hospital can be defined as a specialized lodging facility established to provide medical care for the sick. Hospitals also provide various hospitality-oriented services. They offer sleeping accommodations and many of the same services provided by hotels—including housekeeping, room service, telephone, television, and a pharmacy—and often such additional services as hairstylists, gift shops, and lending libraries.

Hospitality

Hospitality is a term derived from the Latin word *hospitare*, meaning "to receive as a guest." "To receive as a guest" is a phrase that implies a host prepared to meet a guest's basic requirements while that guest is away from home—food, beverages, and lodging.

Hospitality Industry

The hospitality industry consists of businesses that provide food, beverages, or lodging to travelers.

Hostel

A hostel is an inexpensive lodging establishment that typically caters to younger transient customers. Hostels provide little or no service, and many offer very little privacy. The typical hostel provides a bed for the night and offers no frills. Some provide a community kitchen in which guests may prepare their own meals. Everyone staying in a hostel is expected to participate in keeping it clean. There is usually a limit to the number of nights an individual is allowed to stay.

Hotel

The term hotel has been used traditionally to identify a lodging facility of two stories or more that provides sleeping accommodations and other services for its guests. Hotels have commonly offered housekeeping services and luggage-carrying assistance as well as food, beverage, telephone, and other services. The extent of these services varies from property to property. Some hotels provide the full range: restaurants; bars; cocktail lounges; room service; hairstylists; exercise salons; computer, photocopy, and FAX facilities; laundry and dry cleaners; gift shops; check cashing and other financial services; newsstands; travel agencies; drugstores, and other services. Other hotels provide nothing beyond the basics: sleeping accommodations and housekeeping services.

Hotel Representative

A hotel representative, usually called a "hotel rep," is an individual or firm that represents hotels—usually a number of them in many different locations—and sells the services of those hotels directly to individuals, businesses, and groups.

Housekeeping

Housekeeping is a term used to refer to that collection of activities aimed at cleaning and otherwise maintaining and caring for guest accommodations and other areas of a lodging property.

Hub-and-Spoke Routing

In an effort to fill the maximum number of seats on each flight and to simplify scheduling, airlines have developed a system of routing commonly referred to as the hub-and-spoke method. Each airline has several major airports that serve as hubs providing meeting points for planes coming from outlying cities (spokes). Flight schedules are established so that many planes arrive at the hub at about the same time. Passengers then change planes and proceed to their final destinations.

Human Resources Management

Human resources management is the branch of managerial activity aimed at implementing the strategies, plans, and programs required to attract, motivate, develop, reward, and retain the best people to meet the organizational goals and operational objectives of the hospitality enterprise.

HVAC

HVAC is an acronym formed from the first letters of the terms heating, ventilation, and air-conditioning.

Incentive Package

An incentive package is a vacation package sponsored by a corporation and offered to employees as a reward for superior performance, such as high-volume sales of a product or service or some other achievement beyond the norm.

Incentive Travel Firm

An incentive travel firm is one that develops and/or sells incentive packages to corporations.

Income Statement

An income statement is a financial statement that summarizes sales (or revenues) and expenses of an organization for a given time period. That period is normally one year, but income statements can be prepared for any period of time.

Inn

The term inn was brought to the United States from England in the early seventeenth century. Originally, the term meant an establishment that provided rooms, food, and entertainment to both travelers and residents of the local community. Over the years, the term came to be used to describe any one of three different types of hospitality enterprises.

1. A small, typically rural, lodging establishment that may or may not serve food
2. A larger property—or one that may have once been known as a hotel—that wishes to convey an image of smallness and caring for its customers
3. A restaurant or bar that has no sleeping accommodations available

Institutional Foodservice

Institutional foodservice is a term referring to a foodservice operation the principal purpose of which is the preparation of food for those associated with the particular institution. The institution may be any of a wide range of service organizations, public and private, that attend to one or another of many possible public needs. Schools, colleges, hospitals, nursing homes, and prisons are some common examples of institutions.

Internationalization

Internationalization is a term with at least two hospitality contexts. One is the tendency of national hospitality firms to expand operations beyond national borders—to "go global." The other is the special efforts that hospitality firms are making to cater to the needs of international visitors.

Inventory Turnover

Inventory turnover is a ratio identifying the rate at which an inventory is consumed and replaced during an operating period.

Job Description

A job description is a detailed written statement that describes a job. The job description for any specific job should answer three important questions.

1. What is to be done?
2. When is it done?
3. Where is it done?

Labor Cost Percentage

The ratio of labor cost to dollar sales expressed as a percentage.

Liabilities

Liabilities are items on a balance sheet identifying financial obligations to others. Stated another way, liabilities indicate what a business organization owes.

Limited Menu Establishment

A limited-menu establishment is one in which management has made a conscious decision to restrict the number of items on the menu.

Liquidity

The term liquidity refers to the ability of an asset to be converted into cash.

Lodge

The term lodge has been traditionally used to describe a lodging establishment associated with a particular type of outdoor activity, such as skiing or hunting. This type of lodge is a smaller establishment, typically in a rural setting, that provides food and housekeeping services to guests who come to be with others engaging in the same activity. A substantial number of properties are known as motor lodges. For all practical purposes, this is merely another name for a motel.

Lodging House

A lodging house is a boarding house that provides no meals.

Lodging Property

A lodging property may be defined as an establishment that charges a fee for providing furnished sleeping accommodations to persons who are temporarily away from home or who consider these accommodations their temporary or permanent homes. Many of these establishments also provide food, beverages, cleaning services, and a range of other services normally associated with travel and commonly sought by travelers.

Long-Term Liability

A long-term liability is a financial obligation due beyond the current accounting period.

Luxury Bus Tour

A luxury tour is one that offers the best of everything. The motor coach will be as comfortable as any available anywhere. Lodging will be in luxury hotels and similar superior properties, and meals will be excellent. If there are tickets included, they will be for the best available seats. On luxury tours, everything is usually included in the tour price, so those on the tour have no need to pay for extras, except for personal needs.

Mall

A mall is an enclosed structure designed to accommodate numbers of stores and common walkways under one roof, making shopping possible in virtually any weather.

Marketing

For the hospitality industry, marketing is the process of planning service products, finding the right place to locate, and pricing and promoting products to attract sufficient numbers of customers/guests and to create exchanges that will satisfy both their needs and the goals of the hospitality enterprise.

Market Segmentation

The process of appealing to specific groups of potential customers by developing products with characteristics likely to appeal to those groups.

Menu

A menu is a list of the items offered for sale in a food or beverage enterprise. A menu is also a sales tool that influences customers' orders and the dollar amounts they spend.

Merchandising

Merchandising is a term used to describe those actions taken to increase sales to those customers who are already present in the establishment.

Modified American Plan (MAP)

Room rates quoted under the Modified American Plan include breakfast and dinner. Lunch is often available for an extra charge.

Moment of Truth

A moment of truth is any encounter between a customer and a business, whether or not an employee of the business is present.

Motel

The term motel traditionally described a special type of lodging establishment that catered to travelers with automobiles and provided self-service parking on premises. The original motels were single-story properties providing basic sleeping accommodations to overnight travelers. They were inexpensive, offering free parking and housekeeping service, but little else. Staff was kept to a minimum to keep costs down. There were none of the services normally associated with hotels—room service, bellmen, restaurants, and the like. Motels were located on the outskirts of cities and towns and catered to those who did not want the expense and formality of a hotel. Later, many operations had adequate land to expand and to add swimming pools, which helped to differentiate motels from hotels and to attract new customers. Over the years, many motels evolved into properties that so resemble hotels that it is impossible to identify any differences. Many are multistoried, provide full services, and are located in the centers of cities.

Motor Coach Package

A motor coach package is a special-purpose bus tour for those interested in shopping, sightseeing, or attending a particular sports event, for example. They are planned by motor coach operators and other tour companies. If a particular tour is to take more than one day, the price will normally include accommodations, meals, and entertainment.

Motor Inn

Motor inn is a term that came into use as an alternative to the term motel and originally described a motel property whose proprietors wished to convey the concept of free parking and the traditions of an inn—a kind of modern inn. During the 1950s and 1960s, when older hotels were no longer in favor because of competition from motels, many hotel properties that had parking facilities on premises or nearby changed their names from hotel to motor inn in order to compete with motels.

Motor Lodge

See Motor Inn.

Neighborhood Restaurant

A neighborhood restaurant is one that caters to the needs, tastes, and preferences of those living or working nearby. In general, neighborhood restaurants reflect the character of the neighborhoods in which they are found.

Nonperishable Food

Nonperishable food is the term given to those foods that will keep for extended periods before spoiling. They are typically packaged in cans, jars, bags, bottles, and boxes. Some are dried or frozen. Sometimes referred to simply as nonperishables, these foods are ordered infrequently and can be ordered in larger quantities because these items have longer shelf lifes than perishables.

No-Show

A no-show is a guest with a reservation who fails to checkin.

Nursing Home

A nursing home is a residential facility that provides lodging and food-service for people requiring nursing or related care. People residing in nursing homes tend to be temporarily or permanently infirm, physically or mentally.

On Change

A term used in lodging to indicate that a recently vacated room has not yet been made ready for occupancy.

Operating Budget

An operating budget is a financial plan for generating a given amount of revenue at a given level of expenditure in a coming period. Operating budgets are usually based on income statements from the most recent operating periods.

Operating Ratio

An operating ratio measures overall performance in some specific area. Four operating ratios commonly used in hospitality are percentage of occupancy, seat turnover, inventory turnover, and profitability.

Operations Management

Operations management is the collection of day-to-day activities that managers engage in to achieve the goals of the operations they manage.

Ordinary

The word ordinary is an old term, used originally in Great Britain to describe a midday meal served at a fixed price in a tavern to the local inhabitants. The term also came to mean the tavern itself.

Throughout the colonial period, the terms ordinary, tavern, and inn were all used to refer to the same basic institution—an enterprise providing food, drink, overnight accommodations, or some combination of these to travelers, local residents, or both. Over time, tavern became the more common term from New England to New York; inn became favored in the Pennsylvania region; and ordinary was more common in the South.

Organization Chart

An organization chart is a diagram of the formal structure of the business organization identifying positions and reporting relationships with the organization.

Organizing

Organizing is one of the functions of management. It is the process of coordinating the use of resources, human and otherwise, to achieve established objectives. To organize work in a hospitality operation, a manager determines how human and other resources will be combined and activated to achieve established objectives.

Orientation

Orientation is the term given to the introduction given new employees by members of a human resources team. Orientation typically includes a tour of the facility as well as a briefing to explain and clarify the organization's mission, objectives, policies, procedures, and rules.

Overbooking

In a lodging operation, overbooking means taking more reservations than can be accommodated by the number of rooms available.

Owner's Equity

Owner's equity is the term used to describe the owner's share of the value of assets listed on a balance sheet. The term capital is often used as a synonym.

Oyster House

An oyster house was a popular and inexpensive type of restaurant found in American cities in the nineteenth century. Oysters were a very popular food of the period, and they were served in establishments that were also known by such terms as oyster cellar, oyster saloon, and oyster wagon.

Package

See Travel Package.

Palaces of the Public

Palaces of the public is a term used to refer to American hotels that suggests not only the public character of these hotels but also their elegance.

Passport

A passport is a document issued by the government of a nation to a citizen of that nation. A passport officially identifies the individual to whom it is issued, providing such specifics as the passport holder's name, address, date of birth, occupation, and citizenship status. It includes a photograph of the passport holder.

Percentage of Occupancy

Percentage of occupancy is a ratio relating the number of occupied rooms to the total number of rooms available for occupancy.

Perishable Food

A perishable food is one that can be kept for just a short period before it will begin to lose its quality—to spoil and become unusable. Perishable foods are typically fresh foods, such as meat, fish, fruit, and vegetables.

Personal Selling

Personal selling is an approach to sales that requires personal contact between buyer and seller. Personal selling enables a salesperson to communicate directly with a buyer—to ask and answer questions and to use personal powers of persuasion to sell the service product.

Place

Place is one of the four key elements of marketing. The term refers to the location of the enterprise that will offer service products to customers.

Planning

Planning is a function of management—some would say the primary function of managers at all levels. Planning is the process of defining goals and objectives, then determining the appropriate means for achieving them.

Post-House

Post-houses were inns located at regular intervals along established mail routes during the period when the mails were transported by stagecoach. These post-houses were much like coaching inns. They were equipped to provide replacement teams of fresh horses for stagecoaches carrying mail, to feed stagecoach drivers and passengers and, if necessary, to accommodate them overnight.

Price

Price is one of the four key elements of marketing. The term refers to the price to be charged the customer for each of the service products.

Primitive Camping

Primitive camping is the term given to camping on unimproved sites without the benefit of hot and cold running water, bathrooms, electricity, cooking facilities, and other similar comforts.

Product

Product is one of the four elements of marketing. The term refers to the nature of the service product to be offered to the customer.

Product Line

Product line is a term used in marketing and retailing to refer to a group of products having similar characteristics. Some common examples of product lines are shoes, luggage, or jewelry. Foodservice and lodging have borrowed the term and use it to mean a group of service products offered by a hospitality enterprise, based on the concept developed for that enterprise.

Production Sheet

In foodservice, a production sheet is a list of menu items that will be prepared for a specific day or meal period, along with the quantity of each item for production personnel to prepare. Some production sheets will also indicate particular recipes to be used in preparation.

Promotion

For hospitality operators, promotion is a marketing process aimed at informing, influencing, and persuading customers to purchase their service products. There are five types of promotional activities commonly used in hospitality operations: personal selling, advertising, sales promotion, merchandising, and public relations.

Public Relations

Public relations is the term used to refer to those activities and efforts designed to improve or enhance the image or reputation of an organization; promote the organization's name; or improve its relations with employees, customers, suppliers, stockholders, or any other individuals or groups thought to be important to the organization.

Rates

In the lodging segment of the hospitality industry, rates are amounts changed to guests for their accommodations. They are commonly referred to as room rates. They may or may not include meals, depending on the policies of the management.

Ratio

A ratio is an expression of a relationship between two numbers. In hospitality, ratios are calculated for purposes of making comparisons and judgements.

Recreation

Recreation is a term meaning to create anew, to restore, or to refresh. The idea of activity is commonly linked to recreation; people often refer to recreational activities. Thus, recreation has to do with activities aimed at restoring or refreshing one's mind, body, or both, presumably after some sort of work.

Recreational Vehicle

A recreational vehicle is a wheeled vehicle with temporary living quarters. Examples of recreation vehicles include motor homes, travel trailers, park trailers, truck campers, folding camping trailers, and van campers.

Recruiting

Recruiting is a process used by managers to find suitable applicants for jobs.

Reservation

The term reservation refers to an arrangement by which lodging operators hold accommodations for guests who will be arriving at some later time or foodservice operators hold tables for customers who will be coming later to dine. The guests or customers may make their reservations for the same day or for some date in the future.

Residential Hotel

Residential hotels offer traditional hotel services—food and beverages, laundry and dry cleaning, telephone, and the like—to people who choose to live permanently in hotels. By contrast to transient hotels, residential hotels provide accommodations for long-term guests—individuals who consider the hotel their temporary or permanent home.

Resort Area

A resort area is a geographic area that has become well known regionally, nationally, and in some cases internationally, as a center for some recreational activity.

Resort Condominium

A resort condominium is one located in a resort area or on a resort property. The condominium units differ from traditional guest rooms: they have kitchen and living room facilities in addition to sleeping accommodations. Guests also have access to all the recreational facilities of the resort.

Resort Hotel

A resort hotel is a lodging establishment that features recreational activities for guests. These activities may be enjoyable, beneficial, or both: swimming, tennis, and golf are among the most common, although many others are possible. Some resorts have all the necessary facilities for these activities on premises. Others have only limited recreational facilities on premises and provide their guests access to other facilities nearby.

Resort Motel

A resort motel is simply a motel located in a resort area. Many offer traditional hotel services and most have recreation facilities, although these are likely to be limited compared to those offered in resort hotels.

Restaurant

A restaurant is a foodservice establishment with a dining room open to the public where varied foods can be purchased and consumed. There are dozens of variations.

Return on Sales

Return on sales is the ratio of net income to net sales, expressed as a percent. It indicates the portion of each net sales dollar the enterprise earns as profit.

Revenue

See Sales.

Roadhouse

Roadhouse is a term coined during America's period of Prohibition to refer to a roadside restaurant that illegally sold alcoholic beverages, alone or as accompaniments to meals, and that provided live or recorded music for dancing.

Room Clerk

A front office employee responsible for check-in activities in all lodging properties who may also be responsible for some or all information, check-out, and reservation activities in some of those properties.

Room Service

Room service is the term used to describe a form of dining service, unique to lodging establishments, in which customers have their food and beverage orders delivered to and served in their rooms.

Russian Service

Russian service is characterized by food arranged on a serving platter in the kitchen for maximum eye appeal, then transferred from the serving platter to plates that have been previously placed before each diner.

Sales

Sales is a term used to identify the income an organization receives as a result of doing business. The term is synonymous with revenue.

Sales History

A sales history is a record of the number of customers served during past periods as well as the number of portions of each menu item sold in each past period.

Sales Promotion

A sales promotion is an inducement offered by a seller to persuade a buyer to make an immediate purchase. Sales promotions are intended to persuade consumers to take action immediately rather than to wait.

Seat Turnover

Seat turnover is the ratio of the number of diners served in a given time period to the number of seats available in the dining room. It is often called "turns" in the foodservice industry.

Self-Service

Self-service is a service arrangement in which customers select foods from an array of displayed items, carry the items, with or without a tray, to some location in the establishment, and consume them. Cafeterias, buffets, and salad bars are three common examples of self-service arrangements.

Service Bar

A service bar is a bar to which customers have no access. Drink orders taken by servers are given to the bartender at the service bar. The bartender prepares the drinks, which are then delivered to customers by the servers who have taken their orders.

Sexual Harassment

Sexual harassment is a term defined by the Federal Equal Employment Opportunity Commission as "unwelcomed sexual advances, requests for sexual favors, and other verbal or physical conduct of a sexual nature that takes place under any of the following conditions:

1. submission is made a condition of the person's employment;
2. submission to or rejection of such conduct is used as a basis for employment decisions affecting the person; or
3. it unreasonably interferes with the person's work performance or creates an intimidating, hostile, or offensive work environment."

Sparkling Wines

Sparkling wines are those in which the fermentation process is allowed to continue after bottling. This produces the carbon dioxide that gives sparkling wines their characteristic "fizziness." Champagne is the best known of the sparkling wines.

Speakeasy

A term developed to refer to popular establishments found in cities during the period known as Prohibition. Speakeasies featured music, dancing, and entertainment, and they sold alcoholic beverages in violation of the law.

Special-Interest Package

A special-interest package is a travel package designed for a group of people sharing a particular interest. That special interest may relate to a sport or a particular hobby. The common interests around which these packages are developed include golf or tennis, photography, wine, fall foliage, and many others.

Special-Purpose Bar

A special-purpose bar is one that, although directly accessible to customers, is open only for a defined period to accommodate a special need. Special-purpose bars are most commonly used in banquet or catering businesses to accommodate guests at special functions—parties, dances, or the receptions preceding special events.

Specialty Channeler

A specialty channeler is an individual or firm that represents either buyers or sellers of travel services. Specialty channelers make travel arrangements for the parties they represent and do so either directly with the travel supplier or through a travel agent.

Specialty Restaurant

A specialty restaurant is one that features foods of a particular type, such as seafood, pancakes, chicken, vegetables, steaks, doughnuts, omelettes, or sandwiches. The possibilities for specialties are many and varied, as are the establishments that feature them. Some limit their menus almost exclusively to the specialty, while others use the specialty item as the focal point of the menu but add other items to broaden the restaurant's appeal and attract additional customers.

Stand

A stand is a stationary, open-air foodservice establishment with no dining room facility. Customers walk to a counter to order and obtain foods, then consume the foods at the counter or elsewhere, as they prefer.

Standard Purchase Specification

A standard purchase specification is a carefully considered written description of a food item to be purchased. A specification could include such information as grade, size, count, color, type and size of container, degree of freshness, and other characteristics that vary with the product to be purchased.

Standard Recipe

A standard recipe is a recipe that has been established as the correct recipe to use each time a given item is prepared.

Standard Bus Tour

A standard tour is a motor coach tour that, in terms of comfort and quality, is rated somewhat above a budget tour yet somewhat below a luxury tour.

Still Wine

A still wine is one in which the fermentation process has been stopped before the wine is bottled.

Suite

Suite is a term commonly used in lodging operations to describe an accommodation consisting of two or more rooms, one of which is a living room—sometimes called a parlor—plus one or more than one bedroom and bathroom. Many have some type of kitchen facility. Some properties offer suites that have several bedrooms and baths. Sometimes the term is used to describe a large one room accommodation with a living room area and a bedroom area rather than separate rooms.

Support Services

Support services is a term used to refer to that segment of the travel industry that includes the firms and individuals who provide services and supplies to direct providers. These firms and individuals depend on the travel market for all of their business or for a large part of it. They provide the necessary goods and services that make it possible for direct providers to perform travel services.

Table d'hôte

A term used to indicate that a complete meal is available for one single price. See A la carte.

Table Service

A type of service characterized by orders for food and beverages taken from customers seated at tables. The servers taking the orders normally deliver the food and beverages to the customers at their tables.

Table-Service Restaurant

A table-service restaurant is one in which customers are seated and served at tables.

Take-Out and Delivery Service

Take-out and delivery service are two types of service characterized by the consumption of food off premises. Take-out service means that food is taken from the premises by the customer who has ordered it. Delivery service means that an employee of the establishment takes the food from the premises to an address specified by the customer.

Theme Park

The term theme park refers to a tract of land on which a developer has created a series of exhibits, rides, and other elements that tend to be designed around some unifying idea. While theme parks have some such unifying theme, they commonly have other elements that are not related to the theme in any way. These may include exciting and entertaining rides, interesting and educational exhibits, or both.

Theme Restaurant

A theme restaurant is one designed around a particular theme such that the theme is used or reflected in every element of the establishment's ambiance. Possibilities for themes include railroad cars or stations, antique automobiles, colonial America, the old West, medieval dining, World War II, kitchenware—the number is endless, limited only by human imagination.

Tops

Tops is a shorthand term used to refer to food and beverage operations located on the top floors of hotels or other tall buildings, usually situated in some part of a major city where there is an interesting or spectacular view.

Total Quality Management

As used in the service industry, total quality management is a management technique that gives some authority for making decisions about service to the members of staff directly responsible for providing that service. A desired outcome is the tailoring of service to the individualized needs of guests and customers.

Tour Operator

Tour operators are travel wholesalers who devise packages they believe will appeal to the public, then make the necessary contacts and arrangements with those who will provide the travel services identified in the package — airlines, bus lines, hotels, etc. — then sell the packages and conduct the tours.

Tourism

As recommended by the World Tourism Organization and adopted by the United Nations, tourism comprises the activities of persons traveling to and staying in places outside their usual environment for not more than one consecutive year for leisure, business, and other purposes.

Tourism Development

Tourism development is one of three segments of the travel industry in the classification system proposed by professor Chuck Gee. It is the term used to identify the individuals and organizations that have impact, direct or indirect, on direct providers, support services, and individual travelers. This category includes those with an interest in travel and tourism but who would not be classified as direct providers, support services, or travelers. Examples of tourism development include the American Hotel & Motel Association, the World Tourism Organization, and schools and colleges that train cooks, hotel workers, etc.

Tourist

A tourist is the same as a traveler; see Traveler.

Tourist Destination

A tourist destination is any geographic location—country, state, region, area, city, town, or any other—that receives appreciable numbers of visitors, regardless of the means of transportation they use to reach the destination.

Tourist Home/Guest House

Tourist home and guest house are terms that were developed to describe private homes in which the owners rented spare bedrooms to transient guests. There are very few remaining in operation today. In these establishments, no meals were served to guests. They were not normally run as business ventures in the usual sense; they were more often sources of extra income for those whose primary income was derived from some other source. Tourist homes and guest houses have largely been replaced by bed and breakfast establishments.

Tourist Court

A tourist court was a small collection of roadside cabins that came into being during the 1920s to provide overnight accommodations for motorists. The tourist court is commonly considered a forerunner of the motel.

Trade Show

Trade shows are expositions directed toward a particular industry or trade. Trade shows are not open to the public. Admission is restricted to those who are part of the targeted industry or trade.

Training

A process for teaching individuals the skills necessary to perform particular tasks.

Transient Camping

Transient camping is the term given to camping for one or several nights on an improved site with electricity, bathing facilities, and toilets available.

Transient Hotel

A transient hotel is one designed to accommodate temporary guests—people who have need of temporary sleeping accommodations for one or more nights. The guests may be business people, groups of sightseers, government employees, members of the armed forces, students, or any other individuals or groups seeking temporary lodging.

Travel Agent

A travel agent is a professional in the business of selling travel services in a travel agency. Travel agents have expertise in advising clients about travel and in making the necessary arrangements to meet their travel needs.

Travel and Tourism

The terms travel and tourism are commonly linked together to create this special term used to refer to those businesses providing primary services to travelers. These include the traditional hospitality businesses and a number of others closely linked to them in such fields as entertainment, recreation, and transportation, plus travel agencies and tour operators.

Traveler

As defined by the U.S. Data Travel Center, a traveler is any resident of the United States, regardless of nationality, who travels within the United States to a place one hundred miles or more away from home or who stays away from home one or more nights in paid accommodations and who returns home within twelve months, except for those commuting to and from work or attending school. The terms traveler and tourist are commonly used interchangeably.

Travel Industry

The travel industry is made up of firms and people who serve the needs of travelers. According to professor Chuck Gee, the travel industry has three segments:
1.   Direct providers of travel services
2.   Support services
3.   Tourism development

Travel Package

Travel package is a term used to describe two or more travel services bundled together and sold at one price.

Under Bar

The under bar is a work area under the bar surface containing equipment and supplies used by bartenders.

Vacation Camping

Vacation camping is a term given to camping for a substantial number of nights—from four or five nights to a period of several weeks or more—on an improved site with electricity and bathroom facilities. Most vacation camps have stores selling basic supplies and recreational facilities for such activities as baseball, volleyball, swimming, boating, and waterskiing, among others.

Visa

A visa is either an endorsement on a passport or a separate document showing that a passport holder has received permission to enter a country from the government of the country he intends to visit. Visas are usually obtained by applying to a consulate of the country to be visited well in advance of the intended dates of travel.

Walk

A term used in the lodging industry to describe the practice of sending guests with confirmed reservations to other lodging properties because their reservations cannot be honored.

Yield Management

As used in the lodging industry, yield management is a term used to refer to an approach to room reservations aimed at yielding maximum occupancy at maximum rates. The general approach is as follows. Future demand for accommodations is assessed based on past occupancy and current conditions. For periods of low demand, all rates are available to potential guests. For periods of high demand, only the highest rates are quoted. Presumably, only those willing to pay the higher rates are accepted during periods of high demand, and those unwilling to accept the high rates are accommodated only during slack periods.

Index

VAN NOSTRAND REINHOLD VNR

Your Name_____
Title_____
Function_____
Company_____
Date of book purchase_____

Address_____
City/State/Zip_____
Phone_____
Fax_____
E-Mail_____

Thank you for your interest in Van Nostrand Reinhold publications. To enable us to keep you abreast of the latest developments in your field, please complete the following information.

1. With respect to the topic of this book, are you a:
a. student in this field
   name of your institution: _____
b. working professional in this field
c. hobbyist in this field

2. For how many years have you worked/studied in this field?
_____

3. Of which professional associations are you a member?
_____
_____
_____

4. To which industry or general food-related publications/resources do you subscribe for important information?
_____
_____
_____

5. Describe your professional title:
a. chef
b. caterer
c. restaurant owner/manager
d. food and beverages manager
e. student
f. professor/teacher
g. pastry chef

h. sommelie
i. consulting services
j. government
k. librarian
l. education/research
m. other (please specify)
_____

6. How/where was this book purchased? (circle one)
a. bookstore
b. publisher's outlet
c. through offer in mail
d. through book club
e. other _____

7. How/where do you usually purchase professional books?
   (please circle all that apply)
a. bookstore
b. publisher's outlet
c. through offer in mail
d. through book club
e. other_____

8. Do you own or have access to a computer with a modem?
   a. yes   b. no

9. To which electronic on-line services do you have access?
   (please circle all that apply)
a. America On-Line
b. Prodigy
c. Compuserve
d. Internet

e.   World Wide Web
f.   other (please specify)
     _____
g.   none

10. Do you own or have access to a computer with a CD-ROM reader?
    a. yes   b. no

11. Would you purchase updates, supplements and/or additional chapters to this book in an electronic format?
    a. yes   b. no

12. Which format would you prefer?
a. disk (circle one)   Mac   Dos   Windows
b. CD-ROM
c. online
d. other_____

13. What was the primary reason for purchasing this book?
a. professional enrichment
b. academic coursework
c. personal interest/hobby
d. other_____

14. Would you be interested in or subscribe to a Professional Chef's Newsletter? a. yes b. no
    If yes, which do you prefer?
    a. online   b. print

15. In which of the following areas would you be interested in new books?
a. International cuisine
b. catering
c. baking and pastry
d. beverage management

e. buffets
f. wines
g. other (please specify)
   _____

16. Please indicate author/title and ISBN# of book purchased:
_____
_____

VNR is constantly evaluating its services to better meet your needs. If you need further information please contact us by fax at **212-475-2548.**
BE SURE TO VISIT US AT OUR WEB SITE
http://www.vnr.com/vnr.html

I T P

BUSINESS REPLY MAIL
FIRST CLASS MAIL   PERMIT NO. 704   NEW YORK NY

POSTAGE WILL BE PAID BY ADDRESSEE

VAN NOSTRAND REINHOLD
Culinary and Hospitality
115 FIFTH AVENUE
4th Floor
NEW YORK, NY 10211-0025